D1367062

The Analysis of Organizations

The Analysis of

Organizations

Joseph A. Litterer

Graduate School of Business Administration
University of Illinois

John Wiley & Sons, Inc.,   New York · London · Sydney

Library of Congress Catalog Card Number: 65-20156
Printed in the United States of America

To Marie

Preface

As a topic of study, organizations have always received some attention. For the most part such interest has come from specialists in either public or business administration. In recent years workers in a number of different fields—sociology, social psychology, and the newer field of management science—have done a great deal of work in the area of organizations. The unity of their interests, although suggested by the use of a common label, often appeared to be an article of faith rather than an observable reality. Gradually as work in these disciplines continued and broadened, their unity became more apparent. This book is intended to bring together material from these various approaches giving principal attention to the topic and submerging emphasis on the disciplines from which the material was drawn.

At the same time this vast amount of work was taking place, a notable shift occurred in the method of study and the purposes of investigation. The earlier work was largely concerned with the description of actual organizations and the administrative practices within them or the development of normative prescriptions deduced from a few basic assumptions. The result in either case was usually a general plan for use in developing any organization. More recent work has focused on the elements in organizations and the processes by which they develop and influence behavior. This has led to the development of tools for diagnosing organizational problems and making decisions for the design and development of organizations. The manager no longer has a universal plan to follow but mechanisms to develop the plan for his purposes.

The material in this book is designed for the executive who works in and makes decisions about organizations and who will use the findings of empirical research and models in his work much as the physician and engineer do. With such tools he will be able to diagnose more accurately and plan more reliably. Such skill is becoming more urgently needed as organizations grow larger, more complex, and have to make big changes more frequently.

This book is an introduction to the subject. As such, many important but more complex topics concerning organizations have to be excluded and others only introduced. Although regrettable, it is hoped these restrictions imposed by time and space will not deflect the reader from probing deeper into topics of particular concern and interest.

The author of a book of this type is helped by many people. Some, alas, have slipped into the mists of academic absentmindedness. Particular thanks should go to Professor Chadwick Haberstroh who read the entire manuscript and offered many valuable criticisms and suggestions. Professor Donald Christenson read portions of the manuscript and through long discussions helped clarify many points in the author's mind. Thanks are also owed to the students who were in several years of classes where ideas for this book were tested. Their comments and suggestions were extremely valuable. Mrs. Erma Hyland, who typed numerous drafts and did much to improve spelling and punctuation, deserves a special award for patience and thoroughness. Last in order, but first in importance, is the debt owed to my wife and children for their patience, understanding, and support.

JOSEPH A. LITTERER

February, 1965

Contents

The Analysis of Organizations

Part One

Individual and Group Behavior

I

Introduction

T_HE twentieth-century world has often been said to consist of two kinds of people: the haves and the have nots. Indeed, much of this world still knows the meaning of poverty, as is attested by the many nations emerging from colonial status and pressing for a better life for their people. The economic gap between these and the have nations is usually ascribed to differences in technical development, with the have nots short on trained engineers, other specialists, and productive equipment. In other words, technological development constitutes the measure of difference, and is the key to improving the condition of the underdeveloped lands.

Yet technology is not the only factor to be considered. In the latter part of the nineteenth century some segments of the metal working industries in the United States progressed so rapidly that they were able to ship their products to Europe and undersell well-established European concerns. To a number of European businessmen this ability seemed due to the superior manufacturing equipment used by their American competitors. Hence, they eventually purchased similar equipment and set up their own factories in Europe endeavoring to make them as technically like their American counterparts as possible. Though they gained some advantage from this procedure, the results were far from what the Europeans expected. Observers of their efforts concluded that in general the advantage of American competition lay not only in superior manufacturing equipment but also in the way that American factories were organized and managed.[1]

We often hear of the dramatic technological advancement in Western nations over the past two centuries, but we hear little of the parallel-developments in organization. There are countless instances

[1] Joseph A. Litterer, "Systematic Management: The Search for Order and Integration," *Business History Review*, Winter, 35, 1961, pp. 461–476.

of technical advances making possible, indeed often making necessary, developments in organization. Conversely, the present level of American technical development could never have been attained without commensurate advances in organization. Furthermore, organizational developments often bring about conditions that indicate, and occasionally necessitate, advances in certain areas of technology.[2]

This interdependence of technology and organization is but one way of introducing the importance of organizations in the contemporary world. Most of us at one time or another find ourselves caught up in several large, complex organizations—economic, political, and social. Two hundred years ago our forefathers would have found this a unique rather than a typical experience. Business enterprises were far fewer in number then. Government bureaus and agencies were equally scarce. In those days larger proportions of society were self-employed or grouped in small organized units.

Although we may enjoy many economic and other benefits today which were unknown in an earlier day, we pay for these attainments. We are all largely dependent on a highly sophisticated, highly organized society. Who would know nowadays how to churn butter or make his own shoes, if he were forced to do so? What would happen if electric power were cut off for several days in our large cities or if transportation services were eliminated? Even in daily work few of us can undertake our stint until someone else has completed his. A man on the assembly line waits until the worker at the preceding position has finished his task; the secretary waits until her boss has dictated the letter. Commonplace and obvious as these observations may seem they are, nonetheless, extremely important facts of contemporary life. They emphasize the essentiality of large complex organizations not only because these organizations utilize technology, but also because we are very dependent on them, since most of us have become unfit to care for ourselves in the most fundamental ways, except in the special, organized world we tend to accept as normal. These reasons alone seem to justify the study of organizations.

Nevertheless, the dominant role played by organizations in the modern world has not gone unchallenged or uncriticized. Many persons see large organizations as a threat to basic values, as a real danger to the individual's freedom and personal development, both physical and psychological. Such apprehensions are extremely important and

---

[2] For one discussion of this point see Tom Burns and G. M. Stalker, *The Management of Innovation*, Chicago, Quadrangle Books, 1962, particularly Chapter 2.

require careful consideration. However, they are beyond the scope of this book. Here we accept the presence of numerous and large powerful organizations as a fact of contemporary life (a fact unlikely to change in the foreseeable future) and give attention to understanding and to, perhaps, thereby better utilizing this significant component of twentieth-century life.

WHAT ARE ORGANIZATIONS?

An elephant, a building, an automobile: each is a concrete object and can be easily identified. One difficulty attending the study of organizations is that an organization is not as readily visible or describable. Exactly what is an organization such as a business concern? Is it a building? A collection of machinery? A legal document containing a statement of incorporation? It is hardly likely to be any of these by itself. Rather, to describe an organization requires the consideration of a number of properties it possesses, thus gradually making clear, or at least clearer, what it is.

To begin with, an organization produces something. Typically, we think of it as producing an object such as an automobile, or a service such as medical care. Organizations of this kind are called *formal* organizations, because they entail some degree of conscious planning and their purposes or objectives are more observable. What they produce is consumed by portions of society outside the organization itself.

All organizations do not necessarily produce a result immediately visible to the world without. For example, a group of people come together regularly to play chamber music for their own enjoyment. Music, the product of this organization, is enjoyed only by the members themselves. That is, the organization consumes its own product. Except in rare instances, its product is of no interest or use to those outside the organization.

The purposes of the organization, whether it is formal or informal, are accomplished by a collection of people whose efforts—or, to use a term to be employed throughout this book, *behavior*—are so directed that they become coordinated and integrated in order to attain the objectives of the organization. In formal organizations the objectives are usually stated, and the means for achieving coordination are consciously planned.[3] A family, a friendship clique, and other informal organizations usually do not have explicit objectives that are evident to

---

[3] This should not be taken to mean that everyone knows these objectives; the number who do may be relatively small, but among them it is explicit.

the outsider. Furthermore, although they have coordinated effort, the means by which coordination is achieved is largely spontaneous or voluntary.

Is this to say that families do not at times consciously plan efforts or work among their members? No indeed. Nor does it mean that a business concern provides for all coordinated efforts in its plan and that none spring "informally" or spontaneously. But by and large the conscious, deliberate preparation of statements of objectives and plans for reaching them is far more prevalent in a business enterprise, a government bureau, or a hospital than in a family or friendship clique. The distinction is only relative, but it is an important one.

One thing about formal organizations is that they do not depend on the presence of specific individuals. The men running General Motors currently are not the same as those who ran the corporation ten years ago; and in all likelihood, the people in the organization today are almost completely different from those who were there forty years ago. Organizations have a life and existence of their own. If we examine what happens in them as one individual leaves and another replaces him, we see that for the most part the new organizational member does the same things as his predecessor did. How the new man behaves depends a great deal on his particular position in the organization. To put this more broadly, organizations consist of people who have fairly stable, regular sets of activities and interrelationships as determined by the organization.

Boundaries of Organizations

It is often difficult to determine the boundaries of an organization, to know definitely where one organization ends and the next one begins, or more simply, to discover who is a member of an organization and who is not.

For our purposes, an organizational member is someone who participates in the operation of an organization, the selection of its objectives, or both. Using this criteria, we quickly identify employees as members of the organization. This group, quite typically, is the one used to define the boundaries of the organization. Seldom, however, will this boundary be adequate for a full understanding of an organization. Employees, even if the head of the organization is included, may have relatively little to say about objectives, policies, and the like.

Taking a business enterprise as an illustration, we certainly have to recognize the importance of the investors in determining organizational objectives and often making decisions about how the organization will operate. Many businesses recognize this. They do not depict their organizational structure exclusively on the basis of employees, as in Figure 1.1a, but include the owners and board of directors as an integral part, as in Figure 1.1b.

If we turn from objectives to a consideration of whose efforts must be coordinated to insure realization of these goals, we find the boundaries equally hard to draw. Many companies, especially those in newer

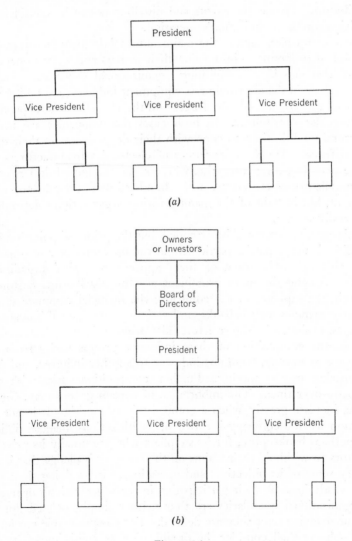

(a)

(b)

Figure 1.1

developing areas, will be concerned primarily with designing and manufacturing products. For marketing, they turn their output over to agents or franchised dealers. Such companies frequently find themselves faced with serious difficulties owing to what they view as apathy on the part of the agents and distributors or lack of attention by the distributors, who seem to be spending disproportionate amounts of effort on products made by rival enterprises. These companies are very much aware that their performance is highly dependent on the distributors. Hence, the agents and distributors can be considered to participate in the organization's operation.

Some companies, such as the major automobile manufacturers, have established programs to insure that their dealers and agents operate in a way that aids in accomplishing organizational objectives. Others, such as those in the electronic test-equipment industry, are taking steps to create their own field sales forces and thereby eliminate dependence on franchise distributors. In both cases the companies are making structural modifications to cope with their dependence on their distribution force. Are the sales forces of electronics manufacturers part of the manufacturing enterprise, whereas, the franchised dealers of the automobile manufacturers are not? In a legal sense the sales forces are different, but in light of the manufacturing organization's dependence they really are not.

This examination could be extended, but the principal point has been established: many parties participate in the operation of any organization, although only some of them appear on typical organization charts. Among the more prominent are the distributors, customers, or both; the suppliers of the company; the financial community, particularly agencies such as banks; and various governmental bureaus and agencies, as shown in Figure 1.1c. The problem is complicated partly because the composition of these influence groups varies from one company to another, from one industry to another industry, and from one market area to another. Further, composition varies with each company over time. The importance of certain groups may, for example, increase greatly when a company faces a crisis. It is not uncommon when a company is threatened with serious financial difficulties, perhaps bankruptcy, for its suppliers who are usually its principal creditors to withhold their claims on the company's pledge that it will modify some of its objectives and operations. In so doing these suppliers vastly increase their participation in the organization's operation.

Organizational boundaries are thus neither simply defined nor are they unchanging once they are defined. For a considerable portion of this book we shall consider the organization as consisting of its em-

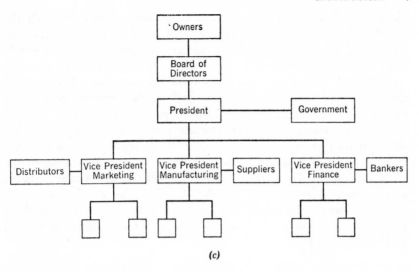

(c)

Figure 1.1

ployees, if it is a business concern or governmental agency, or of its formally registered members if it is a volunteer service organization. This is literary expediency, not a reflection of fact.

Content of Organizations

Thus far we have described organizations by talking about their purposes and the boundaries that delimit them. We have yet to examine the content within these boundaries. What goes on within an organization constitutes the bulk of this book. It is not sufficient to consider an organization as a collection of people and other resources brought together to accomplish an objective. If we want to manufacture washing machines, we have to do more than assemble people, machinery, raw materials, and blueprints in a building called a factory. Something else has to be provided or something has to intervene between the assembly of resources and the accomplishment of objectives.

To use a simple illustration, we make a wall from bricks, but a wall is more than a pile of bricks. It is bricks placed in a particular order. An architect plans, and a mason places the bricks in this order. The *arrangement* of the bricks is the intervening factor that transforms a pile of bricks into a wall. The architect and the mason perform processes which provide this intervening factor.

In a business concern, a government bureau, or a hospital there are sets of intervening factors which link resources and accomplishment of objectives. These factors and the processes that provide them are the essence of organizations. A few we can indentify quickly are: the employees' knowledge of the task to perform, the will to do the job, some way of connecting individual tasks to make a service or product, a method for coping with problems—whether mechanical breakdowns, shortages of parts, absences of personnel, or the like. Some of these take readily observable forms, such as production control systems, cooperation among employees, training programs for employees, job descriptions, company newspapers, and an almost endless list of other items. These factors arise in various ways. Some appear spontaneously. Some are consciously planned by specialists. Others emerge as a means to ease conflict. We shall hardly cover all of them or the processes that are the sinews of organizations, but this book provides a basic framework for showing how the important ones can be identified and how they fit together.

Concepts of Organizations

From what has been said it can be seen that an organization is not a simple clear-cut topic. As a result, depending on their starting place and intent, those who have analyzed organizations have often come up with quite different statements of what constitutes and goes on in them. To some, organizations are arrangements of tasks and an authority structure; whereas to others an organization is a set of relations in a face-to-face group. To some, it is a network of communications, to others a network of interactions. Some points of view support one another; others are in direct conflict, and yet all profess to be talking about organizations.

One student of the subject has likened the situation to the parable of the blind men examining an elephant. In truth, there is considerable justice in this analogy for, as we have seen, it is difficult even to pin down the topics we are discussing. A multiplicity of approaches in discussing organizations is to be expected, even if not desired.

Since this book touches on a number of different approaches or schools of thought about organizations, it is necessary to review some of the principal ones before going on to acquaint the reader with the ground to be covered.

NATURALISTIC AND PLANNED ORGANIZATION. Two principal schools have already been introduced. One maintains that an organization is a set of planned activities and interrelationships logically drawn up to accomplish a specific objective or objectives. From this point of view organizations are formal, rational, planned things. In contrast, the naturalistic school looks on organizations as things that spring spontaneously from the needs of people.   This school points to many social organizations which apparently have no rational planning behind them: families, cliques, economic systems.   In all these there are structures and relationships but the forces bringing them into existence are of a *natural*, informal sort.

BEHAVIORAL AND CLASSICAL SCHOOLS. Another distinction might be made between the behavioral and the classical schools.   The *classical* approach to organization is similar to, and in many ways overlaps, the planned organization approach.   It spends more time, however, on speculating about behavior of people in organizations.   Often it specifies what the behavior of individuals *ought to be*.   It also recognizes that sometimes behavior of individuals does not conform to prescribed standards and therefore compensations, adjustments, and controls become necessary.   The *behavioral* school is much more closely allied and often parallel to the naturalistic approach.   As its name indicates, it too is concerned with the behavior of people in organized settings.

The difference between the two schools lies in the basic assumptions which the respective approaches make in regard to the behavior of people.   The classical school assumes that people should be automatically interested in organizational ends, and that if they do not behave properly it is because they are improperly trained, have received the wrong information, do not have the proper values or standards, or are revealing normal, although unfortunate, human limitations.   As a result, the formal organization must provide means of reporting performance-control devices to take care of normal human lapses, methods of indoctrinating organizational members in proper ideals and values, formal schemes of training to develop skills, clear-cut channels of communication, and precisely defined duties.

The behavioral school, on the other hand, assumes that people are behaving in a way intended to satisfy certain fundamental needs.   Their behavior is designed to acquire desired things or to avoid unwanted things.   Peoples' actions are purposeful and "rational" provided we understand the system of rationality in which they take place.

OTHER APPROACHES. In addition to these approaches to organization, which differ in basic assumptions and viewpoints, there are studies based on the location or type of organization.   In the area of business much attention has been given to formal organizations, particularly in the production function, where such things as the specification of tasks and the selection and training of proper employees have been developed to a high degree. Sociologists have contributed greatly to the study of bureaucracies, which in some ways resemble classical organization concepts, but in other important ways, differ from them.   As bureaucracies have largely been studied in governmental agencies, students in the field of public administration and political science have often shared and contributed to this particular approach.   The political scientist has, moreover, brought his own special interest to this study of organizations, and has often been concerned with the internal political processes which determine the power structure of an organization.   There has also been the work of social psychologists and some sociologists who have been interested in structure and processes of small groups, particularly those at the work level of the organization consisting of the workers and their immediate supervisors.   Last and most recent on the scene has been the work of the management scientists who view the organization in a more inclusive fashion but who use a far more abstract mode of analysis.

All these approaches, and some others not mentioned, are considered by their adherents to be concerned with the study of organizations, and in truth they are.   One can hardly look at a corporation like General Motors or a branch of government, such as the United States Army, and suggest that all this grew spontaneously and naturally. Consequently, there seems more than ample justification for viewing organizations as planned formal entities and for considering them as bureaucracies.   On the other hand, anyone who has been in a large organization for any length of time soon observes that many things take place which are not part of the formal plan and which perhaps do not contribute directly to efficient achievement of organizational ends.   All behavior is not formally planned, and the unplanned portions are very important for us to understand.   Further, there are people who wield power far out of proportion to their formally designated authority, power acquired through political processes.   In short, if we are attempting to understand organizations fully, we need to use many of these approaches.   This is one of the principal objectives of this book: to draw on the many approaches to organizations to understand best what organizations are, how they operate, and how they can be influences.

THE INTENT OF THIS BOOK

This book is intended as a beginning text for those who plan to work in and administer organizations.   Such individuals, whether they are members of an organization or practicing managers, cannot take the limited or specialized view.   They are in the position of the physician or nurse who must treat a whole patient and not just a kidney, a sore eye, or a nervous stomach.

The practicing executive is concerned with understanding organizations to know how to influence them.   Hence, one important perspective of this book is to identify the crucial areas in organizations about which managers have to take action or make decisions.

The work of the practicing manager is made complex by the fact that he performs two quite different roles.   When considering our analogy of a brick wall, we noted that its essence was the structure, or order, among the bricks.   This intervening factor was provided by the planning of the architect and the construction efforts of the mason. Similarly, the need for intervening factors places two demands on the practicing manager: one to see that the factors are established and the other to see that they are operated and maintained.

These intervening factors are significant for the practicing manager because through them he must influence the behavior on which he and the organization depend.   That is, the manager cannot directly influence the behavior of organizational members; he must instead do it through indirect means.   He gives monetary wages to get people to do certain actions at a certain rate.   He bases promotions on skill so that employees will be encouraged to learn and develop their abilities.   His influence on behavior of organizational members occurs in a roundabout way.   The roundaboutness makes his control less sure, less immediate, and a source of much frustration and anxiety.   The situation is further complicated in this manner: while employee efforts toward organizational goals may be encouraged through one creation of the manager, such as a wage-payment plan, they may be deflected or restricted through other decisions of the manager, such as the way in which a job is designed.

The practicing manager then is faced with a difficult situation.   He cannot directly control or influence most of what goes on in an organization but must do so through indirect means.   Moreover, the indirect steps open to him are not mutually exclusive but are usually interrelated.   Frequently they are in conflict or contradiction to one another.   One action, therefore, may have several different effects on the organization—some desirable, some tangential, and still others perhaps of an undesired nature.   The best many managers can hope for is that their actions will have some effect on the part of the organization they intend to influence and furthermore, that the effect will be more favorable than unfavorable.

It is hoped that this is a realistic, if not entirely pleasant, picture of the situation confronting the practicing manager. It contains some of the more important elements of what seem to be the conditions that must be taken into account in designing a book of this type. This book does not propose specific, concrete answers as to what organizations should be. It does not contain the complete program for a factory, a sales organization, a business enterprise, a government agency, or a hospital. Nor is this book able, considering the state of our knowledge, to spell out in complete detail the components of organizations and the interrelationships among them.

What this book can reasonably attempt at this time is to provide some knowledge and conceptual schemes to be used for a better understanding of what organizations do contain, what types of coordination are necessary, and what sort of factors influence the behavior to be coordinated. In this sense the approach is intended to provide conceptual tools which can be used to further knowledge about a specific organization or organizations in general. It is intended more to provide a means of furthering investigation than of presenting a detailed plan or method for solving specific problems or ordering facts. There are, of course, some systematic elements in the book. There is little doubt that in the future greater portions of books of this type will be of a systematic nature. For the moment the book contains as much as our present state of knowledge would seem to justify.

This book draws upon a vast body of research, much of it of fairly recent origin, and works toward building a set of generalizations which can be used as a conceptual tool in understanding organizations. Often the connections among the findings of this research rest on various theories which have been developed to explain organizations. At times the connections rest on what seem reasonable grounds to the author and, hence, are influenced by his personal experience. These generalizations do not constitute a formal theory of organizations, but they do present a conceptual framework to permit more reasonable and adequate organizational decisions to be made.

CONCEPTUAL APPROACHES USED IN THIS BOOK

In approaching a topic such as organizations we have a number of basic intellectual strategies to follow. One approach attempts to develop prescriptions on what should be done. In economic analysis, for example, the prescription suggests that a businessman ought to price his product in a way that maximizes his total profit. This is the normative approach. It designates what *ought to be done* or what a condition *should be*. Yet one has only to know a little bit about the conduct of business affairs to recognize that businessmen often do not price their products to maximize their total profit. Thus, in trying to determine what people actually do as contrasted to what they should do, we have to undertake an entirely different type of investigation.

As indicated, the intent of this book is heuristic. It seeks to provide conceptual tools which will permit people to understand better what happens in organizations. With an understanding of how an organization actually operates it is felt the manager, consultant, or analyst will be able to make far better decisions not only about what should be done but also, more importantly, about what can be done. We take this approach for a number of reasons. Among them is the fact that organizations are far too complex to be analyzed or directed adequately by the limited number of factors usually included in normative models. Second, normative models make unrealistic assumptions (often implicitly) about human behavior, unrealistic to the degree that they result in misleading conclusions.[4] Our emphasis is on people in organizations where managers have to make decisions even though their knowledge and concepts may be inadequate.

As generalizations are made about what takes place in organizations, we shall often be talking about the decision processes that organizational members engage in or the sequence of factors which lead to a particular behavior. We shall at times talk about the possible actions a person may take on receipt of an order from his superior, which he thinks is improper and unwarranted. We shall talk about choosing among the courses of accepting the order completely, protesting, protesting and raising an alternative, or leaving the organization. It sometimes appears as if there were a basic assumption that people consciously bring out all these possibilities and rationally weigh the pros and cons of each. Sometimes they do. A sizable portion of our behavior is of a conscious and even rational nature. Much of it, of course, is unconscious and does not have the deliberate weighing of pros and cons of various courses.

Does the individual at times carry on the same processes unconsciously that on other occasions he perhaps conducts consciously? We hardly know. We are faced with the fact that people sometimes do things and later say, "I never thought that I would act like that under those circumstances." In saying this the individual indicates that he saw other opportunities and that, through some process unobservable to him, he decided among them and chose one that came from

---

[4] For a discussion about the assumptions behind the more prominent theories of organization, see James G. March and Herbert A. Simon, *Organizations*, New York, John Wiley, 1958, especially Chapter 2.

elsewhere than his conscious thought. The distinctions between conscious and unconscious thought are by no means easy to determine, and for our purposes, it is not usually necessary to make them. Considering the development of the field at the moment, it seems reasonable to conduct our analysis at the level at which persons do make decisions, without taking into account whether the choices and decision processes are conscious or not.

Several times references have been made to the intent of this book to provide conceptual tools for the analysis of organizations. As with any other tool models, abstractions and generalizations are useful only when used within their limitations. The person who uses a fine pocketknife as a screwdriver may end up with a broken blade but a screw firmly fastened. Such use of a penknife is foolish and reveals ignorance. The conceptual tools we present also have their limitations, and it would be well to review a few of the more important ones.

Abstraction

In trying to understand what is happening around us we are faced with a fundamental problem. There are just too many facts, details, and items requiring consideration. A man who finds the tire on his automobile flat could gather all sorts of information. He might note that only a portion of the tire is flat, that the tire was made by the Jones Rubber Company, that it is size 7.50-16, that he has an appointment at two o'clock which he can keep if he starts driving now, that the phone is in the house, that the sun is shining, and a host of other details. If he stops to gather all the facts about this situation, he tackles an almost endless task. Actually, in approaching the situation and trying to understand it, he does not attempt to gather all information. Instead he selects certain facts and searches for others. This selection of some items and ignoring of others is a process of abstraction. It is the culling or abstracting from a real—or, if you will, empirical—situation the things seemingly most important to deal with.

Models

Taking the abstracted elements, the man with the flat tire begins to connect them into a pattern. Better yet, he weaves them into a model of the confronting situation, which he can use both to understand his plight and figure out what to do about it. The parts of this model would probably include, among other things, the flat tire, the image of the spare in the trunk, the telephone, the service station, his own forthcoming meeting, and his neatly pressed suit and white shirt.

If he builds a model of how his effort, the spare, and the jack in the trunk can be utilized to replace the flat tire, he will probably see from it that he will get quite dirty and, furthermore, that he does not have the time to do this.   A second model would contain the telephone, the automobile service station, and the repairman there.   The repairman could come out and replace the flat tire, but this too would take more time than is available so this course is also rejected.   Finally, he concludes that he will call a cab and leave his wife to deal with the flat tire as best she can.

These are extraordinarily elementary models, but they serve a very practical purpose.   With them the man in our illustration can see the likely consequences of various courses of action.   He can find out these things by doing them directly, by actually handling the tire himself and observing that he gets dirty, or by calling the repairman and waiting for him and learning that it takes too long.   By using the model, however, he can make some reasonable predictions about what will occur and thereby accept or reject the choices open to him.

In this process of abstraction and model building we deliberately select a few items, ignore many others, and then place the items chosen in a particular relationship to one another.   In doing so we are intentionally ignoring facts or relationships that can influence the type of situation under study.   The problem is to select the most meaningful elements and relationships and ignore the others.

Those who use abstraction skillfully know well that they neither have all the facts nor have considered all the relationships bearing on the outcome of what they are analyzing.   They do not use the abstractions from one situation in another setting without carefully examining the fit.   Neither do they expect a model to handle all aspects of a situation.

For example, the typical organization chart is a useful but limited model.   It identifies planned tasks, titles, and planned relationships among tasks.   It does not show informal communications channels, cliques, activities actually performed, and many other things.   Yet such a chart has been condemned for not doing these and many more things.   Such condemnation is of the same order as the cursing of a penknife blade just broken in prying off the lid of a paint can.

In this book we shall be dealing with many abstractions and models, not with the intention of exactly mirroring the real world but with the objective of clarifying our perception of its most essential features.

Abstractions and models are mechanisms for economizing both time and effort, but like any tool they must be used within their limits.

PLAN OF THE BOOK

The organization of a book always presents a problem. This one uses what might be called a strategy of "development from the center out," which the author has found to be most useful in several years of teaching courses in organization. In this strategy Part One considers fairly basic elements important in any organization, such as the motivation of individual organizational members, their perception, and the like. To these ideas are added additional elements concerning basic interpersonal relationships, such as norms, status, and communications. With these elements developed, we are able to consider more general organizational matters: the division of work, the problems arising from it, and the complex issues of coordination and control. These topics constitute the bulk of Parts Two and Three. Through these first three parts attention is given primarily to the elements of organization, relationships among them, and the processes by which organizations function. Here organizations are examined largely under steady-state conditions. In Part Four the emphasis shifts to a discussion of these elements, relationships, and processes in operating organizations, with particular attention to such things as how individuals adapt to new roles in the organization and how organizations respond to both internal and external changes.

The book has been organized to use much of the material in a building-block fashion. Concepts and relationships developed in one part are used in subsequent parts. For example, the phenomenon of perception introduced in Part One is used in Parts Two, Three, and Four to analyze problems concerning division of labor, line-staff relationships, and adaption of the organization to changes in the environment. Sometimes previously developed ideas are reviewed in detail, whereas at other times they are merely indicated in passing. To avoid monotony and repetition, new material is occasionally developed without specific reference to relevant points previously discussed. The assumption is that the reader will readily recall these points and use them to understand what is currently under consideration.

In general, chapters in this book are organized to make the topic of each the dependent variable. Each chapter is largely devoted to discussing the principal factors that influence the dependent variable it covers and the constraints impinging on these causal relationships.

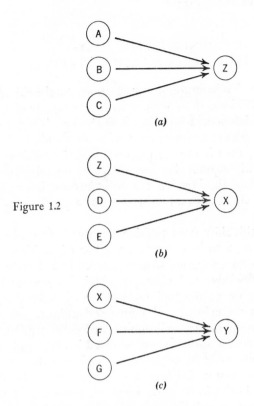

Figure 1.2

Consult Figure 1.2*a*.   The topic of the chapter, Item Z, is the principal dependent variable and the chapter is largely concerned with Items A, B, and C which influence it.   In another chapter Item Z is an independent variable, and its influence on another dependent variable such as X (Figure 1.2*b*) is examined.   Subsequently, Item X is an independent variable in a chapter concerned with Item Y as the new dependent variable (Figure 1.2*c*).

By using this strategy fairly regularly, it is hoped that repetition and overlapping between chapters can be avoided.   It does, however, impose limitations on what is being covered and, admittedly, at times it places things within a chapter in a somewhat unrealistic context.   Yet when the chapters are taken as a whole, this limitation or distortion is less pronounced and far outweighed by the advantages of this approach.   There are times, of course, when this general strategy is ignored: when either a most unrealistic or misleading picture would result or when the substance of a chapter cannot logically be covered in any other manner.

SOUNDINGS IN THE PAST:
AN INDICATION OF THE FUTURE

Not too long ago the literature of organizations consisted largely of principles of organizations; these were didactic statements of absolute and final truths which would hold in all situations. They were, in effect, the one final answer to what an organization should be. Today this is no longer the case; books are prepared which explicitly, as this one does, or implicitly suggest that knowledge of organizations is incomplete, that perhaps the best we can do at present is to use it to guide our inquiries about answers rather than as a precise tool to develop them.

On the surface, this shift from positive statements to qualified less precise ones might seem to be a regression, a loss of position. Actually, it amounts to an enormous step forward. It reflects a major development of knowledge and concepts which has opened up the enormity and intricacy of the topic at hand more fully than ever. The simple faith in the existence of a final and ultimate answer has been replaced by a more mature and sophisticated understanding of the multitude and complexity of the factors involved in organizations.

At one time health could be achieved by banishing the evil spirit. The solution to illness was simple and direct—exorcise the demon. Today the path to health is far more involved, consisting in part of good living conditions, sound diet, and, when illness strikes, in engaging in complex, subtle diagnosis, and often sophisticated and protracted treatment. The requirements for good health are now ramified and far less precise, but the consequences are far more satisfactory. The same applies to the field of organizations. Even now, when our knowledge is obviously far less than desired, we can, through more extended and complicated processes of diagnosis and analysis, develop more satisfactory solutions to organizational problems than would have been possible even a few years ago. It is with this realization that this book is written.

2

Influencing Behavior: Motivation, Learning, and Leadership

I⊤ may appear to be dwelling on the obvious to assert that the individual and individual behavior, in particular, are the basic building blocks of an organization. Nevertheless, this is an extremely important reminder, which suggests quite clearly the substance to be considered early in this book.

Neither the causes nor the effects of individual behavior in organizations are readily observed or easily understood. It would be simpler to understand organizations if people in them behaved only in response to orders from superiors. Very often, as we know from everyday experience, orders are given but ignored or actions are taken when no order has been given at all. Indeed such spontaneous actions are sometimes of great advantage to an organization. This emphasizes the importance of not automatically regarding as undesirable behaviors which do not follow from an order. By doing so we turn attention from merely attempting to find ways to confine individual behavior within certain limits to a more general understanding of the purposes and causes of such behavior.

Frequently behavior is explained in statements such as, "He is behaving in that way because he wants to." That is, we see behavior as purposeful to satisfy desires. As we shall see later in this chapter, there is much truth and utility in this point of view.

People do things to satisfy certain wants, needs, or desires, but this is not the complete explanation. There are many wants of man which do not lead to actions. Man may wish to fly, but he does not simply flap his arms or, for that matter, just glue feathers to his arms. Until our own era, wanting to fly was, for all practical purposes, not to be satisfied through any action. Man's physical form and lack of technology kept him from flight. Behavior is thus constrained in numerous ways; to understand it we must understand some of the principal limitations.

It is easy to fall into the trap of discussing individual behavior by considering the individual in isolation. Analysis of the "Robinson Crusoe" type can be very popular, but its utility is limited in the study of organization. One reason is that man's behavior occurs in an environment shared by other individuals. Much of his behavior is the response to actions and other things initiated by them. Furthermore, as we shall see later in this chapter, many inner needs can be satisfied only through association with other individuals.

We have been considering how to view individual behavior in order to give perspective to this chapter and its place in the book. Concerned with understanding how individual behavior is influenced in an interpersonal setting, let us begin by considering an elementary model of individual behavior. This model will gradually be extended and amplified throughout the chapter. Since it is hardly possible to cover all aspects of individual behavior, we shall cover those elements that seem most essential to understanding such behavior in the particular type of environment known as an organization.

BASIC ELEMENTS THAT INFLUENCE
INDIVIDUAL BEHAVIOR

Current behavioral thinking rests on a number of assumptions. The first is that the behavior of any individual is not a random or chance thing. People do not behave in a particular way just because it is their nature to do so. Instead, it is assumed that the behavior is caused, that every time an individual acts, there is something which produces his action. A second assumption is that behavior is purposeful or goal-directed. These basic assumptions are shown in Figure 2.1. A cause, or as it is commonly called, a *stimulus*, initiates behavior on the part of the individual. The behavior is intended to accomplish an objective which in turn will satisfy, or at least reduce, some need. A simple illustration is a person who, feeling thirst on seeing a drinking fountain (stimulus), walks to the fountain (behavior), takes a drink of water (objective), and quenches his thirst (need satisfaction). To complete the cycle with the need satisfied, the drinking fountain is no longer a stimulus of sufficient influence or effect to lead to behavior.

Like many models used to aid our thinking about the world around

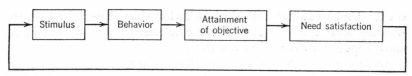

Figure 2.1. Basic assumptions of behavior.

us, this one is very simple. Its simplicity, in fact, may beguile us into thinking that behavior is easily understood. Nothing could be more misleading. Human behavior is extremely complex. This simple model does, however, present a basic framework and orientation helpful in the development of a scheme of analysis for understanding some of the important aspects of behavior.

The Evoked Set

Stimuli may come from inside a person, but frequently come from outside. In industry a common stimulus is an order from a superior. Let us assume that our superior orders us to fly the company airplane to Cincinnati. We can do it, for example, only if we can draw on our knowledge of how to fly an airplane. If we lack this ability, the order is hardly likely to result in the anticipated behavior. In short, to fill the order from a superior, we must be able to draw from memory learned *programs* for performing the action desired.

The importance of learning in determining behavior cannot be over-stressed. Sometimes we may receive a stimulus, such as an order, and have to develop or learn as we go along the steps necessary to execute it. But more often we draw on things we already know. We know a great many things. Some are fairly formal skills, such as how to fly an airplane. Some of the things we learn concern the world around us. For example, if we want food, we do not merely walk into a store and take it. We must first pay for it, which means we must have money.

We often fail to appreciate the vast number of different things we have learned because we use only a small portion of them at any one time. As we use our knowledge of flying an airplane, we are not conscious of, or for that matter even concerned about, how to play bridge. Whereas we may use only a small portion of total knowledge at any one time, all our behavior is influenced by the total fund of knowledge acquired through life. How we behave depends to no small degree on what we know; if different people possess different bodies of knowledge, they are, of course, quite likely to behave differently. Understanding individual behavior thus depends on understanding what a person knows and particularly what portion of his knowledge is drawn on at any one time.

Needless to say, there is no sharp distinction between these "active" (or, as we shall call them, *evoked sets* of knowledge stored in memory) and "passive" elements of our memory content. These are ideal forms or descriptions intended to permit easier discussion of something which in reality must be a series of continual shadings.

The evoked and unevoked elements, that is, total memory, result from *learning*, in which we all engage continuously. This total memory content changes relatively slowly through learning processes. The evoked portions of memory can be changed rather rapidly. At one moment they can be sections involved with driving an automobile but once an individual parks and goes into a store, they quickly change to those portions concerned with the things he came to purchase. The evoked content is a result of an *evoking process* triggered by stimuli.

The first of these processes, learning, is covered in a number of different ways throughout the book. The second process, evoking, is handled, in part, in Chapter 3 on Perception. Thus far we have covered a number of important concepts:

1. That all of us have a fund of knowledge which we collect continuously through our lives.

2. That at any one time a relatively small portion of this knowledge is drawn forth or evoked.

3. That it is only the evoked sets drawn from memory which are used to determine or influence behavior at a given time.[1]

Motivation to Perform

Let us return to the hypothetical situation mentioned in the preceding section. Presuming that we are accomplished pilots, we still may not accept our superior's orders, because we may decide that the weather is so bad there is some danger in being able to fly safely. Therefore, we are faced with these alternatives: to accept the order and fly or to turn it down and not fly. Knowing that our superior is not given to having his orders ignored or disobeyed, we may fully expect that if we do not comply that we shall be fired, be without our next pay check, but we shall also be alive. On the other hand, if we

[1] James G. March and Herbert A. Simon, *Organizations*, New York, John Wiley, 1958, Chapter 3.

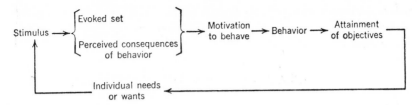

Figure 2.2. Influence on behavior.

fly, we may get through to Cincinnati and get our pay check or we may be dead.

What action we take now will depend not only on the fact that we can fly and on our boss's order but also on additional factors. We resolve this dilemma and make the choice between the alternatives by taking several things into account. First, we consider the weight we place on the alternatives: How great is the certainty of a crash? How certain are we that our boss will fire us? Second, our own needs and objectives are taken into account. Do we very much want the money? Do we enjoy the excitement of a dangerous flight? Do we no longer need the job or the money because we have already agreed to take another one next week?

The illustration reveals several more important elements which influence behavior in a situation. There are (1) the alternatives open to us, (2) the consequences we perceive for these alternatives, and (3) our own individual needs or goals. For convenience sake, let us say that the evoked set, the perceived consequences of alternatives, and our own needs or wants produce what can be called our *motivation to behave*.[2]

We can now extend the model of behavior as follows (see Figure 2.2). A stimulus leads us to an evoked set which, combined with the perceived consequences of alternatives and individual needs or wants, produces a motivation to behave. This in turn leads to behavior intended to accomplish some objective which, when achieved, will satisfy some of our needs or wants. The satisfaction of a need leads to a reduction in the effect or a reinterpretation of the stimulus.

The individual needs of a person play a central role in this model. To begin with, whether a stimulus will have sufficient effect to set off the chain of events leading to behavior depends on these needs. The needs also influence the form of behavior taken in response to an external stimulus. Last, it is to their satisfaction or reduction that the

[2] *Ibid.*, pp. 52–53.

whole process is directed. It is important, therefore, to have a better understanding of human needs. This will be our concern in the next few sections.

CLASSES OF HUMAN NEEDS

One thing most theories of motivation recognize early is that a person can have a great many specific needs. To identify all of them would be an enormous undertaking even if this were possible. There is also no guarantee that even if the specific needs of one individual were clearly identified, they would be similar to those of another person. To avoid this cumbersome problem, we usually discuss classes or categories of needs and assume that these classes or groups of needs are common to all people.

Physiological Needs [3]

Man acts to satisfy many physiological needs. Thirst propels him to seek water or other liquid. Hunger propels him to find food. This concept could be extended easily to include the need for shelter, clothing, rest, exercise, and many other conveniences. These are things man needs to preserve life in its most fundamental form.

Safety Needs

Man can feel insecure in a number of ways. He may be concerned that things important to him will be removed or damaged. In business we are frequently faced with a person's concern about losing his job and by losing the job also losing his income, his status, and prestige. The list could be extended endlessly, but in each case we find man attempting to do something to increase his security. He may work hard to preserve his job. He may take out automobile insurance to protect himself against excessive lawsuits.

Safety needs, however, include other elements and connotations. In varying degrees we are dependent on others. For promotions and

---

[3] This concept of motivation was developed by A. H. Maslow, *Motivation and Personality*, New York, Harper, 1954, and has been restated, elaborated, and extended by a number of other writers. See, for example, Douglas McGregor, *The Human Side of Enterprise*, New York, McGraw-Hill, 1960; and Louis B. Barnes, *Organizational Systems and Engineering Groups: A Comparative Study of Two Technical Groups in Industry*, Boston, Division of Research, Harvard Business School, 1960.

wage increases, we are dependent on our superior to recognize our abilities and to carry enough weight in the organization to make his recommendations effective. When we fly in an airplane our lives may depend on how well a mechanic did his job or on the pilot's skill in an unforeseen emergency. We are so enmeshed with the activities and capabilities of others that almost everything in our daily lives, from such simple matters as receiving the daily paper at the doorstep to the important issues of advancing our careers and preserving our lives, depends in some way on others. No wonder we are often concerned about the capabilities and intentions of those around us. In these de-pendent relationships a person may not actually be threatened but he is in a position where he could be. Hence, in understanding a person's drive to obtain safety, we should look at not only the obvious and existent dangers but also to potential dangers and threats.

Belonging or Membership Needs

Barring a few unusual cases such as hermits, man is a social animal in continuous contact with his fellow man. This is not only because there are a lot of people around him, and he runs into them just as he does into chairs and doors, but also because he enjoys and needs these associations. To gain them a man must be accepted by others. This usually takes the form of wanting to feel that we belong to some group of people, that there are individuals with whom we can have friend-ships and affectionate relations. Men sometimes will go to extremes to win acceptance by others. Furthermore, if the opportunity for asso-ciation with other people is reduced, men often take vigorous action against the obstacle to social intercourse.

Self-esteem

This category concerns the needs for self-respect, self-confidence, a feeling of personal worth, and a feeling of being a unique individual. This is a man's inner appreciation of himself, quite divorced from an opinions others may have. It is a measure of him as an individual in personal private terms.

Recognition or Public Esteem

On the surface, this class of needs appears closely related to self-esteem. Its emphasis is on how others regard a person and his reputa-tion, on how well he is appreciated, and on his recognized uniqueness, his position, or his status.   These are the measures others make of the individual and the place in which they see him.   Although both this and other needs can be considered as involved with a person's ego, they seem to draw on a different basis, thus making a distinction between them necessary.

Self-actualization

With this category of needs we recognize the fact that people have a drive to express themselves or to develop themselves fully.   We hear, or perhaps know, of painters, musicians, or poets who will say, "I do not care what other people think of what I do.   I *must* write (or paint, or play) in order to feel I'm living a full life."   Sometimes we are inclined to think of this as idle bombast or romantic nonsense; sometimes perhaps it is.   But often we recognize in others, as well as in ourselves, a need to develop intrinsic capabilities which lead people to seek situations that can utilize their potential.   This, if you want, is a search for something new to do, a chance to be creative, a chance to do something identifiable with a person.

ACTIVATION OF NEEDS

The recognition that man will act to satisfy human needs and that it is useful to conceive of these needs as falling into broad categories is an important and useful beginning to the understanding of behavior. Unfortunately, unless we have access to a person's inner self, which is usually not the case, we probably encounter considerable difficulty in attempting to analyze what lies behind a particular set of actions or in predicting what type of actions will likely develop in a particular situation.   Knowing that there are categories and needs which may motivate a person does not tell us which category is involved in any particular instance.   We may see a teenage boy running down the street.   Is he running to avoid being caught for some prank (safety need)?   Is he running because he is training for a high school track meet in which he hopes to star in order to gain local popularity (recognition need)?   We really do not know.   It might be almost any one of the classes of needs already discussed.   Also, we are not sure whether there is just one or several classes of needs involved at the same time.

To help understand behavior we can turn to some guides concerning the needs likely to be involved in a given type of situation.   It is suggested [4] that we conceive of the classes of needs as arranged in a hierarchy with physiological needs at the bottom and self-actualization needs at the top. We may assume that at any time only one class of needs will be in effect, or activated, while the others lie dormant, meaning that they have either been activated and are presently satiated or that they are not yet activated. A further assumption is that the needs will become activated in reverse hierarchical order, physiological needs coming first. When they are sated, the next level of needs—safety needs—will be activated; and when these are satiated, social needs will become activated, and so on up the hierarchy.

By way of illustration, a person who is starving to death is hardly likely to be interested in satisfying his needs for recognition. In fact, he may willingly do things that diminish his public recognition to fill his yearning for food. Nor may he be very interested in personal safety and instead may take hazardous risks to obtain the food he desires. Once he obtains food, however, his thoughts may well turn to security matters, such as how to assure himself of a continuing supply of food. After this has been accomplished he may become concerned about getting along with his fellow man and receiving some recognition.

A scheme, such as a hierarchy of needs with only one category at a time activated, offers a distinct advantage. We may often be able to determine which class of needs has been satisfied and which ones remain satisfied.

Although this particular hierarchical arrangement has proved useful, it does not hold for all people. Conceivably there may be some individuals for whom an entirely different arrangement exists. For some people the need for self-expression may be so strong that it comes before almost everything else except perhaps physiological needs. The important elements of this concept are that needs can be conceived of in a hierarchical order, only one need at a time being activated, and that satiation of a need at a lower level generates the next higher one in the scale.

Needless to say, the separation between classes of needs is not as complete as this brief explanation implies. There is considerable overlap between categories, and we should really conceive of the hierarchy as consisting of some highly activated categories, some temporarily satiated ones, and others much less activated, though unsatiated.

Furthermore, safety needs fall into a unique category. Indeed,

---

[4] Maslow, *op. cit.*

every one of the other classes of needs can be the object of concern, as each class can be exposed to danger or threatened. Hence, to consider safety needs as always being involved with protecting the source or the means by which we satisfy physiological needs, such as food, would be erroneous. We can be just as concerned with protecting our good name from danger and preserving the right to self-expression. Hence, we must conceive of safety needs as having a unique position compared to the other classes of needs, more or less paralleling, or underlying all of them.[5]

This preeminence of safety needs crops up many times. One illustration observed in industry concerns high-skilled production workers. They may establish work methods which permit them to meet their production quotas in less than a full working day. They can spend their free time in many ways. Not uncommonly they spend time doing their job carefully so that even on jobs where scrap might be expected they are able to turn in an exceptionally low scrap rate and have almost all their units meet with approval. In short, they use the extra time to supply additional evidence that they are truly the most skilled persons around. Informal work restrictions imposed by employees do not, as is often expected, come about because people are lazy or unwilling to work. Instead the reasons often lie in some attempt to increase their security.

USE OF NEED HIERARCHY CONCEPT TO ANALYZE ORGANIZATION PROBLEMS

Maslow's idea of a need hierarchy has been useful not only in the ways referred to in the preceding paragraphs but also in clearing up many confusing points about motivation. At one time it was not uncommon to find people supposing that the more of a person's needs were satisfied, the harder he would work and, therefore, the more productive he would be. Thus, the person who satisfied three classes of needs would enjoy his work more and be more productive than the person satisfying only one. Sometimes events appear to support this contention but other times the reverse seems to be true. If we consider all needs to be of the same magnitude and activated at the same time, such inconsistencies are difficult to understand. With an arrangement in which we can order needs, such apparent inconsistencies can be more readily explained.

[5] Barnes, *op. cit.*, pp. 167–168.

High Productivity and Low Morale [6]

To illustrate this concept, let us consider a study made a number of years ago in a large industrial plant where one group of long-service employees were found to have low morale, but at the same time were consistently meeting rather high production standards. The group of employees also had a relatively low rate of turnover. Here employee attitudes, productivity, and turnover were falling into what would seem to be a pattern inconsistent with the superficial understanding of motivation theory mentioned previously.

Investigation found that management had a rather firm production orientation. Workers were informed that they should either produce according to management standards or they would be fired. It was also learned that the employees had worked for the company for considerable lengths of time. The jobs did not require a high level of skill, and took little time to learn. These skills were not used by any other employer in the immediate community. In fact, many of these employees had special problems which made it difficult for them to find alternate employment. Loss of a job, therefore, meant either no job at all, accepting far less remunerative work in the same community, or disrupting the whole family to move to a new community.

In terms of a need hierarchy these men had their physiological needs largely satisfied. Their saftey needs for job security were highly activated. Furthermore, the one known way to insure the perpetuation of their jobs was to produce in accordance with standards established by management. This being the case, they worked hard at the one thing that quite clearly would enable them to continue their much desired employment.[7]

Apathy and Blocked Paths of Satisfaction

We have been considering a situation where satisfaction of one need activates another whose satisfaction is not complete or assured. Another situation is one in which the next need to be activated has no

[6] This analysis draws heavily upon a proposal made by James V. Clark in "Motivation in Work Groups: A Tentative View," *Human Organization*, Winter, **19**, 1960–61, pp. 199–208.
[7] See William J. Goode and Irving Fowler, "Incentive Factors in a Low Morale Plant," *American Sociological Review*, **14**, 1949, 618–624.

chance of being satisfied; that is, the path to its satisfaction is blocked. Such a case is reported by Guest in his study of assembly-line workers. He found many employees in assembly-line work where, owing to the distance separating the positions, the fact that the workers had to walk along with the work, noise, supervision, and other factors, that it was very difficult for them to interact and, therefore, form groups of any meaning and stability. In this sense it was extraordinarily difficult to satisfy a need for belonging and membership. In interviews off the job the workers were quite frank in stating that the work was unpleasant because of the lack of social contact, and yet they were reluctant to leave. As one worker expressed it in an interview:

> I'll tell you honest. I'm scared to leave. I'm afraid to take the gamble on the outside. I'm not staying because I want to. You see, I'm getting good pay. We live according to the pay I get. It would be tough to change the way we live. With the cost of living what it is, it is too much of a gamble. Then there's another thing. I got good seniority. I take another job and I start from scratch, comes a depression or something and I'm the first to get knocked off. Also they got a pension plan. I'm thirty-seven. I'd lose that. Of course, the joker in the pension plan is that most guys out there chasing the line probably won't live 'til sixty-five. So they're trapped. You get what I mean? [8]

Let us review this worker's situation. He cannot get a better job outside. Second, what he has is secure through seniority and other provisions. His physiological and safety needs are well taken care of, at least as far as job security is concerned. Higher needs, when activated, have their possible satisfaction blocked. The layout, noise, and other features prohibit him from having good social interaction. Interaction with him is pretty limited to his partner and even there he says, "You don't have time for any real conversation." [9] With some needs satisfied and others activated but denied satisfaction this worker is, in his own words, "trapped." What happens to him? One answer comes from the man's wife:

> . . . he comes home at night, plops in a chair, and just sits for about fifteen minutes. I don't know much about what he does at the plant, but it does something to him . . . I wonder whether

[8] Robert H. Guest, "Men and Machines: An Assembly Line Worker Looks at His Job," *Personnel*, 31, 1955, p. 500.
[9] *Ibid.*, p. 499.

these (things he buys with pay such as TV) are more important to us than having Joe get all nervous and tensed up. He snaps at the kids and snaps at me—but he doesn't mean it.[10]

One answer is that he becomes tense, frustrated, has a feeling of being worn out. He reveals a different reaction in regard to his work. "I don't like to work on the line—no man likes to work on a moving line. You can't beat the machine—sometimes the line breaks down. When it does, we all yell, 'Whoopee!' " [11] Perhaps the most generous adjective to use here is that he is "apathetic" about things on which he works and the company that employs him.

THE MECHANICS OF NEED SATISFACTION

Roundaboutness of Need Satisfaction

In this general model behavior is directed toward an objective which in turn satisfies a need. This apparently cumbersome arrangement is necessary to recognize that needs are seldom satisfied directly. Instead, there is usually a chain of events which culminates in satisfying a particular need. For example, if someone is thirsty, he may be able to get water directly. On the other hand, to satisfy a need for water he may need access to the supply, such as permission to cross another party's property or a bucket to lower within the well. Only when all these things have been provided and used may the need for water be satisfied.

An important objective then for the man wanting water is to get the permission of the other party to walk across his property. His immediate behavior directed to this end may not have any apparent relation to water. Knowing the other person's susceptibility to flattery, he may be spending most of the time talking about this man's fine crops or how shrewd he was in a recent business deal. Only when he feels that he has sufficiently softened the other party may he casually ask, "Oh, by the way, might I get a bucket of water from your well?" We could perhaps summarize this section as follows: Satisfying human needs is frequently accomplished through roundabout paths in which we try to accomplish or realize objectives which function as *means* to need satisfaction.

[10] *Ibid.*, p. 500.
[11] *Ibid.*, p. 499.

LEADERSHIP IN AN ORGANIZATIONAL SETTING

Common Views of Leadership

Everyone is familiar with leaders and leadership situations. They appear in the companies in which we work, in the schools in which we enroll, in football teams, neighborhood clubs, churches, and in countless other settings. Considering how common are manifestations of leadership in our daily lives, it is rather surprising to find how little we actually know about it and, for that matter, how varied are the interpretations of the word and the phenomenon.

To some people leadership is the exercise of power or, we might say, the skillful use of fear. The leader or the boss, in effect, says to his followers, "You do as I say or else I will punish you." For example, the foreman can say, "You do as I say or you will be fired." The sergeant in the army says, "You do as I say or I will put you on trial for disobedience and perhaps mutiny." This approach, the exercise of power, has as its main concept the punishment of subordinates for noncompliance.

There are others who take a different view of leadership and say really it can be better described as sort of an exchange situation. The leader says, in essence, to his subordinates, "If you do thus and so, I will give you something." For example, the foreman can say, "If you produce ten per cent over standard rate of output, I will give you a ten per cent bonus in your pay."

Mutual Dependency of Leaders and Followers

These commonly held interpretations describe some aspects of leadership found in real life. However, these interpretations suffer from a number of serious weaknesses. (a) They are far too simple. (b) They do not seem adequate to explain leadership in many situations as, for example, when jobs are plentiful and, hence, the threat of being fired is far less potent. (c) Last, their orientation camouflages a very important point. They accentuate the dependence of the subordinate on the boss which is, of course, quite realistic as far as it goes. However, such interpretations ignore the other side of the issue, namely, the superior's dependence on his subordinates. His success will be measured by the performance of his subordinates or, more accurately, by the performance of his unit. The superior does nothing in which the organization is directly interested. It is only his organizational unit which produces something really meaningful to the overall organization. Leadership is a mutually dependent relationship, and the skillful leader never loses sight of this.

The Leader and the Means of Need Satisfaction

Earlier we noted that satisfaction of a need often comes through a rather lengthy, roundabout sequence of events. In leading, a superior is often influential in determining whether a person will be able to achieve his objective in order to satisfy his needs. We recognize the control a superior may have over a man's wage, which he presumably can use to satisfy many needs. What sometimes is less obvious is that a superior's influence over the means a person requires ultimately to satisfy his needs extends over far more things than wages, and is manifest in many subtle ways. For example, by controlling the assignment of work the superior influences the type of experience a person will have. This may directly influence the skills the person can develop, and thereby control the possibility of future promotions or pay increases.

Let us make explicit a point which may have been obscured. We have been talking largely of the objective of earning money, usually referring to how this can satisfy physiological needs. Many other needs can be satisfied through the work situation. The functional view of the superior's or leader's role applies to all relevant needs.

Unfortunately, neither the subtlety of the superior's influence on the means of individual need satisfaction nor the range of human needs that must be taken into account in an organizational setting are always appreciated by those in leadership positions. A leader who honestly believes that people work primarily for money, and that the company is primarily interested in production, may be innocently oblivious to the problems he is causing his subordinates, himself, and his organization. He may, for example, adopt a leadership style which attempts to prohibit any conversation on the job. People are to stay in their work places and work. Prohibiting interaction will quite obviously cut down, and perhaps eliminate, the possibility of satisfying any of the social needs of which we have spoken. Yet these may be the very needs activated. The superior in this case may be surprised and disappointed with the apparent apathy of his workers, knowing that they are making above average wages for their type of work. A common interpretation made by superiors of this sort in this situation is that the subordinates are lazy and shiftless and not appreciative of the fine advantages open to them. They, therefore, in all likelihood, redouble their efforts to keep workers on the job and to force higher production, thereby compounding the very causes of their problem.

These considerations help us understand more adequately the number of ways in which a superior's actions influence a subordinate's behavior. Returning to our influence model (Figure 2.2), we can see that many of the superior's actions can influence the consequences individuals see for various courses of action. For example, a person who would like to socialize might think about walking over to one of his fellow workers to have a conversation. Then he recalls the superior has warned that anyone who does this will suffer disciplinary actions. Therefore, the person will probably discount this alternative. A second more cumbersome alternative is to signal the person to whom he would like to speak to go out to the restroom and meet him there for the desired conversation. In spite of the drawbacks this alternative does not have the potential hazards and probably will be chosen.

The Leader's Role in the Organization

In an organization, such as a business concern, a person is appointed to a managerial role with the obligation of running a department or subunit of the organization in such a way that this unit renders a service or in some way delivers something useful to the larger organization. The manager of an electrical plating department is expected to have his department deliver plated parts on time and within the cost requirements of the company. His success as a manager in organizational terms will be measured largely by how well he operates his department to perform this service and to deliver these products to other parts of the organization.

At first glance it might appear that the organizational manager is in an incompatible position. On one hand, he must see that the behavior of his subordinates culminates in satisfying organizational objectives. On the other, he is concerned with facilitating the means by which subordinates satisfy their needs. A foreman may ask, "How can I let people working for me have conversations among themselves so they can satisfy some of their social needs, when in doing so they must leave their work positions and, therefore, cannot be working?" It seems to many people impossible to satisfy both the superior's expectations and the subordinates' needs.

Fortunately, this either/or dichotomy is not an accurate reflection of most organizational situations. It is a challenge, but certainly not an impossibility for a superior to arrange things so that acts or behavior by his subordinates can lead to the satisfaction of their needs at the same time that they contribute to a purpose that is meaningful to the overall organization. This possibility has long been recognized in the existence of incentive programs, which attempt to do as much by giving bonuses for higher production. The problem has been that in applying this concept the process usually has stopped at monetary incentives. However, when superiors are able to arrange things so that one act or behavior can satisfy both conditions, they will, in all likelihood, have developed productive units.

To arrange things in this manner it seems that the superior would have to know both the technical aspects of productivity and the psychological needs of his subordinates. If he examined both areas, he would be better able to arrange the type of situation outlined and have the most productive type of units. This has been found to be the case in an extensive series of studies conducted by the Survey Research Center of the University of Michigan.[12] It has been seen repeatedly that superiors who have an *employee-centered* outlook (in their terms this meant the superior took into account both technical and human aspects of the work situation) were likelier to be identified as managers of more productive units than those identified as *job-centered* supervisors (in terms of the study, a person who looked only at the technical aspects of the job). Figure 2.3 shows typical findings from one of the studies. The point made by these studies is that it is possible for a superior to arrange things so that subordinates can achieve their need satisfaction and at the same time the organization can achieve its ends.

We are now in a position to be much more explicit about the way in which a superior influences the behavior of subordinates (Figure 2.4). The leader can give an order as a stimulus for his subordinates. He can also, through learning, have an influence on the total fund of

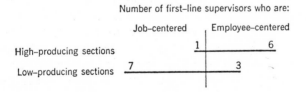

Number of first-line supervisors who are:

	Job-centered	Employee-centered
High-producing sections	1	6
Low-producing sections	7	3

Figure 2.3. (From Rensis Likert, *New Patterns of Management*, New York, McGraw-Hill, 1961, p. 7.)

[12] For an excellent presentation of this research see Rensis Likert, *New Patterns of Management*, New York, McGraw-Hill, 1961.

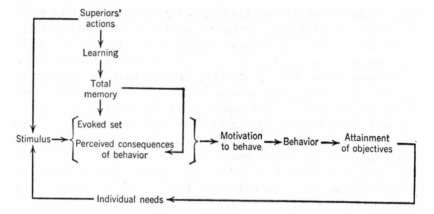

Figure 2.4. Superior's influence on subordinate behavior.

knowledge a person has and from which the evoked set of stimuli will be drawn. The leader can also influence what the person sees as probable consequences of various courses of action. This learning can occur in both formal and informal ways. Viewed in this fashion it is easy to see that the superior has multiple ways of influencing subordinate behavior.

Organizational Influences on Individual Behavior

All too frequently discussions of satisfaction of subordinates' needs revolve around the relationship between the superior and subordinate. This is obviously an extraordinarily important relationship. However, it is not the only relationship to consider when discussing the need satisfaction of people.

As we have seen, the superior, by adopting a particular style of leadership, might keep people from interacting and thereby satisfying some of their social needs. There are many other things, however, which influence people's opportunity to interact. The layout of work, for example, noise, work methods, and many other conditions either hinder or aid the possibility of people interacting. On the other hand, the opportunity for advancement in many situations is controlled either by seniority or merit tests, which are neither designed nor administered by the immediate supervisor but by a central personnel department. We can list many things about everyday work which are of extreme importance in satisfying the needs of people but over which the immediate supervisor has little or no influence. Instead these aspects of work are controlled by decisions made by technical specialists or higher executives, quite removed from the immediate work situation.

As a result of organizational developments, the need satisfaction of subordinates has become an organizational as well as a supervisory issue. To say this a little differently, if leadership is considered the process of facilitating the satisfaction of both organizational and individual objectives and needs, this is first an organizational matter and secondarily a matter of the individual skill and activity of the immediate supervisor.

To understand fully this organizational nature of leadership, we must go one step beyond recognizing that certain classes of things are removed from the decision-making province of the individual supervisor. It is necessary to know that all organizations have in them what might be called a style of leadership which permeates the organization and influences the way in which the individual supervisor will use those elements of decision-making still within his jurisdiction. For example, it is not uncommon to hear a senior executive speaking of a subordinate executive saying, "So and so is too easy on his people. He should be more firm." Nor is it difficult to envision the common result of this, the subordinate manager's learning in one way or another of his boss's views and deciding that he had better appear to be "firmer."

Another aspect of this organizational impact on leadership concerns the way subordinates are brought into the decision-making process. We might conceive of a continuum where at one end the superior makes all the decisions, announces them to subordinates, and tells them to execute their portions of these decisions. On the other end of the continuum is the condition where the superior points to a situation and allows the subordinates to define the problem and develop and adopt their own solutions. Needless to say, there are many points between these extremes having a partial involvement of the subordinates in the decision-making activities.

If, because of the factors we have discussed, high executives in an organization decide, consciously or unconsciously, that it is not good for subordinates to get involved in decision-making, this information probably will permeate the organization quickly, and also act as a guide for subordinate managers in choosing their own immediate leadership style. The result will be that the leadership practices within the organization probably will tend to be homogenous. True, there will be individual variation but taken as a whole we cannot but be impressed with the uniformity of leadership practices usually found within organizations.[13]

Thus, we can see that even within the range of factors that we would normally expect the superior to control, in regard to the need satisfaction of subordinates he does not act as a completely free agent. Rather, many of his decisions will be guided or molded by general properties of the organization in which he finds himself. Hence, leadership quite properly has to be considered primarily as an organizational matter.

SUMMARY

This chapter has been concerned with the influences on the behavior of individuals which are seen as the basic components in organizations. The elements considered and their relationships are shown in Figure 2.4. Stimuli evoke a set of factors in the person's memory, which include knowledge of how to do jobs, other stimuli, and perceived consequences of the various options. These factors in conjunction with personal needs and objectives constitute a motivation which may be strong enough to bring the individual to do something. This results in behavior directed toward an objective which, when achieved, reduces the need felt and eliminates the stimulus effect that brought about the action.

Particular attention was given to the needs or wants of individuals, which were roughly divided into two categories: the physiological and the human or psychological. This last group was subdivided into a number of basic categories of psychological needs. These needs are not all activated at the same time. Instead, they are activated in sequential or hierarchical order with the most fundamental or basic need being the first activated. Only when this one is satisfied to a substantial degree does the need next in order become activated.

The leader's action enters the influence process in two primary ways: (1) through the use of stimuli, which brings about an evoked set; and (2) through learning, which influences total memory content.

These are basic concepts which we shall refer to and extend throughout the remaining portion of this book.

[13] For interesting discussion of how one organization consciously tried to change the style of leadership, see Paul Lawrence, *The Changing of Organizational Behavior Patterns*, Boston, Harvard University, Division of Research, Graduate School of Business Administration, 1958.

3

Perception: The Question
of What We See

If we could be sure of what a given stimulus would evoke, this would be an important but not a particularly troublesome part of our model. As we often do not have a clear idea of this, we are not exactly sure of what behavior response will develop. There are at least three different reasons that a stimulus may have unanticipated consequences.

1. A stimulus may evoke a larger set than expected; or perhaps this is better described as a different set. This situation comes about because we do not have a unique set of memories associated with only one cue. For example, an order from a superior to perform a certain operation may evoke memories of how to perform the operation; but it may also evoke memories of what happened the last time the operation was performed, such as the way the superior criticized the work. Hence, the subordinate may spend a great deal of time thinking about his resentment rather than getting the job done.

2. The stimulus used may include elements which were unperceived or unintended by the person providing it. For example, a superior who has just been told that his automobile needed an expensive repair job and is angry about this may give an order to one of his subordinates in a tone of voice that convinces the employee that he is in disfavor. The subordinate not only has an order to perform an act but also what he regards as additional information on what his boss thinks about him.

3. The person receiving the stimulus may mistake it for another. Perhaps he cannot discriminate adequately between the two or perhaps the stimulus does not clearly define the situation for him. An example of the former is the mock insult often evident among friends. The phrase, "Why, you S.O.B." even with an angry tone might mean

something amusing among friends; whereas, in a less friendly situation it might connote an insult.   A new person in a group not quite sure of how he stands might very well be uncertain or even misinterpret such a phrase.   An illustration of the second situation might be a person in a diner listening to a waitress call out an order, "Two over lightly." This is probably meaningless to a person who does not understand the language used.[1]

To explore these problems more fully, in this chapter we survey the general topic of *perception*, that is, how people form a picture or an understanding of the world about them.

PERCEPTION AND BEHAVIOR

All of us at one time or another have had the experience of watching another person do something or behave in a certain way, saying to ourselves, "He acts as if he thought . . . ," and then filling in some supposition about the way the other person looked at things.   For example, when people give no response to a statement or action we say, "He acts as if he didn't hear (or see) that."   Or the person who has received a rather cold formal response from a clerk in a bureaucracy might say, "He acts as if I were just another set of data."

Simple as the statement, "He acts as if he thought . . ." may be, it illustrates two important points.   First, what the person thinks he sees may not actually exist.   Not too long ago a new young supervisor in a production operation had an experience similar to one most executives have at sometime during their careers.   He had been on the job (his first) a relatively short while when an industrial engineer discussed with him some changes in the work methods used by his subordinates. These changes seemed quite desirable to the new foreman, as they would shorten the work cycle and also remove a number of rather fatiguing aspects of the job.   He was very much surprised, therefore, to find that his employees took violent objection to them.   They pointed out a number of ways in which they thought the changes would not work, and in other ways implied that the proposal was an unfair attempt by "the management" to get more work from them. The foreman followed an understandable course of action.   He tried to explain logically and factually to the employees that this would be as much to their advantage as to the management's.   Although he used considerable patience and tact, he still was not able to remove their

[1] James G. March and Herbert A. Simon, *Organizations*, New York, John Wiley, 1958, pp. 35–36.

objections with logic and facts. It was not until that evening when talking with a friend that he was able to put into words what really was wrong; namely, "They acted as if this simple change in methods was an attempt by management to exploit them." What took him a little longer to recognize was that as long as they had this attitude or belief, any action by management to change any work method would be met, at the very least, with suspicion and probably with hostility.

The second point is that people act on the basis of what they see. Hence, in understanding behavior, we must recognize that facts people do not perceive as meaningful usually will not influence their behavior, whereas the things they believe to be real, even though factually incorrect or nonexistent, will influence it.

Organizations are intended to bring about integrated behavior. Similar, or at least compatible, perceptions on the part of organizational members are therefore a matter of prime consideration. But this situation, like many other organizational matters, is of a reciprocal nature. As we shall see in the remaining portions of this chapter, many things that influence perception are, in turn, directly or indirectly influenced by the organization.[2]

MECHANISMS OF PERCEPTION

Before considering the factors in an organization which can mold or at least influence perception, it is necessary to examine the concept of perception a little more carefully to understand some of the facts about how this phenomenon occurs.

Cues

One of the first things we must recognize is that in learning about things we not only learn what they are, that is, that the round white object is a baseball but we also learn what these things mean, that is, baseball is a sport enjoyed by many people in this country and is a great deal of fun. Upon receiving a signal (sight of a baseball) we perform an interpretative step by which a meaning is attached to it. Many of these "meanings" are so common and fundamental in our understanding of the world that we fail to note them except under unusual circumstances. Who stops to think, for example, that many

[2] For an interesting discussion of both desirability and some of the means for promoting this shared or common perception on organizational matters, see Herbert Kaufman, *The Forest Ranger: A Study in Administrative Behavior,* Baltimore, Johns Hopkins Press, 1960, particularly Chapters 5 and 6.

people tend to view those who wear glasses as more intelligent or women who wear lipstick as less talkative? [3]   One way these meanings are brought home to us is by meeting people from countries different from our own; then we suddenly realize that something we may have deemed very important is unimportant to these people or something very desirable and pleasant to them is repugnant and highly undesirable to us.   Many of the meanings which things have for us thus come from our culture.   They are things all people within the culture share.   These common interpretations of things help enormously in communicating, but they sometimes make it difficult to set factors in perspective so that we can really understand the reasons for behavior.

Of course, there are things that are learned only by certain groups of people in a culture or in a country.   For example, the stop watch is looked upon as a basic tool by the industrial engineer.   He uses it in his work to plan more efficient operations.   To the worker, however, it may be viewed as a repugnant instrument, something which puts him under pressure, an impersonal thing that can cause him great discomfort.   "Holding a watch against them" for many people in industry has the same emotional content as "taking a whip to them."   Here we can see how the same device can have completely different meanings for groups which come quite close together.

Thresholds and the Idea of Selectivity

No doubt we have been all a little disturbed at times when carrying on a conversation with a group of people on a topic of considerable interest, where someone in the group eagerly grasps a side issue in the conversation and through his enthusiasm turns the whole direction of the discussion.   For example, someone relating an amusing story about one of his ancestors mentions casually that he has some of this ancestor's old letters; he may find that the conversation is rather abruptly diverted to these letters, particularly to their stamps, by a stamp enthusiast.   Other members of the group may not even have been fully aware that the old letters had been mentioned until the conversation had proceeded a little way down this new path.

This simple and very common experience illustrates another point

---

[3] There have been a great many studies in the meanings people attach to simple symbols. For example, see W. J. McKeachie, "Lipstick as Determiner of First Impressions of Personality: An Experiment for the General Psychology Course," *Journal of Social Psychology*, 36, 1952, pp. 241–244, and G. R. Thornton, "The Effect upon Judgments of Personality Traits of Varying a Single Factor in a Photograph," *Journal of Social Psychology*, 18, 1943, pp. 127–148.

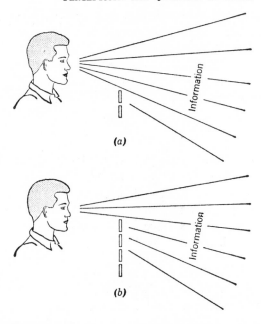

Figure 3.1. Threshold of perception. (*a*) High sensitivity, low threshold; (*b*) low sensitivity, high threshold.

about perception; that we all have certain things (stimuli) to which we are "sensitized," and that when these appear we are instantly alert and eager to examine them. There are other stimuli of relative unimportance to us to which we do not pay as much attention and may, in effect, actually block out. One way of viewing this subject is to suggest that we have *thresholds* or barriers which regulate what information from the outside world reaches our consciousness. On some matters the barriers are high and we remain oblivious to them, but on others which are quite important to us we are sensitized and, in effect, we lower the barrier (see Figure 3.1*a*), permitting all the information possible concerning these matters to reach our consciousness.[4]

RESONANCE. Related to this idea of sensitivity and selectivity is a phenomenon that might be called *resonance*. Through experience and what we see ourselves to be, the understanding of a particular item of

---

[4] For discussion of some of the mechanisms of selectivity and perception, see Leo Postman, Jerome S. Bruner, and Elliott McGinnies, "Personal Values as Selective Factors in Perception," *Journal of Abnormal and Social Psychology*, **63**, 1948, pp. 142–154.

information may be very similar to that of others. For example, a welder knows full well that the diameter of the welding rod, the material of which it is made, and its general quality are very important points in how effectively he can do his job. On the other hand, to a clerk in an office this is a relatively unimportant point, and he would probably have to stop to think about the significance of variations in these elements.

Let us take this a little further. If all the employees in a welding department were involved in welding and the work of one were changed, making it difficult for him to do his job, we would probably expect him to be annoyed and upset by this. We might be surprised, however, to find most of the other welders in the department almost as disturbed about the change as the man directly involved. What we would be witnessing is resonance. It is explained this way: since all the people in the department look upon themselves as welders, they know what the change to the individual welder means in annoyance and inconvenience. They can easily put themselves into his shoes and, once having done so, probably feel almost as disturbed as he. If one welder were placed among various machine operators and assemblers and a change made in his work methods, the people around him might feel sorry for him as an individual, but they would have a difficult time realizing the real significance of this change.

Closure: Filling in the Picture

Most of us at one time have seen pictures like those in Figure 3.2, in which a set of dots or lines are sufficient to see the picture of the shape that we take the dots and lines to represent. On the paper the dots and lines are not connected, and yet in our mind's eye we have no difficulty in linking them to see them represent or portray something. This process of filling in the picture is called *closure*. We do this not only with pictures but also with other types of information which come to us about the world around us. Thus, as someone describes a third party, gives information about his height, weight, general build, color, education, personality, and occupation, he is only supplying bits and pieces of information which our minds fit together into a complete picture. In fact, many times someone describing a person or situation will use just those words, "Do you get the picture?"

Forming this mental image or picture from fragmentary information is not only common but a necessary phenomenon. If we had to wait for all the details before the picture were really clear, life's activities

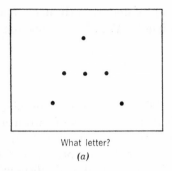

What letter?

(a)

Figure 3.2

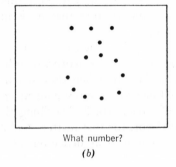

What number?

(b)

would be slowed almost to a standstill. At the same time we must recognize that however useful and necessary the process of closure may be, we are still forming an impression or mental image based on limited facts which may differ from the real thing. The more the difference, the less accurate perception becomes and, therefore, the less suitable our behavior may be. Many things influence closure and the accuracy of perception. First, however, let us examine some other matters relevant to closure and to the phenomenon of perception in general.

INTERNAL CONSISTENCY

One property of the images or pictures formed of the world around us is that they are reasonable, or internally consistent. For instance, we may look at some dots and lines on a page and see them as a dog. One portion of these dots and lines might suggest a hand, but we do not have an image of something half hand and half dog. In fact, if our first impression is of a dog, we may never notice that a portion of the dots looks like a hand. We seem to tune out the elements that do not fit.[5]

Weighted Effect

Another fact concerning the process of forming the bits of information into an image is that some items of information are more important than others. Sometimes it seems that the things learned first have a controlling influence over the interpretation of information acquired later. For example, if we are told at the beginning of a person's description that he is extroverted, very likely the rest of the facts given will be fitted into a picture consistent with this initial information. Conversely, should we first be told that he is introverted, the same patterning would be true.[6]

This is not the only way in which one element of information can order perception. There are some words, or other cues, having such strong effect that regardless of when they occur in the sequence of information they mold or order the resultant image. Hence, if among the words on a list of given words describing the traits of a person were the word "warm" (or, for that matter, "cold"), this word would be likely to have very dominant influence on the type of image developed.[7]

This tendency for one item to influence the total perception is frequently called the *halo effect*, and has been a continual source of difficulty in managerial work, most notably in the evaluation of performance of subordinates. Needless to say, the same sort of problem develops in hiring employees. These are but two of the more obvious and simpler difficulties caused by this phenomenon.

Persistence of Perception Organization

Once we have formed an impression of a person or a situation the impression is likely to have a surprisingly long life. There are apparently a number of reasons for this.

[5] For further discussion on the organization of perception, see Mason Haire and Willa F. Grunes, "Perceptual Defenses: Processes Protecting an Organized Perception of Another Personality," *Human Relations*, 3, 1950, pp. 403–412.

[6] Abraham S. Ouchines, "Experimental Attempts to Minimize the Impact of First Impressions" in C. Hovland (ed.), *The Order of Presentation in Persuasion*, New Haven, Yale University Press, 1957, pp. 63–75.

[7] S. E. Asch, "Forming Impressions of Personality," *Journal of Abnormal and Social Psychology*, 41, 1946, pp. 258–290.

First, the threshold or sensitizing tends to help maintain some organization in our perceptions. We readily admit those things we want to see, or that fit our images, and exclude, or play down, those things that do not seem consistent or supportive. Second, the internal consistency tends to help interpret new information in a way meaningful to the impression already formed. If we have a favorable impression of a person whom we have not met and have learned that he is inquisitive, we should probably say he has an inquiring, curious, wide-ranging mind. On the contrary, should we have an initially negative impression of a person, we may use the information that he is inquisitive to form an image of a person who is, at the least, a busybody and perhaps the type of individual who digs out personal data about people that he can use against them for his own advantage.[8]

Although a particular organization for perception may have considerable tenacity, we are not trying to suggest that it is completely unchangeable. Some impressions which people form do seem to exist relatively unchanged for long periods of time; others change fairly rapidly and easily. The ease with which impressions change depends on many factors, some rooted in the personality of the individual, others in the importance of the particular image to him, and still others in the forces at work to bring about the change.

Social Reality

Behind these processes there is the human being's desire or need to know and understand the world in which he lives, to know the meaning of the information he receives. People are continuously attempting to know what information is important and what it means. Some of this learning comes through experience, as when we learn that a whistling tea kettle is hot and can cause a burn. But a great deal of

[8] There are a number of different proposals concerning the underlying mechanisms for this result. One line of thought says that incoming information to a person may function in two quite different ways. If it comes before an image or impression is formed, it is used to form this conception or framework. Once, however, the framework is formed new information is merely categorized within this framework. See, for example, F. Attneave, "Some Informational Aspects of Visual Perception," *Psychological Review*, **61**, 1954, pp. 183–193. An alternate interpretation is that people are continually comparing new information with what they already "know," and when there is any great difference between the two, a condition known as *cognitive dissonance* develops. People then will act to reduce this dissonance. One way they are thought to do this is by selecting a particular interpretation of new information which will make it fit better with what is already known. See Leon A. Festinger, *A Theory of Cognitive Dissonance*, Stanford University Press, 1957.

this learning comes from being told by others what signals mean. Usually we learn from others that thunder is caused by irate gods or by an electrical discharge called lightning. Whether we understand thunder to be a meaningful sign or a harmless natural phenomenon comes from the people among whom we find ourselves or, better, the culture in which we live.

Man needs to "understand" the meaning of the signals he receives for a number of reasons. We shall consider three.

UNDERSTANDING THE REAL WORLD. We need to know what the real world is like so that we can behave appropriately. When we hear a loud sound from the sky we need to know whether it is thunder, suggesting it might be wise to get an umbrella, or a jet breaking the sound barrier, requiring no action on our part. When a businessman observes a downturn in business activity, he is faced with understanding whether it is a temporary dip, which will require a little belt tightening, or the beginning of a major economic depression, which will necessitate some major cutbacks in the operation of his enterprise. To no small degree his interpretation will depend on whether he sees the economy in a state of long-term growth, meaning that this must be a temporary matter, or sees the past prosperity as having already gone on too long, permitting him to see the current downturn as the beginning of a long economic decline.

CONGRUENCY OF PERCEPTIONS AND COMPATIBLE BEHAVIOR. Most of our life and behavior exists in association with other people, which requires behavior to be compatible, that is, integrated or complementary. Since behavior is determined in part by perceptions, this compatible behavior will be influenced by the degree of congruency of perceptions people hold. On hearing a fire alarm in a public building people understand that it signals danger, and that they should move in an orderly fashion to an exit. The person who finds the bell attractive and starts toward it, in the opposite direction of the crowd, will cause a disturbance.

INTERPERSONAL BEHAVIOR. Often we are more concerned with what a particular signal means in regard to interpersonal behavior than in regard to what it means about the "real" world. For example, a child hearing thunder, perceiving this as a danger, may cry. Its parent, perceiving the sound as something that will frighten the child, acts not with fear but complementarily to comfort the child. In a work group, one worker seeing another having a difficult time with his job, may perceive this as a situation in which he must offer his help.

Someone not of the same group, having the same difficulty, may be viewed as someone having a tough time with his job but not necessarily deserving of assistance. In these situations people are seeking meaning of signals, not to understand the real world in any absolute sense, but as an element to permit them to live more satisfactorily in a social world. As noted at the beginning of this section, the need for this knowledge is great, and people can be viewed as continuously striving to fit pieces into some pattern of understanding. We might further note that once closure has occurred, the organizations of perceptions will persist for long periods.

Consensus

From what has been said we can see that consensus about the meaning of a signal or piece of information is an important aspect of perception in interpersonal behavior. Developing group consensus is a basic process which permits the individual to achieve closure. Checking to maintain consensus is a group mechanism to sustain perception organization. Both group events have their roots in the basic human need for the individual to understand his world.

THINGS THAT MOLD OR INFLUENCE PERCEPTION

Here we discuss the question of the events external to the person which may have an influence upon his perception or, more accurately, on his mechanisms of perception formation. These are the things an outsider may observe and many times control.

Stress

The world in which we live elicits many reactions. A not uncommon one is a feeling of stress. To be called on in the classroom to stand on one's feet and analyze a problem, or, to be asked a question the first time one is attending an important committee meeting, is a stress situation most of us meet at some time. Much of what we say will be dependent upon how we perceive the situation, issue, or question. From what is known, people under stress seem to form their impressions, or complete closure, more quickly than those under less stress. There is some evidence to suggest that under stress they also form less accurate impressions.[9]

[9] See Charles D. Smock, "The Influence of Psychological Stress on the 'Intolerance of Ambiguity,'" *Journal of Abnormal and Social Psychology*, 50, 1955, pp. 177–182.

Group Pressure

We are concerned here not with any overt action of a group toward a person, such as argument or persuasion, but with the effect on a person when he realizes that his perception of a particular item or situation is different from the perception of his group. These differences can be very disturbing, their effect depending on a number of factors. Of particular interest to us is the influence of having support from other group members and the individual's personality. In a word, we are dealing here with *conformity*.

Perhaps the classic studies of conformity pressures have been conducted by Asch. Asch exposed groups of college students to a number of sets of lines, and then asked them which lines matched a standard line also shown. He instructed all except one member of the group to give deliberately the wrong answer on certain displays. The reaction of the "naive" subject was then noted. The naive subject yielded and stated incorrect answers which actually agreed with the majority members of the groups 32 per cent of the time.[10]

EXISTENCE OF ALLIES. Compliance with the group's statements or actions came about not through any overt action but because the naive subject had to stand alone. Asch made some interesting and important variations of his experiment. In one variation he had another member of the group instructed always to give the correct answer and thereby support the naive subject even when the majority of the group were, in accordance with instructions, giving an incorrect one. In this situation the number of pro-majority errors dropped to 5.5 per cent.[11] However, when the ally changed and joined the majority or left the room, the naive subject started to agree more with the majority, and the number of errors increased.

This experiment dramatically shows the effect of having a partner or ally when one person is holding different opinions or beliefs. To put it another way, when one person finds his beliefs, attitudes, or perceptions shared and supported by another, he acquires psychological support to withstand much more easily being different from the majority. The importance of being in a group, even of two, for getting support and assurance in facing the world can be seen easily.

[10] S. E. Asch, "Effects of Group Pressure upon the Modification and Distortment of Judgment," in Dorwin Cartwright and Alvin Zander, *Group Dynamics*, Evanston, Row, Peterson and Company, 1953, p. 157.
[11] *Ibid.*

PERSONALITY.   In his study of conformity Asch divided the naive subjects into two broad categories: those who were independent—that is, they insisted upon stating what they saw even though it was different from the majority opinion—and those who yielded, who went along with the majority opinion.   Each of these broad categories had three subdivisions.

Among the independent subjects were the following types:

1. Those who were quite confident that their perception was correct.   Although they knew they were different from the group, they persisted firmly in their opinions.

2. Those who were withdrawn.   They were characterized more by sticking to their principles of individuality than by vigorously maintaining the accuracy of their perception.

3. Those who felt a great deal of tension and uncertainty about their different perception, but stuck to their opinions because they believed this was necessary to get a job done.

Among the yielding subjects, those who went along with the majority 50 per cent or more of the time, were the following types:

1. Those who apparently experienced a distortion in their perception and who actually claimed to have seen the majority choice as being the correct one.

2. Those who learned to doubt their perception; that is, they knew that they saw the lines differently from the group but thought there must be something wrong with the way they were perceiving things. They were typified by lack of confidence in their own judgment.

3. Those who went along with the majority because they found it too uncomfortable to stand out as different.   They did, however, see differences and had no doubt that they were seeing things accurately.[12]

THE SETTING FOR GROUP PRESSURE.   The effect of group pressure also depends on the setting or situation.   How ambiguous is the situation? The more concrete the item about which the opinions are concerned, the likelier the person will be to "stick to his guns" or at least not to change his own perceptions or beliefs about the correctness of his opinion.   As the situation becomes more ambiguous, shifting from the evaluation of concrete physical to more nebulous things—such as

[12] S. E. Asch, op. cit., pp. 155–156. For further studies, see Richard S. Crutchfield, "Conformity and Character," American Psychologist, 10, 1955, pp. 191–198, and E. W. Bovard, Jr., "Group Structure and Perception," Journal of Abnormal and Social Psychology, 46, 1951, pp. 398–405.

whether an item is beautiful or whether a political opinion is desirable —the more difficult it becomes for the individual to be sure that he is correct and the likelier he is to question his own judgment or, for that matter, even alter his perception.

Interaction

In the studies considered there was no direct interaction among individuals. Let us now consider situations in which there is interaction among group members, for this can substantially influence perception. For example, early in our acquaintance we may like a person and at first think we should like to have him around both at work and during our free time. However, as we get to know him better, we may still like him as a person to socialize with, but may realize that for one of countless reasons he may not be the best person to work with or vice versa.[13] At other times we may learn not only about the person involved but also about the situations in which we are functioning together so that we can better interpret what the other person's behavior means. Thus, through interaction we acquire more information which improves the accuracy of our perception or which may bring about a shift or sharpening of it.[14]

EFFECTS OF PARTICIPATION. It has been noted that participation affects the organization member's feelings of control over the organization, influences his degree of ego involvement, and reduces the visibility of power.[15] In turn, all three of these govern a person's perception. People conceive of and offer new ideas (perceive possibilities they might not otherwise bother with) if given evidence that their ideas are welcome, and they are not in such an inferior power position that there is little likelihood of their ideas being accepted. For our purposes it will be useful to consider participation as an aspect of leadership.

Leadership style can affect perception in still one other way. If the leadership style is autocratic and the superior gives all orders and instructions permitting nothing but compliance from his subordinates,

[13] Ronald Lippitt, "A Program of Experimentation on Group Functioning and Group Productivity," in W. Dennis (ed.), *Current Trends in Social Psychology*, University of Pittsburgh Press, 1948, pp. 14–49.
[14] Jerome S. Bruner and Renato Tagiuri, "The Perception of People," in Gardner Lindzey (ed.), *Handbook of Social Psychology*, Cambridge, Addison-Wesley, 1954, pp. 634–654.
[15] James G. March and Herbert A. Simon, *Organizations*, New York, John Wiley, 1958, p. 54–55.

people will soon develop a mental attitude that will greatly reduce, if not eliminate, the likelihood of their thinking of new ways of doing their job. To this degree their perception of new possibilities will be reduced.

Role

If a person were to walk into a room and see a man hitting a child, he might interpret it in several ways. He might say, "Here is an outrageous situation, a grown man abusing a child," or "Here is a father disciplining his child." There would probably be no dispute over the fact that the child was being struck by an adult, but what this meant would depend on a number of things, principal among them, the way the person viewed the man. If the man were, for example, a stranger to the child, this indeed would be a rather shocking situation and the first interpretation might well be taken. However, if one knew or thought the man was the child's father, the second interpretation would be likelier and the situation more acceptable. What we see, then, depends on what we *expect of a person in a situation*, which in turn depends on the *role* we see him filling.

We live in a tightly constructed society in that social positions are all around us—father, mother, counselor, teacher, boss, subordinate, and many others. These positions are filled by individuals; we expect that when they fill them they will behave in a certain way. That is, we expect an adult man to act in one way toward children who are not his own and differently toward his own children.

Needless to say, all of us fill a number of different roles. During a given day we may be son, student, president of a student club, and something else. We are the same person in each role, but as we move from one to another people expect different things from us, and in all likelihood we will come quite close to filling these expectations. In short, our own behavior is influenced by the roles we see ourselves filling at any one time.

Real difficulties can arise when we see the organization role differently from the way it is seen by other organizational members. A striking study of this was made a few years ago in a plant where the plant manager had died and was replaced by a new man whose interest ran to gaining acceptance and approval from higher executives in the central office. Because he was so concerned with the approval of superiors, and so little concerned with the approval of any other group, there were striking reactions among his subordinates who felt ". . . this pattern of behavior [was] 'unmanly.' He created a situation in which they did not know where they stood and in which they felt powerless." [16]   To his central-office superiors his behavior appeared satisfactory.   Among other things, different role expectations made the difference.

Reference Groups

Many of a person's attitudes or opinions are related or linked to one or more groups.   People use groups in a number of ways to clarify or guide their perceptions.   If the group happens to be the membership committee of a club that an individual would like to join, in asking himself the question, "I wonder what they will think of me if I do such and such?" he is using a *reference group* to understand better some meaning of his current and future actions.   The person who drives through a slum area and sees people in the neighborhood suffering from poverty and other problems may look at his current position more favorably than heretofore, because now he sees how much better it is in relation to the position of others.   Here he is using another group as a reference to locate his current position.   Many times we refer to some group to gain a perspective on life to help understand, evaluate, and form our attitudes.

NORMATIVE AND COMPARATIVE FUNCTIONS OF REFERENCE GROUPS.   Generally speaking, there are two kinds of relationships which a person may have with his reference groups.   One type occurs when the group is important to him, and he wants to be included in it.   In effect, he is concerned with gaining and maintaining the group's acceptance.   In this sort of a situation a person is interested in finding out the values of the group and the attitudes it expects from its members.   He can then use these as guides for his own actions, thereby showing that he has some of the qualifications for acceptance by the group. Here the group serves a *normative function*.   That is, it is used by the person to determine what he ought to think, do, or hold important about certain matters.[17]

On the other hand, people may use reference groups in a different way.   They may not always want to be accepted or gain admission to

[16] Alvin W. Gouldner, *Patterns of Industrial Bureaucracy*, Glencoe, The Free Press, 1954, p. 78.

[17] Howard H. Kelly, "Two Functions of Reference Groups," in Swanson, Newcomb, and Hartley (eds.), *Readings in Social Psychology*, New York, Holt, 1952, pp. 410–414.

the group as, for example, a group of people living in a slum neighbor-hood. Nonetheless, groups of this sort can serve as reference groups. If a person were to place himself, he could position himself above the group in the slums and somewhere below Supreme Court Justices, feel-ing that he does not have the exact position in life he would like, but does have one better than many people. Or he may be applying for a job, and in attempting to evaluate his own prospects he may consider and compare the qualifications of the other applicants with his own. Again, he may have a very clear image of this group (for example, of the graduating seniors from his own college) and yet not be thinking of joining it but of using it instead as a reference to evaluate himself. In these situations the group serves a *comparison function*.[18]

COSMOPOLITANS AND LOCALS. From an organizational point of view we are quite concerned with people's attitudes toward their work and the organizations of which they are members. Attitudes, in turn, are fre-quently dependent on the reference groups chosen. Unfortunately, the number of reference groups which may influence a person's be-havior is almost infinite. Again, to cope with this sort of problem we employ classes of items.

One way to classify reference groups is on the basis of whether they are inside or outside of the organizations in question. For example, a scientist working in a business concern may be quite dedicated to his chosen discipline. As such he may feel that among the important things in life for him is to be recognized as a scientist who has made contributions to his field. This is not general public recognition but a recognition and approval by people who know his discipline well enough to evaluate him accurately; these people are largely other scientists in his field. He then has the recognition that is important to him.

However, the overwhelming majority of scientists who can recog-nize the merits of this individual work outside of his present com-pany. Thus the group whose acceptance he is attempting or hoping to achieve is in reality an outside group of other scientists in his disci-pline. Such a person is a *cosmopolitan;* he is not likely to view with favor any work assignments that take him away from the research which is going to earn him the recognition he desires. Hence, admin-istrative work, filling in reports, worrying about budgetary matters are nuisances to be tolerated only when they cannot be avoided. Any formal job assignments requiring him to spend less time on research (for instance, an appointment to a managerial post) would be a most

[18] Kelly, *op. cit.,* p. 413.

undesirable development. For quite understandable reasons, therefore, he might quickly turn down an offer of a promotion to a post in the managerial hierarchy.

His refusal may be perplexing to executives in the company. They may be very interested in getting a promotion because this signifies to others in the company that they are making the grade, showing competence and ability. Furthermore, since in all likelihood they think quite highly of their organization, they believe that to be a high-ranking member is most important. In short, these people will identify themselves closely with reference groups in, or immediately connected with, the organizations of which they are members. These people we can call *locals*.[19]

For the person analyzing behavior in an organization it will be important to determine the reference groups members choose. If, for example, a company were going to reorganize and its employees were going to have to shift jobs, no doubt there would be internal disturbances during the period of transition. This might lead the cosmopolitans to think that in order to do their real work they would have to go elsewhere. On the other hand, locals, having their reference groups within the organization and loyalties to it, probably would be more willing to tolerate the shifting and confusion feeling that in the long run the change would benefit the organization, which to them is a very important entity. In short, determining which of these classifications applies to an individual will enable us to discern in part how he will perceive organizational changes and to understand better how he will behave.

REFERENCE GROUPS WITHIN AN ORGANIZATION. Within any organization a person may have several different reference groups. For example, people will frequently use their superiors as reference groups, and attempt to find out their attitudes, beliefs, and wants, then try to show that they are in conformance with or supportive of them. This effort may carry over even to minor details of behavior or dress. For instance, subordinates may go to great lengths to wear clothing of the same styling and color as their boss' and perhaps even adopt some of his personal mannerisms. An individual starts to identify with his superiors because they are so important to his life and are also where he intends to be some day. We may find a different attitude toward subordinates. The superior looks on them as props to him and his

[19] Alvin W. Gouldner, "Cosmopolitans and Locals: Toward an Analysis of Latent Social Roles," *Administrative Science Quarterly*, 2, 1957, pp. 281–306; and *ibid.*, 2, 1958, pp. 444–480.

advancement but not as a group with which he strongly identifies personally.[20]

Sometimes a person's peers are his important reference group. This is not at all difficult to understand; these are the people with whom he will associate as equals, with whom he may make his closest friendships and satisfy many of his deep needs for social activities. Wanting to be accepted by his peers, a person may very well be aware of the fact that he has to show attitudes of friendliness and cooperativeness, sometimes even at the expense of violating some of the expectations of his superiors or his subordinates. In situations where people are within the organization only during the time they are actively at work, and during these times are primarily involved with their superiors or subordinates, peer associations may not loom large. However, where one is in residence in the organization all the time, even when not working, as aboard a naval ship, peer relationships may become much more potent.[21] At the worker level—that is, below supervisory ranks—peer relationships frequently are the most dominant of all.[22]

A third major category to which an individual in an organization may relate himself are his subordinates. When superiors give him an order to follow this person is quite likely to ask, "What will my people think if I do this?" rather than "What will my bosses think if I do not do it?" Needless to say, this, too, will influence organizational performance.

Organizational Position

The place or position a person occupies in an organization has considerable influence on the way things appear to him. To illustrate, a person who deals largely with matters of marketing, selling the commodity, anticipating customers' tastes and preference, and reaction to a product frequently tends to view many of the company's problems as marketing problems. People in accounting or finance are likely to look at many company problems as matters of control; just as those in the personnel department may view most problems as being related to selection and motivation of employees. In sum, the type of work a

[20] William E. Henry, "The Business Executive: The Psycho-Dynamics of a Social Role," *American Journal of Sociology*, **54**, 1949, pp. 286–291.

[21] See, for example, a very interesting discussion in Ralph H. Turner, "The Navy Disbursing Officer as a Bureaucrat," *American Sociological Review*, **12**, 1947, pp. 342–348.

[22] We shall discuss this more fully in the chapter on small groups, but among the major items in the literature is Fritz J. Roethlisberger, William J. Dickson, *Management and the Worker*, Cambridge, Harvard University Press, 1956.

person does, defined largely by his organizational position, will seriously influence the way things look to him, making the problems or affairs of the organization seem like extensions of his work.

An interesting illustration of this appeared in a study in which a group of business executives from a wide variety of companies was given a case which described a company with a number of general problems. The executives were asked to analyze the case and state what each thought to be the most important problem facing the company. Their responses were classified according to whether they identified a sales problem, a problem where it was necessary to "clarify organization," or a human relations problem. The responses were then compared with the departmental backgrounds of the executives responding. As seen in Table 3.1, sales executives tended to view the

Table 3.1

Department	Total Number of Executives	Sales	Number Who Mentioned "Clarify Organization"	Human Relations
Sales	6	5	1	0
Production	5	1	4	0
Accounting	4	3	0	0
Miscellaneous	8	1	3	3
Totals	23	10	8	3

Source: DeWitt C. Dearborn and Herbert A. Simon, "Selective Perception: A Note on the Departmental Identifications of Executives," *Sociometry,* **21**, 1958, p. 142.

company problem as being in the sales area; production executives thought that clarification of the organization was necessary; and the so-called "miscellaneous" [23] classification of executives tended to view the company as having primarily human relations problems.[24]

Departmental identification places a person on a horizontal scale, that is, horizontally across the traditional organization chart. However, vertical position also has an important influence on the perception of people. The different levels of an organization reflect not only different hierarchical positions but also vastly different forms of

[23] The miscellaneous classification of executives was composed of two members of the legal department, two in research and development, and one each from public relations, industrial relations, medical, and purchasing.

[24] DeWitt C. Dearborn and Herbert A. Simon, "Selective Perception: A Note on the Departmental Identifications of Executives," *Sociometry,* **21**, 1958, pp. 140–144.

work. Managerial positions at the first and second levels in the hierarchy are confronted with problems of immediate nature which require immediate action and where the corrective action will be effective in relatively short periods of time. As a person moves higher into the organization, the problems faced have longer time dimension and are likely to come up less frequently. Problems at higher levels of the organization take longer to analyze, to start action on, and require longer periods for action to reach fruition. We may find, therefore, that when a first-line supervisor looks at a problem, he may consider it a major crisis in need of immediate attention. His boss, to whom he may have come for authorization to work his department overtime, may view it as a relatively minor disturbance compared to the longer run, more important problems with which he has to cope.[25]

There is another aspect of hierarchial position. In general, the higher a person goes, the greater the range of resources and opportunities under his control. With this greater scope for action, a person in the higher position is likelier to see courses for actions than is one in a lower position.

JOB CONTENT. The content of jobs at a given hierarchical level can vary greatly depending on many factors. Some hold relatively little in the way of opportunities for the position holder to make decisions, whereas others at the same level may have a wide range of decision-making possibilities. The influence of job content on behavior will be explored more fully in Chapter 10. Here we merely wish to identify it as another factor which influences the number of optional actions likely to occur to a person, that is, likely to influence his perception.

POSITION IN A COMMUNICATION NET. Still another way in which organizational position can be of importance is as a place in a communication network. Some positions are so placed that much information flows through them giving the occupant a great deal of data with which to form opinions. Other positions have less centrality, and as a consequence have much less information passing through them giving their occupants less knowledge.

Reward Systems

Several times we have dwelt on the particular aspect of perception which deals with the possible actions a person sees in a situation. To

[25] For an interesting discussion of these various perspectives, see Norman H. Martin, "Differential Decisions in the Management of an Industrial Plant," *Journal of Business*, **29**, 1956, pp. 249–260.

explore this further, we have to recognize the impact of a system of rewards on an organization. At least two different effects can be noted. First, there are some rewards which are directly tied in with the development of new ideas, such as suggestion systems. Here, of course, the person may not even have to use the idea; he has only to produce it. Second, incentives are tied in many times with productivity. Here the person is looking at the consequences of actions in a more constrained way. This is not to say that production incentives do not produce new ideas. In truth, frequently they do, as anyone knows who has had the chance to observe the short cuts and improved work methods often devised by people working under incentive payment schemes. However, the range of ideas evoked is likely to be narrower, and people will be more concerned with the consequences of their actions under a production incentive plan than under a reward plan geared to the development of new ideas.

We could explore this subject interminably. For now, let us merely note that a person's organizational position will have a great deal to do with the perceptions he forms of the organization. In his role his perceptions are formed partially through his job identifications, job requirements, information he receives in his position, and the reward system. For brevity's sake, many other things will have to be left untouched.

SUMMARY

In this chapter we have considered the topic of perception, which is the understanding or view people have of things in the world around them. A person's perception of a thing, a fact, or an act may be quite different from the actual and also may be quite different from the perception anyone else has of that thing, fact, or act. Hence, we note the differentiation between perception and actuality. Perceptions are of extreme importance to understanding organizational behavior, for people act on the basis of what they think they see or understand.

Perception is, in part, a process which entails being sensitized to and developing certain interpretations of stimuli or facts. Some facts enter our consciousness very quickly and easily, and others, because of their high thresholds, enter only with difficulty, if at all.

One of the basic factors in perception is the ability of people to take a limited number of facts and pieces of information and fit them into a whole picture. This process of closure plays a central role in perception. The "picture" formed has a considerable degree of internal consistency in that its parts seem to fit together in a way that makes sense. This consistency comes about in a number of ways. Some ideas or cues are so influential that regardless of when they occur they serve as a central organizing point. However, at other times when such a centrally important cue is missing, the particular organization of perception may be dominated by the information received first. Also, later information is often interpreted or viewed in a way that makes it fit into the emerging or perhaps already formed picture. The impression a person has—or better yet, his perceptual organization—has a considerable stability and in some cases persists over remarkably long periods of time.

Of particular interest are some of the external things which influence a person's perception. Stress conditions were noted as having an important effect on closure. One of the particular types of stress which received attention was that of group pressures where a person finds his opinions at variance with those around him. Another external factor is the interactions a person has with the people with whom he is sharing or comparing opinions. The greater the interaction and the more information available, the likelier it is that a perception will become sharper and more defined. A third factor found to influence perceptions are the expectations people have of a person occupying a role.

One of the key influences in forming attitudes, absorbing values, and obtaining interpretation—in short, in forming perceptions—are reference groups. Reference groups are groups with which a person relates or identifies in one of several ways. Furthermore, a person's perception will be influenced by where he stands as he looks at a situation, a fact, or an act. It was noted that a person's organizational position will have much to do with how he looks at things or the perceptions he has about acts or facts in or related to the organization.

Since so many elements have been surveyed, it may be well to consider one simplified way in which they fit together. Our beginning relationship is shown in Figure 3.3. Our real interest has been centered, however, on the ways in which perceptions are formed. For this reason it is convenient to think of perception formation as preceding the existence of the perception itself.

Perception formation consists of three mechanisms (Figure 3.4). The first is *selectivity*, in which certain pieces of information are

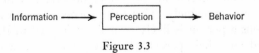

Figure 3.3

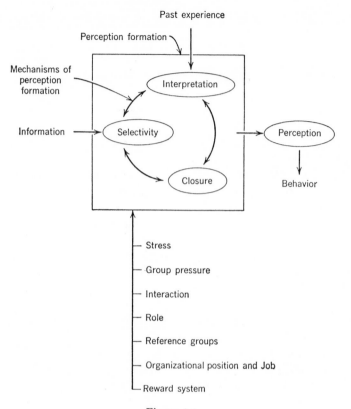

Figure 3.4

separated for further consideration by thresholds. The second is *closure*, where the bits of information are compiled into a meaningful whole. The third is *interpretation*, where previous experiences aid in judging the information collected. Information admitted by selectivity is given meaning by either closure or interpretation, or both; and, of course, both feed back to determine what information will be selected.

The Perceptions and the Evoked Set

In this chapter we have discussed perception in a rather general sense. Our prime interest in this book, however, is in a particular aspect of perception, namely, what this process means in regard to the action-decisions a person is likely to make in regard to the courses of action evoked and their perceived consequences. It would be well, therefore, to extend this summary to draw together those items discussed which influence these two important aspects of the motivation to behave.

The Evoked Set of Courses of Action

We have noted an array of things that influence the content of the courses of action which a person is likely to see. Among them are a number of effects caused by *groups*. Of particular importance are the things others in the group are doing. Do they differ from us? Do they support us? Do they accept us? What we see may help us develop new ideas for action. We also noted the effect of *leadership style on participation*. Affecting participation, in turn, was noted to affect a person's perception of *control over his environment* and the *visibility of power relations*. Still another influence was the position a person held both as to its *content* and its *location in the organization structure*, which materially influenced the evoked set (Figure 3.4).

PERCEIVED CONSEQUENCES. Some of the categories of things discussed also influence the perceived consequences. Principal among these factors are the rewards for performance or production, which may take the form of promotions, wage increases, etc., and also the group in which the person finds himself (Figure 3.4). Not explicit, but to be recognized, is the influence the superior will have in molding various aspects of the reward system, particularly those other than monetary or formal promotion. If we consider the praise and recognition a person may get for a particular type of performance as a reward, this is directly under control of the supervisor and can be included under the general variable of leadership.

4

Status

STATUS is a simple idea. It is the ranking of people in a social system. In everyday conversation we allude to this phenomenon many times. We refer to upper class, middle class, or lower class. We speak of highbrow or lowbrow. We note that old established families in a city move in a different circle from newer additions to the community. Although we may recognize these references to status quite readily, we often do not sense how pervasive our interest in status can be in thinking and behavior.

Consider the case of people in a club or work setting being told that a new member will join their group. They will probably ask questions about the new person, such as, "Where does he come from? Where did he go to school? Who are his family? What does he do? Where does he live?" These questions are extremely revealing, especially about the importance of status. Compare them with another set of questions: "What is his personality like? Does he have a quick mind? Will he be loyal to our group?" This set of questions concerns individual nature or personality. The first set is less concerned with, "What is he like?" than with, "Where do we classify him within a larger social scheme?" The first set really seeks information about his status. That is, where does he fit? More importantly, where does he fit relative to us? It is this almost universal concern of individuals about their place relative to others in a status system which makes this a topic of fundamental importance for understanding organizations.

Status is not an absolute property of people. It is the interpretation others place on certain properties an individual has. For example, a man may have the ability to repair his own automobile. In some

66

quarters this talent would be looked on as a proper, laudatory, perhaps somewhat outstanding thing to do that sets the individual apart as one who is above those who cannot or will not do likewise. In other quarters the man who works with his hands would be viewed as someone who has lowered himself or who is of lower status. Status, then, is a special case of perception. The desire to "place" people is but one type of closure.

Whereas all aspects of status are of interest to the student of organization, some are more important than others for his analysis. There are different ways of classifying status. Perhaps the most fundamental is to distinguish between the roots, or sources, of status. One type of status, called *ascribed*, is the status a person is born to, the caste system in India, for example. Less defined ascribed status is found in other countries. In the United States a child born into a prominent family immediately has status as a member of that family. Although of interest, ascribed status is not of major concern in this study of organizations. *Achieved* status, on the other hand, is. Achieved status is the status a person acquires during the course of life. The person who achieves a college education usually has a higher status than one who does not. The person who has a high school education will in some ways have a higher status than the person who has only a grade school education. At the same time the president of a major corporation may, through his personal efforts and accomplishments, achieve a status level far beyond that into which he was born on, perhaps, "the other side of the tracks."

The key idea is that achieved status comes about because of something a person has done or is doing. It is not permanent or fixed but can be changed in two primary ways. Perhaps we can understand this better if we envision a status hierarchy. A person who can acquire some of the properties or characteristics of positions with higher status attains a higher status. This is one way status can be changed. Since status is, however, a matter of relative position, one person's status can be changed by altering the status structure. For example, when a person keeps the same properties, but the status hierarchy is extended with the addition of three or four positions above him, he is further from the top; relatively speaking, he has lost status.

Achieved status is of primary importance in the study of organization, since an organization influences both the movement of people into positions of status and the number of positions in a status system. In turn, organizations are significantly influenced by people's concern about and reaction to their status.

TYPES OF STATUS STRUCTURES

Status would be much simpler to study if there were but one status structure; actually there are many.   In this section we shall consider a few of the more prominent and common ones.

Occupation

All kinds of work are not given equal status rank by either our society in general or the members of a particular organization.   Some occupations, such as those of judge or physician, rank high.   Others, such as street sweepers or window washers, rate relatively low. Farmers, engineers, and welders fit somewhere between these extremes.   Although it is not standard for all time or for all people, an occupation ranking is nonetheless fairly stable.   Occupational ranking has been studied by many, and the results of one such study are reproduced in Table 4.1.

Table 4.1   Prestige Ratings of Selected Occupations, 1947

1. U. S. Supreme Court justice	96	18. Lawyer		86
2. Physician	93	19. Member of board of large		
3. State governor	93	corporation		86
4. Cabinet member in federal		20. Nuclear physicist		86
government	92			
5. Diplomat in the U. S. foreign		21. Priest		86
service	92	22. Psychologist		85
6. Mayor of a large city	90	23. Civil engineer		84
7. College professor	89	24. Airline pilot		83
8. Scientist	89	25. Artist who paints pictures		
9. U. S. representative in		that are exhibited in galleries	83	
Congress	89	26. Owner of factory that		
10. Banker	88	employs about 100 people	82	
		27. Sociologist	82	
11. Government scientist	88	28. Accountant for a large		
12. County judge	87	business		81
13. Head of department in		29. Biologist		81
state government	87	30. Musician in symphony		
14. Minister	87	orchestra		81
15. Architect	86			
16. Chemist	86	31. Author of novels		80
17. Dentist	86	32. Captain in the regular army	80	

33.	Building contractor	79	62.	Local official of a labor union	62
34.	Economist	79	63.	Owner-operator of a lunch stand	62
35.	Instructor in public schools	79	64.	Corporal in the regular army	60
36.	Public school teacher	78			
37.	County agricultural agent	77	65.	Machine operator in a factory	60
38.	Railroad engineer	77			
39.	Farm owner and operator	76	66.	Barber	59
40.	Official of an international labor union	75	67.	Clerk in a store	58
			68.	Fisherman who owns his own boat	58
41.	Radio announcer	75	69.	Streecar motorman	58
42.	Newspaper columnist	74	70.	Milk-route man	54
43.	Owner-operator of printing shop	74	71.	Restaurant cook	54
44.	Electrician	73	72.	Truck driver	54
45.	Trainer machinist	73	73.	Lumberjack	53
46.	Welfare worker for city government	73	74.	Filling-station attendant	52
47.	Undertaker	72	75.	Singer in a night club	52
48.	Reporter on daily newspaper	71	76.	Farm hand	50
49.	Manager of a small store in a city	69	77.	Coal miner	49
			78.	Taxi driver	49
50.	Bookkeeper	68	79.	Railroad section hand	48
			80.	Restaurant waiter	48
51.	Insurance agent	68			
52.	Tenant farmer—one who owns livestock and machinery and manages the farm	68	81.	Dock worker	47
			82.	Night watchman	47
			83.	Clothes presser in a laundry	46
53.	Traveling salesman for a wholesale concern	68	84.	Soda-fountain clerk	45
			85.	Bartender	44
54.	Playground director	67	86.	Janitor	44
55.	Policeman	67	87.	Share cropper—one who owns no livestock and equipment and does not manage farm	40
56.	Railroad conductor	67			
57.	Mail carrier	66			
58.	Carpenter	65	88.	Garbage collector	35
59.	Automobile repairman	63	89.	Street sweeper	34
60.	Plumber	63	90.	Shoe shiner	33
61.	Garage mechanic	62		Average	69.8

Source: Opinion News, September 1, 1947, pp. 4–5.

Material Worked On

Although all members of the same occupation are, in the broad sense, within the same status position or level, it would be misleading to presume that there are no status differences within an occupational grouping. One way people are classified in an occupational category is by the material on which they work. For example, within large restaurants there may be a number of cooks. Individuals within this category will be differentiated according to the type of food they prepare. The person who works on fish will be ranked lower than the one who works on chickens who, in turn, will be ranked lower than the one who works on beef.[1] Similar differences can be noted in most other occupational groups.

Skill or Knowledge Differences

People within an occupational category can be differentiated according to the skill or knowledge they possess for their job. Thus, within a group of machinists, all of whom may have the same title and even the same wage rate, some are given higher status by their associates because they are assigned to work on more exacting or difficult pieces requiring more skill and ability.

By examining occupation status first, the impression is sometimes given that status ranks are broadly defined. This is wrong. As we have seen, one status scale can be applied to refine another so that it is often possible to give each person a rather precise position which differentiates him from the rest of society. Hence, for example, it is possible within a kitchen for a person to have status according to the general occupational category into which he is placed, cook. Within the cook's grouping he can have position according to the material he works on, let us say, chickens. The first classification places him among the ten cooks in a kitchen of perhaps sixty people. The second classification separates him from the ten cooks into the three who work on chickens. Among these he may be differentiated according to skill and be given the most difficult or demanding chicken dishes to prepare in recognition of his talent; hence, he may be classified as the highest among the chicken cooks. It should be noted that while these three methods of classifying status may be integrated in the way indi-

[1] William F. Whyte, *Human Relations in the Restaurant Industry*, New York, McGraw-Hill, 1948, Chapter 4.

cated, it is equally possible for them to be used separately or in some other combination.

Rank

Let us return to the different forms of status rankings. Hierarchical position in organization gives a definite status ranking. Those at the top of an organization, for example, presidents and vice presidents of corporations, rank higher in the status system than plant managers who, in turn, rank higher than elevator operators. For many persons this type of arrangement is illustrated by the typical organization chart. When they see that the block representing the position occupied by an individual is at the top or close to the top of the chart, they tend to give it or presume that it has a fairly high status. This has been a source of difficulty to planners of formal organization charts, particularly when relatively unimportant positions are placed near the top of an organization, as sometimes happens with certain staff occupations. The planner of the organization may not intend to suggest that the position has a high status, but those viewing its location on the chart may think it has which, in turn, may cause considerable difficulty.

Wages

To recognize that wages are important to people is hardly novel. To understand some of the reasons why wages are important is exceedingly significant and perhaps not as obvious. A number of studies have shown that wages are relatively unimportant to people in comparison with many other things they obtain on a job. Yet when we consider all the difficulty and disagreements that revolve around wages, we sometimes may wonder about the validity or accuracy of such observations. Part of this confusion may be eliminated by distinguishing between wages as a *quantity of money* and wages as *a symbol*.

Perhaps this point can be illustrated by referring to a situation in which an employee protested vehemently to his superior about the inadequacy of his wages. During a long and heated discussion, he mentioned the fact that a relatively new man in the organization and one, in his opinion, inferior to him, was actually making a few cents more an hour. Toward the end of the discussion he finally specified what he wanted. Surprisingly enough, he did not want any large increase. He said, "I don't need much of an increase, but I do need at least six cents." This would have amounted to an increase of two dollars and forty cents a week.   Considering the employee was already making two dollars and sixty cents an hour, this was hardly a major increase.   What this increase would have done, however, would have been to eliminate the three cents an hour difference between himself and the next highest paid employee, and place him three cents an hour more in pay above any other employee in his classification.   The new wage would have placed him in a higher position relative to the other employees with whom he was ranking himself.   The difference between them was not particularly important to him as long as there was a difference and he was on top.

Seniority

Seniority is a common way of ranking people.   The old timers on a job are usually looked up to for guidance and advice by the newer men, and have an almost universal status position.   The fact that seniority has been taken over into the formal job rules, usually at the behest of unions, perhaps signifies the fundamental importance that many people attach to this form of status ranking.

Derived Status

One interesting form of status is that which a person achieves through his associations.   We have already noted that all people within an occupation do not possess exactly the same status position. One other way in which they may be differentiated is by employer or primary agent with whom they associate.   A maid working for the Rockefeller family, even though she may do the same work and receive the same pay, has a higher status than a maid who works for the James Smith family.

Multiplicity of Status Rankings

This discussion by no means exhausts the number of status hierarchies.   Some very prominent ones have not even been touched on, such as age, sex, and race.   However, this list should serve to identify some of those which will be of significant importance in the study of organizations and which will be referred to later in this book.   The important point is that there are a large number of status rankings, and a person may have a place on several of them at the same time.   Sometimes being on several of them will help clarify a person's position, but it should also be understood that at other times he may find himself on several which do not help clarify his position and, in fact, may confuse it. We shall deal with this situation more thoroughly in a later section of this chapter.

STATUS SYMBOLS

Status rankings are often identified by observable symbols. Such symbols, denoting status, are important to people for two related reasons. First, a person can tell where others rank and where he fits relative to them; second, others will, in turn, know his position. Sometimes, of course, it is relatively easy to identify a person's status, as when we walk through a machine shop we can note who are the machinists and who are the sweepers by the tools they use; the tools function both as an instrument and as a symbol. In other situations the work itself does not make such simple visual classification possible.

If we were to go into a large office, we would have a much more difficult time differentiating status merely by observing the tools or the work. All people would seem to be sitting at desks, all people would seem to be working with papers or engaged in conversation, and few would be seen to be doing something which, to the uninitiated eye, would be different. It is very difficult for even a fairly knowledgeable observer to look at two men sitting at desks and be able to tell which is the engineer working on the advanced project, requiring a great deal of skill and knowledge, and which is the engineer working on a rather ordinary project, requiring no extraordinary amount of skill and ability. Hence, we have great difficulty in differentiating many types of status in an office situation. We must turn to other signs to determine a person's status position. We should not presume simply because there are no easily evaluated external clues that status is not important in an office situation.

An observer sophisticated about the ways of an office will probably have no real difficulty in determining the status structure and the place of any one person within it. He will doubtless have learned to read the subtle symbols used to mark these differences. He will be able to note some obvious differences: that some people work in private offices with a secretary having a separate office in front. Others work in offices which they share with their secretaries, and still others work in offices they share with large numbers of other people. This gives him one set of clues. Moreover, he will turn to more subtle differences, and note that even among those having private offices some will have thick rugs on the floor while others will have asphalt tile. Some have large mahogany desks, others have oak or metal, and most interestingly, some have none at all. Within the large offices, which perhaps a number of people share, he will note that some have the positions close to the window and the others do not. Some have a position where they look at the back of the heads of everyone else while others occupy a position where everyone else in the room can see them. All these and many other factors are symbols which the sophisticated observer can use to determine the status position of people within the office.

One noticeable aspect of status symbols is that they are usually developed informally. There are obvious exceptions; the military, for one, formally designates explicit symbols for different hierarchical ranks, which clearly are status positions. But in the large sense, these are symbols which, as a rule, are informally designated. People note observable differences between status positions and then use these as symbols to differentiate among them. Furthermore, these differences once established, though informally, are useful and carefully adhered to, even though there is no formal rule that certain symbols go with certain status.

One interesting study showed how aprons and shop coats were informally controlled status symbols in a machine shop. In this particular plant all employees had the formal right to use whichever they chose. The aprons were provided by the company and rented for a nominal rate to the employees. Very few employees used the coats; only those four or five people at the very top of the status structure, but below the rank of supervision, used them. No one said these were reserved for the most skilled worker, but this informal code was strictly adhered to. In fact, when one new employee violated the use of these symbols and wore a shop coat, he did so for only a week before changing to the proper symbol of his status. In another instance when an employee started wearing clothes symbolic of positions almost two ranks higher than his current assignment, there was a great deal of concern both among the workers and management. The final consequence was that the members of the management hierarchy decided to move the employee "misusing" the status symbols into a higher capacity more in line with what he was wearing. The solution was, in brief, to eliminate the violation by putting the individual involved in a position where what he was doing was no longer a violation. It should be noted that this was done under unusual circumstances of a labor shortage and an expanding company. Here is an interesting and dramatic example of the importance of these informal rules and the concern of members of the formal hierarchy over their infringement or violation.[2]

To summarize, it is seen that various status positions usually have certain identifying symbols: uniforms, tools, work locations, and furniture to name a few. By noting the symbols associated with an individual, his status ranking can be determined even though it may be difficult to detect the base on which this position rests. In fact, the more difficult it is for the casual observer to see the basis for differentiation, the more important the symbols may be.

PREROGATIVES

Closely aligned with status symbols are the *prerogatives* which frequently accompany status. As a general rule, the higher a person is within a status hierarchy, especially in a work situation, the more freedom of movement he has, both as to where he goes and when, as well as access to people and information. The man working at a position on an assembly line, for example, does not have many of these freedoms. He is pretty well fixed in one place during the work day, makes practically no decisions concerning what he does, and the assembly line controls when he acts. Even if he were not pinned down, he would not be in a position to get much information nor would he be able to walk into the plant manager's office at his will and obtain the things he wanted. Contrasted with such a position, the vice president in charge of manufacturing has considerable freedom. He can go around the country to visit plants and attend business associations and special meetings. He is also more in control of when he does these things. He can get a great deal of information automatically and can readily get considerably more by asking for it. Since prerogatives parallel status rankings, they become important in our understanding of people's concern about status. The complaints sometimes heard in plants that "some young punk of an expediter can come and go in the plant while I have to clock out if I even want to go to the infirmary," reflect some of the problems which can arise with prerogatives.

Limitations Imposed by Status

Status, if often accompanied by prerogatives, can also impose limitations on the acts, movements, and information received; these we

[2] Frank J. Jasinski, "How They Dress on the Job: Clues to the Informal Organization," *Personnel*, **34**, 1957, pp. 35–41.

might call negative prerogatives. We do not expect to hear a university president swear. Officers in military services are not supposed to become too friendly or fraternize with enlisted men. Clergymen are not told off-color jokes. These are only a few of the restrictions which accompany higher status positions.

Some Mishandling of Status Symbols and Prerogatives

When it is more difficult to discern status quickly by observation, the use of symbols, as we have seen, becomes greater in importance. This increase in the importance of symbols has not gone unnoted by people in formal organizations and has lead to a number of unfortunate procedures. One of these has its start in confusing the symbol of status with status itself, which leads to the error of presuming that when the symbol is changed the status itself changes. Changing symbols may have a desired short-run effect, but, in general, this soon deteriorates into confusion and frustration. The important factor is not the symbol but the relative positions people have to one another. Once people learn that the old meaning of the symbol no longer exists, they seek some new way either to clarify their current position or to improve it in some real fashion. Hence, changing titles to give a position a fancier or more elaborate label may temporarily soothe the person who has been frustrated because of his low status until he finds out that all others on the same level as he, whom he was trying to rise above, now have the same label.

An interesting and different sort of case came to light a number of years ago when a company employing many thousands of engineers recognized that the men who stayed in engineering could advance only through three ranks before they reached the top engineering position open to them. Men would begin as a junior engineer, advance to a senior engineer, perhaps become a project engineer, and then, unless they were going to go into some sort of managerial work, there would be no higher positions for them to assume. Most engineers would achieve the rank of project engineer five to eight years after graduation. This meant there was no way of using titles to distinguish those who had much seniority in the company or those who possessed a high order of skill and ability. In recognition of this the company established three additional grades of engineers above the project engineer, culminating in the position of consulting engineer. It was presumed that only those engineers of the highest abilities would ever achieve this rank and that there would now be sufficient positions and titles to identify different degrees of engineering competence. This worked well for a while, and the engineers seemed to accept it gratefully.

The company had been expanding rapidly and many relatively young inexperienced engineers were put into managerial positions. After a period of time, it was recognized that some of them were not doing well as executives and would have to be removed from their managerial post. Since they were competent engineers, higher management wanted to retain them and give some recognition of the fact that it had appreciated their efforts as managers even though they had not worked out. The question was: Should these men be put back into the rank they had occupied several years earlier, or should it be presumed that age and experience had increased their ability so that they would qualify for one of the newer, higher professional engineering ranks? The decision was made to give them the rank of consulting engineer partially in recognition of their efforts as managers. Though laudable and understandable, this step proved to be disastrous for the expanded hierarchy of engineering jobs. It soon became known among the engineers that to be offered the position of consulting engineer was almost an insult; as they saw it, this rank had become "the dumping ground for broken-down engineering managers."

A knowledge of status and status symbols is imperative for managerial people to prevent them from acting in ignorance.

SOME BEHAVIORAL ASPECTS OF STATUS

Behavior Between and Within Status Levels

For the moment let us assume that there is only one status structure. What effects will status have on individuals at different levels and on the same level within this structure?

A fairly general observation has been that there are more communicative acts of a nontask nature from lower to higher status positions, or, if not actually communicating, people prefer to communicate with those of higher status than with those of lower status.[3] However, the largest volume of communication occurs between people at the same level or in the same group.

To appreciate the effect of status on communication requires that

[3] See, for example, J. M. Jackson, *Analysis of Interpersonal Relations in a Formal Organization*, unpublished Ph.D. thesis, University of Michigan, 1953; and Harold H. Kelley, "Communication in Experimentally Created Hierarchies," *Human Relations*, 4, 1951, pp. 39–56.

different types of communication be recognized. Lower status people direct more communication upward, but it is of a type that does not have much to do with the work at hand. High-status people, on the other hand, are less likely to express criticism of their own group or report on its confusion or problems. At the same time, they are likelier to feel free to criticize the work of lower status individuals.[4] Hence, the communication upward is likely to take a different form from downward communication.

As we might expect, noting the relative ease with which communications flow among people of similar status, those on the same status level tend to accept one another more easily and quickly than do people on different status levels. Thus, there is less tendency to note aggressive behavior between people on the same status level. This is not to say that people on the same status level will of necessity be bosom friends, or for that matter, be friends at all, but among them there is, if not a warm and personal relationship, at least one of neutral objective acceptance.

What lies behind these variations in communication and other behavioral phenomena connected with status? One explanation is the following. As we have noted, one of the commonly recognized needs of man is for recognition or public esteem, and certainly to hold high status is one way of satisfying this need. People, therefore, strive to acquire more status and to keep what status they have. They can lose status in a number of ways. For example, a person can lose a job as a highly skilled craftsman and be forced to take work in a less skilled occupation. Someone else can receive a pay increase so that he now earns more than a person who thought that his relatively higher salary marked his higher status. An individual can be placed in a group with others he thinks to be on a lower status than himself, which raises the danger that the others may think he is actually on their level. We are all too familiar with the exclusiveness of certain groups and the practice of "blackballing." The problem is that while one person is trying to move up to a higher status position, those already in these positions may be quite concerned that someone of lower status may soon be in their ranks, and they employ a wide range of practices to keep him out. In short, a person's position in a status hierarchy seems to be one of defending his present position against interlopers from lower levels and expending a fair amount of effort and attention in trying to advance upward to new and higher ones. The consequences of this behavior appears many times in our studies.

This defensive-aggressive behavior does not exist in all status struc-

[4] Kelley, *op. cit.*

tures. It is usually found in what might be called *loose* or *open* status structures, those where it is possible either for a person to move from one position to another within the system or for the structure itself to change. Certainly, this definition describes the vast majority of the status structures in this country. Yet there are status systems which, for all practical purposes, are fixed and rigid, where not only the structure itself cannot be changed but also where a person's place within it is unchangeable. When this happens, the behavioral consequences we have been discussing tend to diminish. Lower status persons cannot be a threat to those at a higher level. At the same time, if one cannot rise to a higher level, why should one strive to advance oneself? Under such circumstances, many of the constraints of communication between status levels disappear and communicating becomes more natural. Nevertheless, the converse seems true. The more insecure a person's or a group's status is, or the likelier a structure is to be changed, the more aggressive and defensive will become the behavior of people.[5]

This phenomenon can raise great difficulties for managers. We have noted that within an occupational group there are frequently sharp differences of status which may be completely unknown to high management. In the situation among cooks, for example, if someone had decided that all cooks were the same and had innocently, but unfortunately, shifted a cook working on beef to a position where he had to work on fish, he would have, in addition to reassigning a job, been putting this cook in a lower status position whereupon vigorous protest would have probably resulted. Of course, had the cook previously preparing fish been assigned to preparing beef, he probably would not have protested at all.

Status Congruency

The discussion has introduced the interesting and organizationally important issue of what happens when we place people whose status is different in the same group, such as a department, team, or the like. When this occurs we say that the status of the group is not very congruent or simply that there is considerable status incongruency. From our previous discussion we would expect status incongruency to lead to distortions of internal communication and strain between group members, which, in turn, would effect the group's performance. One

---

[5] For an interesting study where such conditions play an important role in the behavior of groups, see Leonard R. Sayles, *Behavior of Industrial Work Groups: Prediction and Control*, New York, John Wiley, 1958.

study of this factor has revealed that as we go from groups with considerable status incongruency to those with less,

1. social relationships and personal emotional states tend to improve moderately, and

2. technical performance will improve for a while and then deteriorate significantly.[6]

In addition to *group* status congruency, there is another factor called *individual* status congruency.   A person may be placed on numerous status hierarchies: education, age, skill, to name a few.   Whoever finds himself high on one and low on another will, in all likelihood, feel considerable discomfort if both are important to him.   The executive who has reached a high rank in his organization but only possesses a grade school education is one illustration.   To a lesser degree, the effects of increased individual status congruency on personal emotional states and technical performance follow the same patterns just mentioned.[7]

SUMMARY

Status enters our analysis of organizations in a number of ways.   In striving for higher status people seek one means of satisfying a need for public recognition, and in attempting to preserve their status position they search for means of satisfying another need.   A friendly familiar greeting may be welcomed when it comes from some people and rejected, perhaps emotionally, should it come from other people.   The same form of greeting may be seen as acceptance to a higher status level in one situation and in the other as a dangerous encroachment by someone from a lower status position.

In addition to its relationship to motivation and perception status is, or should be, of great concern to a manager in an organization since many of his decisions in regard to the organization will have some sort of an influence on the status of organization members.   Every time he makes a decision about the content of a job, the grouping of jobs, titles of jobs, wages, layout of work positions, the assignment of people to jobs, and a host of other things he is making a decision which will have an implication for status.

Many of the organizational issues regarding status can be approached through the concept of status congruency.   Among group members

[6] Stuart Adams, "Status Congruency as a Variable in Small Group Performance," *Social Forces*, **32**, 1953, pp. 16–22.
[7] *Ibid.*

research has found that going from less to more status congruency reduces both interpersonal and personal strain, first increasing then decreasing the effect on technical performance. The status congruency of an individual can also be examined since there are a number of status hierarchies in which a person can have a position. Research suggests that the more similar a person's position is on the various relevant hierarchies and, hence, the greater his status congruency, the more improved will be his personal emotional state.

5

Groups and Group Cohesiveness

W_{HY} should the topic of groups be included in a study of large formal organizations? One answer is that groups exist in any actual organization. Another answer that is more significant from the management view, in particular, is that groups are essential to an organization's actual performance. Moreover, on the basis of the definitions laid down in this book, an organization's groups are very much a part of it.

Chapter 1 proposed a framework for looking at organizations as vehicles for achieving certain goals or objectives through the behavior of individuals. Organizations were seen as sets of intervening factors influencing or controlling individual behavior. However, research since the middle of the 1920's has shown how much it is the group that really controls such behavior.

Everyone knows in a general way that groups influence behavior. The extent, regularity, and processes of this influence, however, are facts that only careful scientific investigation has made clear. As a topic of investigation, groups came into prominence during the now famous Hawthorne studies which began in the late 1920's.[1]

Many people connected with manufacturing operations[2] have observed that factory workers frequently restrict production below the levels set by management. This has been true even when there has been an incentive wage plan which would have given the workers a higher income for a higher level of productivity. To many observers this has seemed "irrational" and could only be explained by saying the

---

[1] Unless otherwise noted, references to the Hawthorne studies are drawn from Fritz J. Roethlisberger and William J. Dickson, *Management and the Worker*, Cambridge, Harvard University Press, 1939.

[2] Not the first, but perhaps the best known of the earlier observers was Frederick W. Taylor, *The Principles of Scientific Management*, New York, Harper, 1911.

workers were lazy, irresponsible, or mutinous. What the Hawthorne studies did, among other things, was to show that work restrictions were a group phenomenon. They further disclosed that rather than being a capricious, random, unexplainable phenomenon the group processes behind this behavior were orderly and served definite purposes or functions for the group. Last, on certain points, the group could and did exercise tight control over individual behavior.

In short, the Hawthorne studies showed that work restriction was a manifestation, not of chaos and loss of control, but of a high degree of order and control. However, the control was not being exercised by the company hierarchy but by a largely neglected element, the group. Subsequent research has shown that groups exercise control over a wide range of things other than work output. These investigations have also explained much about how this control is achieved.

It would be wrong to presume that groups are significant only in manufacturing. Groups have been found to be important in influencing the behavior of individuals in a wide number of settings. During the Second World War extensive investigations were undertaken of the behavior of troops in combat. Perhaps one of the most significant conclusions drawn from these studies was that it was not patriotism, personal courage, or personal ambition which seemed to be the most significant factor in helping a man maintain his valor in combat; it was loyalty to his unit or particular group of buddies. The authors of one major study asserted that a tight group in which men found themselves ". . . served two principal functions in combat motivation: it set and emphasized group standards of behavior and it supported and sustained the individual in stresses he would otherwise not have been able to withstand." [3]

Shifting to an entirely different area, investigators studying mass communications have observed that if the process is to be understood accurately and the communications to be carried out effectively, more factors must be taken into account than selecting the media, sending out the message, and having it received. The communication must be prepared and sent out knowing that the individuals to whom it is addressed are members of groups which will have a profound influence on what messages they receive and what they understand from them. [4]

So much for groups as elements in an organization; they are important because they are a prime factor in influencing the behavior of

[3] Samuel A. Stouffer, et al., *The American Soldier: Study in Social Psychology in World War II*, Vol. 2, Princeton University Press, 1949, p. 130.
[4] Elihu Katz and Paul F. Lazarsfeld, *Personal Influence: The Part Played by People in the Flow of Mass Communication*, Glencoe, Free Press, 1955.

organizational members.   The remainder of this chapter considers one of the most important aspects of a group and how it is influenced. That is, why people come together in groups and may remain in one group over a considerable period of time.   We shall study these matters by examining an important property of groups, their "stick togetherness" or, in more technical terms, their *cohesiveness.*

When we think of a group sticking together for some period of time, we usually think first of a group of friends who know and like one another.   Then we start to list groups of people who may not actually be close friends or, for that matter, may not be friends at all.   Political parties, some athletic teams, and many other groups attract and hold people on some basis other than friendship.

Our first general observation is that cohesiveness results from the attractiveness a group has for an individual.   Second, there are a number of reasons a person may be attracted to a group.   Moreover, an individual may belong to many long-standing groups each based on a different type of attraction.   Since these groups may be of different types, an individual may have multiple memberships without any conflicting "loyalties."   On the other hand, multiple group memberships can be a source of considerable strain and difficulty when the sources of group attractiveness begin to overlap or become mutually exclusive.   Our third general observation is that people may have multiple group memberships which may or may not lead to problems of group loyalty.

ELEMENTS PRODUCING COHESIVENESS

Let us begin by considering some of the elements which seem to make groups attractive for people.   These will be divided into two major categories: the social elements which are essentially the satisfactions a person achieves or realizes by being a member of the group, and the goal(s) or task objectives which a person wants accomplished outside of the group, but which he accomplishes, realizes, or achieves through being a member of the group.[5]

Social Elements

A group may have several social elements which will make it attractive to a person.   Perhaps the most obvious of these are:

[5] This general distinction follows that developed by Dorwin Cartwright and Alvin Zander, *Group Dynamics,* Evanston, Row, Peterson and Company, 1953, pp. 73–91.

PERSONAL ATTRACTIVENESS OF GROUP MEMBERS. When this exists, people joining a group associate with others whose company they greatly enjoy. This situation, of course, exists most predominantly in friendship cliques, but also occurs in many other types of groups. We hear people say from time to time that they would prefer to work for Company X because the people there are so pleasant and nice, or conversely, that they would like to leave Company Y because they have found the people there so disagreeable.

ACTIVITIES OF THE GROUP. At times people join groups because the activities in which the group is engaged are quite significant and enjoyable to them. An example of this is a regular bridge group whose members assemble because they enjoy the game and, perhaps, only secondarily because they find one another personally attractive. Among other types of groups that people join because they enjoy the activities in which the group engages are sports teams of all sorts, square dancing clubs, and barber shop quartets.

Goals or Means to Goals

The first category of elements that attracts people to groups is that which enables a person to, by merely joining the group, accomplish or achieve something he wants. The second category is a little different in that the group provides a means for obtaining something he wants very much.

GROUP GOALS. People frequently join groups because the purpose to which the group is dedicated is one they would like to see accomplished; typical of these are charitable organizations. A person may want to see cancer eradicated; therefore, he may work with a charitable organization that collects funds to foster research in this field. People join many organizations for these reasons: political parties, charitable organizations, fund-raising campaigns for universities, to name a few.

GROUP LOCOMOTION. Many times as a group advances or accomplishes its goals every member also advances in a personal way. In this situation the goal itself may not be particularly important to the individual member, but the fact that he is a member of an advancing group is. For example, a member of a business concern may work quite hard to advance his company so that it becomes known as a leader of its industry. As long as his company is moving toward this objective, part of the reputation rubs off. The same is true of the person on a rowing team who wants to be known as a member of a winning team.

PERSONAL GOALS THROUGH GROUP MEMBERSHIP.   Inherent in the preceding element, but sufficiently different to be noted separately, is the attractiveness a group may have for a person because it can be the means for him to attain personal goals.   It may not be necessary for the group to achieve its goals for him to reach his own.   For example, a student who wants to become president of the student council has a highly personal goal for which he needs the group; yet this objective is not directly linked to any group goal.

STATUS.   There are status hierarchies among groups just as there are among people.   A person deciding to join a country club, for example, may choose Club A over Club B primarily because Club A has a higher status than B; by being a member of A, he will have a higher status than if he were a member of B.   In many ways this element of cohesiveness is similar to those under the social category, because the status a person can achieve by being a member of a group is attained as soon as he joins.   An important difference is, however, that he obtains this position in the world external to the group or club.   That is, the status he has is most important when he is in the external community where people can say, "There goes a man who is a member of Country Club A."

There are other elements of group cohesion but these seem the most relevant for the present discussion.   Several points should be stressed about even so relatively simple a set of elements.   A person may find a group attractive for any one of these reasons, for several of them, or he might initially find the group attractive for one reason and later for another.   Some of these distinctions can be made clearer by examining the relationships between them and another important group property —its productivity.

RESULTS OF GROUP COHESION

Effects of Cohesion on Group Output

In discussing a group's productivity we should recognize that it is usually considered from the point of view of some person or agency outside of the group.   For example, in work situations productivity is usually measured by units produced or by the cost of production. This is production as it interests higher management.   Members of the group may, however, be more concerned with the group's ability to produce security of employment or stability in personal relationships. The importance of the various ways in which productivity can be

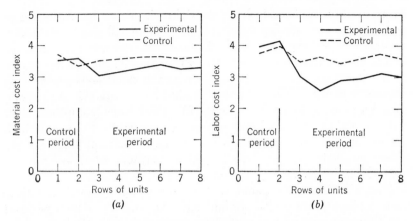

Figure 5.1. (*a*) Fluctuations between experimental and control groups on materials costs compared for entire three-month period. (*b*) Fluctuations between experimental and control groups on labor costs compared for entire three-month period.

defined is developed later in this chapter. For the moment let us concentrate on several illustrations of how some of these elements seem to influence productivity.

In the building trades industry, work groups continually are being assembled, assigned to work for a while on a project (such as a house or an office building), and are broken up when the project is complete. Upon completion, the individual workers need to be regrouped differently for a later project. Usually these groupings are made by the foremen who select men personally known to them, often on the basis of what they perceive to be the worker's competence in his craft. A study was made of one project where some construction crews were chosen in the usual fashion, while others were assembled on the basis of personal choices made by the workers themselves.[6] Each man was asked to indicate a person with whom he would most prefer to work, and work groups were formed to follow these choices as closely as possible.

The results showed rather clearly that those groups assembled on the basis of the personal choices of the members had significantly higher job satisfaction, lower turnover rates, lower indices of labor cost, and lower indices of material cost (see Figure 5.1). Although this instance shows the effects of self-selection in promoting cohesiveness and

[6] Raymond H. Van Zelst, "Sociometrically Selected Work Teams Increase Production," *Personnel Psychology,* **5,** 1952, pp. 175–185.

an apparently resultant high productivity, it would be erroneous to presume that cohesiveness built on such grounds will always yield high productivity as we have been discussing it. In another situation, where groups were formed on the basis of the personal attractiveness of the members, the group tended to stretch discussions out as long as possible in order to continue the pleasant conversations. As a result, they seriously reduced the speed with which they completed their assigned tasks.[7] In still other groups, where productivity was high (or to put it another way, the groups were successful or efficient), the group members did not have any great personal attraction for one another.[8]

Here is an interesting paradox. Sometimes high personal attractiveness and high productivity go together. At other times high personal attractiveness goes with low productivity, and in still other cases relatively low personal attractiveness accompanies high productivity. The paradox can be partially explained by drawing on a number of points previously made. First, all three groups were highly cohesive but not for the same reason. In two cases cohesiveness rested on personal attractiveness, in the other on team success and the purpose of the group. Second, productivity was measured by some system external to the group. In some cases, productivity in group terms was the same or congruent with those of the investigator, whereas in the second case they were to a considerable degree mutually exclusive. In the second case the group would have to turn its attention and conversation to solving technical problems, which would keep members from enjoying one another's company, the basis of their cohesiveness. Hence, productivity based on the assigned task would have been unproductive from the standpoint of the group.

It has been noted that there is usually less variability in productivity within a highly cohesive group than within a group that has low cohesiveness. That is, all members of a highly cohesive group tend to produce at a similar level; in a group with low cohesiveness some members may be producing at a high level and others at a low level. A highly cohesive group is able to exercise control over the productivity of members, as evidenced in the uniformity of the production of the individual group members. If the group control over individual production were fixed at a high rate, management or the experimental investigator would admit that it was getting high productivity. On

[7] K. W. Back, "Influence Through Social Communication," *Journal of Abnormal and Social Psychology*, 46, 1951, pp. 9–23.

[8] Fred E. Fiedler, "Assumed Similarity Measures as Predictors of Team Effectiveness," *Journal of Abnormal and Social Psychology*, **49**, 1954, pp. 381–388.

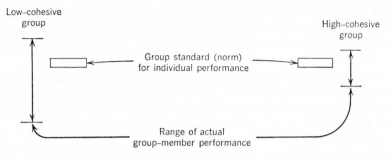

Figure 5.2

the other hand, if the control of the group fixed production at a low rate, management would not obtain the desired productivity. The important point here is that high group cohesiveness promotes high group control over the *variation* in productivity performance among group members (Figure 5.2). The *level* of group production, often specified by a norm (Chapter 6), is dependent on other factors.[9]

Although the relationship between the level of group production—or better, the group standard—and productivity in management terms has not been well studied, we are able to identify some relevant factors. Let us begin by recalling that both the group and management (or the investigator) have their own objectives in regard to productivity, or, to put it more rigorously, there are two systems each with its own standards. If the two sets are congruent, there is little problem. However, if management wants high volume of production to get lower costs, but the work group wants a low volume of production to keep its jobs longer, the two production standards differ. When the production standards of management and the group vary considerably and group cohesiveness is high, it is doubtful that any individual performance of a group member will match the standards set by management. On the other hand, even if the standards differ considerably, but cohesiveness is low, it is likely, or at least possible, that some group member's performance will approach the management's standard.

Many times, of course, group and management standards do not differ along only a single dimension, for example, quantity produced but in several aspects of output. It would be perfectly possible to have a work group that defined productivity in terms of quality first

[9] See, for example, Stanley F. Seashore, *Group Cohesiveness in the Industrial Work Group*, Ann Arbor, Survey Research Center, University of Michigan, 1954.

and quantity second, where management's order of preference was the reverse. Group effort in producing a high-quality output may reduce the quantity produced, giving management both a quality and quantity it does not want.

Some combinations of the output standards of the two units, the work group and management, are illustrated in Figure 5.3. In Figure 5.3a the work-group standard and the expected output of management are the same; thus, the output realized by management is the same as it expected. In Figure 5.3b the group standard is lower than the expectations of management, and the output realized, in management terms, is low. In Figure 5.3c the dimensions of the two units are different, and again only part of management's expected output is realized.

Effects of Cohesion on the Internal Group Events

The more cohesive a group is, the better the group members seem to be able to withstand pressures emanating from outside. Pressure exerted by a supervisor on an individual worker is likely to be less effec-

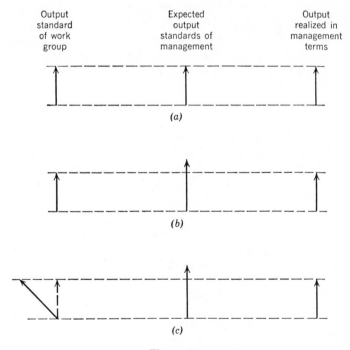

Figure 5.3

tive if the person is in a more highly cohesive group than in a less cohesive one. For example, complaints or abuse coming from clients in a governmental agency are easier to "take" or ignore if an individual is in a more cohesive group.[10]

Several other factors seem to vary directly with group cohesion, although the relationships concerning cause and effect are not quite clear. As group cohesion increases, the amount of interaction between group members increases; and as cohesion increases, the amount of agreement in group opinion also increases.[11] This last point is not surprising in the light of the discussion in Chapter 3, where we noted that increased group pressure led to increased uniformity of opinion. Since greater cohesion seems to make it possible for a group to exert increased pressure on an individual, greater uniformity of opinion readily follows.

Underlying many of these effects of cohesion are some of the relationships discussed in Chapter 2. The greater the group cohesiveness and, therefore, the more attractive the group is to an individual, the greater is its influence on the individual's evoked set of choices and their consequences. The more attractive a group is to an individual, the more congruent his evoked set is likely to be with the norms and opinions of the group. For those courses incongruent with group standards, the individual is aware that the group can make the consequences of choosing them far from desirable. First, it is more disturbing for a person to be dropped from or ostracized by a group that is highly attractive than from one that has relatively little attraction for him. Also, the more cohesive group has clearer opinions about what it expects, making a violation of its expectations easier to detect. Last, opinions being more uniformly held in a highly cohesive group makes it surer that the break will be with all group members.

CONDITIONS INFLUENCING COHESIVENESS

Until now, we have been considering what cohesiveness is and some of its effects. Now let us turn to some of the factors that influence cohesiveness.

---

[10] For discussion of this point see Peter Blau, *The Dynamics of Bureaucracy*, University of Chicago Press, 1955, particularly Chapter 6.

[11] For elaboration and support of this point see James G. March and Herbert A. Simon, *Organizations*, New York, John Wiley, 1958, p. 60.

Degree of Dependency upon the Group

One fundamental factor is the degree of an individual's dependency on a group. The more highly dependent a person is on a group for some result or effect, the greater will be the group's attractiveness, and the greater its cohesiveness. We may consider this situation as a continuum, as shown in Figure 5.4. At one end of the continuum the person is totally dependent on the group for something vital to him. Here the bonding effect or cohesiveness is great. An example of this kind of group is a bomber crew. It recognizes that while on a mission the individual lives of its members are totally dependent on the overall success of the group; should any one member of the group fail, they could all lose. At the other end of the continuum there is low group dependency and low attractiveness to any one group. An example of this type is the person who is looking for a company to employ him and who is faced with the fact that a number of companies need his talents. Such a situation makes it relatively easy for him to join any one of the concerns. Consequently, since many groups are open to him he is not particularly dependent on any one of them; he will have a relatively weaker bond with the particular group he joins.

It has also been suggested, quite reasonably, that the greater the number of individual needs a group can or does satisfy, the greater is its attractiveness and its cohesiveness.[12] Hence, a group that merely satisfies a need for money is less cohesive than a group that also permits social needs to be satisfied during and after work, for both the individual and his family. For example, in military organizations, which through the isolation of their establishments, their well-developed social and recreational facilities, and their rotational policies, make it difficult for military personnel to become deeply integrated into a nonmilitary community, the military personnel tend to satisfy most of their own and their family needs in the organization.

Figure 5.4. Degree of dependency on a group.

[12] For a discussion of this point, see *ibid.*, p. 66.

Size

Other things being considered equal, size has an inverse relationship with group cohesiveness. In one study of almost 6,000 people in industry, it was found that as a rule the cohesiveness of the group declined as its size increased up to about 25 members. It is interesting to note that size was a more influential factor than other elements, such as similarity in age or educational level, for which no significant relationship with cohesiveness was found.[13] Laboratory studies have supported these findings. A cohesive group presumably would view itself as a unit. Consequently, any group tending to break up into factions or subgroups would not be considered as cohesive as one that does not. In experiments conducted in a summer camp, where groups of different size were given problems to carry out, it was found the groups with 12 tended to break into factions more readily than those with only 5 members.[14]

One explanation for this seems to be that cohesiveness increases in part through interaction among group members. This permits them to know and like each other, brings about a greater sharing on values and goals, etc. The difficulty is that as the size of the group increases, the number of potential interactions an individual group member may have with other individuals, pairs, and larger subgroups increases very rapidly, as seen in the equation:

$$PI = 2^{n-1} - 1 \qquad \text{where } PI = \text{Potential Interactions} \\ n = \text{number in group}$$

For a 6-member group, $PI = 31$, but for a 7-member group $PI = 63$.[15] Hence, increasing size makes it progressively difficult for group members to handle all possible interactions; or to put it differently, larger numbers of the potential interactions would go unutilized. As groups become larger, it is less likely that one person will be well acquainted with all other group members, but will tend to direct his interactions to a subgroup which, as noted, will have a propensity to break away.

---

[13] Seashore, *op. cit.*, pp. 90–95.

[14] A. Paul Hare, "Interaction and Consensus in Different Sized Groups," *The American Sociological Review*, 17, 1952, pp. 261–267.

[15] For the development of this mathematical expression, see William M. Kephart, "A Quantitative Analysis of Intragroup Relationships," *American Journal of Sociology*, 55, 1950, pp. 544–549.

Stable Relationships

Size is not the only factor that can influence interrelations among group members and, therefore, cohesiveness. The relationships have to persist for a period of time to permit people to know one another, to develop common understandings of shared goals and values. In other words, cohesiveness seems to depend on some minimal degree of group stability. Such a relationship was seen in wartime studies of California aircraft factories. Groups that were disturbed frequently or rearranged did not achieve cohesiveness, as evidenced by a high degree of absenteeism and turnover.[16]

Competition

Competition is an aspect of group activity that can have profound influences on cohesion. We must distinguish between two major classes of competition: that within the group (between group members) and that without the group or between the group and other groups.

INTRAGROUP COMPETITION. In a company study, great pressure was put on individual production supervisors to keep departmental cost at the lowest possible level. An instance arose in which goods on a production order were damaged somewhere in the production process. Ordinarily the cost of this damage would have to be borne by the department in which the damage occurred. The plant manager called a meeting of subordinate department heads and tried to determine which department should be charged with the expense. Every department head vigorously denied that the damage could have been done in his department. In attempting to prove not only that they could not have been responsible for the damage but also that it must have been done elsewhere, a number of the foremen specifically named other departments where they were quite sure the damage must have occurred. Needless to say, this resulted in harsh feelings on the part of the foremen of the departments so accused. Competition, in this case to avoid assuming the expense of the damage, completely disrupted the foremen's group. It created hostilities and bitter feelings which effectively kept the foremen disunited. The end result was

[16] Elton Mayo and George F. Lombard, *Teamwork and Labor Turnover in the Aircraft Industry of Southern California*, Business Research Report, No. 32, p. 8, Boston, Graduate School of Business Administration, Harvard University, 1944.

that the plant manager had to face the fact that no one would willingly accept the responsibility and that the loss had to be charged against general plant overhead.[17]   Competition here was destructive of what little group cohesiveness may have previously existed.

INTERGROUP COMPETITION.   Whereas intragroup competition can be disastrous for group cohesiveness, intergroup competition frequently has positive influences on such cohesion.   In an interesting experiment [18] groups were first assigned problems on a noncompetitive basis and were then arranged into pairs of groups which competed on a win-lose basis where only one group could win.   It was found that the already reasonably high group cohesiveness increased once the competition period actually began.   This experience of producing positive cohesiveness at a time when a group is in a competitive position is

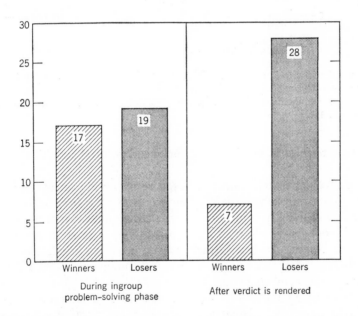

Figure 5.5. Changes in tension, fighting, and feelings of competitiveness after victory and defeat in intergroup competition. *Source:* Robert R. Blake and Jane S. Mouton, "Reactions to Intergroup Competition Under Win-Lose Conditions," *Management Science,* 7, 1961, p. 432.

[17] Chris Argyris, *The Impact of Budgets on People,* New York, The Controllers Institute, 1952, p. 23.
[18] Robert R. Blake and Jane S. Mouton, "Reactions to Intergroup Competition Under Win-Lose Conditions," *Management Science,* 7, 1961, pp. 420–435.

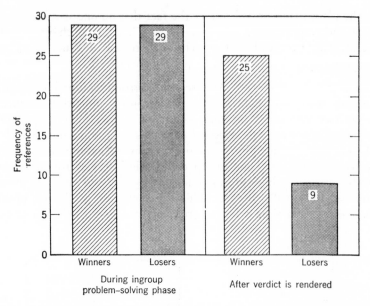

Figure 5.6. Change in work and cooperation after victory and defeat in inter-group competition. *Source:* Robert R. Blake and Jane S. Mouton, "Reactions to Intergroup Competition Under Win-Lose Conditions," *Management Science,* **7,** 4, 1961, p. 431.

common to most of us—in sports, social and political activities, and the like.

Equally interesting, however, is the result or impact of success or failure on group cohesiveness. The group that has been successful in competition has a new view of itself, a recognition that from its con-certed, cooperative effort as a group it is able to produce unique and tangible results. It has further proved itself to itself. Individual members can feel that this group does have unique properties and that they are not members of just any group.[19]

In comparing the effects of success or failure on groups, several different points have been noted. The group meeting with success feels sure of its abilities to succeed in the future, hence, feels relaxed, confident, and unified. The group meeting with defeat feels consid-erable tension, anger, and competitiveness both within the group and toward things outside the group. On the whole, it is under much more strain. In Figure 5.5 the general tension and feelings of com-

[19] Leonard R. Sayles, *Behavior of Industrial Work Groups: Prediction and Control,* New York, John Wiley, 1958, p. 113.

petitiveness of two groups are compared during competition and after, when one group has been declared the winner. The general tension and competitiveness is roughly comparable between the groups during the competition, but when the winner is declared the index drops heavily for the winning group and rises abruptly for the losing one. Furthermore, cooperativeness changes only slightly for the winning team at the end of the competition but drops markedly among the members of the losing team (see Figure 5.6).

To summarize, the effects of intergroup competition should be viewed in two ways: first, the effects on the group during the period of competition; second, the effects when competition is over and the groups have to adjust either to success or failure. In general, competition increases group cohesiveness, and success increases this cohesiveness even further. In the losing groups there is considerable tension and generally disruptive forces which, to an extent, upset the internal relationships. If the group does not fragment but instead maintains continuity, things again begin to stabilize in a pattern not too different from that which existed previously.

Status Position of the Group

As a rule, the higher the status of the group, the greater is its cohesiveness. This general proposition, however, must not lead us to conclude that all low-status groups of necessity have very little cohesiveness and that all high-status groups, in contrast, have very high cohesiveness. This is perhaps true if we do not consider the effects of change, actual or potential, in the group's position. In an experimental situation, where groups were arranged in a status hierarchy, it was found that the low-status groups whose members could not leave the group even when unsuccessful in realizing group goals frequently had correspondingly high cohesion, as measured in the sociometric attractiveness among group members.[20] The same experiment also noted, as shown in Table 5.1, that the high-status group which had been unsuccessful in achieving its goals, and therefore had lost status, had a lower index of cohesiveness. What we seem to observe here is that when group members see no possibility of bettering themselves, as would happen in leaving an unsuccessful group and joining a more successful one, they tend to adjust to the circumstances "to make the best of it." The same sort of phenomenon has been noted in other circumstances as, for example, among the Japanese who were relocated

[20] John W. Thibaut, "An Experimental Study of Cohesiveness of Underprivileged Groups," *Human Relations*, 3, 1950, pp. 251–278.

Table 5.1 Differences Between Presession and Postsession in Average Indices of Sociometric Attractiveness of Own Team, for Central, Peripheral, and Total Team Members in the Various Experimental and Control Treatments*

Teams	Central Members				Peripheral Members				Total Members			
	N (Teams)	M	SD (Among Teams)	t †	N (Teams)	M	SD (Among Teams)	t †	N (Teams)	M	SD (Among Teams)	t †
Unsuccessful low-status	9	.319	.173	5.50	9	.198	.840		9	.266	.469	1.71
Consistently high-status	9	.265	.451	1.71	9	.530	.633	2.51	9	.402	.390	3.09
Successful low-status	9	.039	.351		9	.102	.921		9	.048	.439	
Displaced high-status	9	.004	.463		9	.160	.434		9	.077	.395	
Control teams (combined)	4	.094	.214		4	.126	.399		4	.108	.250	

* When the average index is positive, as it is throughout this table, it indicates a shift toward choosing within own team.

† The t computed tests the hypothesis that the obtained mean is zero. A t is reported only if $p < .20$. For 8 degrees of freedom, a t of 3.36 is at $p = .01$, 2.31 at $p = .05$, 1.86 at $p = .10$, and 1.40 at $p = .20$. Source: John W. Thibaut, "An Experimental Study of Cohesiveness of Underprivileged Groups," Human Relations, 3, 1950, pp. 251–278.

into camps in this country during the war.   Among them many cohesive subgroups developed partially on the basis of the individual's inability to disassociate himself from the group.[21]

Disruptive Forces

For the most part, we have been considering those things that promote cohesiveness and only a few factors, such as intragroup competition and group failure, that disrupt or decrease cohesion.   One study suggests that factors disrupting group cohesion fall into three categories.   In decreasing order of importance these are: [22]

1. When group members or subgroups within the group tend to use different tasks to accomplish the same goal.   The question is not what to accomplish but how to accomplish it.   This situation nicely describes the general circumstances frequently found under conditions of competition.   The objective is usually rather clear cut, to win by accomplishing a certain result.   Disruption can be expected to result in disputes over how to win; that is, the choice of strategy, and techniques to be used in accomplishing this.

2. Differences regarding the goal(s) to accomplish.   Although this problem does not exist in the win-lose type of competition, such conditions can arise in many other types of group situations where the group may have two or more goals of importance to different members.   It is interesting to note that differences concerning goals are less frequently disruptive than are differences about methods of achieving a single universally recognized goal.

3. The individual goals of group members.   When the goals of individual group members are in conflict about such things as their status in the group, the cohesive bonds of the group are weakened.

The increase in cohesiveness with the advent of competition need not always occur.   If we have a group wherein cohesiveness is primarily based on personal attractiveness, and then introduce competition, which in turn makes a task of the group much more important, there will be an interference with the opportunities of group members to interact on a social basis.   As a result, cohesiveness from this source would diminish with the possible development of resentment that the task was interfering with social pleasures.   This resentment might reduce the cohesive bonds arising from working on a common task.

[21] Alexander H. Leighton, *The Governing of Men,* The Princeton University Press, 1945.
[22] John R. P. French, Jr., "The Disruption and Cohesion of Groups," *The Journal of Abnormal and Social Psychology,* **36,** 1941, pp. 361–377.

Ritual

One thing groups do to promote cohesiveness is to employ rituals. We may at first think of rituals as something used by primitive tribes as a means of providing a common knowledge, a common bond, a common experience. However, we can find some form of ritual, more sophisticated and perhaps less obtrusive, in groups in all types of society. Thus, the social fraternity that has a password, a handclasp, an order in which its meetings are conducted, portions of the meetings allocated to special offices within the group, group recitation of pledges (chants), etc. uses ritual. We can find a rich array of ritual in many contemporary organizations, from the Loyal and Benevolent Order of the Owl to a business concern.

Ritual serves first to give group members something, both in knowledge and experience, which they as members of the group share and nonmembers do not. Second, it serves to remind them that they are different, set apart, have certain unique characteristics and properties which are the benefits of being a member of the group. Third, although hardly last, ritual serves as a barrier to keep others out; or to put it another way, learning the ritual is usually one of the hurdles and tasks a newcomer must overcome in order to gain membership in the group.

SUMMARY

Cohesiveness is a central property of groups. It is a characteristic which differentiates a group from a mere collection of people. Cohesiveness is the attraction of the group for the group members resulting from two basic elements: social—comprising the personal attractiveness of group members and the activities of the group itself—and means to goals—where the group serves as a vehicle for individuals to accomplish something outside the group. Other classes of elements doubtless exist, but these seem to be of major importance.

Cohesiveness is the resultant of a number of forces coming from these various elements—some of them positive and additive in nature and others negative or subtractive in nature. If the sum of them is a positive force toward the group, it can be thought to be a cohesive one. It is important to recognize that cohesiveness depends on a relationship among a number of elements not all of which may be additive. Furthermore, the relationships between these elements may change. These relationships are influenced by a variety of conditions or factors.   One is an individual's dependency on the group to obtain certain things important to him.   If a person is not particularly dependent on a group, group cohesiveness will be relatively weak; whereas, if the person is dependent to a greater degree on the group, cohesiveness will tend to be much stronger.   Second, increased size decreases cohesiveness.   Third, intergroup competition generally tends to increase cohesiveness.   However, this is mitigated by the initially dominant element in the cohesiveness and its importance to group members.   Intragroup competition is destructive of group cohesiveness.

The results of competition, that is, success or failure, can have marked effects on group cohesiveness.   In general, success promotes cohesion, whereas failure, producing great strains, reduces it.   Cohesiveness is also influenced by some general group properties. Among those noted were the group's current status or rank and the prospect of change.   For low-status groups with no prospect of change there may be high group cohesiveness just as when a high-status group continually meets success and thereby maintains its position.   In general, status and cohesiveness seem positively correlated.

6

Group Processes

THE preceding chapter dealt with general group properties: cohesiveness, productivity, and some of the factors influencing these. Here we turn to the internal elements of groups. First, we examine more thoroughly what a group is, various types of groups, and the internal characteristics differentiating them, and then we discuss group processes and structures.

WHAT IS A GROUP?

Crowds and Groups

Though composed of people, a group is more than a collection of individuals. In a railroad station or in an elevator, we are in proximity to others, and yet we would not claim that we are in a group. In a group we interact through conversation, gesture, or some other means. Even so, it is more than mere interaction. If while walking through a crowded railroad station we accidentally bump another person, look at him, and say, "Pardon me," we would be interacting with him, but would hardly be in a group. Interaction among group members has a stable or predictable quality to it, at least as far as the group members are concerned.

This stable and predictable aspect of group interaction pertains to many things. When a member of a group turns to another for help, he is usually confident he will receive it; whereas if he goes to another individual who is not a member of the group, he might receive an abrupt refusal or perhaps no attention at all. Furthermore, the individual has not only a pretty good idea of how other group members will behave toward him but he also knows how he is expected to behave toward them.   Last, the individual knows that most of certain types of interaction will be with members of his group and few, if any, with others.   Hence, members of a friendship clique may well expect the group to spend most of its social life together; any member of the group who engages in substantial amounts of social activity outside the group may soon find himself viewed as an outsider rather than a member.

Types of Groups

THE FAMILY.   Within these general characteristics of continuing stable interactions there are many different types of groups.   One with the strongest ties and perhaps the longest existence is the family.   This group frequently gets intense loyalty and is a source of many satisfactions.   The relationships among its individuals are spontaneous, warm, and frequently self-sacrificing.

FRIENDSHIP CLIQUES.   Perhaps one of the first types of group other than the family which comes to mind is groups of friends, cliques, or the gang.   These are the people with whom we have fun, with whom we socialize.   It may be a street-corner gang, a group of people with whom we socialize regularly on Friday and Saturday evenings, or a collection of people with whom we take our lunch hour while on the job.   It is important to recognize that friendship cliques can exist in a work environment; in fact, their absence might cause high rates of absenteeism and turnover.[1]

Figure 6.1 shows in schematic form the people who were in the bank wiring room in the Hawthorne plant,[2] and indicates those who were friends.   Each circle indicates a person with an identifying label such as I_1, W_4, or S_2, and the arrows indicate pairs of men who were friends.   For all practical purposes, there were two friendship cliques. Clique A (C_A) consisting of W_1, W_3, W_4, I_1, S_2, and Clique B (C_B) composed of W_7, W_8, W_9, S_4.

TASK OR WORK GROUPS.   The type of group that has received much attention in industrial studies has been the task or work group.   This type of group is made up of people whose jobs are closely related. They usually form a department, work gang, etc., and work close

---

[1] Elton Mayo and George F. Lombard, *Teamwork and Labor Turnover in the Aircraft Industry of Southern California*, Business Research Report, No. 32, p. 274. Boston, Graduate School of Business Administration, Harvard University, 1944.
[2] Fritz W. Roethlisberger and William J. Dickson, *Management and the Worker*, Cambridge, Harvard University Press, 1939, p. 507.

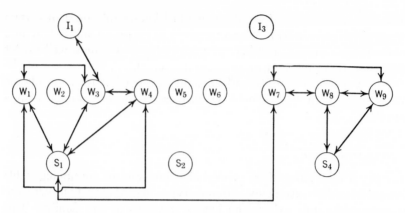

Figure 6.1. Bank wiring room: men who were friends. *Source:* Fritz J. Roethlisberger and William J. Dickson, *Management and the Worker,* Cambridge, Harvard University Press, 1939, p. 507.

together in both time and space. People with interdependent jobs may be spread out geographically, may work in the same area, or on the same machines on different shifts. We have already noted that work groups or task groups can control the output of individuals. They can also influence work methods and even work assignments.

It would be erroneous to assume that the influence of work groups is always to the disadvantage of management or overall organization objectives. Many times groups are supportive of such objectives. In fact, at times the actions of the group are supportive of organization objectives even though on the surface they may appear to be, and perhaps are, contrary to specific management directions.

One illustration of generally supportive behavior by groups were some efforts at informal coordination found in a study of British coal mines. In an attempt to increase productivity, the work in some mines had been rather drastically reorganized. In doing this, the cycle of mining operations was spread over three shifts so that each shift had its own specific duties which were quite different from the other two shifts. Difficulties frequently developed between the shift that drilled holes and dynamited the coal and the following shift which removed the coal. If the dynamiting were not done correctly, it was extremely difficult for those on the following shift to do their job completely or well. To insure that work on the preceding shift was done thoroughly, miners responsible for removing the loosened coal made contact with members of the previous shift outside the work situation, and attempted through personal persuasion and sometimes bribes to make sure that they completed their work properly.[3]   Here the workers engaged in the managerial activity of bringing about coordination, and also expended some of their own money to assure that their job and also the work of the organization was done well.

There are times when workers take actions which are definitely at variance with management policies but which have results beneficial to both the group and the larger organization.   For example, many companies have strict regulations against exchanging jobs.   When these regulations are circumvented by employees, however, investigators have found this permits reduction of tension, a chance to develop additional skills which enable people to substitute in different jobs, the perfection of short cuts, or, frequently, a chance for fatigued workers to rest.[4]   Work groups have at times developed new methods to make inadequate or incomplete managerial directives or plans workable.[5]

The people in a department may not all be members of the same work group, just as they may not all be members of the same friendship clique. Figure 6.2 shows which men traded jobs (one of the characteristics of a work group) in the bank wiring room. W_2 trades jobs with S_1, but they are not in the same friendship clique; and W_9 and S_4, who are friends, do not exchange jobs.

THE COMMAND GROUP.   Implicit in this discussion is that groups are composed of peers; many groups are.   However, to assume that all groups are made up of equals is erroneous.   In organizations, one of the extremely important groups is the command group, which consists of a superior and his immediate subordinates.[6]   The inclusion of a group of people on different hierarchal levels makes the internal affairs of the group more complex.   Much of this increased complexity revolves around a superior who has greater authority over his subordinate group members, but at the same time is dependent on them to accomplish his assigned responsibilities.   We examine this particular situation more thoroughly later, particularly in Chapter 23.

GROUPS, SUBGROUPS, AND MULTIPLE GROUP MEMBERSHIP.   As noted in chapter 5, a person can be in several groups at the same time, and fre-

---

[3] E. Trist and K. Bamforth, "Some Social and Psychological Consequences of the Long Wall Method of Coal-getting," *Human Relations*, 4, 1951, pp. 3–38.

[4] William F. Whyte, "The Social Structure of the Restaurant," *The American Journal of Sociology*, 54, 1949, pp. 306–307.

[5] For a very interesting description of such practices, see Donald Roy, "Efficiency and 'The Fix': Informal Intergroup Relations in a Piece Work Machine Shop," *The American Journal of Sociology*, 61, 1954, pp. 255–266.

[6] Elliot Jacques, *The Changing Culture of a Factory*, London, Tavistock Publications, 1951, p. 274.

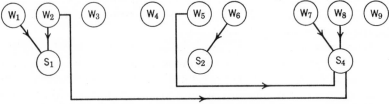

Figure 6.2. Bank wiring room: men who traded jobs. *Source:* Fritz J. Roethlisberger and William J. Dickson, *Management and the Worker,* Cambridge, Harvard University Press, 1939, p. 504.

quently these groups have overlapping membership. This situation is well illustrated in the study of the bank wiring room. All persons in the bank wiring room, shown in Figures 6.1 and 6.2 were members of a single group as far as working together on such things as restricting output and helping one another were concerned (see Figure 6.3). Within this group there were two friendship cliques previously designated as Cliques A and B. In accord with the more social activities expected in a friendship clique, Roethlisberger and Dickson noted the following distinction between the two. Most of the gambling games occurred in Clique A, and most of the "binging" (a game which attempted to see who could hit the other man hardest on the arm) in Clique B. Clique A bought chocolate candy in small quantities; Clique B bought less expensive candy but in large quantities. Clique

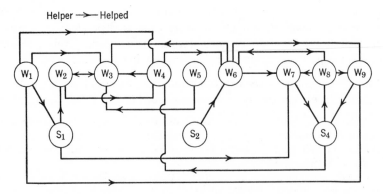

Figure 6.3. Bank wiring room: men who helped one another. *Source:* Fritz J. Roethlisberger and William J. Dickson, *Management and the Worker,* Cambridge, Harvard University Press, 1939, p. 506.

A argued more, whereas Clique B engaged in more horseplay and noisy activities.[7]

In addition to this configuration of cliques, all persons in the bank wiring room were in a command group that included their supervisor. An individual in the bank wiring room was thus in at least three distinct groups. These groups were of different types, existing for different purposes, and hence, did not present as much conflict as we might expect. Even in the contradiction between the command and work groups, the conflict was more apparent than real. Though work was being restricted regularly and rigidly, even the foreman professed to feel that production was more than adequate and that the group was performing well. This is not to say that multiple group membership is universally comfortable, for as we shall see in Part Four, many times it is not. However, this need not be an impossible situation.

To avoid confusion, we discuss group phenomena as if there were only one group. The phenomena we analyze is universal to all groups although our illustrations, for the most part, come from task or work groups.

ELEMENTS OF GROUPS

In addition to interaction, groups may be described as having four principal features or elements.

1. Goals or purposes. Group members share one or more goals, purposes, or objectives. Thus, we may find that they are interested in helping one another get a job done which is their livelihood; or, that they come together to have fun, or to get a political candidate elected.

2. Groups develop norms or informal rules and standards which mold and guide the behavior of group members.

3. When a group continues for any length of time, structure develops which, among other things, has individual members more or less permanently filling different roles.

4. When the group continues to exist for any period of time, the members develop attractions for other group members, the group itself, and the things it stands for. At this stage they see themselves as liking or perhaps disliking other group members. They see that the group has an identity which stands for something such as, "We discuss important topics"; or, "We do not engage in rowdy activities." [8]

[7] Roethlisberger and Dickson, *op. cit.*, pp. 5–10.
[8] Adapted from A. Paul Hare, *Handbook of Small Group Research*, New York, The Free Press of Glencoe, 1962, p. 10.

The first and last of these elements have already been examined closely. Norms and group structure occupy the remainder of this chapter.

Norms and Social Control

Norms have received a great deal of attention by investigators of group phenomena. One reason for this is that norms frequently affect things which are of importance to people outside groups. Some are also easily observed, such as output or production restrictions. Norms are one of the most important ways in which groups control the behavior of individuals.

A norm is an agreement or consensus of group members concerning how individuals in the group should or should not behave. Norms are supported by group processes that insure compliance of actual with desired behavior.[9] Provision for enforcement is important; without it a norm would be the same as an ideal or a value judgment. We may have many ideals we strive for, but no one expects us to adhere to them always in everyday living, such as the ideal that a person should be courteous. Norms are more rigorous, more like laws; people are expected to comply with them regularly as they are expected to comply with laws against murder and theft.

There are two basic types of norms, *prescriptive* and *proscriptive*. Among the latter, in industrial work groups at least, we frequently find such norms as, "Don't be a rate buster by working too fast"; "Don't be a chiseler by working too slow"; "Don't socialize with the boss," that is, "Don't Brown Nose." Prescriptive norms might include, "Help your buddy if he's stuck on the job or is under the weather," or "Be sure to report all useful information about management plans to people in the group." Proscriptive norms are usually easiest to enforce because their violation is easier to detect. Violations of prescriptive norms are harder to sense. For example, is a person expected to help one's buddy only when he asks for it or is he expected to volunteer to help him when he thinks his friend needs it?

FUNCTIONS OF NORMS. We can well ask the question, what purpose do norms serve in group operations? The answer is many, but here we can only review some of the more general functions which norms appear to fill.

Let us begin by examining what would be likely to happen in groups if norms did not exist. If there were to be any sort of united action

[9] John W. Thibaut and Harold H. Kelley, *The Social Psychology of Groups,* New York, John Wiley, 1959, p. 239.

on joint goals, each act would have to be preceded by a rather long period of discussion unless, of course, some member or members of the group were able to wield personal power that enabled them to determine the action for other members. Under these conditions group action would occur when (1) each new required act was considered individually and decisions were made about it, (2) the decision made was a result of discussion and the reaching of accord among all members of the group, or (3) the exercise of power of one or more members over the remaining members of the group was obvious. The use of norms avoids or, at least, reduces all of these possibilities.

A norm serves as a guide for the behavior of all members of the group in regard to fairly common types of situations which require action. The decision made is in effect from that moment and thereafter. Because the decision is made once and is applied to many similar situations, the amount of time employed in discussion is greatly reduced. Hence, time and channels of communication are made available for other topics of interest to group members. Furthermore, the use of norms eliminates or, in any case, reduces the necessity and often prevents the exercise of personal power to bring about group action.[10] Last, norms frequently function to strengthen group solidarity and prevent competition or conflicts among members of the group, which would disrupt and perhaps destroy the group, thereby reducing its effectiveness in achieving other ends.[11]

These functions are basically internal to the group, factors which make the group itself stronger, more effective, or pleasanter to be in. Many other norms center on achieving group purposes and, in fact, can best be understood by determining their relationship to the objectives of the group in regard to the world around it. For example, work restrictions, during the depression particularly, were seen to be a way of extending work; or, to put it another way, to work hard and complete more production than absolutely necessary would only shorten the length of time people would have work.[12] Perhaps the main point can be stated as follows: Norms will develop in those areas where group members find it necessary to influence one another, and this condition will occur where members are particularly interdependent.[13]

Compliance with Norms

Three social processes of particular interest aid in bringing about compliance with norms. Two of these, enforcement and internaliza-

---

[10] *Ibid.*, pp. 130–139.   [11] Roethlisberger and Dickson, *op. cit.*, p. 531.
[12] *Ibid.*   [13] Thibaut and Kelley, *op. cit.*, pp. 135–136.

tion of norms, are considered here. The third, group pressure, was discussed in Chapter 3.

ENFORCEMENT OF GROUP NORMS. Much attention has been focused on the overt processes by which groups bring about compliance. This process has at least four principal phases:

1. *Education.* When a new man enters an existing group, commonly the important norms of the group will be brought to his early attention. This process has been very interestingly described by Donald Roy, an industrial sociologist who went to work in a machine shop. When he first went on the job, he was made aware of norms about output restriction in the following manner.

> One of Starkey's first questions was, "What have you been doing?" When I said I had worked in a Pacific Coast shipyard at a rate of pay over $1.00 an hour, Starkey exclaimed, "Then what are you doing in this place?" When I replied that averaging $1.25 an hour wasn't bad, he exploded:
>
> "Averaging, you say!   Averaging?"
>
> "Yeah, on the average. I'm an average guy; so I ought to make my buck and a quarter. That is, after I get onto it."
>
> "Don't you know," cried Starkey angrily, "that 1.25 an hour is the MOST we can make, even when we CAN make more! And most of the time we can't even make that! Have you ever worked on piecework before?"
>
> "No."
>
> "I can see that!   Well, what do you suppose would happen if I turned in $1.25 an hour on these pump bodies?"
>
> "Turned in?   You mean if you actually did the work?"
>
> "I mean if I actually did the work and turned it in!"
>
> "They'd have to pay you, wouldn't they?   Isn't that the agreement?"
>
> "Yes!   They'd pay me—once!   Don't you know that if I turned in $1.50 an hour on these pump bodies tonight, the whole goddamned Methods Department would be down here tomorrow?   And they'd retime this job so quick it would make your head swim!   And when they retimed it, they'd cut the price in half!   And I'd be working for 85 cents an hour instead of $1.25!" [14]

2. *Surveillance of Group Members.* Established members of the group observe the new man or any other possible deviate to detect

[14] Donald Roy, "Quota Restriction and Goldbricking in a Machine Shop," *The American Journal of Sociology*, **57**, 1952, p. 431.

departure from the norm. Any member may, and apparently most members of groups do, carry out this surveillance function.

3. *Warning.* When a deviation is detected, there is an increase of interaction by group members with the deviate.[15] Initially this increased interaction may be quite friendly, indicating that the group is still supporting the man, that perhaps he is making an innocent error. This is well brought out by Roy.

> From this initial exposition of Starkey's to my last day at the plant I was subject to warnings and predictions concerning price cuts. . . . Jack Starkey defined the quota carefully but forcefully when I turned in $10.50 for one day (the norm was $10.25) or $1.31 an hour.
>
> "What's the matter? Are you trying to upset the apple cart?"
>
> Jack explained in a friendly manner that $10.50 was too much to turn in, even on an old job.[16]

4. *Disciplinary or Rewarding Actions.* However, if explaining and the educational approach does not bring the deviate into line, the interaction takes on a different form characterized by razzing, argument, or threats of discipline. When it becomes clear that the deviate is not going to come back into line, actual discipline can be imposed by the group. In a way the razzing and heckling are one form of discipline. A common severe discipline is isolation or ostracizing the individual from the group. In some cases punishment may take a physical form, such as violence or tampering with the deviate's personal possessions.[17]

INTERNALIZATION OF NORMS. Thus far we have been considering situations where the person is bringing his behavior into compliance with an external standard. Much behavior, of course, is controlled by what a person individually feels to be right or proper. Most individual standards are those taken from the world around us and made personal guides for behavior. Norms set by a group can become personal standards of conduct that we feel to be right. We, in effect, internalize them. In essence this is a learning experience. The individual

[15] Stanley Schachter, "Deviation, Rejection, and Communication," *Journal of Abnormal and Social Psychology*, 46, 1951, pp. 190–207; see also, Leon Festinger, H. B. Gerard, B. Hymovitch, "The Influence Process in the Presence of Extreme Deviates," *Human Relations*, 5, 1952, pp. 327–346.

[16] Roy, *op. cit.*, pp. 430–431.

[17] H. W. Riecken and George C. Homans, "Psychological Aspects of Social Structure," in Gardener Lindzey (ed.), *Handbook of Social Psychology*, Cambridge, Addison-Wesley, 1954, pp. 786–832; and E. C. Hughes, "The Knitting of Racial Groups in Industry," *American Sociological Review*, 11, 1946, pp. 512–519.

now acts in accordance with what he knows to be right rather than in accordance with what he knows will earn him rewards or punishments. Perhaps the most extreme and striking form of this behavior was found when some inmates of concentration camps came to adopt the values and standards of their captors.[18]

Irregular Conformity

All members of a group do not conform to group norms or majority opinions to the same degree. One factor related to this variation is the status of both the group and the individual within it, and also the length of time in the group.

Within a group it has been observed that "*. . . the higher the rank of a person within a group, the more nearly his activities conform to the norms of the group.*" [19]   This close compliance of the leader with norms may be for a different reason, however, than the compliance by lower status members. The leader is many times the formulator or at least the enunciator of a group norm. The norm, in effect, is his *and* the group's, whereas group members later accepted are brought into line with *it*.[20]   However, this relation between status and compliance with norms does not hold in every case. There are times when leaders are able to deviate more from norms than are lower status members.[21] Homans explains this in part as follows: "Up to a point, the surer a man is of his rank in a group, the less he has to worry about conforming to its norms." [22]   There are norms, however, which even the leader cannot violate, such as playing favorites with some members of the group or passing confidential information concerning the group or some of its members to outsiders.

We can perhaps summarize this in the following way. The higher status a person has in a group, the likelier his activities will comply with group norms because they are substantially influenced by him, because he has risen to a higher status level, or because he "naturally" fills their requirements. Having achieved a higher status, a person may, if he wants to, deviate from norms of the group with more

[18] Eugen Kogon, *The Theory and Practice of Hell*, New York, Farrar, Straus and Cudahy, 1950.

[19] George C. Homans, *The Human Group*, New York, Harcourt, Brace and Co., Inc., 1950, p. 141.

[20] Hare, *op. cit.*, p. 41.

[21] James E. Dittes and Harold H. Kelley, "Effects of Different Conditions of Acceptance upon Conformity to Group Norms," *Journal of Abnormal and Social Psychology*, **53**, 1956, pp. 100–107; and Hughes, *op. cit.*

[22] Homans, *op. cit.*, p. 144.

impunity provided the norms involved are not central to the group goals or the maintenance of the group.

LENGTH OF TIME IN THE GROUP. Seniority in a group influences the degree to which a person will comply with norms. The new person in a group may be expected to adhere more closely to group norms than a person who has been in the group for some time.[23]

NONHOMOGENEOUS CONFORMITY. The reason variation from conformity is permitted by a group is open to speculation. A common interpretation is that some members of the group are so important, such as leaders or those who possess special resources, that a certain degree of deviation is tolerated in them without driving them from the group. In a sense, some balance is struck where their greater actual contribution is found to compensate for their deviation.[24]

COMMUNICATIONS WITHIN GROUPS

Communications move easily within a group. As soon as one member obtains information which is of importance to the group, he quickly spreads it to all others.

In groups, many of the psychological barriers to communication are greatly reduced. Here people know they are accepted, and although there are distinctions and status differences, they tend to be much closer in status, abilities, and outlooks than they are with nongroup members. Hence, group members feel freer to say things and to ask for information. A person in an organizational setting may be reluctant to reveal to those in superior or subordinate positions that he does not know something relevant to his job, but the same person may feel perfectly free to turn to peers or members of his group to obtain help.[25] Being in a group, therefore, permits a person to feel freer in sending out certain information about himself and in seeking certain information from others.

In addition to a more compatible psychological climate, groups also develop their own special languages. All of us know that in our families or among our friends certain words or phrases take on very special meanings which would, in most cases, be completely unknown to an outsider. These special languages of groups often have a structure or order of terms which help convey a great deal of meaning. One of

[23] Hughes, *op. cit.*, p. 517.   [24] Hare, *op. cit.*, p. 45.
[25] Abraham Zaleznik, *Worker Satisfaction and Development*, Boston, Graduate School of Business Administration, Harvard University, 1956, pp. 36–41.

these structures, which has gained fairly wide use, is a series of numbers such as 36, 24, 38.   Among those interested in such matters there is an instant recognition that a person is talking about the bust, waist, and hip measurements of a presumably attractive young lady.   The development of words with special meanings and the use of special structures permits a great deal of information to be conveyed quite accurately and economically within groups.

The purpose of a group often leads to values and norms that restrict topics considered to be relevant for communications.   In a social group meeting for a good time, the person who tries to raise a serious political question for discussion may find himself the object of rather blunt comments as, "Oh, don't spoil the evening by raising something like that," or being completely ignored.   A similar reaction might occur if a person attempts to engage in a little light conversation in a group working to devise a solution to some serious social problem.

Groups, then, can facilitate the quick and accurate transmission of important information within the group by providing special languages and by censoring irrelevant communications.   An action or communication to one member of the group on something very much related to the group's purpose, values, etc., will be rapidly communicated and have a significant impact on other group members.

One factor which should be noted is that groups serve as a prime source of information for individuals.   We learn a great many facts about our world and learn even more, perhaps, about how to interpret them from the groups in which we are members.

Communications Patterns and Groups

Investigation has shown that within groups there are fairly regular patterns of communication or, as they are often called, interaction. Some of the more regular and important patterns are:

1. The person who initiates the most interaction tends to receive the most interaction.[26]

2. Low-status members of the group direct more communication toward high-status members than vice versa.[27]

3. As a group increases in size, more interaction is directed to the

[26] Robert F. Bales, Fred L. Strodtbeck, Theodore M. Mills, and Mary E. Roseborough, "Channels of Communication in Small Groups," *American Sociological Review*, 16, 1951, pp. 461–468.
[27] Harold H. Kelley, "Communication in Experimentally Created Hierarchies," *Human Relations*, 4, 1951, pp. 39–56.

high-status person and smaller relative proportions to other members.[28]

4. As groups grow larger, the top interacting person tends to direct more of his interaction to the group as a whole rather than to individuals.[29]

THE INFORMAL LEADER

As groups continue in existence, separate roles become established with members filling one or more of them. Perhaps the commonest, certainly the most widely discussed, of these roles is that of leader. Complementary to the leader's role is that of follower, hence in accepting one of their members as leader, the other group members accept the role of followers. This is not always the easiest thing for people to do.

The key distinction of the informal leader is his acceptance by the group. He is a person the group turns to, a person whom the members want to be the leader. What power he has is given him by the group. This is in contrast to the formal leader who is appointed and exercises his influence by manipulation of the powers given to him by someone outside the group.

The distinction between the formal and informal leader is primarily in the *source* of power or influence rather than in what he does. The informal leader's function is to make it possible for group members to achieve their private goals along with the group's goals. His success in filling this function, and therefore his likelihood in being followed, depends on his personal ability to identify, plan for, and facilitate the attainment of these goals.

Since the informal leader has his position at the wish (in effect) of the group members, they can readily change whom they accept. Informal leaders can change frequently; however, they often hold their positions for long periods of time.

Informal leadership is made difficult because there are usually two different and sometimes conflicting classes of needs to be satisfied. One is the need to advance individuals and the group toward their goals; this requires ideas, plans, direction, etc. The other is the need to satisfy some maintenance requirements of holding the group together: promoting an adequate level of harmony, mutual liking, etc.,

---

[28] Robert F. Bales, "Some Uniformities of Behavior in Small Social Systems," in Guy E. Swanson, Theodore M. Newcomb, and Eugene L. Hartley (eds.), *Readings in Social Psychology*, New York, Henry Holt, 1952, p. 155.
[29] *Ibid.*

among group members. It is often difficult, perhaps impossible, for one person to satisfy both needs. As a result there are often two leaders: a task or work leader and a "social-emotional specialist." In this sort of an arrangement the leader involved with getting the job done for the group does not have to divert his attention to maintaining the group as a pleasant social place. Needless to say there must be some considerable support between the two if the group is to be both productive and stable.[30] One man may start filling both roles but may eventually be forced to choose one over the other. When this occurs, the evidence indicates that the work or task-specialist role will be dropped.[31]

These distinctions between formal and informal leaders reflect "ideal" types which may not accurately describe actual leaders. Appointed leaders who rely only on formally granted authority most likely, as noted in Chapter 2, will not have sufficient influence over the group to have a really successful unit. This situation indicates that something more than formal authority is necessary to have sufficient influence. Even if appointed leaders had all the authority described in our ideal type, this would be true. Formal leaders, as we shall see in Chapter 22, usually have considerably less authority than this stereotype would suggest. Most formal leaders therefore take steps to promote their personal acceptance by their subordinates; [32] that is, in effect they build an informal-leader segment into their leadership activity. At the same time the informal leader may have to draw on sources other than his personal skills to obtain and maintain his leadership pattern. For example, the leader of a neighborhood gang may have to spend more money than any other gang member for beer, entertainment, food, etc., for his gang.[33]

The informal leader, as we have noted, is usually a person who best knows the group's objectives, values, norms, etc. More than knowing, he usually best represents these attributes. To this extent he is the group's "ideal," a person it can look up to, one with whom its members can identify. In such a position the informal leader can have great influence on people's perception of what ought to be done and how it should be accomplished.

[30] Robert F. Bales, *Interaction Process Analysis*, Cambridge, Addison-Wesley Press, 1950.

[31] Robert F. Bales, "The Equilibrium Problem in Small Groups," in Talcott Parsons, Robert F. Bales, and Edward A. Shils (eds.), *Working Papers in the Theory of Action*, Glencoe, Free Press, 1953, pp. 111–161.

[32] See Chapter 23.

[33] William F. Whyte, Jr., *Street Corner Society*, University of Chicago Press, 1955, pp. 257–263.

How does this congruency among the objectives, values, and norms of the group, on one hand, and the statements and acts of the leader come about? There are several explanations, and probably one or more are involved in each case. One explanation is that there is a natural match between the wants and needs of the group and the thoughts and abilities of the leader. What this person by nature thinks and does is just what the group needs and wants. Another explanation is that the leader, wanting to be leader, examines the group and adapts himself to fill the necessary role. Perhaps it is more accurate to say that a person who is reasonably close to meeting the group's expectations about leadership makes some moderate adjustments to fit himself better. We find some evidence of this adjustment in the leader's dropping one of two roles he holds. Interviews with informal leaders suggest they often do things not quite of their choosing but which they see as necessary in their role as leader.[34]

A person in a leader's role has dictinct advantages when it comes to improving his knowledge of what the group wants and needs; as noted earlier, much more information flows to him than to anyone else in the group. Much of this information in one way or another relates to members' aspirations and values. However, position is not the only way a person may obtain a marginal advantage in knowing group needs and wants. Time in the group or seniority give a person an opportunity to learn about a group and, by knowing the history of many group ideas, enable him to sharpen and clarify them with a time perspective. Leaders are often old timers in the group.

The leader is also in a position to mold group objectives and values, often changing them over time to be more congruent with his own talents and wishes. One advantage the leader has in doing this is that when he speaks people listen and are quite likely to be influenced. The same idea expressed by a high-status person, which the leader certainly is, is much likelier to be acted on than if it were proposed by a low-status person.[35] Another advantage is that he is likely to be the person who educates new members of the group about group values and norms, as we find Starkey doing in the passage quoted earlier.[36] We might note that although the leader may be more influential than anyone else in molding group opinions and values, even he can change them only slowly. The leader who attempts a great and rapid change

[34] *Ibid.*
[35] Robert F. Bales, "Small Group Theory and Research," in Robert K. Merton, et al., *Sociology Today: Problems and Prospects*, New York, Basic Books, 1959, pp. 293–305.
[36] See p. 110 of this book.

in group objectives and values may find the objectives unchanged and himself no longer leader.

STATUS

Groups have structures other than functional roles; one such is status. Needless to say, those filling leader roles often acquire higher status for doing so, but there are other ways people achieve status in groups. Not infrequently, seniority in the group is a source of status. Skill in doing one's work can be a source of status. On the other hand, some investigators have found that high status goes with not being the highest producer, as may be the case in groups that have strong output restrictions.[37] This may seem confusing until we recall that the situation occurring is one where status is acquired by individuals who excel in and satisfy some of the principal norms of the group as determined by the objectives or values of the group. Hence, when skilled work is an important group value, those with skill have status. When work restriction is a norm, high producers do not obtain status.

SUMMARY

Groups are among the most important of the intervening factors which weld an organization. They influence the behavior of people in organizations in a number of distinct ways.

1. They influence people's perception.
2. They teach individuals many things about their job, the organization, and the world around them.
3. They control behavior.

This chapter has focused on some of the principal ways in which groups are able to accomplish these things.

Groups greatly facilitate communications making the movement of information on relevant topics among group members very easy. This is achieved because groups (1) reduce many of the psychological barriers to communications, (2) develop special languages which include not only words with unique and precise meanings for the group but, frequently, rules for the ordering of communications, as well. However, the interaction patterns through which much information is communicated show that the flow of information in the

[37] Homans, *op. cit.*, p. 141.

groups is not uniform but varies with certain structural properties of the group.

As groups exist over time a number of structures develop within them. First are a set of roles, including several leadership roles and several follower roles. Status also develops based on both roles within these groups and on norms and values of prime importance to the group.

Groups establish norms which are agreements regarding what constitutes acceptable behavior and also create means of enforcing these norms. The enforcement process consists of (1) education, (2) surveillance of group member behavior, (3) reeducation and support of the individual to have him change the error of his ways, and (4) discipline through razzing, caustic remarks, and finally rejection from the group, or violence.

To understand fully any of these processes or the behaviors in a group, we must look toward the objective or purpose of the group and its principal values. Without this orientation group behavior and phenomena often appear contradictory or confusing. With this orientation both become understandable and logical.

7

A Framework for
Organization Analysis

INTUITIVELY one may feel that phenomena such as groups, motivation, and perception bear directly on organizations. Indeed, it is easy to rationalize about why this is so. Yet neither intuitive feeling nor rationalization provide enough substance to support rigorous analysis. Something more than insight is necessary. To achieve a more sophisticated analysis we need the aid of a conceptual scheme or model as a tool. For this reason, we devote this chapter to the consideration of a broad model which can tie together the more limited and specific models previously discussed, and in particular, groups and the factors that mold them.

This is both an easy and difficult task.[1] At first glance, the ideas may seem so simple that they hardly need elaboration; this is exactly why it is difficult to see their real significance. The concepts to be discussed do not form an exact model of organizational behavior. They form instead a general model of social behavior which, in fact, can be best described as a framework. It is important to take time to grasp this framework clearly, to work through its elements and their relationship enough times so they become a comfortable part of our thinking, for this approach underlies many of the remaining portions of the book. Sometimes this framework is used directly and referred to explicitly; other times it is the foundation of both the selection of the material included and the organization in which it is presented. With this framework clearly in mind and easily at our disposal, many portions of the book are more easily understood; without it, they are complex and confusing.

[1] Material in this chapter is based on the work of George Homans in his book, *The Human Group*, New York, Harcourt, Brace, 1950, unless otherwise noted.

INTERNAL AND EXTERNAL SYSTEMS

Let us begin by imagining ourselves in a situation where we are watching an industrial engineer and some supervisors plan a new department. This is to be a plating department, to be housed in a new wing of a factory, utilizing new equipment, and staffed by personnel hired for this particular operation. As plans for the new department are formed, decisions will be made as to exactly what machinery or equipment will be necessary and the jobs which will have to be performed. Decisions as to how the jobs are to be performed will be recorded in job descriptions and job instruction sheets. Hence, from the job descriptions, job instruction sheets, and other prepared data, we can form an idea of some of the things which will go on within this department once it is established and staffed.

If we look into this new department shortly after it begins operations, we shall in all likelihood observe the employees at their assigned equipment doing the tasks assigned. At first this statement may not seem too remarkable. After all, what is wrong with employees doing exactly what they are hired and told to do? However, if we have the opportunity to go into the same department a few weeks or months later, we may see quite a few different things. Some employees will be performing their assigned tasks. Several may gather as usual for their morning chat at the water cooler. Others may have exchanged jobs, and still others may be gluing closed the lid of another worker's lunch box while he is in the rest room. In short, a number of things are going on which are not called for in the plans made earlier. These activities have *emerged* in the particular work situation; they grow out of, or are added to, the things *required* by management and the engineers.

This is an important distinction: the difference between things required and things that emerge. In Homans' terminology it implies the existence of two aspects of a social system, an *external* system and an *internal* system. The former embraces required behaviors, the latter emergent behaviors. In our illustration, a large element of the external system is management, which makes decisions that bring particular people together in particular ways. Management molds or forms part of the external system by job specifications, work methods, prescribed layouts, and selection of personnel.

As for the internal system, the people brought together by management may be strangers at first but eventually they come to know one another, develop friendships and cliques, socialize on (and perhaps off) the job, help one another in their work, perhaps agree to hold down production, etc.   In other words, they have a new basis on which to associate, one that modifies and influences their behavior over and above the effects of the external system.   This new form of behavior is a product of and a response to the external system.   Thus the external system constitutes "an outer hull" [2] which, though not part of the internal system, bears directly on it.

Differentiating between an external system of required behaviors and an internal system of emergent behaviors can be very useful as an analytical tool.   We should never lose sight of the fact that the two are highly interrelated.   The principal value of Homans' concepts is that they provide a framework with which to understand the interrelatedness of the two systems.

ESSENTIAL ELEMENTS IN THE FRAMEWORK FOR ORGANIZATIONAL ANALYSIS

Homans holds that the elements of a social system can be sorted into three categories: activities, interactions, and sentiments.   Into these categories fall aspects of both the external and internal systems.

Activities

Activities are the things people do, the acts they perform.   Some acts are dictated by written instructions, orders, etc.   These are activities prescribed or required by the external system.   Other acts which spring out of a situation, such as horseplay on the job, extra motions to hold down productivity, etc., are products of the internal system.

Interactions

Activities and interactions are closely related yet distinctly different.   Interactions occur when two people in some way come together so that one party has an effect on the other.   To be more precise, interaction occurs when one activity is linked to another.   Many times this takes the form of a communicative act, such as one person speaking or writing to another.   The act of speaking by one person is followed by the act of speaking by a second person.   An act of speaking by one person may be followed by an act of walking by another.   But not all interaction is in this form of communication.

[2] For further discussion along these lines, see Kurt Lewin, *Principles of Topological Psychology*, New York, McGraw-Hill, 1936.

For example, one person may leave a room into which has walked another person he hates.

We can differentiate interactions in many ways. One is on the basis of the duration of an interaction. Some are relatively short, such as a brief greeting in which we say "hello" and the other person responds with, "how are you today?"; others can be long and extend over hours or even days. Another basis of differentiation is the frequency of interaction. We interact with some people daily, perhaps many times daily, whereas there are others with whom we rarely interact. A third basis of differentiation is order or direction. Interactions, since they involve one person acting and another responding, have a direction to them. If we note the interactions between two parties always occurring in a particular order, we may conclude that the one who begins the interaction is a superior and the one who responds or receives the interaction is a subordinate.

As remarked, activities and interactions are closely related; indeed, at times their separation is difficult. On the other hand, these two classes of events in a social system or organization have a distinct advantage in that they are observable. We do not have this advantage with the third class of elements in a social system, sentiments.

Sentiments

This is an enormously broad category of elements and an elusive, difficult one. Sentiments are the internal states of a human being. Such states include a person's emotions or feelings, his beliefs or values, aspirations or objectives, frames of reference or ways of looking at things, his needs or drives—in short, all the factors within a person which motivate his activities and shape his perspective of himself and the world around him.

Suppose we were to ask an employee who was planning to go "on the town" with some of his fellow workers why he was going out with the same people he had worked with all day. He, in all likelihood, would say, "They are my friends. I like them." The sentiment here, of course, is one of friendship or mutual liking that emerges from the external situation, in that he is going with some people he has met through his work. That is, it is a sentiment in the internal system. Employees' feeling of dislike for their boss or a belief that producing a thousand parts a day instead of the fifteen hundred required by management is reasonable and just, is a similar sentiment in the internal system.

Sentiments in the internal system are rather easy to identify and understand. But what are sentiments in the external system? Actually, there are two different types. One set of external sentiments are those a person brings with him into a particular situation. For example, an employee has certain prejudices, ideals, hopes, and fears acquired prior to taking a job, which he brings with him when entering the organization. One woman may feel that her job as a clerk-typist is not a very prestigious form of work, perhaps because her family and neighbors have always been employed in professional or semiprofessional categories such as teachers or laboratory technicians. Another woman might see the same job as being highly desirable since most of her family and friends work as factory laborers. These are simple illustrations of two of the host of attitudes, prejudices, fears, and outlooks that any of us bring into a situation from which new patterns of behavior emerge.

There is another and different set of external sentiments. They are the sentiments required by the organization, or the external system. An example of this type is loyalty. Men entering the army are expected to be loyal to their country, to the army, and loyal to the point where they will even sacrifice their lives if necessary. The same is true for people within companies. Business executives many times talk about the need for company loyalty among their employees, how pleased they are when they find it, and how disappointed when they miss it. Loyalty is only one of the many sentiments the organization may prescribe as necessary for organizational members. Not all organizations have this particular sentiment, but any organization has some type of required sentiments. Later we shall explore this more fully, particularly in the area of decentralization.

Values and Norms: A Distinction

Under the topic of sentiments we have considered elements known as values and another set known as norms. Since these will come up many times in many ways, it is perhaps important to make a distinction between the two. Values are ideas people hold as hopes and assumptions in the form of an ideal, a standard, a belief, an objective so great or so encompassing as to be actually unattainable, but which at the same time serve as a guide to people. Contrasted to this, norms are much more specific. They designate particular behaviors, attitudes, or beliefs to which people must adhere. When it is understood by a work group that none will produce more than a thousand plated parts a day, even though the management requests fifteen hundred, a norm exists.   A norm is measurable, people can understand it clearly, and it is attainable.

AN EXAMINATION OF PAIRED RELATIONSHIPS

We now have a framework consisting of six major compartments: sentiments, interactions, and activities in both an external system and an internal system.   This framework would be useful even if it merely provided a convenient way of sorting different elements in a social system.   However, its major utility and real importance is that each element is related to all the others.   For ease of presentation, we shall begin by considering the relationship between pairs of elements in the external system and then between pairs in the internal system, eventually examining longer chains of events where three, four, or more elements are involved.

Activities and Interactions in the External System

In chapter 9 when we examine division of work, we pay particular attention to the fact that as work is specialized, the tasks performed become highly interrelated.   One of the most difficult and universal problems in organizations is to achieve the integration of work that has been divided.   Without digging too deeply into that issue at this point, we merely state that a division of labor automatically creates the need for a means of integration.   The jobs or tasks resulting from a division of work have to be carried out in a particular way in a certain order or time sequence; these are the activities of the external system.   In short, they are linked activities, and some interaction takes place to facilitate the linkage.

The important point is that any one division of labor resulting in a particular set of jobs or activities requires a specific set of interactions to promote the necessary integration.   Any change in activities, of necessity, changes the required interactions.   As with all paired relationships, this is a reciprocal one; that is, any change of the interactions in an established system is matched by a change in required activities.

In the past management planning of work has been influenced by industrial engineering, which in many instances has looked exclusively at the activities to be performed, ignoring the required relationships. The presumption seemed to be that the relationships would take care of themselves and that it was the activities which were the controlling factors.   This point of view has led to many problems.

Sentiments and Activities in the External System

As we noted when examining sentiments in the external system, we have to deal with two different types: those given or brought in by organizational members and those required by particular external system or formal organization design.

GIVEN OR BROUGHT-IN SENTIMENTS.   A person develops many sentiments, values, ideals, or objectives throughout his life which he brings into any particular organized setting.   In college or from his professional colleagues, an engineer may have adopted the belief that to do really professional work he must continually tackle a variety of new tasks or design problems.   On getting a job he may find that his activities are the same so that having solved one particular type of engineering problem, he is given others of a similar nature.   The activities are routine.   They do not match his feelings of what constitutes truly professional work.   To summarize, the activities people perform, or are expected to perform, are connected closely with their inner needs and values, that is, sentiments.

REQUIRED SENTIMENTS.   Let us return to the example of required sentiments of loyalty in an army; when a person has this sentiment, he will act in specific ways.   For example, he will not desert his unit when under fire but will follow commands of superiors and support his organization.   Another example is the organization having the required sentiment that supervisors fill a distinctly different role from subordinates; both must think and act differently.   That is, an executive or supervisor who engages in activities assigned to his subordinates is definitely doing the wrong thing.   The list could be extended, but the relationship between the required sentiments and required activities should by this time be clear.

Sentiments and Interactions in the External System

Just as there is a close relationship between the sentiments and activities of the external system, so there are close bonds between sentiments and interactions.   Again, the beliefs and values people develop before coming into an organization often have coupled with them implications for the interactions which will occur.   For example, persons from an authoritarian culture might well expect on moving into an organization that subordinates would not speak to superiors except when spoken to.   They might be distressed to find differences in the organization.   At the same time, there are some required sentiments which have required types of interactions associated with them.   If a company assumes that its managers will view themselves as independent businessmen, it presumes they will initiate a fair amount of interaction with their superiors rather than the reverse.   Hence, sentiments are related to both the initiation and content of interaction.

Sentiments and Interactions in the Internal System

Let us turn now to the mutual relationships between pairs of elements in the internal system concerned with emergent behavior or sentiments, as contrasted with required or prescribed behavior.   A broad, general proposition here is that people who interact frequently will develop positive sentiments or friendly feelings toward one another.   This is sometimes stated a little more explicitly as: the more frequently people interact, the stronger will be their feelings of friendship or liking.   This relationship holds in two ways.   We interact frequently with those we like and learn to like those with whom we interact.

However, there is one definite proviso; there must be no extenuating factors.   For example, when a person interacts with another toward whom he has strong prejudices, repeated interaction may bring about intensified feelings of dislike.   In terms of this chapter's analysis, when interaction is required between persons—one of whom has an externally developed negative sentiment toward some features of the other, for example, race—the particular sentiments developed by the prejudiced individual toward the other will be strongly negative.   For this reason the relationship between interactions and sentiments can be best expressed as an increase in interaction between two or more people which brings about an increase in the strength of their sentiments. The direction of the sentiments—positive or liking, negative or disliking—is determined by other factors.

Sentiments that influence interaction need not be mutual; they may also be shared.   An example of such a situation may be seen when people do not have particularly strong feelings on important issues yet come together to talk about these points.   Anyone who has ever worked in an industrial situation where the management has been forced to take some unpopular action recognizes that people will be drawn together to talk about their common complaint just as readily as they will be drawn together to talk as a result of friendship.   This emergent interaction may, of course, lead to emergent positive sentiments toward one another.

Sentiments and Activities in the Internal System

In many situations we can observe people who like one another (that is, who have strong positive sentiments toward one another) coming together to share activities, games, parties, etc. Some of them do not even have any obvious direct interaction. They may sit silently, for example, while sailing a boat just "enjoying each other's company." In this relationship there is a suggestion that the sentiments people have has a strong influence on how well they work together on shared or related activities. As we saw when discussing cohesion in Chapter 5, when people who like one another are on the same job, they work together better than those who do not like one another.

We should look at this relationship from both sides. People will often have definite sentiments about activities and the individuals who perform them. They seem to say, in effect, "Well, if he does thus, he must be all right" or vice versa.

Activities and Interactions in the Internal System

It is perhaps belaboring the obvious, but to stress a frequently neglected point, people do seem to need and require certain amounts of association with other people. Interaction with others is, therefore, something pleasant and sought after in the natural course of events by human beings.[3] Pure interaction, however, is difficult to attain. Hence, we usually do it in conjunction with some activity. This situation leads one to suspect that much of the activity in which people engage—games, dances, and the like—are created primarily to provide a vehicle or means through which people can interact and enjoy associations with others. The two, activity and interaction, as noted before, go closely together.

Sentiments, Interactions, and Activities in the Internal System

Having considered various paired relationships, let us examine how all three categories of phenomena relate in the internal system. We discuss first a particular class of sentiment, namely, a norm. Members of a group may notice that one of them is doing certain things, performing certain activities that violate the norm. The interactions

[3] See, for example, Leonard R. Sayles, "Work Group Behavior and the Larger Organization," in *Research in Industrial Human Relations, IRRA,* New York, Harper, 1957, pp. 131–145.

among group members and the person who is deviating no doubt actually increase as they try to persuade him, through argument or ridicule, to stop his deviate behavior. If, however, he persists, the group will probably reach a point where it will decide it can no longer hope to persuade him to change by interaction, ultimately cutting it off altogether and ostracizing the deviate.

The group may even go further. Having failed by persuasion and social ostracism to bring the deviate into line, they may take actions, which assume the form of harassment, such as hiding his lunch or tools, or perhaps even physical abuse. By use of these concepts we can explain how certain situations will emerge and, further, how different sets of factors develop.

We have traced a line of analysis from a sentiment to different patterns of interaction that might bring about a correction in the action of the deviate member. If these efforts do not, this situation might well lead to new actions by the rest of the group. In short, the factors that emerge at one time in the internal system may very well set up conditions which develop subsequent sets of activities, interactions, and sentiments.

USES OF THE HOMANS MODEL
OF A SOCIAL SYSTEM

The basic variables in the Homans model—sentiments, activities, and interactions—were included or implicit in the earlier discussions of motivation, leadership, groups, status, etc. Status, for example, was identified as a ranking, but behind it is a value scheme that says a certain person or a certain position should be ranked above another. We have also noted that values are one of the components of sentiment and that there are problems of congruency between what an individual believes himself to possess in the way of status and the status he actually receives from his position, seniority, associations, etc. We also reviewed the problems that can occur when a person's job is changed (activity), which may influence his acquired status (sentiment) or lead to strong feelings of pleasure or disappointment with his new position (emergent sentiment), and possibly to subsequent actions such as complaining to the boss, filing a grievance, etc.

In our discussion of groups, the Homans variables came up in several ways. Norms, as we have noted, are closely related to values and are therefore a part of sentiment. The roles of emergent interactions in enforcing compliance with group norms and of required interaction in initial group development were discussed. In examining cohesive-

ness we considered sentiments when reviewing the attractions a group
or its activities might have for a person.   We also reviewed the importance of interaction among group members to increase the sharing of
sentiments, how these interactions are influenced by the activities of
the group, and whether they are ends in themselves or merely means to
an end.   This list could be extended but, as we have noted, the point in
dealing with specific aspects of behavior in earlier chapters, that we
were continually referring to variables included in the Homans
model.

Unity Revealed by Second Level of Abstraction

Homans' first essential observation was that in many specific and
different types of social phenomena there are basic elements common
to all.   Identifying these elements gives us an extraordinarily valuable
conceptual tool.   Without it we are talking about numerous discreet
phenomena which we find difficult to relate to each other in any
meaningful fashion.   With this tool we have a common set of dimensions we can apply to each phenomenon, permitting more meaningful
comparison and integration.

Basic also to the Homans model is the interrelatedness of the variables.   The nature of one influences the nature of all others.   Change
in one influences all the others.   *If the more basic variables of sentiment, interactions, and activities are interrelated, so too are the more
specific phenomena and processes of status, groups, perception, motivation, and the like.*   This model tells us that a change in a person's job
changes his activities, which changes his status and his sentiment.   We
also know that a change in activities will bring about a change in
interactions; a change in sentiment will influence interaction; and a
change in interaction will affect the nature of the group the person is
in.   The model more than points out the interrelatedness of group
organization properties such as status, group cohesion, etc.   It helps to
understand the *way* in which these properties are interrelated.   It
gives us a guide to analysis.

Last, the Homans model provides a uniquely valuable bridge that
links systems.   It ties the emergent system of people's actual everyday
behavior to organizations and the external system of formal plans,
culture, and other groups that mold emergent behavior.   Such a
bridge permits us to trace the effects of a change in the external system
on the behavior of the internal system and, we might add, vice versa.
It is, therefore, a powerful tool for analyzing what has occurred and

why and for predicting what might occur if a proposed change were made.

This framework is by no means the only way of analyzing social phenomena. However, it is one of the simplest and at the same time most inclusive and effective means available. On the surface it is deceptively simple. Once a person becomes familiar with the concepts and their multiple simultaneous relationships, this system provides a highly useful tool, and constitutes the framework for the analysis and presentation of many later sections of this book. Sometimes the use of the model is clearly identified and other times it is not. It will be helpful, therefore, to understand this model clearly before proceeding further.

Part Two

Formal Organization: Dividing Work

8

Formal Organizations

Part One examined some important elements in formal organizations. In Part Two we turn attention to the formal organizations themselves. In this and following parts we shall be concerned primarily with details of organizational structure and operation. Before becoming immersed in these details, however, it will be useful to consider some overall concepts of organizations. These will provide a framework for keeping subsequent parts in order and an orientation for reminding us that the details examined later are only components of a whole.

The Nature of Formal Organizations

Organizations are purposeful entities. We have seen that small groups or cliques are organizations since they have objectives. These objectives may not be clearly stated; they may be of no purpose to anyone except members of the organization, but they are there. The distinction often made between a formal organization and a group or informal one is that the former is a planned organization. A formal organization's objectives are more explicit. Its structure is the result of conscious decision making. Many of its internal processes are also consciously planned, more explicit than a group's, and usually more observable. The distinction between formal and informal organizations is then, in part, a matter of planning, explicitness, and observability of such properties as structure, processes, and objectives.

To say that formal organizations are planned organizations should not be taken to mean that the study of formal organizations is only concerned with the planned part of organizations. Classical organization theory was often restricted to these matters. Current theory is not. We have already noted how decisions in regard to such things as work layout, job content, work pace, etc., form part of the external system within which the internal system develops and molds behavior. Formal organizations in this book are looked on not only as including the planned portions of the organization but also the behavior of individuals and groups influenced by these organization prescriptions.

ORGANIZATION GOALS

Many people observing organizations are confused and disturbed by the fact that what the organization is doing runs counter to what its objectives say it ought to be doing. A business concern may declare that it is using science to serve society and yet may have only a mediocre, lackadaisical research program, or perhaps may purposefully hold back new discoveries in order to protect its profits on established products. A prison system may have declared objectives of rehabilitating its inmates but, in fact, may provide primarily custodial care. These are distinctions between *official* (that is, for public consumption) and *operative* goals (those actually pursued, which mold the operation of the organization). Operative goals need not be completely different from official ones; they may differ only in degree of specificity.[1] Nor need we assume that operative goals are always hidden, secret, or hard to find. In examining organizations the point is to find the operative goals; to focus on the official goals, especially when they are considerably different from the operative goals, would be confounding and misleading.

Types of Operative Goals

It is hard to conceive of an organization which has only one goal. Organizations usually have multiple goals that are of different types. Failure to recognize the existence of both different types of goals and their multiplicity can cause great confusion.

Business concerns are often described as organizations whose objective it is to make a profit. Such a statement, however, does not help to understand much about the organization we are observing or the directions in which it might be moving. A number of writers have pointed out that many times organizations do not seem to be concerned pri-

---

[1] For further discussion of official and operative goals, see Charles Perrow, "The Analysis of Goals in Complex Organizations," *American Sociological Review*, **26**, 1961, pp. 854–865.

marily with the pursuit of profit or, at least, the maximization of profit. Furthermore, they have remarked that the profit motive is relatively useless for organizational planning and direction.[2]

In planning an organization, one of the key concepts is division of work. Organization objectives should certainly be useful in determining how work is to be divided. We might ask, "How do we divide the work of making a profit?" An objective such as profit does not provide a usable answer to this question. However, an objective of "making and selling washing machines" is useful in determining how work should be divided. Here we know that we want some units to be concerned with manufacturing and others with selling. But we quickly run into other questions such as how far should we continue to divide the work of selling the washing machines? Should we plan a selling effort that turns the product over to some national retailing chain? Should we have a selling effort that involves manufacturing under our own label and distributing through our own regional warehouses to private dealers operating retail stores? The statement of the objective to make and sell washing machines does not help to decide the degree of vertical integration for the marketing effort. Yet an objective of profit or, preferably, profit maximization does help to answer this question. We may find that maximum profits occur when we distribute through our own regional warehouses, which then turn our products over to retail outlets owned by other companies. Thus, to answer some of the questions that occur in planning an organization, we obviously need more than one objective. More important, we need different types of objectives.

Deterministic Goals

Briefly stated, deterministic goals are those that specify the end or direction toward which the organization applies its efforts. Statements like "Our bureau is going to provide police services to the city" or "We are going to make a popular line of low-price washing machines" are deterministic goals. They identify the end product or service of the organization. On the basis of such statements many organizational decisions can be made, such as those concerned with the division of work.

[2] See, for example, Peter F. Drucker, *The Practice of Management*, New York, Harper, 1954, p. 36.

Constraint Goals

In our illustration the company was obviously not willing to manufacture washing machines under any circumstances, but only if a profit could be made and only in that particular way in which profits could be maximized. By constraint goals we mean those that specify the condition under which an organization will be permitted to operate. These can be many. In some organizations the constraint goal is to make a good profit every year, but in others a very important one is to perpetuate the organization even if profits are not made every year. Constraint goals are numerous; to have safe working conditions and to provide economic security for employees are but two of them. A police department may have a deterministic objective of achieving a low crime rate. However, it may achieve this end only as long as police functions do not interfere with individual liberty and reports of crime are consistent and accurate.

Mutual Dependency of Deterministic and Constraint Goals

We have already noted that we cannot make decisions on the basis of deterministic goals without considering the requirements of constraint goals. The reverse is also true. A sales manager concerned with profit may see that there is an opportunity for the washing machine company to set up coin-operated laundromats. But to do this new deterministic goals will have to be added, for example, the maintenance of the equipment in laundromats, the purchase of detergents, water softeners, and the like. In short, the internal structure of the organization may have to be revamped considerably. If this reorganization does not come about initially through a clear recognition of the new organization goals, it may come about slowly and expensively in response to problems which emerge over time.

This actual, if not explicit, change in goals also entails a change in the environment with which the company comes into contact. Heretofore it did not come in contact with the ultimate user of washers, local governments, labor unions representing truck drivers, etc. It now will, and these add further constraint goals for the concern to consider. If these new environmental contacts are not recognized, the manufacturer may be taken by surprise by a number of different and difficult problems.

Hierarchy of Importance of Goals

Although organizations have many goals, seldom are two of them of equal importance. Consequently, most organizations have a hierarchy of importance for their goals. In some, maximization of long-run profits is more important than maximization of short-run profits, but both are subordinate to perpetuating the organization; in others, the reverse may be true. Our point here is not to cite any particular set of hierarchal importance but to note that such a set will exist in any real organization.

Means-ends Chain

Accompanying any decision concerning goals to be achieved or ends to be obtained is another decision about how this is to be accomplished or the means by which this is to be attained. These means, in turn, become subgoals about which still further decisions have to be made regarding the means by which they are to be achieved. These secondary means, in turn, become sub-subgoals and so on, until the statements of means become sufficiently specific or reach a level of concreteness to permit action to be taken. This sequence of means-ends, means-ends is called the *means-ends chain generated through means-ends analysis.*

We might illustrate this process as follows. The board of directors of General Motors states that the corporation's objective or end is to make and sell automobiles to all classes of customers and that it will do this by means of establishing a series of car styles suited for different consumer income levels. For the president of the company at the next level these decisions on means, in effect, become objectives which he must achieve; and he may decide to accomplish them by setting up major organizational units devoted to making and selling cars geared to specific economic levels. One line of cars will sell at low or "popular" prices, other lines will sell at the middle range of prices, and at the very top will sell the most expensive range of cars. These means he has established, in turn, become the objectives for the vice presidents in charge of each of these divisions. The manager in charge of the popular price line of cars may decide to carry out this objective by setting up factories to make the cars, design units to plan them, and marketing units to sell them. The same will be true for the other divisions. The heads of these various functional units will take these means decisions as ends and, in turn, make their own means decisions and so on

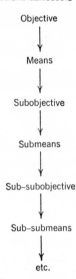

Objective

Means

Subobjective

Submeans

Figure 8.1.   Means-ends chain.

Sub–subobjective

Sub–submeans

etc.

down to the very lowest level.   Hence, there is a hierarchal structure of ends or goals ranging from broad general ones at the top of the organization to quite specific and delimited objectives at the lower levels of the organization (see Figure 8.1).   It is to be noted that the means decision at one level is the end to be achieved for the next level.[3]

The question can be raised as to how far this is to be carried. When does the means-ends chain end?   At what point does the chain become sufficiently concrete or specific enough to be useful?   Essentially, this depends on the circumstances surrounding the organization and the resources available to it.   This process must be continued until a particular means decision can be carried out by existing programs of action or in other concrete ways.

For example, in building a house we might go through a series of decisions such as the following: the house will have walls; they will be of masonry and made of brick; we will buy the brick.   When we have finally reached the decision to buy the brick, we have made the

---

[3] Figure 8.1 might indicate that each link in the chain coincides with an organizational position or level.   This need not be so at all.   There may be several links before an operational goal is defined for a department and several more before the next operational goal is defined for the next level.   Several links in the means-ends chain may cluster at one position or subunit.   In fact, there is no reason why they all could not.   See James G. March and Herbert A. Simon, *Organizations*, New York, John Wiley, 1958, pp. 194–195.

last means decision necessary.   However, let us assume that we have been making the decision to build a house in colonial times when there was no convenient market for brick.   If the only way to obtain bricks had been to make them, the means-ends analysis would have had to be carried considerably further; we would have had to make other decisions, such as to buy land with an adequate clay deposit, to dig a clay pit, to make a kiln, to make brick molds, to hire people to operate the kiln and the brick molds, to prepare the schedules under which they would work.   We would have continued along the ends-means chain with progressively more specific decisions being made until an existing means for accomplishing an end could have been used.   If, in making bricks, we could have hired trained brick makers who possessed skills (or, as we shall call them, programs for performing work), the ends-means chain could have ended with the decision to hire these workers as the means to get the bricks made.   On the other hand, if no one had these skills, we would have had to make another decision about how to obtain competent help and may have chosen to train unskilled help ourselves, thereby extending the means-ends chain further.   To sum up, then, the means-ends chain of analysis continues until a means decision can draw on existing products or programs available in the organizational environment.[4]

To leave this discussion of means-ends analysis here might lead to a possible misinterpretation that the analysis always yields a nice, tightly fitting progression of objectives or ends.   This is not the case.   If several people are involved in developing various sections of the means-ends chain, some of those carrying out the analysis at a later stage may not be fully acquainted with the original end to be achieved.   They receive a more restricted, specific statement of an objective.   By interpreting this situation from their own point of view and making subsequent decisions as to how this objective is to be realized, they may take a direction which makes full accomplishment of the overall end impossible.   Hence, in a prison system, a prison board may decide that rehabilitation is one of the key tasks of the system; but officials farther down the hierarchy, in interpreting some specific objectives, such as operating a prison, may so arrange things that their primary task is to keep prisoners within the prison and that one of the ways to accomplish this is to keep them occupied with handicraft or occupational duties.   As a result, tasks given to people are primarily intended to keep them from being idle rather than to fit them with skills they can

---

[4] For further discussion of this topic, see March and Simon, *op. cit.*, particularly pp. 190–193.

use when they are released from prison.   As the means-ends analysis is continued, such distortions in the hierarchy of goals can occur since the analysis is often carried out by a number of people, each familiar with only a portion of the chain, who approach their decision-making task from different organizational levels and functions and from different environmental backgrounds.[5]

ORGANIZATION SPECIFICATION

To arrive at a hierarchy of goals is an important step in developing an organization; however, there are many things to be resolved before an actual organization exists.   Should departments and positions have one or several goals, and if several, which ones?   Should people be assigned to tasks or should tasks be assigned to people?   These and many other decisions specify the nature of the organization which will emerge.

Patterns of Organizing to Handle the Means-ends Chain

There are business executives who say, "In our business we have no organization chart.   We do not worry about organization.   We just hire good people and put them to work."   If we were to examine how such an executive works, we would probably note that he acquires people in whom he has confidence and whom he feels are loyal and think as he does, and then assigns them an area of the company to operate or a problem to handle.   Furthermore, a person assigned to handle a problem in one area might at a later time be assigned a different problem in a totally different area.   His skills in the new area or his knowledge of it apparently are secondary to the fact that the top executive has confidence in him as an individual.   Those who read the history of governments, especially in the smaller, earlier states, find this happening frequently.   An individual who had the confidence of the king might at one time receive an assignment as general of an army and later be assigned as a diplomat to negotiate the marriage of a daughter. In these cases the subordinate involved usually has the overall objective

---

[5] To make explicit an important point implicit in this statement, there is no need to consider the hierarchy of goals arrived at by means-ends analysis as the result of a unified planning process, or the people who carry it out as members of some unifying authority system. The connections between the people who carry out the analysis may be very tenuous, each of them conducting the analysis in the way and on the premises they perceive best.

identified by his superior and then must commence to develop for himself the rest of the means-ends chain. It is up to him to determine what skills or programs will be used at the end of the chain and, if necessary, to train people, perhaps himself, in them.

Such an arrangement is often expedient, but it raises several fundamental problems, among them, that the means-ends analysis and often the programs developed to accomplish the objectives exist primarily in the mind of the subordinate assigned the job. If he were to die or for some reason leave, another person inheriting the task would have to develop all the steps for himself.

Quite a different way of handling the means-ends analysis is found in our "ideal" bureaucracy. Here the chain is clearly and formally developed, often by a central agency or individual. As a result, the purposes of jobs, tasks, and duties are clearly specified as are the ways or programs for accomplishing them. People are chosen for these jobs on the basis of their ability to carry out the programs to accomplish specific ends. In this sort of situation if an individual were to die or leave, a new person could be brought in and trained in the programs necessary to accomplish the needed subgoals. The whole arrangement is far less dependent on the existence and skills of any one individual.

What all this shows is that organizations can have different degrees of *institutionalization*. Institutionalization is the process of establishing standard roles, duties, and behaviors. This is a relative concept. One degree of institutionalization exists when the objective or ends of each position are clearly spelled out. A higher degree of institutionalization exists when the programs (rules and procedures) for each position are defined. In the first illustration, which we call a *personalized* organization, there is very little institutionalization. In the *bureaucratic* situation there is a high degree of institutionalization. Figure 8.2 summarizes some of the essential differences between the two conditions. The personalized or noninstitutionalized situation rests on high personal regard in the form of loyalty, etc., existing between the superior and the subordinate, the absence of programs, very little of the means-ends chain being prepared by the superior, and a real need for the subordinate to understand the overall end to be accomplished. In the bureaucratic situation there is almost complete institutionalization, and the opposite exists on almost every count. Individual jobs are precisely defined regarding both what is to be accomplished by the job and the means by which these ends are to be achieved. The means-ends chain and the program specification are

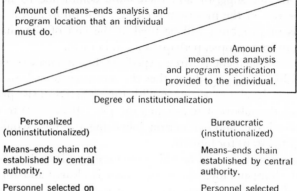

Degree of institutionalization

Personalized (noninstitutionalized)	Bureaucratic (institutionalized)
Means–ends chain not established by central authority.	Means–ends chain established by central authority.
Personnel selected on basis of personal preference.	Personnel selected on the basis of competence.
Personnel have to develop much of means–ends chain themselves.	Personnel do not have to develop means–ends chain.
Personnel need to know overall objectives and ends.	Personnel need to know means activities.
Personnel need to be able to develop or find adequate programs.	Personnel are trained in existing programs.

Figure 8.2

often carried out on a centralized basis. People are assigned jobs on the basis of personal competence, not personal attraction. Theoretically at least, there is no need for the individual to know the overall end of the organization or the means-ends chain.

Figure 8.2 makes clear something which until this time has been implicit. As we proceed along the continuum from personalized to bureaucratic end points, the amount of the subordinate's job which is spelled out for him increases, and, conversely, the amount of the job left to his discretion decreases. The importance of the subordinate being able to perform specified duties grows, and the necessity for his ability to develop, or find new ways of doing things, declines.

Needless to say, we are dealing with ideal forms of organization. No actual organization would ever meet the conditions at either end of the continuum in Figure 8.2. It would be found instead somewhere toward the middle. Nonetheless, such an arrangement helps to make important distinctions among existing degrees of institutionalization and what these imply for carrying out such vital processes as means-ends analysis.

The Overdefined Organization

The personalized and bureaucratic modes of organizational definition do not cover all possible conditions of organization. That is, the bureaucratic form is not the ultimate in definitions. There is still the *overdefined condition*.

To elucidate the overdefined condition, let us consider a plant manager who is about to make some decisions in regard to production scheduling. He can schedule production runs for a product as soon as orders, however small, are received, and in doing this can assure prompt delivery to customers which will doubtless please the sales department. However, this procedure will probably result in short and irregularly scheduled production runs of any given product, causing high setup and production costs. The manager can, on the other hand, hold small orders until he has enough to justify a relatively long production run, thereby reducing setup costs but at the same time leaving some customers' order unsatisfied for a long period. If he were in a situation where he had been told by his superior to "go run the factory," it would be within his province to decide which of these alternate strategies to choose, and doubtless he would do so on the basis of what he thought to be the important objectives to maximize. We could call his position *underdefined*, leaving him free to establish policy and standards to be met.

In a completely bureaucratic setting this situation would not be the case. Exactly what the manager was to do would be clearly spelled out. There might be flexibility in the sense that under certain conditions, such as few or no competitors for the company's products, he could schedule production to minimize costs, but for those products for which there were competitors he would have to schedule production to meet customer demands. In any case, what he was to do would be specified in exact detail. We call this the *exactly defined* organization.

However, the plant manager may well have been told that he must fill customer orders immediately and that he must also keep production costs low. Here standards are clear and explicit but also conflicting. The plant manager is in that peculiar situation where by satisfying one of the objectives given him he must violate another. In the sense that he has more specification than is useful, the situation is identified as being overdefined.[6]

If this situation is not modified by a decision rule, such as "whenever faced with conflicting standards, always choose the one which minimizes cost," the plant manager must make some decision himself as to which rule or standard or objective to follow.   This means, first, that he must make the policy of organizational significance by himself; second, that the existence of conflicting objectives or standards actually puts him into a freer position than in the exactly defined organization.   It should be noted that this condition also places him in a more frustrating, tension-producing situation.   Last, we might note that unless the tension or frustration is particularly severe, such conditions might actually promote inventiveness of new solutions which will enable him to cope more adequately with conflicting standards.   We shall have more to say about these situations in Chapter 21.

The overdefined situation, rather than being unusual in large organizations, is all too common.   The conflicting objectives or standards usually come from different channels of authority.   Typical among such situations are those in which a manager may receive one set of standards or instructions from one staff department, another and conflicting set from a second staff department; when going to his line superior for help, he receives the answer that he is to "follow the advice" of staff as he sees best.

This discussion of "ideal types" may lead to the conclusion that we are dealing with terms which can describe a whole organization. Actually, it is perfectly possible for an organization to be underdefined, exactly defined, and overdefined all at the same time.   The plant manager referred to earlier may find things overdefined in regard to production scheduling, exactly defined in terms of recruitment procedures, and underdefined in terms of safety matters.   Needless to say, to consider all three at the same time makes discussion and analysis extraordinarily complex.   Following our regular rule, therefore, we shall discuss organizations as if only one of these conditions existed, recognizing that in reality things are not so simple.

The person faced with multiple objectives or programs is also usually faced with alternate authority structures.   The decision as to which one to obey or which to put first is seldom completely open to his discretion.   In any actual organization situations usually develop in

---

[6] This terminology is drawn from Andrew G. Frank, "Goal Ambiguity and Conflicting Standards: An Approach to the Study of Organization," Paper presented to the American Sociological Society, 1958.

which one channel of authority (or set of objectives) takes precedence over the others.   Often this preeminence is not determined by "legitimate" factors but by what is most essential for the organization at a given time.   When an organization such as a business concern or a hospital is new, the acquisition of capital may be of such enormous importance that the parties involved with this activity have an overwhelming influence.   As time goes along, as the investment is committed, new problems arise, such as making the organization successful, which may give a prominence to certain technical or managerial skills. Hence, the executive who can develop a new marketing scheme or develop market outlets may, because of his importance to the organization at that time, have an influence far exceeding other executives. Still later, after the investment has been developed and the markets established, the problem may be to operate efficiently to combat cost advantages of competitors.   Here internal routine operations may receive paramount attention, and those individuals involved with maximizing this type of activity become most powerful.[7]

In summary, the role of the individual executive is not simple.   In contemporary organizations he is often faced with an overdefined situation.   He must choose among conflicting objectives and standards, and his decision is both aided and confused by the existence of multiple channels of authority which have different and changing degrees of influence.

TWO BASIC FORMS OF ORGANIZATION THEORY

Although there are many different theories or models of organizations, they tend to fall into two broad generic types.   We briefly examine each of these at two levels of abstraction: (1) where we consider the entire organization as a unit, and (2) where we consider the basic internal elements of the overall unit.   If we were discussing automobiles, for example, the first approach would have us consider them as a unit: their purchase cost, their maintenance cost, their fuel consumption, weight, etc.   The second level of abstraction would have us examining their types of motor and transmission, and the way motors and transmissions were connected to wheels, etc.   The distinction between these two levels of abstractions is fairly elementary. However, if it is not taken into account, the following discussion of theories can be confusing.

[7] For discussion of this see Perrow, *op. cit.*

The Goal Model

Most of the discussion thus far has centered on goal models. These are models of organizations which have as a central focus the goals (in terms we have been using, the deterministic goals) of the organization. The goals are used in two ways. The first is to determine the relative success or failure of the organization. If it meets its goals, such as winning an election, it is a successful organization; if not, it is to that degree unsuccessful. Second, goals function as the starting point of means-ends analysis which leads to a hierarchy of goals and to a definition of organizational subunits, such as departments, divisions, and positions.

A great deal of the literature and thinking about organizations has in the past been in some way connected with goal models. We have already referred to some of their important properties and use them in a more extended form in Chapters 9 and 11. At the same time, we have to recognize that goal models do not explain or permit explanation of all organizational phenomena and do not seem suitable as a guide for making the many types of decisions required in organizations. Many of these difficulties are cleared up, or are at least better handled, through a different type of model.

The Systems Model

Unlike the goal model, the systems model focuses on an organization's general properties and processes. Such an approach does not give prime attention to organizational objectives but to those attributes of an organization which are relevant to the achievement of any goal.[8]

Perhaps a more general way to put this is that any organization must fulfill several important functions if it is to survive. Among these are: (1) goal achievement which defines overall objectives and develops sets of subgoals to be accomplished by positions, departments, and the like; (2) an integrating function which sets up or facilitates those relationships that permit the efforts of individuals and organizational subunits to be effectively coordinated; (3) the adaption of the organization to both the environment and its own internal requirements and, to some degree, the adaption of the environment itself; (4) the acquiring and maintaining of necessary resources in the form of per-

[8] For a distinction between these two general types of organization models, see Amitai Etzioni, "Two Approaches to Organizational Analysis: A Critique and a Suggestion," *Administrative Science Quarterly*, 5, 1960, pp. 257–278.

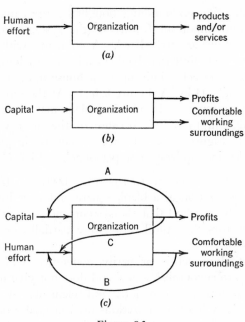

Figure 8.3

sonnel, machinery, technical knowledge, etc.[9] The first of these functions is the concern of goal models; all of them are the concern of systems models. The two approaches are thus not divorced; more important, they are not in opposition but are instead intimately connected.

These are by no means the only functions found in organizations, however; because they seem to be among the most important, they receive considerable attention in this and Part Three.

THE SYSTEMS MODEL AT THE OVERALL UNIT LEVEL. The systems model requires us to consider the organization as receiving inputs from the environment and, in turn, delivering outputs to the environment. In short, we tend to think in "flows." One flow might be that of human effort entering the company (Figure 8.3a) and products or services leaving. Another flow might be funds coming in from the environment as capital, or loans from banks, and profits or payments leaving to banks and owners, as well as satisfactions received by employees from

[9] These functions have been adapted from a number of sources. Most important among them is Talcott Parsons, *Structure and Process in Modern Societies*, The Free Press of Glencoe, 1960, particularly pp. 17–47.

working in attractive surroundings bought by the capital (see Figure 8.3*b*). A second important feature of the systems model is that it considers these flows as interrelated. A company with a diminishing profit (output) may find that bankers take a dim look at lending it money and say, in effect, "Tidy up your house first, and then we will make you a loan." (Line A, Figure 8.3*c*.) At the same time, a company that cannot renovate its physical plant may find that new employees are difficult to recruit because of the poor working conditions. (Line B, Figure 8.3*c*.) Hence, a decrease in profit leads to a greater difficulty in acquiring new personnel. (Line C, Figure 8.3*c*.)

THE SYSTEMS MODEL INTERNAL TO THE ORGANIZATION. If we stop considering the organization as a blank square and start looking at what goes on internally, we find that the systems model continues to focus attention on factors that, until now, were partially or perhaps completely neglected.

The goal-based model is primarily concerned with dividing the work necessary to accomplish a goal and does not give much attention to the relationships between jobs and elements of organizations. Ideally, if the analysis of organizations used in goal models were carried out completely, we might expect all aspects of the relationships among jobs as well as the content of jobs to be included in the plan. Unfortunately, the model is not that elegant, nor is our skill in using it that advanced. The tendency, while using the goal-based model, is to give inadequate and sometimes no attention to the relationships among jobs or elements of the organization.

The systems model focuses directly on this deficiency. The essential idea behind a system in an organizational sense is the connectiveness,[10] or perhaps, a better word would be the *interconnectiveness*, of the parts of an organization.

Systems are so prevalent in our lives that we seldom acknowledge them as ways of looking at or analyzing the world around us. A typical example are the brakes in an automobile. We push a pedal on the car floor which, in turn, actuates a number of links. These eventually cause a piston to press on fluid in a cylinder, the fluid transmits the pressure through pipes to other pistons at each wheel. As these pistons move, each presses against a brake shoe which, in turn, presses against a brake drum and causes the wheel to slow down. These parts are connective; they constitute a brake system, which functions to slow and stop automobiles. In a business organization, such as a restaurant, a system might consist of a customer giving an

[10] Stafford Beer, *Cybernetics and Management*, New York, John Wiley, 1959, p. 9.

order to a waitress who, in turn, takes the order to a cook, who prepares some food and gives it eventually to the waitress, who brings it to the customer.   In this sense, the customer, waitress, and cook are interconnected in a customer-feeding system.

We could list illustrations endlessly.   These two, however, will be sufficient to bring out some other important properties: (1) the parts in these systems are in a dynamic state; they move. (2) They not only move but they also interact with one another, and an event occurring at one part is in some way transmitted through the system.   We might describe this patterning of interactions as a *network*.   This interaction transmits or conveys information.   It is, in a sense, a communications system.

Let us go back to the brake system.   If we look at the piston in the master cylinder and really want to understand what it does, we have to look at more than the piston itself.   Studying only the one part, all we can say is that here is a piston which presses on some fluid.   This does not help to understand what the piston really does, that it is involved with stopping automobiles.   To comprehend this, we have to look at the piston as a part in a system; then we can understand its real purpose and, furthermore, how it operates.   So too, with the waitress.   If we could envision focusing attention merely on a waitress and nothing else, her activities would be meaningless.   It is only through seeing her as part of a customer-feeding system that what she does becomes meaningful.   This elementary point is stressed at length because people tend to look at various activities and situations as isolated elements rather than as components of a system.   By doing so, especially in the study of organizations, it is possible to miss the true significance or purpose of an element.

Multiplicity of Systems

We have already mentioned that any organization comprises a great many systems; or to put it differently, an organization is a system composed of subsystems and sub-subsystems.   We should further point out that many times individual parts or elements may serve in a number of systems.   For example, the waitress and cook, in addition to being part of a customer-feeding system, may serve as members of a union bargaining committee, and in this sense also represent parts of a collective bargaining system.

We should also note that a part in one system may be the container in totally different systems.   For example, the waitress is a part in the customer-feeding system and the collective bargaining system, but

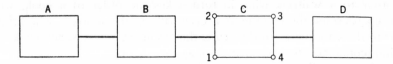

Figure 8.4. An item as a part of a system and as a container of a system.

within her body, there are a great many physiological systems, such as the one that regulates the temperature of her blood.   Another illustration of the systems within systems phenomenon might be an inventory-control system which operates within a larger production-control system, which in turn operates within the larger manufacturing system of a company.   Figure 8.4 illustrates such an arrangement.   One system consists of Blocks A, B, C, and D.   Blocks, such as C, are made up of elements 1, 2, 3, and 4.   In this case, C is a part of a larger system and is, at the same time, the container of another system composed of the numbered elements.

The systems concept focuses not only on the interconnectiveness of parts and the multiplicity of systems but also very importantly on the interconnectedness of the systems themselves.   Hence, a variation in any one system or a part of it can and probably does have some influence on all other systems.   In one way we might think of the systems models as being similar to a bowl of gelatin.   Touching one portion brings about some response in all other portions.   Thus, if the waitress has a day when her physiological systems are out of order, this will affect her performance as a part of the larger system.   She might be curt and careless in the customer-feeding system, and she might be arbitrary and unreasonable in the collective bargaining system.   Since these two systems are parts of larger systems which we might identify as the restaurant business system and the restaurant workers'-union system, the effect of her physiological upset might spread widely.

The systems model is extremely valuable in pointing out how far the effects of changing one part of a system may be carried.   On the other hand, it would be wrong to assume that organizations are highly unstable, that a headache by one employee could upset a vast, complex of individuals.   As we shall see in Chapter 13 on control, organizations have ways of dampening and compensating for disturbances, which keep the upsets from spreading indefinitely.   This discussion leads us to another important point about the systems concept.   Not only are systems, such as organizations, made up of interconnected parts and systems, they are also always in a state of movement either responding to a change in one part of the organization or adjusting to the effects of this response.

Arbitrariness of Defining a Particular System

Many times throughout this book we shall refer to a particular system. From what has been said this is obviously an arbitrary designation. When one particular network of organizational elements is under discussion, the other networks to which the parts belong and the interconnection between systems are deliberately ignored. This is necessary for purposes of exposition, but we should never lose sight of the properties of systems we have been discussing.

Purposefulness of Systems

In general, when discussing a system, we are talking about a particular network of organizational elements directly involved with achieving a purpose. In the restaurant illustration, there are a number of people (Figure 8.5), some of whom are interconnected for the purposes of feeding customers (solid black line). At other times, the parts are connected for purposes of settling labor-management differences, the collective bargaining system (dashed line).

Viewing systems as purposeful, that is, as structures which produce an effect or result, opens up a valuable way of analyzing organizational problems. Too often when something fails in an organization, the general strategy taken by management is to find out what is wrong and what is causing the problem. The search is for the guilty party or part. If, however, we conceive of all organization phenomena, problems as well as desired results, as outputs of a system, the strategy might better be phrased as which system is producing the undesired effect. If, for example, the quality of a product is falling off because one of the parts is frequently found to be inferior, the situation could be improved by setting up an inspection procedure to screen out the

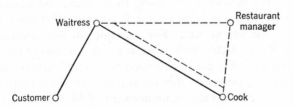

Figure 8.5. Purposeful systems.

inferior parts before they enter the final product. An analysis which raises the question, "Which system produces this inferior part?" might disclose that the parts are being transported in containers, which permits them to knock about and perhaps become damaged, and that by providing better containers their quality can be maintained and the costly inspection process made unnecessary.

Deterministic and Probabilistic Systems

The illustrations might suggest that once a system has been isolated by knowledge of the change or input at one end, we should be able to predict accurately the output at the other end. This is sometimes true. The brake system of an automobile is of this nature. Pressure on the pedal invariably causes the brake shoe to press against the brake drum. When the operation of the system is completely predictable, it is called a deterministic system.

Many systems, particularly those in organizations, are not deterministic. The customer giving the waitress an order for fried clams may not get what he ordered if, for example, the restaurant has just served its last order of clams. In fact if the customer thinks that because of the hour or some other factor the supply of clams has been exhausted, he may take this into account by saying, ". . . and if you're out of clams, bring me a swordfish steak." When the outcome of a system performance is not completely predictable, it is a probabilistic system. If we could examine the inner workings of the restaurant customer's mind, we would probably find him saying, "Well, if there's a fifty-fifty chance of getting clams, I'd better give the waitress an alternative." For purposes of simplicity, we are treating all systems as if they were deterministic and we shall continue to do so in this book.

Closed and Open Systems

The first three parts of this book are primarily concerned with what could be called closed systems. That is, we look at a limited number of parts and the relationships among them alone, and assume that the rest of the world around this system is constant, that there are no influences outside the system. For example, in the customer-feeding system, we know pretty well what is going on among the customer, the waitress, and the cook, provided the world around them stays fairly stable. If, however, this restaurant were in a railroad station, and the customer heard the announcement of his train's impending departure, he might instruct the waitress to cancel his order, a message of a totally different type.   In a brake-mechanism system, we understand how the parts are interrelated to slow or stop the car provided, of course, that a stone from the road has not bounced up and caused a serious leak.   In attempting to understand systems, we usually assume them to be closed.   This introduces an artificial note, for actually, in some way, all systems of interest are open.

Many times "outside" factors remain constant over sufficiently long periods of time; thus, to view a system as closed does not introduce any serious distortion.   An economist, in trying to analyze systems involved with individual economic decisions, is on fairly safe ground when he says, "Let us assume that income is constant."   For, although individual income does change, it changes relatively slowly compared to the length of time involved in most individual economic decisions.

We might summarize and clarify what has been said in this way: in reality there is no such thing as a closed system.   However, as an intellectual expedient, it is frequently desirable to assume that systems are closed and, in light of the slowness with which many of the "exogenous" variables change, relative to the "endogenous" variables of the closed system, this is not an unrealistic or unworkable assumption.

Equilibrium of Systems

Systems vary greatly; some exist for long periods of time.   Others are so fleeting they are difficult to detect.   For the most part, we are concerned with stable organizational systems, those that persist in organizations long enough to be considered fairly permanent.   A system is continually receiving shocks and influences from other systems and from its own internal elements.   A system, therefore, is continually adjusting and if it is stable, it must be adjusting toward some point of equilibrium.   Unfortunately, in this book we shall be able to do little more than introduce these extraordinarily important and complex topics of system stability and equilibrium.

We might also note that some organizations are very tight.   The elements in them directly and significantly influence one another.   They are closely coupled, whereas other systems are quite loose and a change in one element in these latter systems influences many things other than the next element, and this only in an attenuated form.

As already indicated, organizations cannot be effectively understood by using only one model.   Both goal and systems concepts are necessary. Perhaps the most reasonable approach has been suggested by Parsons; that is, that goal defining and derivative activities are only one of the basic functions of an overall systems concept.[11]

The remaining portions of this book are concerned with the major issues introduced in this chapter. The next few chapters of Part Two concern themselves with the definition of duties, largely as parts of a goal model of organization. Two principal issues are division of work and assignment problems. Part Three deals with issues of providing coordination and integration. The nature of this problem is analyzed, and some of the principal organizational means of providing coordination are explored. Part Four primarily covers organizational and individual adaptation and the problems of facilitating organization by attracting and holding critical resources.

In a chapter that is essentially introductory and summary in nature, it seems hardly profitable to offer a summary at this time. It might be well, however, to return to the observation with which we began; namely, that the topic we are pursuing is extraordinarily complex and elusive. To understand it we need some scheme to keep our ideas straight and orderly, and to acquire tools with which to discuss and manipulate these ideas. This chapter was intended to provide some of the basic concepts and terminology necessary for the more detailed analysis to follow.

[11] Parsons, *op. cit.*

9

The Division of Work

Probably the most important single concept in analyzing organizations is the division of work. It is both an exceptionally old concept and an exceedingly common phenomenon. If we pause to look, we see it in use everywhere in modern life. Within the family there tends to be a fairly standard division of work, one group of activities being involved with the economic support of the family, another group concerned with informal tasks of cooking, housekeeping, child raising, and the like. We find the work of operating a food store divided into a number of separate jobs, such as putting stock on a shelf, operating a cash register, etc.

Closely associated with dividing work to be done into separate assignments is the practice of having people restrict their activities to one (or a few) work assignments; that is, people specialize in the work they perform. In the course of a day we are likely to come into contact with many specialists: the physician who treats our physical ailments, the TV repairman who replaces a tube, the butcher who cuts meat, the school teacher who trains the young. If we examine formal organizations, we notice people who clean the building, others who operate machines or do clerical work. Division of work and the resulting specialization of labor is in fact so common, widespread, and familiar to all of us that we are likely to give it very little attention, thereby overlooking both its extreme importance and the complexity of the problems involved in its utilization. Neglecting or perhaps not understanding these problems, often we may not apply division of work wisely or, at least, well.

REASONS FOR ADOPTING A DIVISION OF WORK

Before undertaking a detailed examination of the concept of the division of work, it might be useful to examine some of the general reasons it is employed.

Scope of Task or Knowledge Necessary to Perform Task

At times we are faced with a job which is too big for any one person to handle. The only way it can be accomplished is to bring more people in and divide the work among them. Building a pyramid, a battleship, a dam, or an irrigation project requires the labor of huge numbers of people, and the only way we can really use them effectively is to divide the overall task among them.

Physical size is not the only task property that may be too large for one man. To no small degree, what we can accomplish depends on how much we know. A person cannot build automobiles unless he knows a good deal about internal combustion engines, metals, paints, suspensions, structures, etc. It would be virtually impossible for anyone today to know all the facts necessary for designing and making an automobile. This situation has made it necessary for people to specialize in what they will learn; hence, we have mechanical engineers, metallurgists, production specialists, and many other persons who bring specialized collections of knowledge to the task of making automobiles.

Still another type of situation occurs that may force us to divide labor when the work of administration becomes too large for one person to handle. Perhaps the earliest reference to this situation is found in Jethro's advice to Moses to divide up the work of administering the Tribes of Israel, and to assign some of it to subheads.[1]

Efficient Production of Products or Services

The limited work capacity of the individual is not the only reason we turn to a division of work. It is often a far more efficient way of accomplishing a purpose. Among the earliest detailed analyses of this aspect of division of work were those made by Adam Smith and

[1] *Exodus* XVIII: 21, 22.

Charles Babbage.[2]   Both men very carefully examined the manufacture of pins.   Although this is a somewhat limited area and these are relatively old studies, they do bring out crucial points.

Making pins, Babbage found, had essentially seven basic steps, or as he called them, "processes": drawing the wire, straightening the wire, pointing, twisting, and cutting the heads, heading, tinning or whitening, and papering.   At least one person, and sometimes several people, was assigned to the performance of each of these operations.   Babbage noticed the difference in the skill required as well as the time required through each of these processes or operations, and pointed out that if a workman were to make a decent daily wage performing all operations (that is, without any division of labor) the pins would have to cost three and three-quarters times as much.[3]

Division of work produces goods which are more *uniform*, in design, dimensions, and quality.   The excellence of design and quality is often thought to be lower when work is divided to a considerable degree.   Division of work does raise problems in obtaining higher quality, but it also has some advantages.   Actually when a lesser degree of excellence accompanies extensive division of work, the loss in quality is often "caused" by other factors.

These are not the only advantages, but they are the major ones, of using division of labor for the production of goods and services.   The reasons for this and the conditions under which division of work becomes more efficient are the topics for the remaining portions of this chapter.   First, however, let us make some further distinctions about what this chapter covers.

BASIC DIRECTIONS FOR THE DIVISION OF WORK

One of the factors that makes the study of the division of work difficult is the fact that there are so many different ways in which work can be divided.   For example, we can divide work by the different operations or tasks people perform, such as digging ditches, making concrete, and hammering nails; but we can also divide it so as to separate operations from the factors in the control or integration of these operations.   One distinction of this kind is between the type of work a worker does directly on a project and the work the foreman or manager does in coordinating the efforts of his employees.

[2] Adam Smith, *The Wealth of Nations*, London, Strahan and Candell, 1776; and Charles Babbage, *On the Economy of Machinery and Manufacturers*, London, Charles Knight, 1832.
[3] Babbage, *Ibid.*

We can briefly distinguish these tasks by saying that there are two different directions in which work can be divided: horizontally, where we separate the tasks or operations people perform, and vertically, where we separate or divide work on the basis of the scope of the work a position controls or integrates. We shall call the first the *operating system* and the second the *managing system*.[4] The person employed in a particular job on an assembly line controls only the work specifically assigned to him. The foreman is concerned with controlling and integrating the work of all the employees who report to him. The plant manager is concerned with the coordination and control of all the workers who report to all the foremen, who in turn report to him, and so on. In this chapter we are concerned primarily with horizontal division of work. The vertical division of work is handled in Chapter 16.

PROGRESSIVE DIVISION OF WORK

In brief, division of work is involved with differentiating the tasks necessary to accomplish an objective or goal. Each differentiated task can be handled separately (by different individuals or the same individual at different times). This division can be repeated several times. The differentiated tasks at one level are divided into subtasks at the next. We have already noted a hierarchy of objectives in Chapter 7. Accompanying this is a progressive division of labor.

In making a product, we might first divide the product into its basic subassemblies, the subassemblies into their component parts, the work of making each part into separate operations, and, finally, each operation into the basic motions involved. Suppose, for example, we make washing machines. The washing machine is constructed of parts assemblies—among them the cabinet, the drum which contains the clothes, the agitator which imparts the washing motion, the motor, and the controls (see Figure 9.1). Each of these assemblies consists of several parts. The agitator has, among other things, an aluminum casting and bearings which permit it to oscillate easily. The casting (the fin-like apparatus) is made in a number of different operations. Among the operations involved in making the casting are the preparation of a mold, pouring of the molten aluminum into the mold, removing the casting from the mold, and a de-burring process.

---

[4] For further elaboration of this distinction, see A. K. Rice, *Productivity and Social Organization: The Ahmedabad Experiment*, London, Tavistock Publications, 1958, particularly pp. 41–42.

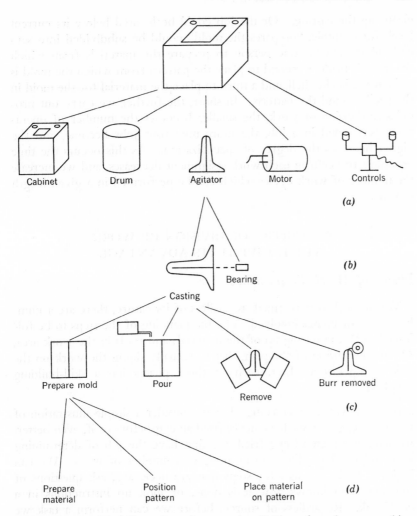

Figure 9.1. Simplified illustration of progressive division of work on a washing machine.

Degree of Specialization

Let us call the operation at the bottom of Figure 9.1 a *job*. The scope of work here defines the job, which is assigned to a person. This job could be located in a number of different places. It could be located at a level where one person performs all operations in making a casting—prepares the mold, pours the metal, removes the mold, and cleans up the casting. Or the job could be located below its current level; for example, "prepares the mold" could be subdivided into several suboperations—one person to prepare the materials from which the mold is made, a second to place the pattern from which the mold is to be made in the shell, and a third to place the material for the mold in the shell around the pattern. In short, the further we carry out progressive division of work, the smaller becomes the number of operations performed in a job, the more numerous jobs become, and the higher becomes the degree of specialization. As this occurs the time necessary to perform each work assignment decreases, and we increase the number of work cycles which can be performed in a given length of time.

PROPERTIES OF DIVISION OF WORK
WHICH GIVE IT ITS ADVANTAGE

Phases of Work Performance

When work is performed, regardless of its nature, there are a number of major phases involved: (1) the planning of the steps to be followed, (2) the setting up of the materials and tools in the work area, (3) the execution of the plan, that is, actually doing the work on the task or operation. Last, each of these phases has a skill-building subphase.

PROGRAM DEVELOPMENT TIME. Let us consider a simple illustration of frying an egg. If we have never fried an egg before or if, even better, we have not seen an egg fried, we first have the job of determining how to proceed. This can be done in a number of ways. We can logically think through the steps that are necessary, ask questions of someone who knows how it is done, or look up instructions in a cookbook. Regardless of source, before we can perform a task we must know what to do, have a plan, or in today's terms, a *program*.

SETUP TIME. With a program available, the next step is to assemble in one place the egg, frying pan, spatula, and other necessary utensils. These are setting up activities necessary to prepare for actually doing the work.

EXECUTION OF THE TASK. Finally, with a set of steps planned and the materials assembled we are ready to fry the egg, or to execute the program.

DEVELOPING SKILL TO CARRY OUT PHASES OF WORK PERFORMANCE. Following the instructions to fry an egg is much simpler for the person who has fried similar things in the past. Adjusting the heat of the range, using the spatula, and other parts of the operation are easier because he has developed skills. A person can build skill in any one of the phases just mentioned: developing a program, setting up a work position, and carrying out a program. Hence, each of the phases we have been discussing have a skill-building subphase.

Separation of Phases of Work Performance

The phases in work performance do not have to be performed by the same person. In the egg-frying illustration we can obtain a program for cooking the egg by asking someone else or by referring to a cookbook. We may find, when we begin to fry an egg, that someone else has just prepared one for himself. We thus have the advantage that many of the items needed are already assembled at the stove. Separation of phases of work performance is quite common in mass-production industries. Planning of work and the preparation of detailed instruction sheets is the work of the industrial engineers. Preparation of work positions, which includes assembly of parts and tools to be used, is the work of another group. When these tasks are finished, the worker goes to the prepared work position and performs operations in accordance with the instructions he has received.

We have noted that the work involved in accomplishing a technical purpose can be segmented into a series of tasks or operations. Thus, to fabricate a simple product we may first make each part and then undertake operation to obtain a completed product (Figure 9.2a).

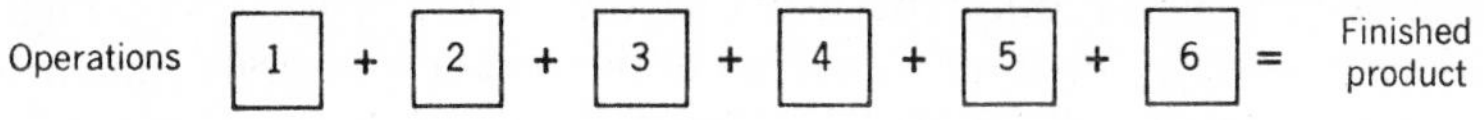

Operations $\boxed{1}$ + $\boxed{2}$ + $\boxed{3}$ + $\boxed{4}$ + $\boxed{5}$ + $\boxed{6}$ = Finished product

(a)

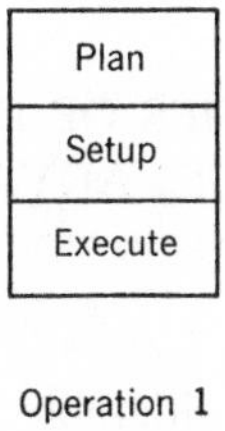

Plan
Setup
Execute

Operation 1

(b)

Figure 9.2

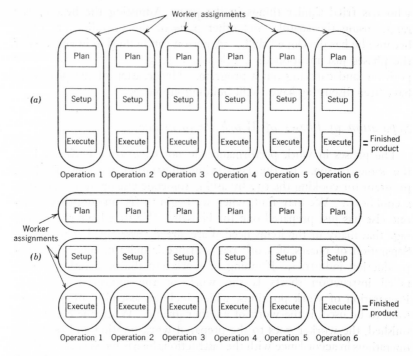

Figure 9.3

Each operation has several phases in its performance: program development, setup, and execution (Figure 9.2*b*). Therefore, we can choose a number of different ways to divide the work. We might divide the work by operations, giving each worker a separate operation and letting him do all its phases (Figure 9.3*a*). However, we could divide the work by having, for example, one man do all programing of operations, two persons set up the work, and a separate person execute each operation (Figure 9.3*b*).

HOW THE PROPERTIES OF DIVISION OF WORK GIVE IT ITS ADVANTAGE

Reduction of Phases

It probably would take a considerable period of time to fry the first egg in the preceding illustration. It would take the length of time to work out a program (t_p), plus the amount of time to set up the work area (t_s), plus the time to execute the program (t_e), or: $t = t_p +$

$t_s + t_e$. If, however, as soon as we finished the first egg, someone walked into the kitchen and said, "That looks quite good. Will you make one for me while I make our coffee?", the time to make the second egg would be $t = t_e$.

Development of Skills

The time to carry out the execution phase of frying an egg is not the same on the second egg as on the first. We would expect skill to increase on each subsequent egg, thereby reducing the execution time

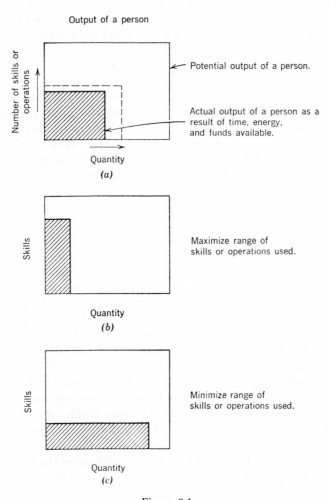

Figure 9.4

for each egg until for all practical purposes we reach a point where skill develops no further so that all subsequent t_e's are the same.

The time spent in developing skills is influenced by a number of factors. First, the higher the degree of specialization, the smaller is the range of skills contained in any one task. As a result, it takes a shorter amount of time to train a person to do his work, and the sooner he will reach his optimal level of operation. Second, the further the division of work is carried, the shorter each work cycle becomes. This means that the person is using his skill more regularly, and skills once developed are less likely to deteriorate. The further division of work is carried, the lower are the costs of developing skills.

With a given capacity for work there is a distinct relationship between the range of skills (or operations) a person employs and the quantity of goods (or services) completed (see Figure 9.4).

Employing People with Skills Developed

Whereas repetition of work may permit people to develop skills, we may want to avoid this expenditure of time by hiring people who already have the skills we need. Again, the further we carry division of labor, the greater may be the advantage. The more restricted the range of skills in a job, the likelier we are to find people who possess them and, presumably, the less they have to be paid. The way we divide work can, therefore, determine the labor market open to the organization.

Optimal Use of Abilities Available

Let us go back to Figure 9.1. If the job is established at the (b) level, where the worker makes the complete agitator casting, he must have a range of skills which permit him to do any of the operations involved in making the casting, such as preparing the molds, pouring it, removing it, etc. Suppose that preparing a mold requires a much greater skill and more training than removing the mold from the casting. To hire an employee who has the level of skill necessary to prepare a mold costs $3.50 an hour. To hire someone who has just the skills necessary to remove the mold from the casting costs $1.50 an hour. In this situation every time the more highly skilled worker, receiving $3.50 an hour, is employed in removing a casting from the mold, he is overpaid for the work performed. On the other hand, if the job were located at the (c) level, we could assign the high-priced worker to the job which fully utilized his skills and hire another employee, at a lower wage, for the less skilled job.   To put this in more abstract terms, division of labor opens the possibility of matching the requirements of a job more exactly with the abilities a person has. The same, of course, is true with machinery.

Concurrent Operations

One advantage of division of work is that work on different aspects of the same objective can be carried on at the same time.   Returning to the making of washing machines, we would not find them being fabricated in a long series of steps.   We do not first make the agitator, then the washing drum, then the cabinet, and then the other major parts.   Instead, the parts for any one washing machine all can be in the process of manufacture at the same time.   The length of time it takes to make any one washing machine is thereby greatly reduced.

We may say "This is fine when you are making large quantities of the same item, such as hundreds, thousands, or perhaps hundreds of thousands of washing machines," and ask, "What happens when you are making only one or at least a very few units?   Is there this advantage?"   The answer is yes, but at a cost.   For example, in developing the first atomic bomb, the work was divided among a number of subprojects which were carried out simultaneously so that when it became time to assemble the bomb, the parts were available.   In short, the advantage of reducing the overall production time can be realized whether producing one or many items.   The cost, however, can be very high if there is only one product and a lot of people have to be brought in to work on only one part or operation, with nothing following on which to use their special skills and talents.   At times, of course, the reduction in time is cheap at almost any price.   We do something similar to this in the development of military weapons. The time between the inception of a new weapon and its completion, the so-called *lead time*, has become progressively longer.   It would now reach staggering proportions if all the work were done in a serial fashion.

These factors all concern concurrent rather than serial performance of operations.   There is also a distinct advantage to concurrent tackling of phases of work performance.   For example, if separate workers undertake each phase of work performance, the planning of the next item of work can be carried on by one person while another is engaged in executing the current project.   This arrangement is common in industry.

REQUIREMENTS FOR DIVISION OF WORK

It is important to understand that the advantages of division of work are to be realized only if certain conditions are met. We consider some of the technical requirements and limitations in the following section and devote Chapter 10 to the social requirements.

Volume of Work and Degree of Specialization

Earlier in this chapter we noted the relation between the extent to which we carry out progressive division of labor, that is, degree of specialization and the number of work cycles which can be performed. Referring to the washing machine illustration and Figure 9.1, it would be silly to divide the work further, if it takes eight hours of work to produce the casting for an agitator, and we have only sufficient orders to require the fabrication of one agitator a day. Men assigned to work which had been divided further, say at the (c) level, would spend most of their day sitting idle. The relationships involved are covered in Figure 9.4. If we have a relatively low volume of work and want to keep one man employed full time, we shall probably have an arrangement like Figure 9.4b. If we have a relatively high volume of work, we can divide it into a number of jobs, each with a reduced range of skills as in Figure 9.4c. In short, the further the division of work, the larger must be the volume of work to support it provided there is a constraint goal of trying to reach the minimum cost position.

In passing, a precautionary note might be made that the illustrations deal with one way of dividing labor. In this section we are discussing general characteristics of a division of labor regardless of the way in which it is divided. We shall see in later sections how these general conditions exist with many different types or ways of dividing work.

Stability

Another general condition required for an adequate utilization of the division-of-work concept is stability. This concept includes stability of all factors involved with a particular division of work.

VARIATIONS IN THE VOLUME OF WORK. There is little advantage, for example, in dividing work on the basis of a temporary high volume. As soon as the demand falls off we run into problems created by the division of labor established. Thus, if the volume of demand drops, we find ourselves in the condition where people have jobs with less work than is necessary to keep them fully employed. If we determine that future demand will remain at this new lower level, making it necessary to redivide work, we may shift the job in Figure 9.1 from the (c) level to the (b) level. The only difficulty here is that no one is trained to perform the more extensive range of operations now contained in jobs, and no setups are established for the single work positions at the (b) level. Consequently, to change the degree of specialization requires expensive or costly transitions.

On the other hand, if the volume increases and there might be a distinct advantage to having work subdivided further, for example, from the (c) to the (d) level, we are faced with the problem that handling the larger volume at this new level reduces the range of skills in a job utilized by its occupant. Under these circumstances do we take current employees at the (c) level and retrain them to fill some of the positions at the (d) level, thereby reducing their skill and presumably their pay? Or do we fill these new positions at the (d) level with new employees whom we hire with a lower skill level, and presumably at lower pay, and then transfer or fire the employees who have filled the positions at the (c) level?

VARIATIONS IN RAW MATERIALS. Any variation in the raw material used in the productive process can have significant effects. Suppose, for example, the quantity of raw material being delivered is sharply reduced as sometimes results from a strike in a transportation service. We can have a high volume of demand, people well-trained and sitting in their positions ready to work, but unfortunately no material on which to work.

Variations in quality cause difficulties which become more acute as the degree of specialization increases. As we define a job and train people to handle it, we are also training them to use specialized or precisely defined raw materials. What happens in the egg-frying situation if instead of always getting an assured supply of fresh eggs, we receive eggs of lower quality, occasionally having spoiled ones among them? If we have trained people to work with good, uniformly fresh eggs, and they have a request to scramble a number of eggs, they probably would open all of them into a bowl before beating them without noticing until too late that the last egg opened was spoiled. As a result, all the previously opened eggs would be ruined. They have to be scrapped and work has to be started all over again. Had we trained people to handle a lower quality egg, doubtless we would have trained them to break each egg into a separate cup and then, after examining it, empty it into the bowl.

Variation in quality of materials requires additional steps before the materials can be used. If we have not trained people in these operations, they are likely to operate exactly as they have in the past with unfortunate consequences. Even if they do note the deviation in the raw material, they will not know what to do and again the effectiveness of the division of work will be influenced.

ABSENCE OF WORKERS. One of the things that happens with an advanced degree of specialization is that each worker ends up with a unique job. No one else in the organization fully knows this job. Consequently, should a worker be absent work in his position will stop, as will work at positions supplied by him. One advantage to this gloomy situation is, of course, that the further we divide work, the lower the skill level becomes, and the more quickly people can be trained as substitutes. The problem now becomes, "Where do we get someone to act as substitute?" Do we move them from another position creating another hole in the production system? Do we have the supervisor step in and ignore his own work? It is not an insurmountable problem, but it is a messy one. When we consider how many different types of work there are in an organization using a fairly high degree of specialization, we can appreciate the staggering effect of even a moderate amount of absenteeism.

Needless to say, an organization faced with this condition has to take some corrective measures such as having "floating" workers who are trained and always available to step into a wide number of *different* specialized jobs. But as soon as we hire these additional personnel who do have this ability, and who therefore draw relatively high salaries, we reduce proportionately the efficiency (or productivity) of the system.

CHANGE OF PRODUCT OR PURPOSE. It should be obvious that any change in the product of a system of division of work has ramifications on the particular set of jobs which have been established. If it is a fairly abrupt change, the whole system may be obsolete. Let us envision, for example, a manufacturer of closed car-top carriers, which have in recent years become popular among people going on vacation. This company has been making them largely from fabrics, such as canvas or plastic sheeting, and the basic production operations have involved cutting, stitching, and others of this sort. Then a competitor places on the market a molded fiber glass carrier which gains a wide and immediate acceptance by the public. The company is faced with an agonizing decision. Does it change over to make molded fiber glass car-top carriers, or does it go into some other type of cutting and stitching business? At the moment none of its current operations are suitable for making the new car-top carrier; its previous division of work is obsolete.

Many times, of course, we are faced with less extreme changes, such as the same car-top manufacturer faces should the preference go from having the openings in the carrier closed by snaps to having them closed by zippers. Some of the operations could stay pretty much the same. A few, such as those involved with sewing in the snaps, would be dropped and new ones added for sewing in zippers. Each time we make a change in some of the positions, we scrap some of the programs we have established and have to substitute new ones. We scrap some of the setups established which may include fixtures, jigs, etc., and have to get new ones. We scrap some of the skills of the employees and train them in new ones. These changes are difficult and expensive.

CHANGE IN TECHNOLOGY. The last of the types of changes we shall consider involves a change in technology. Let us presume, for example, that developments in plastics reach a point where it becomes possible to make the agitators in a washing machine from plastics rather than from aluminum. These plastic agitators may be both lighter and cheaper, but the company has a commitment. It has people with skills in making castings, plus a considerable investment in equipment used in this type of manufacture. To change and make a new type of agitator requires scrapping the skills of people, and perhaps the people themselves, in addition to scrapping the equipment or special facilities established.

We have considered the relationship between division of work and stability at some length because of its importance. The further we carry a division of work, the higher must be the volume of work to support this division of labor and the stabler must be all factors entering into the system. To put this another way, as division of work is carried further in an organization, it becomes progressively less flexible. This is not to say, however, that it becomes less flexible or more dependent on stability in the same proportion in all directions. The way in which inflexibility develops varies considerably depending on many things, such as the type of division of work, involved.

Perhaps this concept can be summarized by stating two general points.

1. Any division of work creates a need for some type of stability along at least one dimension and perhaps many.

2. A division of work or specialization of labor delimits the skills to be used or the technology to be employed, making it difficult for the organization to deal with anything outside of these delimited areas.

Interdependency Created by a Division of Work

Closely allied to stability is the observation that in any division of work the effectiveness of the whole system is highly dependent on the effective operation of all elements of the system. Within an organization the effectiveness with which a person at any job can carry out his work is highly dependent on how the jobs preceding his in the work flow or supporting his have been done. Hence, the ease with which a person pouring the aluminum into the mold can do his work depends partially on whether the proper raw materials are purchased and on how well the mold was prepared by the person preceding him.

We examine a number of aspects of this interdependency in Chapters 11 and 12. One point of interest now concerns the observation made by almost anyone with experience in large organizations; not only does division of work make the elements of the system interdependent but it also seems to make the necessary coordination more difficult to achieve. Often people seem to be far more interested in what their department does than in accomplishing the overall goals of the organization. As a result, they may do things they deem important to show that they or their departments are doing a good job rather than direct their efforts to the overall objective. In the washing machine company illustration the person responsible for knocking the burrs and rough edges from the casting of the agitator may decide that he wants to put a fine finish on the casting. Therefore, instead of just grinding the rough edges, he spends a great deal of time searching out minute blemishes and removing them. As a result he produces some finely finished agitators, but he spends so much time doing it that he is not finishing enough agitators to keep the following positions working. This is an interesting phenomenon with a number of roots, only one of which will be examined now.

DIVIDING WORK DEFINES THE OBJECTIVES OF THE UNIT OR POSITION. When being assigned a job people are usually told what operations to perform, tools to use, etc., but seldom are they given the specific subobjective(s) of their department and information concerning where their job fits into the departmental objective. Commonly people infer the objective of their job and its position in the means-ends chain from the program given them and from their own perceptions of where their jobs fit into the department. The immediate tasks and program assigned may loom so large in this perception formation that great incongruencies are causes between the perceived objective of a position and what is required. Many times in organizations the division of work is carried out in such a manner or to such a degree that it is difficult for a person to comprehend adequately or, at least, to feel himself and his work associated with the overall objective.

The issue before us is that dividing work creates a simultaneous need for some means of integrating the subdivided work. The matter is further complicated by the fact that the greater the degree of specialization, the more difficult it becomes to satisfy this need for integration. This important issue is discussed in Part Three. First, it is necessary to consider some additional technical and important behavioral matters connected with division of work.

WAYS OF DIVIDING WORK

Until now we have not touched on the ways that work can be divided; these are numerous. In choosing one of them we have to consider two points. First, what are the various methods in which work in question can be divided? Second, how can we choose the best of these for our purposes? In this section we consider the first of these points. The second is reserved for Chapter 11.

Writers on organization typically list between five and ten ways of dividing work.[5] In an effort to both simplify and clarify these we arrange them into two major classifications: those ways of dividing work based on the item or recipient of output of a unit or position, and those based on how the unit performs its work. In short, these classifications are largely concerned with questions of what (or for whom), how, and with what? There are still one or two ways of dividing work which fit none of these classifications and that are treated separately at the end of this chapter.

[5] Materials for this section are drawn largely from Ernest Dale, *Planning and Developing the Company Organization Structure*, New York, American Management Assn., 1952, particularly pp. 23–37; Luther Gulick, "Notes on the Theory of Organization," in Gulick and Urwick, *Papers on the Science of Administration*, New York, Institute of Public Administration, 1937, pp. 1–45; and L. Urwick, *The Elements of Administration*, New York, Harper, 1943, particularly pp. 56–62.

The Item or Recipient of Unit Output

1. *Purpose or Product.* Here work is arranged to contribute to a particular output: a product or purpose. For example, in General Motors the Chevrolet Division is concerned with producing that particular brand of automobile. In the local city government the Health Department is concerned with producing a particular type of service or, if you will, achieving a particular type of purpose (Figure 9.5). In a position elements in a job would be grouped on the basis of its output.

2. *Customer or Client.* When work is divided in this way, main attention is given to the recipient, usually referred to as the customer, of whatever the organization is delivering or in service and governmental institutions, the client. For example, a company may set up two divisions: one to deal with the general public, probably called the Consumer Division, and the other to handle government work, perhaps called the Government or Defense Department. Both divisions may actually make fairly similar products, maybe identical ones, but they are concerned with delivering them to different types of customers. Similarly, we find that large railroads may have several different ticket-sales units: one to the general public in their various stations and another to large users of railroads, such as companies and government agencies (Figure 9.6). A department or a position within an organiza-

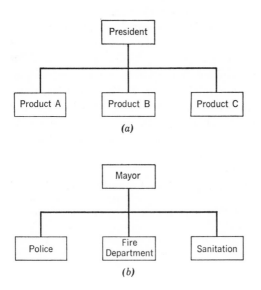

Figure 9.5. Division of work by product or purpose (by what is delivered outside the organization).

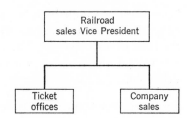

Figure 9.6. Dividing work by customer (who receives product or service).

tion may group elements necessary to serve some other particular position or department. For example, a secretary's job might consist of many elements—typing, answering telephones, filing—assembled to serve a single client, the manager to whom she reports.

3. *Location, Area, or Geography.* Many organizations extend over a large geographic area and have found it desirable to divide work according to particular locations. When returning to our example of railroads, we find many times that they have divided the company into different geographical sections with perhaps a vice president in charge of each. This man is responsible usually for operating what is, for all practical purposes, a separate railroad in a given location (see Figure 9.7). A company may need both personnel and public relations work performed in all areas in which it operates. It may not be able to have one man handle each of these activities in each area. It may decide to

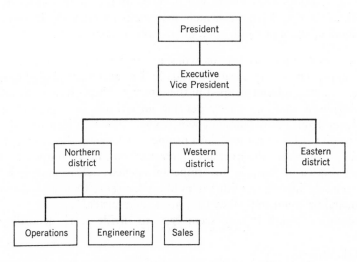

Figure 9.7. Dividing work by area or location (where work on product or service is done).

have one man handle both in one area rather than have one man handle either activity in two areas.   Here job elements are being grouped on the basis of area served.   The idea is that the subunits or positions are formed on the basis of where work is to be done or where it is delivered.

ADVANTAGES OF DIVIDING BY ITEM OR RECIPIENT OF OUTPUT.   There are a number of definite reasons for choosing one of these ways of dividing work.[6]   One is that such a method brings together under a single head all the work on a project or purpose.   Hence, the work is likelier to receive continuous and undivided attention.   Second, the unit is less likely to be dependent on other units doing their work; that is, it does itself most of the things really necessary to completing its purpose. For example, in General Motors, the Chevrolet Division does not have to wait for the Pontiac Division to do something or vice versa.   From this develops a third point: the unit can operate fairly autonomously if higher authority chooses to give it that autonomy.   (Let us be specific on this point.   Just because the unit could have autonomy does not guarantee that higher executives will necessarily delegate that auton-omy to it.)   A fourth advantage is that the work of subunits defined on this basis is more clearly recognized and does not get lost in the activities of the parent unit.   Hence, if customers have a complaint about a Chevrolet, the overall company executives have no problem in defining who is responsible and who should take action.   Last, this way of dividing work makes the purpose of the subunit more easily identified and understood, which may help enormously in enabling members of the unit to identify themselves in their work.

SOME DRAWBACKS TO DIVISION OF WORK BY ITEM OR RECIPIENT OF OUTPUT. Any approach in organizations usually has accompanying disadvan-tages.   First, a subunit defined in these terms, when given a considera-ble degree of autonomy, may develop an attitude or degree of inde-pendence from the parent unit which will ultimately lead to unfortu-nate results.   There is the serious problem of keeping the subunit from drifting away from the overall organization control or purpose.   This is sometimes a problem in governmental agencies where units may get more closely identified with the public they serve than with the gov-ernmental program and policy they are to administer.[7]

Second, although it may seem easy to divide work according to

---

[6] Gulick, *op. cit.*

[7] For further discussion of this point, see Herbert Kaufman, *The Forest Ranger*, Baltimore, Johns Hopkins Press, 1960.

output, often it is not.   What at first seem to be clear lines of demarcation are often actually blurred or overlapping.   For example, in situations where companies make quite different products but sell them to the same customers, the question comes up, "Are we wearing out our welcome with the customer by having two people badger him to buy products from our company?"   Or in a railroad where the basic divisions are on the basis of geographic area, we have to face the fact that the trains pass from one area to another; hence, the success with which one department or subunit performs its task is actually more interrelated with how other units have done theirs than might at first seem to be the case.

Third, in an effort to make a good showing for a unit set up on this basis, its managers may be unwilling, or perhaps unable because of limitations of size, to utilize the latest technical advantages.   Consequently, the company may not be able to produce things as cheaply as it would if work had not been divided in this fashion.

Fourth, subordinate units within the subunit may be submerged.   In this way they lose their effectiveness, as may happen in the case of an engineering department which is too small to have a group devoted to handling the problems of transferring engineering designs into manufacturing methods.   Consequently, the design engineers may be called in continually to handle production problems, a condition which seriously undermines their designing efficiencies and may create conditions which will cause some of them to leave.

The Way in Which a Unit Performs Its Work

The first major category of ways of dividing work dealt with those methods that centered on the output of an organization (or a subunit) or their target.   It was an external orientation.   Now we look inside the organization or unit to ask, "How does it do this?"

FUNCTION.   In listing ways of dividing work, the term function is commonly used and vague.   Since it contains some extremely important ideas which are used in later sections, let us elaborate some general aspects of a function before examining its specific application in dividing work.

One factor that contributes to confusion in the use of this term stems from discussions which focus on the types of functional classifications rather than on the nature of functional relationships.   Perhaps we can explain this point by noting that when we discuss a function, we are really talking about the role of a part in a larger entity.   Or we might say we are talking about the contribution of a partial activity or partial institution to a larger activity or institution. In short, the important point to recognize is that we are dealing with a part of a system.

This leads to two important points. First, if we are going to understand the function of an activity, we have to understand the system of which it is a part. For example, we would be hard pressed to say what function a new automobile was to serve unless we had further information about its purchaser or the purchase. We might be tempted to say that it was going to serve to transport its owner from one place to another, and that this was the reason he made the purchase. But is it? Our experiences or even the advertisements of automobile manufacturers suggest readily that many times people buy new automobiles for other reasons. One of these reasons may be that they feel it gives them some status; hence, by buying perhaps a Cadillac rather than a Ford a person may feel he has enhanced his status position. If this is the case, the function of the new automobile is to give the owner status; since he could just as well have gotten transportation from his former automobile. Similarly, in looking at organizational subunits, the only way we can really determine what, if any, functional properties they have is to know the type of system in which they exist. Since we have discussed departments or subunits created on the basis of functional division of work as parts of a system, we must recognize that, as a part, each of these for all practical purposes is useless by itself. Again, by analogy, the heart removed from the body is useless by itself. It only has purpose or meaning in association with the whole system.

Let us summarize what we have said thus far; in functional groupings we have subunits which contribute a part objective to an overall objective of the parent unit.

1. *Business Functions.* We can look at the basic purpose of organization in the world in which it exists. For example, the purpose of the washing machine manufacturer can be put this way: to make and distribute washing machines. We are really defining the business of the company in these terms. There are a number of very obvious functions involved in conducting this business. One we have already discussed is making the washing machines. Another is distribution or the marketing function. Still another is the purchasing or acquisition of the material or parts which make up the washing machines. Departments or positions defined along these lines serve a function relevant to the basic nature of the business. We call this a division of work based on business functions. This is the type of departmentalization used in a large percentage of manufacturing companies in this

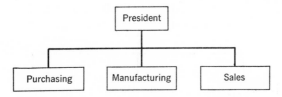

Figure 9.8.   Division according to business function.

country; hence, we commonly see this form of organization (see Figure 9.8). If the objectives of the organization were stated a bit differently, the resulting business function departments would also be different. For example, if the company had defined its objective as designing weapons systems, the nature of the business would be to provide an engineering service and its business functions would be different from those in Figure 9.8.

2. *Managerial Functions.* Let us return to our use of the word function; a unit may serve a purpose which is not directly involved with accomplishing a business objective of the company, but instead may perform a function in assisting the management of the business. For example, one of the things we would expect the management of a business to do would be to make plans for the company. What products should it make now and in the future? Should it expand or contract? A department concerned with aiding in or, for that matter, doing this sort of planning would therefore be classified on the basis of the managerial function it performed. There are many different classifications of managerial functions. We note here only the more common ones: planning, organizing, motivating, and controlling. In many organizations we find positions or departments which are directly involved with these classes of work. Accountants are intimately involved with controlling, as are quality control specialists. It is not at all uncommon to find departments of an organization concerned with analyzing and developing the organization of the business. The function these and similar departments fill does not contribute directly to the objectives of the business of the company. They do contribute quite directly, however, to the execution of the management function. Many companies will have departments which can best be classified according to the managerial function they perform (Figure 9.9).

3. *Technical Function or Process.* When work is divided on the basis of process, activities are grouped by the way in which they are performed. For example, a company may make a number of products, all of which have some sort of painted finish on them (Figure

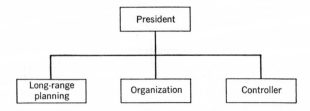

Figure 9.9. Division of work according to managerial function.

9.10). Therefore we may group all of the painting operations together in a single department, and paint all products there.

Technical function or process-type departments have at their roots either a particular technology, a particular type of equipment, or both. The term "technology" is used very broadly here; that is, it could mean a particular manufacturing technology, such as casting or welding, or it could be any other technology which is useful in the business. Thus, accounting becomes an area of knowledge which provides a technology usable in business, and in many companies we may find all the accounting work grouped into one department, that is, being grouped on the basis of process.

The question may arise, "Well, is not accounting a control function?" The answer is, "It can be, but it does not have to be." That is, some accounting departments function strictly in the fashion of collecting and processing certain types of data according to pre-arranged methods or, if you will, a technology. They may help to a degree in performing a control function, *but* they do not cover the *full scope* of the control function. The solution then lies in the answer to the question, "What does the department do?" If it brings together people working on a common technology, it is a process department. If it provides control, it is a managerial-functional department.

ADVANTAGES OF DIVIDING WORK BY THE WAY IT IS PERFORMED. We might begin by noting that this is probably the commonest form of organiza-

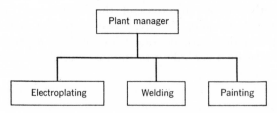

Figure 9.10. Division of work by process.

tion for smaller business firms.   The frequency with which this form occurs suggests that it has a number of very distinct advantages.   Among them we may find (1) that grouping together certain activities permits a sufficiently large volume of them to realize a good many of the efficiencies which come from a high degree of specialization; (2) that placing the major emphasis on a particular function enables people to acquire a high degree of specialization and, therefore, efficiency (In addition, people probably will be strongly motivated to continue advancing themselves in their specialty.   Hence their high level of technical competence is inclined to be not only perpetuated but also extended.); (3) that dividing work by performance is very likely to encourage people within a subunit to exchange information freely about their particular form of specialization (Therefore, a technical discovery which may be of advantage to a great many of the company's products or manufacturing methods can be quickly transmitted to others in the concern who can use this knowledge; whereas, division on the basis of purpose, product, or service may make it very difficult for a piece of technical information to move from one subunit to another.); (4) that this type of arrangement usually promotes easier use of centralized control; (5) that with such an arrangement we are apt to have larger groupings of professional employees providing many more levels through which they can advance than would be true of the smaller professional groupings likely to occur under a product or purpose organization (Hence, specialists will be tempted to improve in order to gain promotion and to stay on so as to realize the benefits that are open through this vertical advancement, an opportunity which may not be possible with other forms of organization.).

Of course, there are disadvantages to this way of dividing work. For one, the advantage of a high degree of specialization may tend to make the occupants of these subunits more concerned with their specialty than they are with the end purpose of the organization.   Consequently, they may not support organizational objectives as effectively as they should.   Second, because of their interest in their specialty, people may find it either difficult or not in their interest to communicate and associate with other organizational members.   Therefore, we may have difficulties in obtaining transmission of necessary information between and coordination among various subunits divided this way, as, for example, between engineering and manufacturing. Third, at the same time that this coordination and flow of information is becoming more difficult, the need for it has been increasing. Fourth, in many instances people who have risen through several levels of the organization within a functional specialty have advanced within a very unique professional environment and, consequently, may be poorly equipped eventually to assume overall organization responsibilities. Hence, a company may have a very difficult time in finding presidents and key vice-presidents within its own ranks.

Other Ways of Dividing Work

1. *Similar Tools or Techniques.* There are so many different ways in which work can be divided that we shall hardly attempt to enumerate all of them. Let us merely mention that work can be divided by a common type of machine or tool. It can also be divided by similar techniques which can be carried out by slightly different tools, and by many other variations.

2. *Time.* By time we mean the interval in the day when work is done within a position or a unit. For many organizations this is a relatively unimportant issue for they work on only one shift and everyone works the same hours. However, there are other organizations which work different shifts; some, in fact, work twenty-four hours a day, seven days a week. The particular dimension here, of course, is *when* work is performed.

3. *Skill.* Within a department using a range of skills where skill is important as, for example, in some process-type departments, we may find employees being divided according to their skills. We can note the distinction among craftsmen, journeymen, and apprentices in many types of work. All may have the same range of skills, although not necessarily. The deciding dimension here is the degree to which these skills have been developed.

MULTIPLE WAYS OF DIVIDING WORK

If we examine any reasonably large organization, we shall in all likelihood find a number of different ways of dividing work being used at the same time. We may find that at the top of the organization the method used for dividing work is on the basis of products; therefore, the major organizational units reporting to the top executive are product divisions. At the next level, reporting to each of the product division managers, we may find the work divided on the basis of busi-

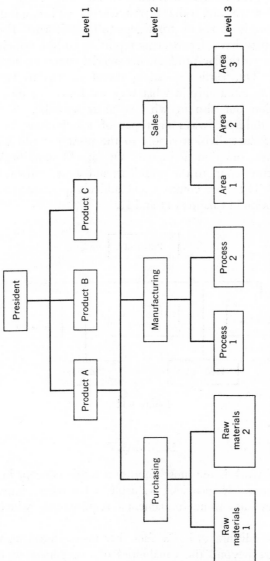

Figure 9.11. An illustration of multiple ways of dividing work.

ness function and that each of these business functions has an entirely different basis of subdividing: sales on the basis of area, manufacturing on the basis of process, and purchasing on the basis of item (see Figure 9.11). Needless to say, other arrangements and combinations are possible. There is no reason for things to be uniform. For example, the president may have departments reporting to him which are characterized by a particular product, managerial function, and area (see Figure 9.12). Our earlier question, therefore, has to be extended. We are not interested only in what *way* work may be divided within the organization but also in what *ways* it may be. Second, how should these different ways or types of subdivisions be grouped? Should the product division report to the president and have underneath it business function divisions? Or, should some business function departments report to the president, and some of them be divided by product? These are complex and difficult questions to which we turn our attention in Chapters 11 and 12.

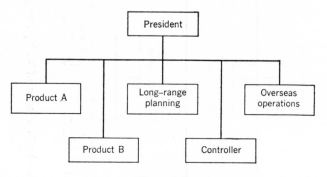

Figure 9.12

SUMMARY

Division of work is the most important single concept in the study of organizations. It provides valuable advantages, imposes some limitations, and has some fundamental requirements which must be met.

Among the advantages is the fact that many things man wants to accomplish are beyond the capabilities of one person or even small groups of people. Instead, they require vast numbers of people, employing a multitude of skills, and drawing on a vast store of knowledge. In short, the sheer magnitude of the task to be performed requires combined effort. With any combined effort there will be a necessity for dividing the work to be done. Even if there is no differentiation of the actual work on the project, the great numbers of people used will make it necessary for the work to be divided into managing and operations systems.

There are many other reasons for dividing work besides making some large tasks possible, and ways other than the elementary separation into operating and managerial systems already mentioned. Basically, division of work permits work to be done more efficiently by reducing the number of man-hours and costs needed to complete a unit of production. We have given most attention to the ways in which work can be divided to produce these advantages and the conditions that must be met to use them.

Division of work is primarily the separating or partitioning of duties or work into positions or departments. Although there are a great many bases for this partitioning, we have grouped them according to two primary types: item or recipient of output and ways of performing work. The work of any position or subunit will have a number of phases and subphases. The phases are program development, setup, and execution. Each of these phases has a skill-building subphase. The advantage of any of the ways of dividing work comes from eliminating one or more of these phases and subphases.

In general, the higher the degree of specialization used by an organization, the less flexible it becomes; that is, the less able it is to adjust to changes in objectives, environment, resources, or technology. However, organization flexibility must be viewed as having several dimensions; hence, it may be very inflexible along one and relatively more flexible along others. The way in which work is divided or partitioned will be the major influence in determining in which dimensions an organization will be most inflexible.

The Social Consequences of
Division of Work

ALL jobs within an organization are not alike. Some are quite interesting and pleasing to hold, others are most unpleasant, the sort of thing we might hope, if possible, to avoid. In this chapter, we turn to some of the ways in which the process of dividing up work influences the nature of jobs. In short, we analyze some of the social consequences of a specialization of labor. The analysis rests on the Homans model. As we know, a substantial portion of the external system is determined by the formal organization in which people find themselves. Our particular concern here is with the manner in which the division of work influences the activities and interactions expected of people as a result of a formal organization plan. More specifically, we examine the influence of division of work on the external system and its resultant effect on the behavior and satisfaction of organizational members. We shall also consider some of the consequences of different types of division of work.

Sociotechnical Systems

In earlier chapters we noted that to understand a person's behavior we have to understand the social system he is in and how it influences his choice of behavior. Among other things, Homans' model of a social system explains how an internal system emerges from or is molded by an external system (Figure 10.1).

The question is, what molds or determines the external system? In the previous discussions this part of the matter was left rather loose and open. It was allowed to stretch back rather vaguely from the internal system to include families, culture, higher management, and

Figure 10.1

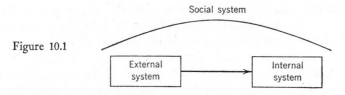

other factors. For the purposes of analysis, this process needs to be more specific, more ordered. Let us, therefore, delimit the external system to think of it as a hull or mold which forms the internal system and ask, what are the things that determine its form or shape? Delimited this way culture, family, and the like become the determinants of the external system. The number of such determinants is obviously large. Here we consider only those most important for large-scale organizations.

One of the factors which determine the activities and interactions of the external system is the division of work developed. However, a division of work cannot be chosen with complete freedom. It, too, is constrained by many things, among them the technology employed (Figure 10.2). A technology and the set of operations needed to employ it, of which a subpart is the division of work, let us call a *technical system*. We have two closely interconnected systems which can be recognized as components in a more inclusive system.

Technology and division of work molding the external system are all "outside" the emergent behavior of the individual, and in the group they are "internal" to an organization, such as a company or government agency. At the risk of being repetitious, let us note that for purposes of exposition we have been discussing systems in isolation or in simple pairs and then noting only one direction of influence. The multiplicity, interconnectedness, and reciprocal influence of systems should never be overlooked. Hence, division of work is as much social as it is technical.

The particular focus of this chapter is on the relationship of division

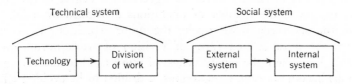

Figure 10.2. Sociotechnical system.

of work to the social system.   Division of work has two general levels of influence.   It determines the particular set of jobs and people from which the internal system emerges.   If the division of work establishes technical departments, a man hired as a machinist associates while working mostly with other machinists, people of the same skill, class, and level.   Departmentalization by product, however, might group the same individual with welders and painters, workers of different skill classes and skill levels.   In addition, the division of work does much to determine the relationship among those who are brought together.   This level of influence is the essence of this chapter.

THE INFLUENCE OF DIVISION OF WORK ON THE MEANING OF A JOB

Work has a meaning to people; in part, this is a matter of what they do.   The activities they perform, the tasks they carry out, can be important sources of satisfaction for them.   Sometimes, however, it is not a matter of the work itself but rather of the significance of the work.   What does it mean that a person has a particular job with a certain job of responsibility?   To find out we consider two categories of what work can signify to people: job content and job meaning.

Job Content

Someone commenting on his job might say, "There just isn't much to it."   It is evident that he does not mean there is not much to do.   There is probably a great deal to keep a person busy.   However, there might not be much substance or content to the job.   What is involved in content?

JOB SCOPE.   Jobs vary greatly in the number of operations a person performs.   There may be many so that it takes a person a day or perhaps even several days to complete all of them and begin to repeat the cycle.   Contrarily, the scope of some jobs is so narrow and the operations so few that the work cycle can be repeated hundreds, perhaps thousands, of times a day.   The greater the degree of division of work, the fewer the number of operations demanded by a job.   As noted, the shorter a work cycle, the more repetitious it becomes.   Perhaps the most refined form of division of work occurs on the assembly line where the repetitiveness of work can become very great, and jobs become boring, monotonous, a drudge to be avoided (Table 10.1).

Table 10.1

Operations Performed	Very or Fairly Interesting	Not Very or Not at All Interesting
1	19	38
2–5	28	36
5 or more	41	18

Source: Charles R. Walker and Robert H. Guest, *The Man on the Assembly Line*, Cambridge, Harvard University Press, 1952, p. 54.

JOB DEPTH.   A second dimension for determining job content concerns the number of phases of work a job contains. For example, how much planning of how and when work will be performed is left in the job, and how much is assigned to another, for example, to the job of the industrial engineer? Even jobs with a small scope of skills or operations may have all phases of the work in them. For example, a person working in an office may be assigned to the most rudimentary job and know that it must be completed at the end of the day. However, the same office worker may be able to decide the order in which elements of the job are to be performed, how they will be done, and to some degree the pace at which he works. This is not always the case in production work, especially when the work is of a highly integrated fashion. Returning for the moment to the assembly line, we observe that here the person has absolutely no control over how he does his work. He is told exactly the sequence of operations and motions he is to follow. Second, he has no control over when he works, because he works when material comes in front of him, and he must finish before the work goes on to the next position. The worker does not control the pace nor when he works; the machine does. The reactions to this situation are sometimes dramatic. "The work isn't hard, it's the never ending pace. . . . The guys yell 'hurrah' whenever the line breaks down. . . . You can hear it all over the plant." [1]

It should be clear that by carrying division of labor to an extreme level, the content of the individual job is stripped of so much that the job itself does not have much left in it to produce real personal satisfaction. The job becomes undesirable, a source of frustration, and negative sentiments develop toward work. The pay can be good, the working conditions adequate, but as one worker put it, "You know it's

[1] Charles R. Walker and Robert H. Guest, *The Man on the Assembly Line*, Cambridge, Harvard University Press, 1952, p. 51.

a funny thing, these things are all good but they don't make the job good; it is what you spend most of the time doing that counts." [2]   In jobs such as this, the work itself holds so little fascination that people are strongly tempted to leave either by quitting or absenteeism. Table 10.2 shows how, in the study of 175 workers, absenteeism correlated very well with the overall content of the job.   Here the job factors scored consisted of six elements.   Even if people do not actually leave the unsatisfactory job because of its high pay or the depend-

Table 10.2   Absenteeism Related to Job Factors (175 Workers) *

	Below Median Job-Factor Score † (0–5 points)	Above Median Job-Factor Score (6–12 points)	Total
Lower than Median Absentee Record (0–6 points)	35	54	89
Higher than Median Absentee Record (7 or more points)	54	32	86
Total 89		86	175

* Line and column totals do not divide exactly at the median of 175. In each case the nearest point-score figure to the median was used.

† Job factor score consisted of six factors: degree of repetitiveness, degree of mechanical pacing, skill as measured by length of learning time, frequency of break in job routine, frequency of social interaction, size of interacting group. Each factor rated 0 for high mass-production characteristics, and 2 for low mass-production characteristics. Hence, low score indicated repetitive, dull job. *Source:* Charles R. Walker and Robert H. Guest, *The Man on the Assembly Line*, Cambridge, Harvard University Press, 1952, p. 120.

ency of their families on the high pay, they still feel a strong yearning to get away from it.[3]   Here division of work has lead to jobs which in themselves do not satisfy.   People stay on such jobs from economic necessity.   As a result, the wages received for some jobs having very low skill requirements are considerable higher than for jobs with greater skill content.   This inconsistency with the assumed relationship between skill and wage levels can be understood by recognizing that people in such situations are being paid largely to stay on the job, and are only partially paid for the skills contributed.

[2] Robert H. Guest, "Man and Machines: Assembly Line Worker Looks at His Job," *Personnel,* **31,** 1955, pp. 496–503.
[3] *Ibid.*

What can be done by management to improve the situation? Several things have been tried quite successfully. One set of actions fall under the title of *job enlargement*, which really has two branches. The first of these is to take a job that has been reduced to an elementary number of operations (for example, five or six) and increase the steps, thus giving the person more to do, a bigger job. The result of such action has been fairly consistent improvement in employee satisfaction and productivity.[4]

The second way of enlarging the scope of the job is to permit the employee to engage in some degree of planning rather than telling him exactly what to do. He is told what is desired and allowed to determine the ways in which the work is to be performed. Again, when jobs are enlarged in this direction, both productivity and employee satisfaction have been shown to increase.[5]

If what we have been saying suggests that division of work is not a useful concept, this is not so. We are trying to suggest that division of labor is not something that can be carried out through successive divisions, resulting in ever-increasing specialized work, and always yielding great efficiency. What we are suggesting is that the further we carry specialization, the greater will be the advantages up to a point, provided, of course, the conditions for the division of labor are met. Once past that point the advantages probably start to decrease, and in fact, very likely reach a juncture where they actually begin to erase some of the advantages previously achieved. There is, in short, not only a point of diminishing return but also of negative return.

For a long time when considering division of work, the thought was to design a job to promote minimum per-unit cost.[6] To obtain economic efficiency, the focus was on adjusting people to the requirements of the machine in their jobs. In doing so, people lost sight of a point made by Henry Ford: "Machines alone do not give us mass production. Mass production is achieved by both machines *and* man and while we have gone a long way toward perfecting our mechanical

[4] Set, for example, Danse L. Bibby, "Enlarging of the Job for the Worker," *Proceedings of the 17th Conference, Texas Personnel and Management Association*, Austin, University of Texas, 1955, pp. 29–31; and James C. Worthy, "Organizational Structure and Employee Morale," *American Sociological Review*, **15**, 1950, pp. 169–179; F. L. Richardson, Jr. and Charles R. Walker, *Human Relations in an Expanding Company*, New Haven, Yale University, 1948.
[5] See, for example, Lester Coch and John R. P. French, Jr., "Overcoming Resistance to Change," *Human Relations*, **1**, 1948, pp. 512–532.
[6] For further discussion of this point, see Louis E. Davis, "Job Design and Productivity; A New Approach," Personnel, **33**, 1957, pp. 418–430.

operation, we have not successfully risen to our equation, whatever complex factors represent man's human element." [7]

We have been singling out some of the limiting conditions which human beings place on a division of work. Unfortunately, the point at which diminishing returns become serious cannot be determined exactly, but at least we can indicate that carried to an extreme degree division of work has undesirable consequences.

Job Meaning

So much for job content. Jobs are also sources of satisfaction for what they mean to people.

One source of job meaning is the status it gives a person. As noted in Chapter 4, different occupations have different places in the status hierarchy. In assigning a person to a job, we also assign him an occupational status. Needless to say, an employee assigned to a low-status job is likely to have fewer feelings of satisfaction than one assigned to a higher status. The real issue is the congruency between the status a person believes he occupies and the status of the job assigned him. Hence, people in an industrial setting who have high-status positions may refuse to do work, or at least may be reluctant to do work they consider belonging to a lower status of occupation. A machinist, for example, who has a high-status position may be most reluctant to push a container full of parts to the next department, a job normally handled by a materials handler who has a very low status. Many of us have seen or heard of situations where certain men have refused to wash dishes or diaper babies because they consider this to be "women's work," something beneath their masculine status.

In an interesting study conducted by the Tavistock Institute it was found that the status of a position closely paralleled its amount of responsibility, responsibility primarily being reflected by two conditions: (a) the extent to which the job occupant could commit the organization in the future and (b) the length of time the job occupant could work before he was checked on by his superior.[8] Job content, in this instance the amount of responsibility involved, influences the meaning of a job by determining one aspect of its status.

[7] Henry Ford, II, "The Challenge of Human Engineering," an address to the Society of Automotive Engineers, Detroit, 1946.
[8] Elliott Jacques, *Measurement of Responsibility*, London, Tavistock Publications, 1956.

JOB RELATIONS

In the process of creating jobs by division of work, the result is not only individual jobs but also jobs in a particular relationship to one another. There are several categories of such relationships. One set concerns the proximity of one position to others. For example, a clerk attached to a vice president's personal staff may be doing essentially the same work and receiving the same pay as a clerk working in the factory reporting to a foreman; yet the clerk attached to the vice president's office probably feels that she has the better job.

Social Interaction

The other principal categories might better be called *interactions*. The way that work is divided and a job is designed determines two classes of interactions in the external system: those required and those permitted. Almost any organizational activity, particularly those related to a productive function, is connected with a flow which means the work moves from one job to another. In many instances if a person can do his job, not only does he have certain operations he must perform but he must also dovetail these operations with those performed by others. When he does this, he almost inevitably comes into contact with other people, and many times has to exchange certain information in order to synchronize his work with theirs. This is not the only common pattern of interaction; another person with whom the worker doubtless interacts is his superior.

There are certain required contacts a job holder must make with other people. The number of people with whom he comes into contact and the frequency and duration of the contacts is drastically influenced by the way work is divided. In brief, the more specialized work becomes, the fewer, less frequent, and the shorter become required, interpersonal contacts. Let us assume we have a group of executives, each with a private secretary. The secretaries, among other duties, function as receptionists for their bosses, take dictation, and type letters. If these jobs were subdivided and rearranged so that one employee functioned as receptionist for all of the executives, and the others were assigned to a typing pool under a supervisor where they worked in transcribing letters from dictating machines, we change the number of required interactions. That is, those interactions legitimately necessary to carry out the job of the employees in the steno pool become sharply reduced. They probably would have little required interaction amongst themselves, little primary inter-action with their direct superior, and no longer would meet the varied array of people coming into the different executive offices. For the receptionist, on the other hand, the frequency of interaction and the number of people with whom she would come in contact would in-crease enormously. However, the duration of any of these contacts probably will be quite short, and gone will be the longer, and perhaps more substantial, contacts she had earlier with the executive who was her superior.

Table 10.3   Temporal Analysis of Occupational Roles and Tasks

		Tasks Connected With:		
	Short Stops	*Long Stops*		*Depart-mental Duties*
Occupational Roles	*Weaving*	*Loading-Unloading*	*Loom Maintenance*	
Weavers	x			
Battery fillers	x			
Smash hands	x			
Bobbin carrier	x			
Gaters		x		
Cloth carrier		x		
Jobbers			x	
Assistant jobbers			x	
Feeler-motion fitter			x	
Oiler			x	
Sweeper			(x)	x
Humidification fitter				x

Source: A. K. Rice, "Productivity and Social Organization in an Indian Weaving Shed," *Human Relations,* **6**, 1953, p. 311.

Division of work not only determines what interactions are required or necessary but also substantially influences which ones are possible or permitted. For example, a night watchman, even though he may have ample time when he has nothing to do, is unlikely to have anyone to interact with simply because of the particular nature of his work. A receptionist meets a great many people. However, the job also precludes the associations from being long or predictable. Others, such as messenger boys, have job assignments which take them into a great many places making it possible for them to exercise greater dis-

cretion over the duration and recipient of interaction. A person assigned to a job on an assembly line must stay in that position. He
cannot walk off to talk with another whenever he chooses. If he
should, disciplinary action would be instigated. Here the job does not
take him into contact with many people, and he is not permitted to
make voluntary contacts.

This is not the only way in which job design or division of work
influences the interactions that are permitted. Ordinarily we might
say that people, though they may not be able to interact on the job, are
free to do so on their break period; but are they? In a study of a
textile factory in India it was found that the way jobs were designed
gave some people relatively short rest periods and other people relatively long rest periods (Table 10.3). Even if people with both long
and short rest periods were free at the same time, the differences in the
time they could spend together would make it difficult for them to
develop the same social relationships as might have developed if they
had shared the same period of time free. But this is not the important
factor, for again, Table 10.3 notes that some of those having long stops
were responsible for loading and unloading the looms. This could
only be done when the looms were stopped, which was at the time
when the loom operators were taking their rest periods. Hence, the
jobs were so designed that the rest periods of people did not occur
concurrently.

Job design can also influence, and perhaps to a degree eliminate, the
possibility of required interactions leading to emergent interactions.
As can be seen from Figure 10.3, personnel on a loom may be required
to interact, for example, with repairmen when notifying them that
maintenance on their equipment is necessary and explaining in some
degree what the difficulty is. However, since their periods of work
and rest are reciprocal to each other, they have little opportunity to
develop social contacts beyond the required relationship. Conversely,
employees working on one loom have no required interaction with
those on other looms, nor do work conditions permit them to initiate
interaction voluntarily. Yet, since there is some likelihood that their
machines may be shut down at the same time (for example, while new
materials are placed on the loom), they may be able to share rest
periods in which they can voluntarily group together, should they
choose to do so. This is still a chancy proposition because the looms
may not shut down at the same time. Consequently, in this sort of a
situation, the opportunities for stable social groups to develop are
sharply reduced.

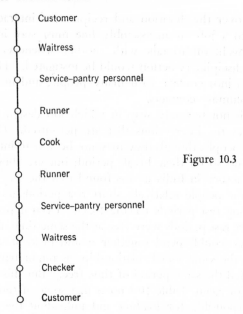

Figure 10.3

Shared Perceptions

One point to be noted is that the way in which work is divided places positions, and therefore, the people assigned to them, in a particular context. Hence, a welder in a welder's job on an assembly line is in a department organized on a product basis. Each of the jobs along the assembly line is quite different. They all share, however, in the product in which all their efforts culminate. A change in the product, even though it may influence only one or two positions, is likely to be of interest to all members of the department. On the other hand, if during an economy effort, the company buys a smaller diameter welding rod making it necessary for the welder to spend more time to complete each weld, this does not change something common to all positions, but only to one. Other people on the production line may sympathize with the welder as an individual, but not really feel it is their problem. Should there be a process rather than a product form of organization, the welder would be in a department composed of other welders who would handle a variety of products. Here a change in one or two features of the products would be of little interest to them. On the other hand, should one welder be given inferior or smaller size welding rods, all members of the department would understand the problem and be able to place themselves in the unfortunate welder's shoes.[9]

WORK FLOW

Thus far we have been considering separately those elements of the external system influenced by the division of work: job content, job meaning, job relations. Although identification of these elements is important in organizational analysis, their interrelation is the bedrock of our conceptual scheme. It is, therefore, necessary to examine them in combination. For this discussion we consider a common organizational element, work flow.

In any organization we find a number of work flows. One may be a product flow consisting of the steps or operations through which the raw materials entering a plant are transformed into a finished product. Another flow is that of money or funds, for example, from the time it is received from a customer until it has been spent and given to some supplier or vendor. Still another flow deals with information. Although differing widely in nature and purpose, flows have common characteristics. They specify a sequence of events which takes place in order to accomplish some result. In this chapter we are particularly concerned with the type of flow called *work flow*.

In work-flow analysis we identify the sequence of activities involved in producing a product or service. A study of a large restaurant has described the work flow involved with handling customers' orders.[10] This is shown in an abbreviated form in Figure 10.3. The work flow begins with a customer giving an order to the waitress. The waitress takes his order to the service pantry where the order will be assembled. Many of the foods are, of course, already here, but certain elements such as meats frequently have to be prepared specially, particularly when there is any sort of a rush. Runners are assigned to take requests for meats, fish, or poultry from the service pantry to the cooks in the kitchen, in this case on a different floor, who prepare these dishes. If the cook does not have the particular item requested already prepared, on receiving this information from the runner, he begins to cook the required dish. When completed, the runner takes the meat

[9] For other influences of division of work on perception, see Chapter 3 of this book.
[10] William F. Whyte, Jr., *Human Relations in the Restaurant Industry*, New York, McGraw-Hill, 1948. Material in this section is taken largely from Chapters 4 and 5.

to the service pantry where the customer's order will be completed. The waitress then takes the assembled order to a checker who makes sure that the portions are the proper size, that the plates and trays are neat, and that the customer's check has been properly prepared. If all of these are correct, the waitress then takes the order to the customer.

In observing this rather elementary work flow, Whyte noted that there were places along the flow which could be described as "hot spots," where there seemed to be clashes or difficulties between people filling various positions. One such hot spot was between the runners and the cooks. The heart of these difficulties involved two principal factors.

Status

In these kitchens, the highest status among nonsupervisory employees was that of the cook. Other positions within the kitchen were ranked lower in status than cooks. Almost at the very bottom was the position of runner, one requiring little or no experience or skill. The point of difficulty arose when a person of high status and a person of low status came into contact. It would be erroneous, however, to presume that contacts between people widely separated in status would of necessity cause difficulty. The problems which arose were the result of the nature of the contact between these people.

Initiating Work

The difficulties between the cooks and runners were likeliest to occur at certain times during the day, notably during rush hours. Usually the cooks prepared standard meat dishes on a minimum-maximum basis; that is, they would prepare a certain quantity of food and try to maintain the quantity on hand between stated lower and upper levels. Therefore, many times when a customer's order came, for example, pork chops, these chops would be available for the runner to pick up immediately to take out to the pantry. However, during rush periods, the cook might get behind in work, making it necessary for the runner to ask for certain dishes to be prepared. These were the times when the most serious difficulties between the two were likely to occur. At such moments, the runner was *initiating work* for the cook. That is, the runner, by conveying the customer's order, made it necessary for the cook to do a specific task. The cooks found it intolerable to think that they, the highest-status persons in the kitchen, were in effect, being ordered to work by someone who held the lowest status in the kitchen.

To summarize in terms of concepts we have been developing, the division of work employed in the restaurant leads to two developments: jobs (activities) which have occupational status differences (different job meanings) and a particular form of interaction which has required the person in the lower status position to initiate action for a person in a higher one.

The purpose of the illustration was to show how the models under discussion can be used to analyze organizational situations, not to show *the* way organizational elements fit together to cause difficulties. The same concepts can be used to analyze a broad array of organizational issues. Let us consider a situation where the division of work chosen by determination of job content, and thereby job meaning, leads to incongruencies between the status of positions people hold and the status they think their jobs should have, based on the values (sentiments) they bring with them into the organization. Here work flow is again an important factor, because the sequence of work performance determines important differences in job content.

ANALYSIS OF ENGINEERING WORK FLOW. In the engineering department of a very large manufacturing company, the subdepartments are organized on the basis of engineering specialties.[11] The two particular divisions with which we are concerned are mechanical engineering and electrical engineering. These two divisions are similar in many ways. Members of both departments have professional engineering backgrounds. There is about the same portion of Bachelor degrees, Masters, and Doctorates in each. Salaries are similar for the same level of work. Actually, a person walking into the two divisions would notice quite a difference. In the electrical engineering division, he would hear engineers say that their work is interesting, challenging, and stimulating, and that they are quite pleased with their present position and prospects. In the mechanical engineering division, he would hear far more criticisms of the company and the work in the department. Many people in these departments might say that they found the professional climate so bad they wished they could or were thinking of leaving the company.

To understand the rather sharp differences in morale between the two departments, we have to look at several factors. The first of

[11] Material for this section is largely taken from Raymond R. Ritti, "Engineers and Managers: A Study of Engineering Organization," unpublished Ph.D. thesis, Cornell University, 1960.

these is the value of structure of the engineers. In brief, the engineers, looking at themselves as professional men, feel they are doing true engineering work when they draw on their knowledge of the physical world to solve major technical problems. This point of view clearly recognizes several phases in engineering work. The first phase, in which the problem is defined clearly, the overall approach decided on, and the basic design of the solution or product laid out is the highest or "true" form of engineering work. Once this basic design has been developed, there are many subsidiary designs which have to be produced to make a final product or achieve a solution to reality. These are of a lesser importance requiring less engineering competence. For example, in designing a bridge initial design considerations may involve determining the length, the basic structure, for example, whether it is to be a suspension or cantilever bridge, and other overall design characteristics. Once this is done, designs on many subparts of the bridge can be carried out: girders, plates used to hold beams and girders together, the form and number of rivets and bolts, etc. There is a succession of engineering tasks, each subsequent one constrained by the preceding one, allowing less originality and requiring less competence. As we move toward the tail end of this sequence involved with the making of drawings, the counting up of rivets, and designing of relatively minor or unimportant subunits, the work tends to be classified by engineers as "hack work," something fit only for the least competent of the professionals or for subprofessionals such as draftsmen.

The second point of contention was the flow of work between the divisional units within the engineering division. The company had largely developed as an electrical manufacturer. The work of this engineering division was concerned with designing electrical or electronic units for the military. When a contract was signed by the company for the development of a new apparatus or weapon, the design work would begin in the electrical engineering division. Once the electrical system and circuits had been designed and the basic electrical components selected, the work was then moved to the mechanical engineering division. In short, the electrical group always made the basic, overall design, and the mechanical group always made supportive or secondary designs. The work flow fixed the mechanical engineers into what, by their value system, was a low-status position. With no opportunity to rise to the point where they could do "true" engineering work, the frustration, poor morale, and potential turnover problems became understandable.

SUMMARY

In Chapter 9 we considered work as a technical property. "What are the technical elements of work?"; "How can they be handled?" were considered. In Chapters 2, 5 and 7 we noted that individual behavior was influenced by the social system in which people found themselves. These two threads were connected in this chapter by recognizing that work is carried out by the behavior of individuals. How the technical aspects of work are carried out is determined by the form of social systems in existence, and the social system is determined by the technical structure or system which exists. Since neither could adequately be considered separately, it was necessary to consider, on a more general level of abstraction, what has been called a sociotechnical system.

The link between the technical system and the social was provided by considering the external system of the Homans' model as a set of activities, interactions, and sentiments which was in part molded by the technical system, and which in turn molds the internal system. Through this intervening mold, the technical elements of the division of work were translated social elements which determine behavior. Such an intellectual tool has a number of valuable applications. First, it aids in diagnosing existing problems in organizations. Second, it makes predictions about the performance of proposed organizational forms. Third, it points out the factors that limit the extent to which such concepts as division of work can be used.

Requirements of Organizational Differentiation

Dᴵꜰꜰᴇʀᴇɴᴛ ways of dividing work create various conditions which require satisfaction through the provision of support structures and activities. Furthermore, the ways and degree to which work is divided are influenced by these conditions or requirements. Knowing them permits more adequate decisions to be made about the division of work.

BOUNDARY CONDITIONS

When work is divided, boundaries are drawn between various work elements, grouping them into jobs, positions, or organizational units. These boundaries are drawn on the basis of interunit differences, intraunit similarities, or both. Whether the units grouped (or divided) are similar depends on the criteria used. For example, suppose we have a pile of boxes that could be classified according to three dimensions: height, depth, and length. One difference among the boxes is that some are two inches long, some seven, and others ten. If we divide the boxes on the basis of length, we get three piles. Boxes within each pile are homogonous, at least on the basis of length. Let us suppose further that the boxes could be one, two, or three inches high for each of the three lengths. If the pile of five-inch long boxes were also to be homogonous in height, we would have to subdivide boxes further.

If all the boxes had the same width and we used this dimension to group them, we would have only one pile. The simple but important point here is that whether factors are considered to be the same or different depends on the criteria (or dimensions) used. That is, units

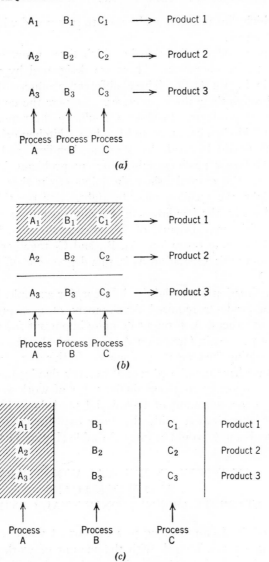

Figure 11.1. Boundary to divide work into departments based on unique features of product.

can be different along one dimension, while similar along another. Thus, the sales department is different from the production department in some respects and similar to it in others. In dividing work, among the most important decisions to be made are those that determine which dimensions must be used to group and which to divide the work elements.

Let us consider a situation in which three processes are used in a manufacturing operation. These are designated by the letters A, B, and C in Figure 11.1a. Three different products—1, 2, and 3—are made through these three processes. Suppose the company is making sheet-metal products. Product 1 could be sheet-metal fishing boats, Product 2 kitchen canisters, and Product 3 kitchen cabinets. All three products would be made by shearing, bending, and welding operations. Different products raise different problems for some of these processes. For example, since the joints of the sheet-metal boat have to be tight, the welding must be tight. But for this process to be handled easily, the bending and shearing operations must be handled with special care. Because of this interdependency, it might become essential to group operations A_1, B_1, and C_1 together (Figure 11.1b). But in doing this, Operation A_1 is, to a degree, cut off from Operations A_2 and A_3.

If the situation were slightly different, for example, if the making of all three products required development of new procedures for all aspects of process A, it might be quite important for new ideas developed by persons in Operation A_1 to be quickly disseminated to other workers doing the same type of work. In this case a boundary or wall, such as we have mentioned would be very disadvantageous. It might be more important to group similar types of work so that there could be easy communication of technical knowledge. Hence, a process-type of organization with the boundary between process A and processes B and C would be more desirable (Figure 11.1c).

MATCHING INDIVIDUAL WORK CAPACITY
AND WORK LOADS:
STABILITY OF ENVIRONMENTAL CONDITIONS

One of the factors leading to a division of work is the necessity of matching a person's work with the amount of work he is capable of doing. A person's work capacity can be underutilized either because his assignment is too "small" or because the items to be worked on are not available. A break in a conveyor belt which interrupts the flow of materials to a work position creates the second condition. We might also note that a worker in a position preceding the broken conveyor probably would be forced to stop, as he would have no place to send his completed work. Likewise, a plant that makes a product for which the public's taste has changed, or whose supplies are inter-

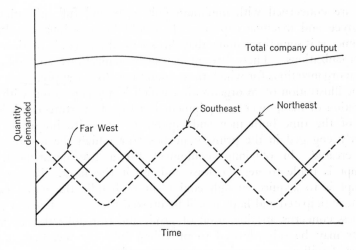

Figure 11.2

rupted by a railroad strike, would be faced with the same situation. An important constraint on division of work is the stability of the environment, which gives inputs to or receives outputs from an organizational unit.[1]

Let us envision a company that manufactures products distributed throughout the entire country. It is trying to determine whether it should build one plant to supply all customers or several plants located in three geographical areas, the Northeast, the Southeast, and the Far West. The company may have noted a fairly uniform demand for its products throughout the entire year. However, closer examination reveals that each geographical area has a different demand pattern. At one time of the year the demand is high in the Northeast section and low in the Southeast. Several months later, the pattern is reversed (Figure 11.2). Given that transportation costs are not a major problem, the company may decide against dividing its manufacturing, in favor of concentrating it in one plant, thereby reaping the advantage of stabler levels of production.

SUBOPTIMIZATION OF ORGANIZATIONAL UNITS

Among the difficult issues facing any organization is determining a hierarchy of goals. Business organizations are frequently concerned with maintaining a profit, or better, maximizing profits. Therefore,

[1] Provided, of course, that a major constraint is efficient utilization of employee or member time.

they are concerned with minimum unit costs and full utilization of employee and machine capacity. It would be a serious mistake to presume, as is sometimes done, that this set of objectives is pertinent to all organizations. There are numerous organizations and subunits within organizations for which these conditions do not apply.

One illustration of an organization which is not concerned with full utilization of manpower or equipment is a Fire Department. A large part of the time both men and equipment in a fire house are not directly engaged in the primary purpose for which the organization was created. In obtaining equipment for a fire department, no attempt is made to get the least and use it the most. Rather, the attempt is to acquire enough equipment to handle the worst catastrophe anticipated and hope it will be utilized the least. Even in some business concerns, maximization of profit and full utilization of manpower may be subordinated to providing jobs for members of the owners' families or promoting security of employment.

There is another aspect to this, however, which might be called maximizing utilization of major resources. Many elements of organization, just as many parts of machines, exist to support or facilitate others. For example, consider the battery in a car. It is usually used in starting an automobile. The rest of the time it is not being used at all or it is being charged. No one feels particularly upset that the battery spends most of its time in an unused state. It is worthwhile to have the battery there when needed in order to make a larger, more expensive piece of equipment easier and more comfortable to use. The same is often true of organizations. A company may have a $6,000-a-year secretary working for a vice president who earns $40,000 a year. The secretary's time may not be fully utilized, but she is deemed necessary nonetheless since she permits the executive to apply his time to things which are his real work rather than lesser chores, such as opening mail, getting files, and answering telephones. Needless to say, the same thinking can be applied to a whole department.

WORK CYCLES

In any job or organizational unit defined by a division of work, there is a sequence of operations. The time from the beginning of the first operation until the same operation starts again is called a *work cycle*. With the completion of each work cycle, some output in the form of a product or service is produced, which goes to the next unit where another work cycle is performed. Hence, as an item is manufactured it often goes from one unit to another having a number of work cycles performed on it.

Harmonic Work Cycles

Ideally, as one work cycle is completed the next should be ready to receive its output. This effect would be most simply achieved if all work cycles were of the same length; but this is seldom the case. It is often desirable to attempt to develop work cycles which are multiples of each other. Then if Cycle One takes 10 minutes and Cycle Two takes 5 minutes, we can achieve a balance by having two positions performing Cycle One and one performing Cycle Two. Needless to say, in the long sequence of operations characteristic of many manufacturing enterprises even this harmonic balancing of the volume and timing of work is difficult.

Shift Problems

At times the technology used dictates that a work cycle expand beyond the control of one position or even one department. For example, it may take 10 hours to prepare a batch of chemicals. Unless employees are to work overtime, the work has to be completed by the next shift. This can, and often does, raise many problems. If the work turns out to be of poor quality, who is to blame? Is it the crew that happens to be there ready to take the reprimand, or the crew which started the batch and has long since gone home? There may be numerous special instructions about adjustments made by the first crew in starting the batch which have to be transmitted to the second group. How is this to be done efficiently? These are a few of the problems that can affect a work cycle that extends over more than one shift.[2]

The problems pertaining to a work cycle that extends over two shifts often are handled by moving them up in the organizational hierarchy to a level of supervision to which both shifts report. This point may be several levels up; thus, some executives are concerned with details considerably distant from their place in the organization. Furthermore, the time delay in the transmission of the problem upward and of the solution downward can greatly compound the difficulty.

Timing Between Jobs or Units

The ideal expressed in the preceding paragraph was that as one work cycle ended, the next would be ready to utilize its output (Figure

[2] For further discussion, see Eric Miller, "Technology, Territory and Time," *Human Relations*, 1959, **12**, particularly pp. 254–256.

11.3a). We might say that here the work cycles would be closely coupled. Such conditions are difficult to obtain. The slightest variation in the performance of one work cycle will be transmitted to all subsequent work cycles. If a disturbance is entered at several units causing variation to several work cycles, the system would have a very jerky movement if it operated at all. To avoid such overly rigid conditions, actual work systems are made more flexible or are accorded more "give" by the inclusion of stocks between positions. These stocks serve as cushions for disturbances entering the system. Hence, in Figure 11.3b, if something interferes temporarily to delay the work cycle in work position 1, position 2 can draw on the stock of material in front of it and keep going. Furthermore, if something should go wrong in position 3, position 2 would not have to stop, but could pile work in the stock between the two positions. Needless to say, this in-process inventory has some costs attached to it. Efforts are made to keep it as small as possible. Such an inventory serves as sort of a balance wheel for the system.

All this information applies to officially created stocks. However, organizational members often unofficially create their own stocks for the same basic reasons: to serve as cushions or buffers. For example, when a worker knows that he is to maintain a certain level of produc-

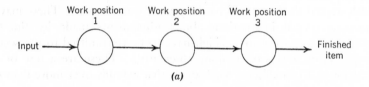

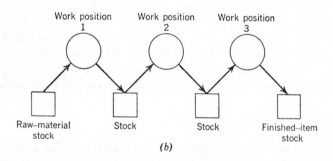

Figure 11.3. (a) Material moves directly from one work position to another. (b) Material moves from stock, to work position, to stock.

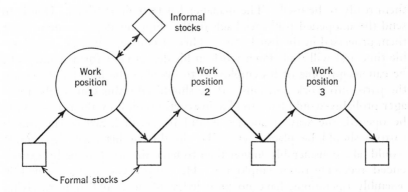

Figure 11.4. Production in excess of standard quantity moves into informal stocks and out of informal stocks to meet production deficiencies at a position.

tion, he may build his own unofficial stock of parts on days when he is over the standard so that he can draw against it on days when his actual production may be below standard, and in doing so he avoids censure by his superior or his fellow workers [3] (see Figure 11.4). Hence, we may find officially designated stocks between positions and unofficially created stocks within positions serving to cushion variations in perhaps the same but often different systems.

STANDARDIZED INPUTS

Thus far, in noting that division of work increases a unit's sensitivity to inputs, we have principally given attention to the quantity and timing of the input. Division of work also increases the unit's dependency on specification of the input.

Let us suppose that a department regularly receives, unpacked in tote pans, the parts it employs in an assembly operation and that the parts are counted into exact quantities ready for use. One day parts come just as they have been received from the supplier: uncounted in unopened boxes. The manager in charge of the department now has a problem. His employees are trained and allocated to assembly work. They are accustomed to having parts in open tote pans in front of

[3] For discussion of this situation, see Fritz J. Roethlisberger and William J. Dickson, *Management and the Worker*, Cambridge, Harvard University Press, 1956, particularly pp. 432–436; and Donald Roy, "Quota Restriction and Goldbricking in a Machine Shop," *American Journal of Sociology*, **57**, 1952, pp. 427–442.

them ready to be used.   The manager has two alternatives.   One is to send the unopened packages back to the shipping department to have them processed in the usual way.   This, of course, will take considerable time and will shut down work in his department for a while.   Or, he can assign some of his employees to opening the boxes and putting the parts into work positions.   If he should take this course, the manager probably would have to give instructions on how the boxes should be opened, the way quantities should be verified, where the empty cartons should be placed, etc.   To do this in his own department would take considerably longer than to have the work done by experienced receiving-room employees.   His employees, being trained in assembly operations, have no knowledge of how to handle receiving work; they have no program for it, and are consequently relatively unsuited to this type of work.

In short, the standardized assignments resulting from division of work require standardized inputs.   When inputs vary from the established standard, additional work of a nonstandard variety is required, for which programs, setups, and execution time must be provided.   In this simple illustration, the nonstandard work could be reasonably handled by members of the department.   But suppose it could not, as when the preceding operations were very complex or required special equipment.   Then there might be considerable delay in bringing about a correction.

The Role of Standards and Tolerances

The response to the need for congruency among inputs, outputs, and work methods means that as work moves from one unit to the next, whether it is a position or department, it must comply with a set of standards.   If work moving across this nexus does not meet these standards, additional nonroutine or nonstandard work will have to be performed.

One of the consequences, interchangeable parts, is so common that we fail to realize that this is not the only way in which goods or services can be produced.   Even in highly technical industries it was quite common, until relatively recent times, to use a manufacturing method whereby each part was carefully fitted to those with which it came into contact.   Fine products can be made in this way, but there is usually no opportunity to transfer parts from one assembly to another.   Under this method it would be impossible to walk into a store to buy bearings for a car and have them inserted to replace worn ones.   Each bearing would have to be made separately for the car.

Producing to standard, making interchangeable parts, may decrease quality or individuality, but it also greatly reduces costs.[4]

Merely to state that there are standards for transactions between organizational units is not sufficient; for in reality, no standard is ever met. We merely come acceptably close to meeting them. We cannot say that a part must be exactly two inches in diameter, because it would be impossible to machine anything to exactly two inches; however, it is possible to specify that it should be no more than two inches and no less than 1.98 inches. The actual dimensions can vary within a range of two-hundredths of an inch.

A newcomer to the group is expected to adhere more closely to the group norm than is the old, established leader. The new man may be permitted one violation of the standard before he receives discipline, but the old established member may be able to violate the norm several times before someone seriously raises questions about his behavior. In short, there are permissible variations from norms as well as permissible variations from physical measurement. These permissible variations are called *tolerances*. They are the actual critical factor in controlling interorganizational transactions. The further the degree of specialization of labor, the narrower is the range of variation which can be tolerated.

We can perhaps summarize some of the main points in regard to tolerance by recalling some of the principal properties mentioned in relation to division of work   First, as noted in Chapter 9, a division of work usually requires a large volume of work or that the elements of work be repeated many times. For standardized work methods to be employed with a high degree of repetitiveness, we must be sure that the work coming in will meet necessary standards. Work going out also must meet certain standards. In short, both the work method and the items worked on are predictable in a number of different ways. When something does not meet the standard, it is not predictable and some new steps must be taken to compensate for this contingency.

Depending on how they are established, various organizational systems have differing tolerances for contingencies. A crucial question for an organization planner is, what tolerance for contingency must be built into the organization? Should there be inspectors checking the work as it moves from one department to another? Should there be all-around repair men in the assembly line to correct errors and devia-

[4] For specifications and interchangeable parts, see James G. March and Herbert A. Simon, *Organizations*, New York, Wiley, 1958, p. 160; and Joseph A. Litterer, "Systematic Management: The Search for Order and Integration," *Business History Review*, **35**, 1961, particularly pp. 464–468.

tions? Should one choose a product or a process-type of departmentalization to produce a higher tolerance for contingencies? These are not easy questions. They rest on the knowledge of what results from choosing various organizational forms and also from the requirements of the particular technical and social systems being dealt with.

SUMMARY

This has been a brief coverage of some of the more important factors to be considered in making a choice about division of work. Merely choosing a division of work imposes some conditions or requirements which must be met in some way. If these can be met easily, of course, there is little problem. But often such conditions are difficult to meet and therefore should be avoided or reduced. Our effort has not been to discuss solutions but to identify things which must be taken into account in developing solutions.

The items considered have centered in a number of topics. One was the general objective of maximizing man or machine utilization and the requirements this raises for stable inputs, outputs, and work methods. This stability—or as we have later called it, predictability—can be enhanced by adequately taking into account the requirements of the work cycles in organizations, the problems in timing and integrating them, and the development of standards for more accurate tolerances for items that have moved through an organization. Perhaps the central idea has been to identify those things that influence an organization's tolerance for contingencies.

The illustrations chosen have usually centered on manufacturing situations and parts or at least raw materials. Needless to say, the conditions discussed are pertinent to all things which move in and out of an organization. A large organization, such as General Motors, could not operate, at least in its present fashion, if it were not sure that it could get fairly standard types of employees from the labor market: metallurgists, computer programmers, and the like. It could not operate if it did not know that in most of its financial dealings with other business organizations certain practices were considered proper form. In any area where division of work reduces an organization's tolerance for contingency below the normal level of variation in that area, the division of work must stop.

Part Three

Achieving Coordination

Coordination

Most of Part Two was devoted to matters relating to the development of jobs or activities for the individuals and subunits in an organization. This division of work, however, constitutes only one of the two basic phenomena of organizations. The other element, which is equally instrumental in making an organization effective, is the fitting together of job performances for the accomplishment of a specific purpose or *coordination*. Many writers have stressed the theoretical importance of coordination in an organization.[1] Yet in actual practice the managers responsible for planning organizations have often given the major part of their attention to dividing the work, largely ignoring coordination with serious consequences for actual performance.[2] An assumption implicit in much of such planning seems to be that if work is divided artfully enough and jobs are described in sufficient detail, coordination will fall into line automatically.[3] As a matter of fact, this does not happen.

Coordination principally concerns the relationships between tasks or activities which must fit in both form and time into an integrated accomplishment of some overall goal or purpose. In discussing coordination we do not consider totally different factors from those discussed in division of work. It is the emphasis or direction that is different. We are concerned with what one job or activity should be in relation to another, and are interested in the content of jobs and when they are performed, that is, in timing. In division of work the

[1] See, for example, James D. Mooney, *The Principles of Organization,* New York, Harper, 1947, pp. 5–13.
[2] Joseph A. Litterer, "Systematic Management: The Search for Order and Integration," *Business History Review,* **35,** 1961, pp. 461–476.
[3] See, for example, James G. March and Herbert A. Simon, *Organizations,* New York, John Wiley, 1958, pp. 25–26.

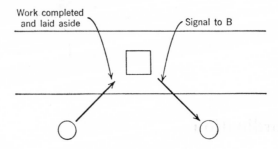

Figure 12.1

major emphasis was on the economy of effort, here it is on the integration or synchronization of effort.

In this chapter we look first at the basic elements of coordination, at the factors which influence a need, and the possibility of providing for coordination. Last, we review the principal administrative strategies for achieving this goal. In Chapter 13 we examine the basic processes by which coordination or control is achieved.

THE ELEMENTS OF COORDINATION

In a crude way division of work is concerned with breaking a big task into smaller ones. The resulting jobs or activities are therefore interconnected or linked. Coordination is the process of facilitating these *linked actions*.

Linked Actions

On an assembly line a worker often picks up a part, does some work on it, and lays it down when he finishes. The next worker, seeing the part laid down, knows that it is now ready and the time has arrived for him to perform his operation (Figure 12.1). The important point of this simple illustration is that the first employee's act of laying down the part is a signal (communication) to the second employee that it is time to perform his activity. One activity leads to another particular one through interaction.[4] Thus we can now describe more specifically the condition of interpendence referred to in Chapter 8. The dependence is on a particular set of linked activities facilitated by the

---

[4] Using slightly different terms this point is made by George Homans, *The Human Group*, New York, Harcourt Brace, 1950, pp. 101–103.

communications contained in a particular pattern of interaction.   This is a more dynamic, kinomatic aspect of work.

Multiplicity of Means for Facilitating Linked Actions

In the illustration the device for linking activities was the signal given by one employee in laying down the part on which he had been working.   Such signals, however, can be and frequently are carried out by more roundabout methods.   For example, when completing his task the first worker could notify his superior who would, in turn, direct the second employee to get the part and perform the next operations (Figure 12.2), or the sequence could be even longer.   Perhaps it could flow through several supervisors or a production control system.   The important point is that coordination occurs only when the proper actions are linked.   Much of the content of this chapter and those following consists of examinations of the ways in which this linkage can actually be facilitated.

Elements in Coordination

Coordination has two essential elements: the work, tasks, or activities performed and their timing through a communication process.

ACTIVITIES.   Work performance, as already noted, requires a program to specify the nature or elements of the task and how it is to be executed.   Organizations are likely to vary widely in the degree to which they provide such programs.   Some using assembly lines, for

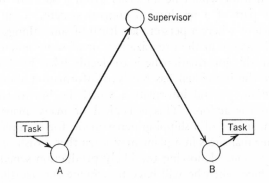

Figure 12.2. (1) On completing his task, A notifies his superior; (2) supervisor notifies B to perform task; (3) order from supervisor is a signal to B to begin task.

example, may devise very detailed programs for jobs of small content. Other organizations in effect permit a person to "write his own ticket" on what he will do. Both extremes are misleading. No one ever completely writes his own ticket because the output of his efforts and the way he performs his job must still fit into an overall organizational scheme. Even in the most circumscribed job on an assembly line there are some things not specified in a job description or job instruction sheet for which a person will have to acquire more information, in some fashion, to further programs.

To some degree, a person in an organization has to search for and choose among additional programs to round out those given to him. The adequacy of this search and collection process depends on many of the points discussed in Part One. Frequently individuals attempt to reduce the search. As a result, existing programs are often adapted or modified to meet new assignments. Hence, the adequacy of the new program is dependent to no small degree on the programs the individual has previously learned and the skill with which he adapts them. The process has two main components: classification of existing usable or adaptable programs with the immediate needs and a creative phase in which a program is adapted to a new purpose.

COMMUNICATION. Timing and coordination is provided through communication. We are concerned with two aspects of communication: the content of the message and its transmission.

The content of information flowing to an individual in an organization can vary widely. It may include specific instruction as to the activities or end result desired and the time it is to be provided. Such precise information would be an order from a superior or schedules developed as part of a production control system. Contrasted with this are situations where a person may learn of some things which have been done elsewhere in the organization, or of some new organization needs. From this information he is to decide what he should do and when. Here the individual has received information about a *state of the organization*, general information which he has to translate into specific plans for action. This is typical of many managerial positions. The manager of a shipping department, for example, at a meeting with other managers in a plant may learn that a rush order is to go through very soon. Knowing the likely production schedule, he will probably deduce when he will have to arrange for overtime workers, extra packing materials, and perhaps extra trucks or railroad cars.

In doing this he takes the general information he has received and through "rules of thumb" or standard operating procedures (that is, stored programs) determines his needs and has these provided for by the time the work load reaches his department. Some of these stored programs may be elements in other control processes, such as keeping manpower in line with existing labor agreements.

For communication, information or message content must get from one person to another. This process of transmission is neither simple nor easy. There are many things which block, distort, or delay transmission of information. Division of work raises partitions between people, departments, and other organizational units. A functional form of divisionalization may make the transmission of information about products difficult, but the transmission of information about technical aspects of the function easy. Processes of communication will be discussed more thoroughly in Chapter 14.

Factors Which Influence Need for and Facilitation of Coordination

All organizations or subunits in them do not have the same need for coordination. Within some organizations we may find departments which are essentially self-contained or autonomous. These are units which, in order to carry out their activities, need little or no help or assistance from other components of the organization. Needless to say, this is another ideal form; no subunit of an organization ever fully realizes it although some come close to it. For example, the Buick Division of General Motors is highly autonomous in regard to many other divisions of the company, but it does have a very close dependency upon certain top level departments of the corporation. Such a division designs its own automobiles, has its own outlets, and may very well have a good year when some of the other divisions are meeting with financial difficulty. In contrast, a factory within the Buick Division has far less autonomy. Its production schedules are prepared by a central office, purchasing is handled at a division office, and another unit arranges for the material to be transported from the factory, to name but a few items for which such a factory would be dependent on others. The more self-contained an organizational unit is, the less need for coordination with other organizational units.

An organizational unit may be highly self-contained or autonomous in some areas and not in others. A manufacturing plant might have complete discretion when buying its own raw materials and parts but may have to check everything that relates to personnel with higher authorities. Let us review some of the implications resulting from an organizational unit's degree of autonomy.

ADDITIVE AND INTERDEPENDENT SUBGOALS. Even in an organization where there are several subunits which are highly self-contained, there are important relations among them. They contribute to and share a common organization which means there are at least two ways in which they may be related.

When the subgoals of organizational units are similar or identical, they are additive in nature. An example would be the retail outlet in the Sears Roebuck chain. Each outlet contributes dollars of sale and profit to the overall organization. If one store fails to make a profit, it drags down the profit of the entire company and reduces the combined success of all subunits.

A more demanding form of this condition exists when the overall organizational goal cannot be realized unless all subunit goals are realized, even though each subunit may be able to achieve its subgoal independent of all other units. Let us consider a dance given by a social organization. Tickets have been sold by one group, the hall has been decorated by another, refreshments have been prepared by a third group. The guests arrive expecting to have a good time, but unfortunately the band, which was to come from out of town, was given the wrong date by the group responsible for that arrangement. All groups did their work, but their total effort was meaningless.

Dependent Units

A more common type of organizational situation is for subunits to be dependent on one another. One unit cannot do its work and meet its subgoals without other subunits doing theirs. We consider two forms of dependency here.

MUTUAL DEPENDENCY. Subunits are mutually dependent when together they depend on still another unit in order to carry out their activities. Manufacturing departments of a company, for example, are mutually dependent on other departments, such as the finance department or the personnel department. Usually this dependency revolves around some resource. The several manufacturing departments may know there are limits to the amount of capital or skilled personnel available; this makes them very much concerned about how these various resources will be allocated. In such situations often we find departments in competitive or, at best, bargaining positions. We have already noted some of the disruptive effects competition can produce; it has no small influence on the ease with which coordination is supplied in an organization.

INTERDEPENDENCY. Organizational units are interdependent when, to carry out their activity, they depend on the actions or activities of other units, which is a typical condition.   In the interdependent situation there is a sequential set of actions in different organizational units that are usually divided on the basis of function.   The coordination problem here is to cope with the interdependency and is concerned with making sure that proper actions, in proper quantities, are performed at the appropriate times.   This is essentially a scheduling problem.[5]

Division of Work

Underlying much of what we have just discussed is the point that one of the most significant influences on the need for and the possibility of facilitating coordination is the division of work chosen.   In general, the need for coordination resulting from a division of work depends on how the means-ends chain is allocated among organization units.   For any organizational goal there will be a cluster of means-ends items.   If this cluster is grouped within one organizational unit, the problems of coordination will be simplified.   If they are scattered over several units, coordination becomes much more difficult.[6]   If a company makes gardening tools, such as hand trowels, the manufacture of the metal blade, the wood handle, and the assembly of these parts can be grouped into one division, simplifying the coordination problem, or it may be scattered in three different units—metal working, woodworking, and assembly—thereby increasing the coordination effort in regard to the product.

It is not only the place but also the degree to which division of work is carried that creates coordinative problems.   In general, the further division of work is carried, the greater becomes the interdependency among jobs and organizational units and, therefore, the greater the coordinative task.   We have noted earlier in this chapter, and in Chapters 10 and 11, some of the ways this can affect coordination by influencing perception and the flow of communication.   Decisions influencing coordination do not begin after the division of work has been determined; they are made at every step in arriving at a division of work.   Often such decisions are made unknowingly through default or neglect, and as a result they increase coordinative problems rather than minimize them.

The Effect of Organizational Environment

In Chapter 11 we noted the ways in which variations in organizational inputs and outputs or in process make it difficult to achieve

[5] March and Simon, *op. cit.*, p. 122.
[6] *Ibid.*, pp. 163–165.

organizational efficiency or even effectiveness. The problem is simply that variations require an increase in the flow of communications to carry necessary information about the changes, the development, and utilization of new programs, which are the two essential ingredients in a coordinative system.

If the world facing an organization were completely unchanging, the problem of coordination would be greatly reduced. Actually, the real coordinative problem comes from the unpredictable factors. No organization is faced with a completely stable environment. However, we often know the time, direction, and magnitude of changes which will occur. Many companies can predict seasonal variations in a demand for their product quite accurately. They know that they can hire new college graduates most readily in June. Since these and many other variations can to some extent be predicted, organizations can plan accordingly. A separate program will often be developed in advance for these known variations which can be looked for, adjusted to, or possibly avoided. The less predictable the variations in the environment are, the more difficult the problems of coordination become.[7]

Coordinative effort is expensive and, therefore, one of the principal constraints on the degree to which division of work can be carried out. However, division of work can be carried further where the environment with which the organization contends is stablest. Often organizations, notably business concerns, go to considerable lengths to increase the stability of the environment facing them. This is particularly true when there are great advantages to having a high order of functional specialization. Vertical integration in industries, like steel, is one example of this situation.

Types of Coordination

Variations in the environment facing an organization affect not only the magnitude of the coordinative task but also the type of coordination used. In stable situations coordination can be carried on by pre-established programs which specify what activities are to be performed and when. This is called *coordination by plan*.[8] On the other hand, if the situation is fairly fluid, long-standing programs become less possible, and provisions have to be made to adjust them to meet new conditions. Variations in the conditions facing an organization are often detected first by those executing a program. Since these people usually have not established the program, they must have some way of

[7] *Ibid.*, pp. 25–29.
[8] *Ibid.*, p. 160.

transmitting information about their problem to those who prepare schedules and plans so that the latter group, in turn, can prepare a new program.   An example of this situation is the arrangements built into modern production control systems.   The type of coordination with provisions for adjusting to variations is called *coordination by feedback*.[9]

ACHIEVING COORDINATION

How is coordination achieved?   To put the question simply, how does the individual perform the right action at the right time?   There are two basically different ways this occurs; one is by *voluntary* means.   The individual or group of individuals sees a need, finds a program, and applies it when deemed necessary.   Contrasted with this is the *directed* method where individuals are told what to do and when.

Voluntary Coordination

The idea of individuals in an organization being self-starting and self-directing in providing coordination is appealing.   This does occur to some degree in almost any organization.   But a number of things frustrate the use of this form of coordination, particularly in larger organizations.   To have voluntary coordination, an individual has to have some knowledge of the goals of his unit, his position, and of the conditions internal and external to the organization which have to be accommodated.   Such knowledge is often incomplete.   As we have noted, information flows are often distorted or blocked.   A surprisingly large number of people have jobs whose purpose has never been fully explained to them.   In smaller organizations this may not be too serious as an individual may readily be able to see what the organization is doing and where he fits into this effort.   But in larger organizations, where a person may be one of thousands in one of hundreds of departments, it is much harder to develop an adequate perspective. As a result, people can have widely different opinions of what the organization is after or what the purpose of a job is.   This variation can cause mismatching of individual programs and schedules.   To balance these problems of perception and program selection there is the vitally important asset of motivation, which comes from this enriched job content.[10]

Related to these issues, but at a different level of abstraction, are a number of elements important to voluntary coordination that revolve

[9] *Ibid.*
[10] See Chapter 2.

around the individual's identification with the organization. How willing and likely an individual is to do the extra things necessary for voluntary coordination depends on how meaningful they are to him.

INDIVIDUAL IDENTIFICATION WITH THE ORGANIZATION. Commitment to the organization and devotion to its purposes is thought by some to be the prime factor in an effective organization. Such identification makes people willing to put forth extra effort and put up with trying circumstances. Such an approach is typical of an army, particularly in wartime. The same emphasis exists in many other institutions such as hospitals, charitable institutions, and even business concerns. To develop and maintain such identification with the organization is believed by some to be a central factor in establishing an organization.[11] In terms used in Chapter 7, these are efforts to bring about the internalization of external sentiments or organizational values. Whereas a person's identification with an organization can be a valuable organizational element, to depend exclusively on it or to think that without it no organization can exist is to miscalculate its importance. Effective (even if not optimally effective) organizations exist where many members have little, if any, feeling of identity for the organization.

When people have a strong commitment to an organization and share a concept of organization tasks, rapid and effective voluntary coordination is possible. People have been found to keep close contact with those with whom their efforts must coordinate, such as design engineers and production technicians, when there are shared concepts of organization tasks *and* an easy flow of necessary information.[12]

ROLE PERCEPTION. The role in which a person sees himself substantially determines what he believes he should coordinate. An employee in a manufacturing function department, such as a welding department where great emphasis is placed on welding skill, may see a definite need to coordinate with other welders and quickly transmit new knowledge about welding techniques. But, not seeing himself as a worker who makes widgits, he may not think it very important to bring to anyone's attention the great number of widgits erroneously piled in a corner.

There are many different types of roles. One such might be described as the subservient role. Here an individual sees himself as a

[11] See, for example, James D. Mooney, *The Principles of Organization*, New York, Harper, 1947, pp. 10–13.
[12] See Tom Burns and G. M. Stalker, *The Management of Innovation*, Chicago, Quadrangle Books, 1961, Chapter 5.

person who accepts orders and does willingly what he is told, but does nothing else.   Under these circumstances he may not extend himself voluntarily to coordinate work.

ORGANIZATION PRACTICES TO PROMOTE VOLUNTARY COORDINATION.   A list of factors which influence the probability of an individual engaging in voluntary coordination could be extended much further.   This brief list is intended to establish the point that voluntary coordination is likely to be substantially influenced by the organization itself.   Hence, as managers design and operate organizations they determine, often inadvertently, the possibility of voluntary coordination.   We should not fail to mention overt practices in this direction, such as the selection of organizational members and their training.

Where self-coordination becomes more important, the processes of selection often become lengthier and more subjective.   A production worker may be selected largely on the basis of tasks and previous experience in a very short period.   Selecting an executive will have many more subjective factors and take much longer.   His apparent willingness to work hard and put in whatever time is necessary and pick up jobs which have to be done will usually weigh considerably more than his grade in education and tests on any score.   Other executives' feelings that he is a person they can rely on to deliver the goods may count more than years of experience.

Training will also increase and become more continuous in jobs requiring self-coordination.   Of course, we mean by training far more than formal educational programs about the mechanics of a job.   Such formal training programs are visible for production workers but, for all practical purposes, nonexistent for the executive.   For the lower level organization member, the training of the classroom or other forms of education usually end very quickly after employment.   For the higher executive training is likely to be a continuing thing: an executive development program, planned job rotation, and regular (often quarterly, sometimes even monthly) meetings with other executives where the company, its purposes, plans, and expectations are continually brought out and reinforced.

GROUP COORDINATIONS.   Groups can have a major influence on the amount of voluntary coordination.   We have already reviewed the impact of norms—for example, norms of helpfulness—the manner in which groups will pass on information about the jobs to make them easier, and we have seen how individuals may often identify more easily and completely with a group than with an organization.   Therefore, individuals often extend themselves to coordinate work for the group, which they can comprehend in a way they cannot for the larger aggregation of which the group is a part.

Since groups can be so important in promoting coordination, it seems important to have group boundaries coincide with or extend beyond the really important coordinative tasks of an organization. Let us presume that coordinating tasks 1, 2, and 3 in Figures 12.3*a* and *b* is a very difficult problem. Furthermore, let us presume that workers A, B, and C form a tight cohesive group generally supportive of the organization. Here the general orientation of the group is not toward the coordinative problem. Also, in bringing about some coordination between workers A and B with positions 1 and 2, interactions are established which may eventually weaken the existing-type group. Were workers A, B, and C in positions 1, 2, and 3, the existing social groups would support the coordinative problems and technical systems (Figure 12.3*b*).

PREFORMING DECISIONS. In an actual organization situations are seldom as disorganized as the preceding discussion might indicate. Even though precise instructions concerning what to do and when may not be given, individuals often receive guidance in a number of ways. In an organization elements are developed which mold or *preform* decisions that individuals will make, thereby enhancing the likelihood of coordinative action. Voluntary coordination is still used, in that it is self-starting and in detail self-directing, but it is now guided.

Policies are among the most general of such devices. A policy is a broad statement of an organization's intent in a particular area, and the general way in which this end will be achieved. Any large organization has many policies. Some are formally prepared and published, many just grow and are informally disseminated. A policy maintaining prompt shipment of customer orders guides an individual in making decisions so that his efforts fit well with overall organization activity. He might make a totally different decision in regard to the same problem if the policy were to keep operating costs at a minimum. Policies, as a rule, are fairly general statements, and consequently leave broad areas of discretion. Also, some areas of organizational activities are more critical making this latitude undesirable; other ways of preforming decisions become preferred.

One way of increasing coordination and, in general, of tightening decision-making activities is to limit or restrict an individual's scope of decision making. Common forms of such restrictions are limits on the

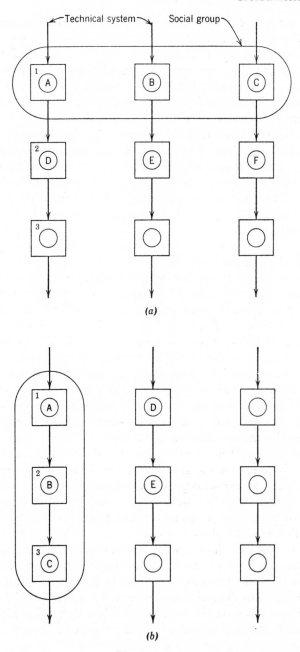

(a)

(b)

Figure 12.3

funds a manager can spend, the length of time he can commit the organization through contract, etc.

Although not always obvious, such restrictions are usually intended to eliminate or reduce one type of coordinative problem. A foreman may know, for example, that he is to complete work on a job by a certain time. To meet this deadline his department will have to work a considerable amount of overtime, more than he is authorized to use. Such a restriction may exist because of other problems the company has had with the union in regard to an unbalanced overtime work schedule. Limits to authority often keep efforts to increase coordination in one area from interfering with necessary coordination in another. The limits to the foreman's authority force the problem to another level in the organization, where someone will be in a position to determine which coordination problem is to be given priority.

Another device is a *decision rule*, an instruction that says, "When that sort of condition comes up, do this." A common form of decision rule is found in buying or purchasing. For example, "When buying any capital equipment costing more than one thousand dollars, bids must be received from at least three suppliers. Lowest bidder receives the order." Even this simple decision rule is often modified so the lowest bidder who also gives delivery within six weeks will receive the order or the lowest bidder who manufactures the product that can be serviced by a company's maintenance department will receive the order. *Wage plans* are another common type of decision rule. Wage plans spell out that individuals be paid for the work they do, with perhaps some bonus for seniority or higher output. Such decision rules are so common today that we hardly think of them. Yet most of them have developed within the last one hundred years, and constitute one of the vital ingredients in any large organization.

These ways to performing decisions leave considerable areas of discretion open to individual organization members. Any organization is concerned with how its members will make decisions within these areas. For example, does a salesman make a decision to coordinate activity to best serve his employer or does he choose those possibilities within the area open to him which are best for his customers who are often his friends? Does the individual policeman select those courses within his area of discretion that support an overall judicial system or choose those that serve the neighborhood in which he has his beat? In other words, does the individual identify more with the organization he is employed by or with the local community or environment?

One step taken by the organizations where this is a problem is to enforce rotation to keep systemic linkages with the nonorganization world from becoming too strong. The area of a policeman's beat is changed periodically; the forest to which a ranger is assigned is changed with regularity. In doing this the thought is that the individual will not be able to get so closely identified with the community that he will place its interest above the employing organization.[13]

Rotation can also influence coordination in another way. Men are sometimes rotated through organizations to broaden their outlook and contacts. A design engineer is given production experience, a production executive is put into the personnel department, etc. As a result they are expected not only to get a different view of the organization but also to make personal contacts with people with whom their efforts must be coordinated.[14]

Directive Coordination

Contrasted to voluntary coordination, directive coordination involves an individual receiving instructions both as to what to do and when to do it.

HIERARCHAL COORDINATION. In *hierarchal coordination*, activities are linked by having them under a central authority. In simplest form, as one employee finishes his job, the supervisor tells the next one to pick it up and perform the next operation. When the number of persons to be supervised becomes so large that one person cannot supervise all of them, the supervisory task is subdivided among two or more supervisors, and their efforts are coordinated by a position to which they all report. Hence, there is one central position which directly or indirectly can coordinate all linked activities. Although this is an appealing ideal, there are several fundamental flaws in this concept. First, it would be impossible for any one person to cope with all the coordinative problems which could come up to him through the chain of command. Second, there is great difficulty in having adequate information about the state of affairs in the organization, in facing the organization flow up the chain of command, and also in having accurate and sufficiently prompt orders or instructions flow down. This is not to say that coordination through hierarchal action is not possible. It does point out, however, that there are serious limitations to extending it too far. Furthermore, because of the difficulty of using

[13] See, for example, Herbert A. Kaufman, *The Forest Ranger*, Baltimore, Johns Hopkins Press, 1960, pp. 115–117 and 176–183.
[14] Victor A. Thompson, *Modern Organizations*, New York, Knopf, 1961, Chapter 9.

this form of coordination, thought should be given to reducing the necessity for it and for providing other ways of accomplishing the same result.

ADMINISTRATIVE SYSTEM.   A great deal of coordinative effort in organization is concerned with a horizontal flow of work of a routine nature. *Administrative systems* are formal procedures designed to carry out much of this routine coordinative work automatically. Some are exceedingly simple—so much so that their importance can be easily overlooked. A simple form of administrative system is the traveling work order or traveling ticket. This is a form which may be filled in by production-control clerks specifying a customer's order number, product number, quantity, and departments or operations to which the materials worked on will have to go. If we were making pulleys, the ticket might go first to the casting department where the proper molds would be brought from stock and the desired quantity of castings made. Then the castings and the ticket would be moved to the next department indicated, probably the machine department, and so on until eventually the ticket and the completed parts arrived at the shipping department. Here clerks would refer to the original order, find the customer's address, and send the order off. Often such a form has a detachable coupon which each department, on completing its work, detaches and sends back to the production-control clerk, who then has feedback regarding where the customer's order was at any one time. Even such a simple procedure can greatly simplify the coordinative problem, relieving supervisors of much running around and reducing the need for individual employees to engage in extensive amounts of voluntary coordination.

This simple form of administrative system is an essential element in integration, a long sequence of complex activities; yet it is only one part of an administrative system. For it to work, organization members have to be educated in use of the form. It contains essential information which is often meaningless to the uninitiated. Members of the organization, therefore, have to learn special symbols or arrangements of symbols which are used to record information. Second, organizational members have to be instructed as to what to do with the form. They must accept it as a legitimate order and do what it says: return the coupon, move the materials on to the next position, etc. In this sense administrative systems are a coordinative, or managerial, technology often unique to an organization and to be learned by its members; only then can it really be effective. In the last seventy or eighty years managerial technology has developed enormously.

Starting with simple production control (systems to coordinate work within a department or perhaps a factory) this managerial technology, with utilization of computers, has grown in recent years to extend across the whole span of company purchasing, manufacturing, selling, and distribution activities.

In essence, administrative systems are developed to take over portions of the routine coordinative work which otherwise would have to be handled largely by the managerial hierarchy and thereby free managers, particularly those in the higher positions, to handle more non-routine items.[15] Such developments, however, make organizations more specialized and therefore less flexible. Changes in objectives, technology, or environment then become progressively more difficult to deal with.

In reality most organizations use a combination of these ways of achieving coordination. Even where quite elaborate administrative systems are used there are still some areas where voluntary coordination becomes essential. Even where organizational members are most predisposed to voluntary coordination many organizations are so complex and have so many interdependencies that it would be impossible to get adequate coordination through these means. The problem is the classic one of management: to determine what the situation needs and then to assemble the best combination of partial solutions.

SUMMARY

This chapter stressed that coordination is not only an extremely important organization phenomenon but that it also has its own unique properties which require specific attention. Division of work, being concerned with the allocation of activities in order to achieve economies of effort, does not automatically provide for coordination. The needs and the facilitation of coordination must be analyzed and planned separately.

The need for coordination was seen as being influenced by two principal items: (1) the degree and type of division of work and (2) the environment of the organization. To satisfy this need two principal types of coordination are used: (1) coordination by plan wherein long-term, fixed plans and schedules are used and (2) coordination by feedback, where provisions are made for the flow of

[15] For more detailed discussion of the development and the details of administrative systems, see Joseph A. Litterer, "Systematic Management: Design for Organization Recoupling in American Manufacturing Firms," *Business History Review*, 37, 1963, pp. 369–391.

information about the work being coordinated. Except under extremely stable conditions only the second type can be used profitably.

Coordination is seen as the task of facilitating linked activities. This process has two fundamental elements: (1) determination of adequate programs for these activities and (2) communications to signal what program is to be used or the conditions for which a program is necessary and when action is needed.

Faced with a need for action, an individual might have a range of conditions to contend with in selecting a program—from those where programs are available, complete, and detailed to those where a program will have to be developed either through searching somewhere else for it, adapting an existing one, or creating a new one. Communications were also seen to have a wide range of forms from the specific, precise instruction or order to the general information about the state of the organization and its environment. The existence of these wide variations and the basic elements of coordination suggest the need for multiple means of achieving coordination from which the most acceptable element or a combination of them can be chosen.

Two principal strategies for promoting coordination were discussed: voluntary and directive. Each had two principal subdivisions: individual and group coordination and hierarchal and administrative systems coordination. The essential task in providing coordination is to find the best combination of these possibilities that can satisfy the coordinative needs of the organization.

Coordination is essentially an organizational problem. The extent and magnitude of the coordinative task is substantially influenced by other organizational decisions. The task itself can be accomplished by a number of combinations of several different means. This chapter has laid out some of the essential aspects of coordination. Many of these details are explored at considerable length in following chapters.

13

Control Processes and Systems

Control is a word that has a number of meanings. Those in popular usage differ considerably from the meaning used in this chapter. In everyday conversation, control is frequently used in the context of one person dominating another, that is, in a confining or coercive sense. In this chapter we are concerned with control in relation to matching performance with necessary or required conditions to obtain a purpose or objective. The essence here is on directivity and integration of effort, required accomplishment of an end. As we shall see later in the chapter, there are a number of different processes which produce control. Some of them fit the popular image of coercion and confinement; many others operate quite differently, more effectively, and, from a human point of view, much more favorably.

From what little has been said, it can be seen that control and co-ordination are closely related. In fact, recent developments in the area of control, or cybernetics, have shown the two to be the same in principle.

Control is concerned not only with events directly related to the accomplishment of major purposes but also with maintaining the organization in a condition in which it can function adequately to achieve these major purposes. For example, when a person exercises violently, he generates excess heat. His body adjusts to this state and starts a complex series of operations. Among other things he perspires, which cools the surface of the skin bringing more blood to it, which in turn can be cooled, etc. This whole series of events is intended to keep the body temperature within desired limits so that a person can continue to function instead of collapsing with heat exhaustion. Although this *organization maintenance* aspect of control, frequently neglected in organizational studies, is of extreme importance, it is touched on only lightly in this chapter.

Timing and Control

First, however, let us distinguish a number of types of control practices. Differentiation is based on the time relationship between the controlling effort and the act being controlled. When the controlling effort takes place prior to the act, we have *precontrol*. Much precontrol is concerned with avoiding or preventing undesired things from occurring, and frequently this means eliminating, removing the possibility of, or in some way preventing an undesired act from taking place. For example, parents who have small children keep their treasured bric-a-brac from being broken by placing it on high shelves which children cannot reach. In a business concern, junior managers are kept from making expensive blunders by restricting the amount of money they can spend.

Current control is concerned with the adjustment of performance still taking place in order to achieve an objective or standard. Turning the steering wheel on an automobile as it weaves slightly is one illustration, easing one's foot back from the accelerator when the speed of the automobile exceeds a safe level is another. Current control is likelier to consist in a person or machine making its own adjustments than to have some outside influence become involved with control, as usually occurs with precontrol.

Postcontrol, or evaluation, occurs when there is an effort to check on whether events did come out as desired. For example, the business concern balances its books at the end of the year to see whether it made the profit it desired. The higher officers in the army make inspection trips every few weeks or months to see whether military units are being maintained at a desired level of performance. This is checking after the fact, which means that information may be gathered regarding where people stand, but may not permit any corrective action to take place in regard to the performance completed. It provides an opportunity to evaluate and adjust the parameters of the system for future operations. Such changes might include relocating a plant, changing work flows in a government office, changing the size of an area covered by a charity drive, etc.

The process of control discussed in the following paragraphs can, if considered in a general way, include all three of these control practices. We should also note that in many organizations all three can be utilized at the same time. For the most part, the illustration and remaining portions of the chapter pertain to current control situations.

THE CONTROL PROCESS

In recent years the study of control has received a great deal of attention by people in a number of different fields. This has come about with the realization that control is basic to an extraordinarily wide array of things. Physiologists are concerned with how our bodies control temperature and blood pressure within very narrow ranges. The ecologists are concerned with why most animal populations seem to stay about the same size. The economist is concerned with why our economy can only increase at a certain rate or what prevents it from falling into a permanent depression. The engineer is concerned with how to keep a rocket on its course. The business executive is concerned with how to keep costs down and income high enough to maintain a desired profit. Although the mechanisms of control are different in each of these situations, analysis shows the process is the same. Therefore, people have begun to study control as a universal process, a topic which can be studied in its own right. So important is this area of inquiry that it has been given a name, *cybernetics*.[1] Much of the work in cybernetics is quite abstract and often uses complex, mathematical analysis. The basic element in the control process, however, can be simply presented.

A typical illustration of control is the thermostat regulating the temperature of the house. This elementary application of control begins when the temperature in the house drops below desired level, for example, 65 degrees. A temperature-indicating device in the thermostat detects this low temperature and causes a circuit to be closed, which turns on the furnace, heating the house, and causing the temperature to rise. The thermostat detects when the house temperature reaches a maximum point, say 72 degrees, and opens the circuit causing the furnace to stop operation, keeping the house from getting any warmer. When the house temperature drops to 65 degrees the sequence is repeated. This simple application contains all the basic elements of the control cycle. There is a data-gathering phase in which a device, in this case a thermometer, generally called a *sensor*, gathers information about the temperature of the room. Then comes a comparing or examination phase when the desired temperature is compared with the standard by a unit called a *discriminator*. After

---

[1] There are two excellent introductory books to this area: Norbert Wiener, *The Human Use of Human Beings*, New York, Doubleday, 1954, and Stafford Beer, *Cybernetics and Management*, New York, John Wiley, 1959.

this comparison is made and, for example, the temperature is noted to be too low corrective action is instigated; the furnace is turned on by a unit which we will call a *decision maker.*[2] Once the furnace is running, the first phases are repeated until the discriminator determines that the temperature has reached or exceeded the upper limit; then another action is instituted, and the furnace is shut off.

The basic steps in the control process identified thus far are: gathering data on performance, comparison of data with a standard, and taking corrective action if performance does not match the standard properly. These phases are carried out by a sensor, discriminator, and decision maker.

Let us carry the illustration one step further and suppose that the weather becomes very cold, so much so that when the furnace operates continuously, it is still not able to maintain temperature in the house at the desired 65 degrees minimum. The homeowner may note (a) that he is using a great deal of fuel and (b) that the continual operation of the furnace is threatening to damage the motor which circulates air through the furnace. He may then decide that the best thing to do is to bundle himself and his family into sweaters and coats and to lower the adjustment on the thermostat to 40 degrees, which is sufficient to keep the pipes from freezing but not high enough to impose any strain on either his pocketbook or the furnace motor. This is a major alternative in any control cycle; instead of taking corrective action one adjusts the standard. These elements and their relationship in the control process are shown in Figure 13.1. In the long run the homeowner may decide that living in a house heated to only 40 degrees is too uncomfortable. This makes comfort a higher order standard and leads him to insulate his home, thereby changing the parameters of the system.

An illustration of the control process in a business organization might consist of a clerk gathering cost data, passing them on to an accountant who compiles them and compares them with a budget figure, and then calls deviations to the attention of a line executive who takes some corrective action to bring performance into line with the budget.

[2] Sometimes this is referred to as the *controller* or *control;* however, using this term in conjunction with the control processes or control cycle seems to lead to confusion. The reader may find it difficult to think of an inanimate object as a decision maker; however, in the broad sense of the term decision making is the choice between alternatives. In effect, the thermostat is making a choice of turning the furnace on or leaving it off. Since most of our decisions of control are in organizations, the use of the term "decision maker" should not be too awkward.

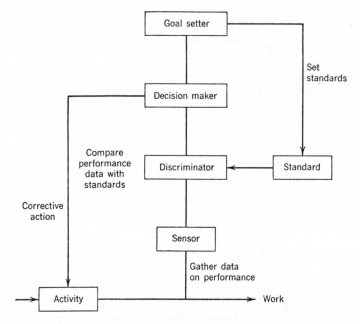

Figure 13.1.   Basic control cycle.

Closed and Open Control Loops

The thermostat illustration is a *closed control loop*. That is, the current performance provides information which is used to control future performance; the information and direction of future perform-ance goes through a feedback loop (Figure 13.2*a*), through a sensor, discriminator, and decision maker to activity.   Contrasted to this sys-tem are *open loops*.   Here, activities may change in accordance with a plan or program, but there is no way to evaluate current performance to modify future ones (Figure 13.2*b*).

An example of an open loop is an automatic washer.   Clothes are washed for a predetermined time, since the machine operates a pre-determined time whether clothes are clean or even if they are not there.   To put this differently, the presence of dirty clothes does not start the machine nor does the presence of clean clothes stop it.   Looking at the washer as a clothes-cleaning system we see that the sensor and the discriminator are missing; they have to be provided by an outside element, the housewife.   In a closed loop the sensor, discriminator, and the decision maker are all part of the same system.   In an open loop, one or more elements are missing thus preventing

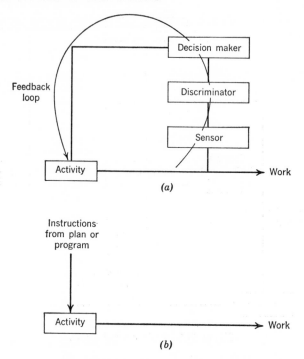

Figure 13.2. (*a*) Feedback loop, and (*b*) open loop.

feedback. The functions of the missing elements must be provided from outside the system, as when the housewife decides that there are sufficient dirty clothes in the machine and starts it or when she decides that one washing cycle has not washed the clothes clean enough and takes corrective action by putting them through another cycle. Coordination by plan, discussed in the preceding chapters, is an open-loop control system, and coordination by feedback is a closed-loop system.

The Closed and Open Control Systems

In the thermostat illustration all the elements involved in the control process were focused within the house. Although it was the outside temperature that caused the house to cool off which was, therefore, the real source of deviation from standard, this was never taken directly into account. When factors external to a system influence it, we have an open system. When a system is isolated or sealed off from external disturbances, it is a closed system. The thermostat illustration is a closed-loop open system. Insulating the house would make it more of a closed system permitting the control-loop elements to operate more predictably.

Control systems, such as production-control systems, budgets, etc., are sometimes designed to be closed systems with the assumption, often implicit, that no external influences have to be considered. However, organizations are open systems. In some areas they are becoming more open as, for example, happens when more groups feel they have a right to, and learn how to, bring pressure on government agencies and business concerns. In some areas they are becoming more closed. Automation, air conditioning, and other developments are making production systems more nearly closed systems. Analyzing open systems is far more complex than analyzing closed systems, often making it a practical necessity to assume a closed system, but this should be done knowing the limitations this imposes on the analysis and the decisions resulting from it.

SELF-REGULATING SYSTEMS

The illustration of the thermostat is so simple and commonplace that one of its important properties can be easily overlooked. Once established, this control process takes place continuously, keeping the temperature of the house at a desired level. Although the temperature varies slightly, it tends toward the desired level. It therefore tends toward equilibrium.

In Chapter 8 we noted that parts interconnected to accomplish a purpose are identified as a system. The thermostat, the air in the room, the furnace, and the radiator constitute a system—a temperature controlling system that continuously and automatically tends toward equilibrium. This is a contrived system. However, there are many others occurring naturally, which have this same property called *homeostasis*.[3] The ability of the body to control the temperature of blood is one example of homeostasis. In an organization, modern production-control techniques not only plan production schedules but also build in ways to check whether these schedules are being maintained; should there be any variation there are procedures established for corrective action, which are self-regulating to keep production flowing smoothly without the higher executives getting involved in the process.

We have already noted that organizations are complexes of systems.

[3] Beer, *op. cit.*, p. 22.

We are now establishing that many systems are self-regulating, or to put it directly, organizations are self-regulating. Most of the illustrations used thus far have been deliberately created self-regulatory systems, such as production control or budgets. Whereas there are many of these planned cybernetic systems in an organization, there are also a great many unplanned ones.

An illustration would be the type of event which is familiar to anyone who has worked in an actual organization. Periodically there are drives on certain areas of organizational performance. Not uncommonly, every few months or so top executives announce that costs are out of line and must be reduced. Great pressure is put on everyone in the organization to make better use of materials and labor in an effort to eliminate all unnecessary expenditures. After this has gone on awhile, costs probably are reduced and this topic will be quietly dropped while some other drive, such as quality or housekeeping, is taken up. These drives, occurring intermittently and often being rather general, are usually deplored by observers of organizational affairs.

It should be noted that from the standpoint of earlier theories of an organization, such practice is improper and an evidence of bad management. Costs should be controlled regularly, earlier theory insists. In fact, it is hard to envision anything of an intermittent nature being consistent with traditional concepts. However, if we use cybernetic concepts to analyze what occurs in organizations, these drives become understandable. Top management, having taken a periodic check on costs, noting they are high, brings this undesired situation to the attention of lower managers insisting that they do something about this. When costs are reduced, the pressure is removed until, of course, costs again appear to rise and the cycle is repeated. In this way the intermittent pressure for reducing costs is not at all unlike the intermittent operation of the furnace in the thermostat illustration.

This is not to say that a drive technique is the best way of achieving cost control; however, it is at least understandable using cybernetic concepts. Furthermore, recognizing these events for what they are we can use the same concepts to devise better ways of achieving these ends. Without cybernetic concepts, and using only earlier concepts, the tendency was to say a practice was wrong and should have been eliminated. In effect, this would have eliminated necessary, if not very sophisticated, self-regulation of the organization. There are a vast multitude of self-regulating systems in any organization. We shall discuss some of them in more detail later in this chapter.

AREAS OF UNDECIDABLE DECISIONS

One of the factors that makes the functioning of self-regulating systems difficult at times is that they have blind spots where elements working with them are incapable of adequately understanding what is going on. For example, envision an individual, who has never seen an airplane, going to an abridged dictionary and finding under the word "airplane" that it is defined simply as "a heavier-than-air ship." Not knowing what this is, he turns to the definition of the heavier-than-air ship and finds that it is an airplane. At the end of this search this person has no more idea of what an airplane is than when he began. Another example of this situation might concern examination of deeds to real estate. A person reading the legal description of the property he is about to buy may find that it runs ". . . due east to the Thompson property thence turning south along this property. . . ." A crucial question then is, "Where is the boundary line to the Thompson property?" Investigating further in the Recorder of Deeds' office he finds the description of the Thompson property reads ". . . running a quarter of a mile, more or less to the property owned by Ivan Morse. . . ." which happens to be the farm he is buying. When this occurs in a language, the language is said to be incomplete and not self-sufficient.[4]

No natural language is entirely complete or self-sufficient. The same is true of systems and, in fact, has to be since "language" is vital to the transmission of information in a system; but the problem can enter systems in another way. Suppose that on detecting the temperature of the air, the thermostat in a house sends electrical signals into a wire that goes to an entirely different building. There a person is expected to read the meter, and, observing that the temperature as indicated by the meter has fallen to a certain level, throw a switch which starts the motor on the furnace back at the house. How does the observer of the meter know positively what the temperature is in the house? The fact that the meter indicates 70 degrees may mean that the temperature in the house *is* 70 degrees. However, if there is some error in the system, such as the temperature-sensing mechanism in the room not working right or the needle being positioned incorrectly on the shaft in the meter, the temperature of the house may not actually be 70 degrees. The only thing he knows is that the needle on the meter points to 70. This system cannot tell with certainty that the needle is registering correctly.

[4] *Ibid.*, pp. 69–75.

To cope with these "blind spots" we have to make use of another vocabulary or system outside the one in which the doubt exists. In describing an airplane, we might break out the problem by going to another means of communication, such as finding a picture of an airplane. In the meter-reading situation, we could cope with the arrangement by having an alternate temperature-detecting system. The observer might use the telephone to call the house and ask someone to read a wall thermometer. The strategy in these solutions is the same. The incompleteness of the system or language is compensated for by resorting to something outside of the system—by using another language or another system.[5]

VARIATIONS IN THE ALLOCATION OF ELEMENTS IN THE CONTROL PROCESS

The control systems of an organization can be implemented in a number of ways. One variation is in the manner in which the elements in the control process are allocated to different organizational members.

A common situation exists when a superior gives a worker instructions that tell him what is to be accomplished: "Make twenty-five widgets of good quality." Here the foreman is giving a standard to the worker. The rest of the control operation is left in the worker's hands. The worker himself will gather data on how well he is performing by counting the items produced and by measuring them to determine their quality. He will make decisions about whether more will have to be made, whether adjustments are necessary on his machines, etc. This type of situation can be seen in Figure 13.3.

However, there are times when the worker is primarily concerned with executing instructions and makes relatively few, if any, decisions about when work is to be performed or when it is complete. For example, foundries are sometimes organized so that the furnaces in which metals are processed are under the direction of a furnace chief. Each furnace chief may have one or more assistants whom he directs. In operating the furnace, the furnace chief, for all practical purposes, makes all decisions. He may, for example, tell a worker to start putting scrap metal into the furnace. The furnace chief watches the material being added until finally he concludes there is enough for his purposes and tells the subordinate to stop. The furnace chief probably makes his decisions based on the instructions he has received from his boss or from the production-control department, which tells him

[5] *Ibid.*, pp. 76–81.

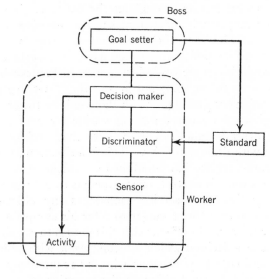

Figure 13.3

how many tons of what type and quality metal are to be produced. Where the worker is primarily concerned with performing the activity, the sensing and decision-making activities are handled by the furnace chief, and the production goals are established by the manager of the production-control department (Figure 13.4). We might note that with the production standards established the situation can be kept in control by the furnace chief unless something rather extraordinary happens, such as running out of a needed alloy. In this case, the furnace chief will probably turn to his superior to ask whether he should produce a smaller quantity of the desired type of metal using the limited amount of alloy or a larger quantity of a different type of metal. This would cause the superior to restate in some way the standards toward which the furnace chief is to guide his performance. In traditional management literature, this phenomenon is called the *exercise of exception principle*. That is, the furnace chief knows what to do under ordinary circumstances and does not go to his boss except when some unusual event arises.

It is possible for all elements in the control process to be under one person or a group of people. An interesting example is the operation of the forest service.[6] The problem here is that the United States

[6] Herbert Kaufman, *The Forest Ranger*, Baltimore, Johns Hopkins Press, 1960, pp. 6, 66–67.

maintains extensive forests throughout the country. These are managed by forest rangers who have to make many decisions in the light of local situations. However, these decisions are made in the context of overall forest service policies, many of which are established by Congress. Many decisions are made in response to requests by individual citizens who want to use some portions of the forest, for example, for logging operations or grazing. With thousands of forest rangers scattered throughout the country making a wide array of decisions, it is difficult for central authorities to be sure that decisions are always made in line with desired policies. This is a situation in need of control. The forest service has established a number of ways providing feedback loops for this control; one of these is to use the public. As a general policy the forest service encourages any citizen dissatisfied with the decision of a forest ranger to refer his complaint to a higher authority for review. In effect, what this does is to say that if a forest ranger has made a decision which is incompatible with policy, it probably will be challenged by someone who, by requesting a review, will bring the unsatisfactory decision to the attention of higher authorities. Figure 13.5 shows this relationship: the forest ranger is engaged in certain activities, the public functions as the sensor, higher executives are the decision makers who bring about corrective action

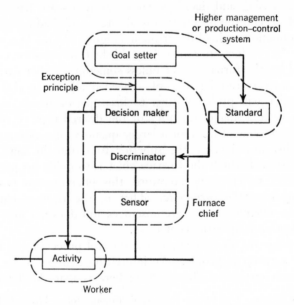

Figure 13.4. Allocation of control-process elements in a foundry.

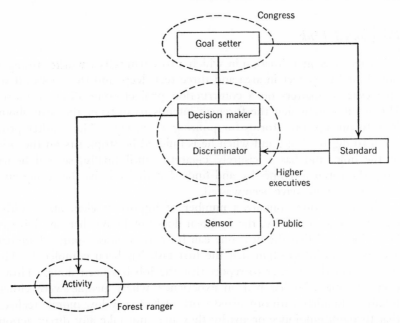

Figure 13.5. Allocation of control-process elements in the forest service.

through revoking or amending the ranger's decision. The decision maker, of course, uses standards established by still higher authorities, in some cases Congress itself.

These illustrations should give some indication of the variations that can occur in the allocation of elements of the control process. Needless to say, these variations have a significant affect on the effectiveness with which the control process is carried out. As noted when discussing division of work, the further work is subdivided, the greater becomes the problem of coordinating the parts. Hence, as we go from having most of the control elements in the hands of one person to having them spread out over a number of people or groups who, in turn, may be widely separated geographically, psychologically, or organizationally, the problem of maintaining effective control becomes greater.

CONTROL AND COORDINATION

Having covered the essential core of control let us now consider how several control loops are connected to provide that synchronization of effort we think of as coordination.

Programed Link

Let us envision a situation in which a foreman tells a worker to dig a hole four by six feet in area and three feet deep, and then goes off to take care of matters on a construction project some distance away. When the hole is dug the foreman intends to instruct the man about how to put up some forms for pouring a footing. The worker proceeds to dig the hole, and when he is finished he stops, sits on the side of the hole, and has a leisurely cigarette until finally, several hours later, the foreman comes by and finds that the hole has been dug and that several hours have been wasted.

This illustration contains a number of important elements. Without chancing to pass by, the foreman does not know that one job has been done and that the next one can be started unless some additional act occurs to inform him that the first task has been completed. He may expect the worker to report that the job has been done. However, anyone who has had an experience where people were either totally unfamiliar with organized work or had very low morale realizes that through ignorance or apathy they may not take any direct action to inform the foreman. If, however, the foreman had given instructions to dig the hole and put into the program the additional instruction to report to him immediately on completion of the task, this difficulty could have been avoided or at least diminished. Since this instruction facilitates linking the completed act with the next one through an information transfer, we call this a programmed link.

The foreman, of course, may detect that something is wrong through another control cycle. He can then take corrective action by including or adding this programmed link or perhaps by attacking the more difficult problem of apathetic attitudes and motivation his employees are displaying. Supplying the step is essentially a coordinative act, the necessity for which has been revealed through a control process.

Progression of Goals

In Chapter 8 we noted that organizations have progressions of goals which result from a division of work. A subdivided goal becomes the standard of control process contained within a specialized organizational unit. We also noted that this nesting of goals is contained in the means-ends chain. Let us now consider how these elements are connected in an organizational hierarchy (Figure 13.6).

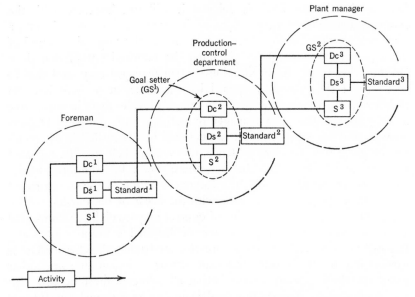

Figure 13.6. Progression of goals or standards and control loops.

Assume a factory situation in which the foreman gives detailed in-structions to his workers regarding what activities they are to perform, but he conducts most of the control process relevant to those activi-ties. Hence, in Figure 13.6, the foreman would be acting as sensor (S^1), discriminator (Ds^1), and decision maker (Dc^1). To keep the performance of the activity in line with the standard (Standard^1) he has been given by the goal setter (GS^1), which in this case is the production control department, he takes corrective action as necessary. Let us suppose that a machine breaks down, and the foreman sees he is not going to be able to meet the standard by producing the necessary quantity of goods within the required time. He calls the production control clerk responsible for that particular order (S^2) asking that the standard be changed by giving him extra time to meet the quantity, that the quantity be reduced to what he can produce within the time, or that he be authorized to work overtime to meet the original stand-ard. The production-control clerk knows that there is some slack time in production schedules, but is not in a position to determine the use of this extra time. Consequently, he refers the report from the foreman with other related schedules and information to his superior, the production-control manager; the manager compares what is going on with the overall schedule of work in the department and makes the decision that if the work is delayed it will not interfere with the company commitments for which he is responsible as spelled out by his standard (Standard[2]).   Hence, he modifies the original standard of the foreman (Standard[1]) by changing the required completion date. On the other hand, the production-control manager may find that to take any of the courses proposed by the foreman he will have to violate one of the standards given to him.   Thus he may, in turn, have to consult with the plant manager or perhaps with the Sales Department to find out whether the customer will be dissatisfied if the goods are shipped a few days late.   Hence, this whole cycle may be repeated through an S^3, Ds^3, Dc^3.   In fact, there could be additional cycles which would permit, ideally, the foreman's activities to be controlled so that they are perfectly in tune with the needs of the outside world.

Needless to say, the hierarchy of control loops which are connected with the progression of goals may be handled a number of ways. Regardless of how the elements are allocated (that is, whether Ds^2 is carried out by the production manager or a person in some other position), the important factor is that all elements must be provided for in some way.   Hence, our model supplies an extremely useful tool in analyzing complex control situations by telling us what basic functions must occur and in what sequence, even though initially we have no idea as to where or how they are executed in the organization.

Loops within Loops

Since organizations seldom have one-for-one reporting relationships, the actual pattern of control loops is more complex than shown in Figure 13.6.   Let us take a simplified manufacturing situation which consists of a production department under a production superintendent, a procurement department under a purchasing manager, and a shipping department under a shipping foreman, all of whom report to a plant manager (Figure 13.7).

The details of individual control loops are not shown but are presumed included within one position signified by a circle.   Hence, we see the individual worker in the production department, for example, checking the performance of his own activities (shown by a square) and correcting them.   He, in turn, receives standards and instructions from the production superintendent, who may develop some of these from observing the performance of his department.   The production superintendent, in turn, receives instructions from the plant manager, who may base part of them on observations of the whole plant performance.   In this situation the production superintendent is a key

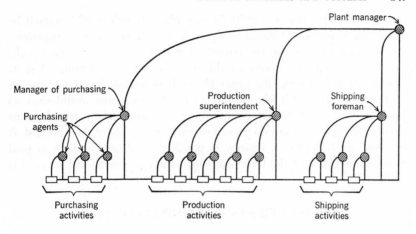

Figure 13.7. Simplified schematic of control loops within loops.

element in the control system, for he is in one loop with the production worker and in another with the plant manager.

Feedback and Goal Formation

In the illustration, the feedback loop containing information about organizational performance and conditions leads to definition of subunit goals or standards. We also showed how a situation in one area could lead to modifications in a number of organizational units at higher levels. Presumably this solution could even result in reformulating the basic goals of the organization. For example, the company may establish the goal of getting into a certain market. After working toward this end, it may find that the short-delivery-times demands by customers in this market cannot be met by its production facilities, and the feedback may result in company executives deciding that the goal of entering this market will have to be abandoned and a new market sought. Feedback is essential to adequate goal formation.

This leads us to an important point which, when stated without the type of development presented, appears to be a somewhat mystical statement; namely, organizations automatically take actions to bring about their continuity or to perpetuate themselves. In the foregoing illustration, if the organization had not changed its goal and had attempted to enter the initially desired market, it probably would have been faced with either losing customers or incurring exceedingly high costs to meet the delivery times unless, of course, it was going to carry on a massive investment activity in new plant, which would in itself be a shifting of goals. Without this plan, however, to persist in maintaining the goal of entering the particular market would leave two paths open to the company; both would mean failure—one through loss of customers and income, the other through incurring losses because of high costs. To put it bluntly, either the organization would shift its goals or face disaster. Of course there are times when organizations do not change goals and do go out of existence. Many, however, shift to those goals feedback defines as possible; feedback leading to goal redefinition is one of the basic ways by which organizational survival is achieved.

DIFFICULTIES IN OBTAINING CONTROL

Whether control systems arise naturally or are deliberately planned, they do not always function effectively. There may be changes in the organization which interfere with one or more elements in the control process. For example, action by higher management can substantially influence the filtering [7] that takes place as information flows from superior to subordinate. Without elaborating in detail, it can be seen easily that actions of management which influence any of the basic concepts discussed earlier—communications, motivations, perception, groups—can, but not necessarily must, influence one or more elements in the control process. Needless to say, the difficulties that can arise in regard to control are endless. We shall restrict discussion to a few of the more common types which arise in regard to planned or formal control systems.

Incompleteness of the System

We began this chapter by noting that the term "control" can have several meanings, some of which are not very close to the concept we have been discussing. However, since these different interpretations exist we should expect that at times inadequate control systems are designed.

This is true if a control system is only partially developed, that is, some elements fully developed and others hardly at all. Such a situation has been effectively described in a study on the use of budgets.[8] In this study, where budgets were to be used for control, it was found

[7] Reducing or modifying message content. See Chapter 14.
[8] Chris Argyris, *The Impact of Budgets on People*, New York, Controllers Institute Research Foundation, 1952.

that members of the finance department who were responsible for handling budget procedures would gather data on the performance of departments. These, in turn, would be compared with the departmental budgets, and when there was a deviation of performance from standard this was brought to the attention of the foreman in charge who was expected to take corrective action. On the surface, this sounds like a fairly complete system. There was a problem, however, in that while the data collected were in sufficient detail to determine whether total cost expenditures, for example, were within budget limits, there was insufficient detail for the foreman to analyze the problem and take adequate corrective action. This placed the foreman in a frustrating position. The budget procedure brought to the foremen and their superiors a continual flow of data on performance, which often was at variance from standard. As a result the foremen were under continuous pressure from their superiors and members of the budget department. The budget became a system for developing pressure and frustration,[9] not a means of achieving control.

Time Discrepancies

Another problem that can exist with control is that the feedback of information on performance takes so long it became impossible to correct performance. For example, in a department working on a job-lot basis where each job is unique, if department costs are inspected only after the entire job has been completed, the data received may be useless for purposes of control. Such systems are useful for finding out whether performance is adequate but not for taking corrective action. In short, they are better suited to punishment than correction.

There is another aspect of time which should be mentioned. As we shall note in Chapter 16, the time horizon of people in an organization gets progressively shorter as we come down in a hierarchy. Foremen can be described as working in a relatively closed time horizon; that is, they deal with immediate problems, today's difficulties or next week's or, at the most, next month's production schedule. Consequently, what may happen six months or a year from now is so far off that it does not receive attention. Hence, as in the preceding illustration, if the feedback is about a project just completed (therefore, itself not suited to being controlled), but one which may be repeated eight months or a year in the future, the feedback information could be used to improve operations on the repetition. The problems created by time horizons suggest strongly that the information will still not be

[9] *Ibid.*, pp. 18–20.

used by the foremen.   Hence, by taking into account the perceptions of organizational members along with the time during which work is being performed on a project, we can begin to define a time period within which feedback must occur if adequate corrective action is to be taken.[10]

Communication Distortions

An important aspect of control is the adequacy of the communications which occur.   We are interested in any organizational conditions which interfere with communications; we identify but two of the many here.

POOR CHANNELS.   One way of getting feedback, as already noted, is to use a third party as a communications' channel.   For example, in discussing the forest service, it was pointed out that the higher management of the service receives useful feedback on the performance of the local forest rangers from individuals who have to deal with the rangers through the public's right of appeal.   The use of the "right of appeal" to get feedback would seem to be a simple and effective device.   However, it is often set up in such a way as to limit its utility seriously.   An example of this situation may be seen in the military where the private, if he feels he is being unfairly treated by his sergeant, can appeal to his commanding officer for relief.   The difficulty comes when he finds that in order to see the captain, he must first get the permission of his sergeant.   Even though he is told that his request for a personal interview with the captain will never be denied and that this is just a way of seeing that the captain's time is not abused, the consequences of this provision are obvious.

NONCONGRUENT GOALS.   In Chapter 8 we noted that organizations have many different goals of subunits, departments and individuals, and that although these do not have to be identical, at least they have to be congruent or supportive of one another.   If they are not, one of the numerous and serious troubles is that people will be talking about things that do not match, and the effect is a great deal of noise in the control systems.   An example of such a situation might be two people who are greatly concerned with eliminating juvenile delinquency.   They may talk for some time before it becomes clear that although both are interested in reducing this social problem, one wants to do it through punitive action, arresting and putting in prison anyone

[10] *Ibid.*, pp. 28–29.

suspected of being a juvenile delinquent, and the other wants to do it through education and social services which change attitudes and living conditions.   Should these two attempt to work together and establish some control systems for their united efforts, the distortions introduced by this noncongruency of goals would seriously hamper the likelihood of effective coordination or control.

OVERLY SIMPLIFIED SYSTEMS

At times those responsible for designing control systems will feel that the simpler the control system, the less likelihood there is of difficulties arising and the more likelihood there is of success.   Needless to say, unnecessary extension of any system through more details or steps can increase the possibility of the system developing problems and functioning improperly.

At the same time there is a possibility that some control systems can become so simplified that they suit only very special conditions.   Let us suppose that a production system which we are attempting to control is to produce blocks of wood six inches square.   We could check to see whether we were meeting this standard by handing the inspector or workmen a standard which consisted of a stick cut off at exactly six inches, and telling him to reject any piece that was longer or shorter than this standard.   This would be fine until the day we decided to make blocks seven inches square; then our control system would be inadequate until we prepared a new standard stick.   In a situation as tangible and obvious as this, the inadequacy of an earlier specialized system is so obvious that it presents no real difficulty, just inconvenience.   However, in other matters which are not so easily seen or understood, oversimplification of the control system may lead to serious but less obvious problems.   Since we live in a world where there are constant changes and variations, our control systems must have enough slack in them to cope with reasonably expected variations.   As Beer succinctly summarized, the problem with overly simple systems is that, ". . . so far from not going wrong, they cannot go right." [11]

SUMMARY

In this chapter we dealt with relatively few ideas, noting them in simple fashion.   It is hoped that this treatment will not lull the reader into thinking that these ideas are unimportant or easily applied in

[11] Beer, *op. cit.*, p. 50.

practice. Nothing could be further from the truth. They are extraordinarily important and they are extremely difficult to deal with in practice. Control systems or cybernetics systems are so extraordinarily complex that it is difficult to deal with them in any detailed fashion. We are likely to find analyses which discuss the performance of organizational elements in handling the control process but relatively little discussion of how this is accomplished. Doubtless as time goes on our knowledge of these details will grow. We mention the inadequacy of our knowledge at this time for two reasons: (1) so the reader will have an appreciation of the complexity of the problem and (2) to point out that even if we do not know many details, we are still able to use cybernetics systems to cope with many important problems. Our ignorance of the details of cybernetics systems may limit our ability to cope with these problems; it does not, however, prevent or cripple us.

Control systems are to a considerable degree influenced by a number of basic organizational phenomena already discussed. Principal among them are perception formation, motivation, and communications. Variations in these phenomena will influence the effectiveness of any organizational control system.

The basic elements of the control process were few in number: (1) gathering of data about performance by a sensor; (2) comparison of performance with standard by a discriminator; (3) when a difference between performance and standard is noted, two courses of action are likely to be taken by a decision maker: (a) to undertake corrective action which will bring performance back into line with standards perhaps by selecting or developing a new program or (b) to direct information about this difference to a goal setter for the establishment of new goals or the redefining of old ones.

When these elements exist, there is control through self-regulation of whatever entity contains them. The elements, however, may be allocated in a number of ways within the entity. They may all be performed by one person or each element may be performed by a different person or, for that matter, by different departments. As the work of carrying the control cycle is divided further, coordination of this effort becomes more difficult.

Control as we have been discussing it is one type of system. Hence, we find control has many of the same properties as systems in general; numerous systems interlocked in many ways. One such way may be seen when there are hierarchies of systems paralleling progressions of goals. There are also control systems within control systems or, as we have more frequently referred to this, control loops within control loops. Since control is also a system, it can influence other systems and in turn be influenced by them. Looking at control as a particular type of system makes us appreciate how extraordinarily complex a topic it is, and at the same time gives us an extremely valuable approach to this difficult subject.

14

Communication Systems

COMMUNICATION involves transactions between people. Its interpersonal nature makes it singularly important for the study of organizations. Indeed, so essential are communications to an organization that some analysts maintain that if we could identify all the channels conveying information and the means by which information influences the behavior of the organization, we would be close to understanding the organization itself.[1]

The importance of communication emerges from review of a number of aspects of organization for which communications serve as an independent variable or a constraint. As a flow of information communications constitute an essential component of a system of coordination, a person in a position to receive a great deal of information can acquire both power and status. Groups are characterized by a relatively easy flow of information. This property is one basis for their cohesiveness. By giving a person information, groups help him form his perception of the world. Through communication people receive stimuli which evoke sets of alternative actions and induce them to behave.

This brief and partial inventory of the ways in which communications are significant to the functioning of organizations clearly demonstrates the importance of the topic. Communication, however, is extraordinarily broad and complex. One sector, semantics, concerns itself with the meaning of symbols and words. Another sector, syntax, is concerned with the systematic properties of communication, that is, the relations between the symbols used. In communications such as the written or spoken word, syntax is concerned with the relationships among letters forming words or the relationships among words in a

[1] Karl W. Deutsch, "On Communication Models in the Social Sciences," *The Public Opinion Quarterly*, 16, 1952, p. 367.

sentence, grammar.   A third part of communication is concerned with pragmatics and focuses on the relationship between communication and purposeful action.[2]   Each of these approaches to communication represents an enormous field of study with many subdivisions.   Although this chapter also touches on all three aspects of communication, its general orientation is more directed.   The central question here is "How does information move through an organization?"   Our concern is with a general communications system.   Much of the communications that occur in organizations primarily involve people, and, hence, many times the specific illustrations of the general system pertain to communications among individuals.

A BASIC MODEL OF A COMMUNICATIONS SYSTEM 1

The following presentation of the communication systems is developed from the ideas advanced by Claude Shannon.   Shannon originally developed his model of communications while working on problems of telephone communications.   Analytical and highly mathematical rather than empirical, these ideas have been the foundation for many new concepts, a large number of them grouped under the title of "Information Theory."   The interesting and important aspects of these concepts are that they have been found applicable in analyzing not only problems of communications by telephone and radio but also in mechanical systems with links and levers and in social systems with human beings.   Shannon's model is a general model of communications useful wherever there is a flow of information.[3]

The basic elements in the Shannon model are shown in Figure 14.1. The block labeled Sender identifies the place, person, or equipment, which produces the message and sends it out.   For the message to move between sender and Receiver requires some way of its being conveyed, a Channel.   Channels can take many forms; a simple illustration is telephone wires.   Channels may also be radio waves, light waves, sound waves, pieces of paper, etc.   They constitute one of the important topics of this chapter.   We are concerned here not only with the various forms of channels but also the ways in which organizations create them or facilitate or impede their creation.   We might note that channels may function to convey information in either one

[2] For further elaboration of this concept, the reader is referred to Colin Cherry, *On Human Communications*, New York, Science Editions, 1961, particularly pp. 2–16 and 217–255.
[3] See Claude E. Shannon and Warren Weaver, *The Mathematical Theory of Communications*, Urbana, University of Illinois Press, 1963.

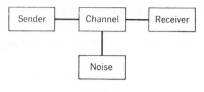

Figure 14.1

direction or two.   The telephone illustrates a two-way channel.   On the other hand, a television program is a unidirectional channel.

Channels are not perfect devices to convey messages.   They are subject to innumerable disturbances, many of them unpredictable, which distort, confuse, or even block and therefore interfere with the accuracy of the transmission of information.   This interference is called *noise* and is comprised of anything moving in the channel apart from the actual signals or messages wanted by the sender.[4]   In a telephone conversation, noise would be both the static from a passing thunderstorm and the words of another conversation which might be coming on the line through cross talk.   To be realistic, we have to take into account not only the noise of the channel, as the figure shows, but also of the sender and the receiver.   Hence as we listen to a radio, we are concerned not only with the static generated as a result of an electrical storm but also with the background buzz or hum which comes from thermal disturbances in the receiver or perhaps from the broadcasting station.

Reducing Errors in Communications

Noise in a communications system is not only a nuisance but also the source of error.   For example, during an electrical storm, a sudden flash of lightning may cause so much loud static on a telephone line that it becomes impossible to hear a portion of the conversation.   The listener will probably ask to have the message repeated.   This simple illustration includes the way one type of noise can interfere with communication and the basic way of reducing error due to noise: repeating part of the message, or as it is called, *redundancy*.   Redundancy is a repetition of any information contained in a message.   This definition includes both redundancies applied to specific disturbances, as in the illustration, and those built into language and used regularly in communication.   One example is the bank check; the amount to be paid is

---

[4] Cherry, *op. cit.*, p. 42.

indicated as an arabic number and also as a word.   Another common illustration is the business letter that places an order and reads, "Please enter our order for twenty-six (26) widgets."

Repetition of this sort is inefficient in the sense that some information must be sent twice requiring effort, time, and use of some of the capacity of the communications system.   On the other hand, since the purpose of communication is the conveyence of information, it is valueless unless transmitted accurately.   Hence, redundancy promotes efficiency to the extent that it increases the accuracy of communication.

A language, such as English, has a great deal of redundancy built into it in the rules by which words are spelled or sentences constructed.   Although it is hard to compute exactly, some investigations have indicated that the redundancy of English is about 50 per cent.[5]

This means that half of the letters or words used in writing are required by our rules of spelling and grammar and therefore are not used because we specifically think they will convey information.   In situations where the need for accuracy of communication is great, redundancy increases even further.   For example, in the communication between the control tower and an aircraft an error can be disastrous to life and property.   Anyone who has listened to such communication realizes that pilots and control-tower personnel have a special way of speaking.   It is English in the sense that we are all familiar with the words being used, but the words are used with precise meanings and in very special structures.   In short, this is really a special language.   An analysis of control-tower language has indicated that the redundancy runs approximately 96 per cent.[6]

THE CONCEPT OF ERROR-FREE TRANSMISSION.   Common-sense analysis suggests that since there is always some type of noise in a communications system there is always some error in the communication which we can best hope to reduce to a minimum level.   One of the interesting factors Shannon's analysis has shown is that this is not the case.   It is possible, if certain conditions are met, to achieve error-free transmission.

To explain this necessitates the introduction of the idea of *channel capacity*.   Although difficult to compute, it is relatively easy to imagine that any channel will have some upper or maximum limit on the amount of information it can transmit.   Through mathematical

---

[5] Shannon and Weaver, *op. cit.*, p. 104.
[6] F. C. Frick and W. H. Sumby, "Control Tower Language," *The Journal of Acoustical Society of America*, **24**, 1952, p. 596.

analysis Shannon has shown that it is possible to achieve error-free transmission by the use of proper coding provided the capacity of the channel is not exceeded.

CODING. Essentially *coding* is transforming the message into a special form for transmission. In a sense it is a special language which enables us to convey more information in an individual communicative act. In this way the transmission rate of information can be increased. The problem is that the original message must be translated into the code, and the process of coding takes time. If the time spent in coding is relatively small and the gain in transmission rate correspondingly large, this is an efficient step.

Thus far we have been talking in terms of error-free transmission. Needless to say, our objective could have just as well been defined as transmission with 2 per cent or 10 per cent error. Shannon's concepts enable us to think in terms of precisely defined transmission error with one point being zero error.

FEEDBACK. Another step in promoting accuracy in transmission is the use of feedback, that is, having some information come back from the receiver. Of course this method of promoting efficiency consumes part of the channel capacity.

The term, feedback, is used in a number of contexts; one such is in the area of control, which we discussed in Chapter 13. Here we are interested in the development of error-free transmission through response and learning.

Perhaps a simple way to illustrate feedback is to describe a simple experiment that has been performed innumerable times and which makes an interesting class project or even a party activity.[7] In this experiment an individual was asked to describe with words certain patterns composed of rectangles which listeners were then to draw (Figure 14.2). The description was presented under two conditions. In the first, the persons to whom the speaker was communicating could hear him but could in no way communicate with him. Usually this was done by placing the person giving the description behind a screen and not permitting any of his listeners to make a sound. This was called a one-way communication condition. In the second situation, a two-way communication, the person speaking was placed where he could observe his listeners and they could ask any questions at any

[7] The original experiment was performed and described by Harold J. Leavitt and R. A. H. Mueller, "Some Effects of Feedback on Communications," *Human Relations*, 4, 1951, pp. 401–410.

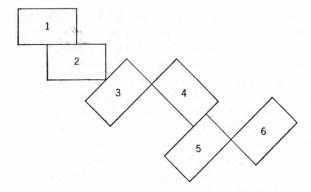

Figure 14.2

time.   The only provision was that the communications had to be carried out in spoken words.

A number of factors were measured: (1) the length of time it took
for the description to be made, (2) the accuracy of the figures drawn
by the listeners, (3) the confidence both listeners and speaker had in
the accuracy of the figures.

In general, one-way communication was faster than two-way.
However, the two-way communication was far more accurate in that
the listeners drew figures more closely resembling those held by the
speaker, and the listeners felt more confident about the accuracy of the
figures they had drawn.

The one-way communication *appears* to be much neater.   Two-
way communication is characterized by interruptions, discussions,
sometimes arguments about what has been said or should be said, sometimes sarcastically cutting comments about the statements the speaker
has been making, and repetition when a slow listener realizes that he
has missed something and insists on going back to a point discussed
before.   All of this is hard on the speaker.   He is aware that his words
are not being accurately understood, which is often a blow to his
pride.   All too frequently there are manifestations of lack of respect
for his descriptive abilities with the result that he feels somewhat
inadequate and perhaps defensive.

An observer of this exercise is likely to note some other things
taking place.   For example, the speaker may have a difficult time describing how the various sides of rectangle are oriented on the paper.
In a two-way communications situation someone may suggest, "Why

don't you describe the directions as we did in aerial gunnery, that is, twelve o'clock to the top of the page, three o'clock to the right hand side, six to the bottom, and so on?" Ideas like this are almost always adopted and used to both speed up the communications and make it more accurate. They are, in effect, a code. Let us note two things about this: (1) the code is developed by the group during the process of two-way communication, (2) everyone hears the proposal and agrees to it. They all learn the code at the same time, and are able to use it with maximum effectiveness. Development of codes or special languages is, as we have noted, one of the ways of improving communications, but these take time to perfect, and they are only effective when both sender and receiver understand them.

It is perfectly possible, of course, for the sender to develop a code, but he must make sure that the receiver learns it. Sometimes in one-way communication the speaker attempts to develop his own codes and may tell the group, "When I say such and such I mean this and that." This sounds simple, yet before many words are spoken it usually becomes clear that some members of the group have not understood his instruction and therefore do not understand the code. One aspect of two-way communications or feedback is that it is extremely useful in developing adequate special languages and having them learned quickly by all parties involved.

Second, an observer may note that in a two-way communication the speaker in describing the figure looks up at the group, and even though they say nothing he pauses, apparently makes a decision, and then goes back to repeat his point. What he is doing is getting a response from the general appearance of his audience that lets him know whether or not he "got through."

Feedback, then, is a process of two-way communication. Two principal aspects of interest are: (1) the response it gives the sender regarding the understanding the receivers have of his message, and (2) the development and learning of special languages or codes.

A BASIC MODEL OF A COMMUNICATIONS SYSTEM 2

Encoding and Decoding

Introduction of the idea of a code and the process of coding a message makes it apparent that the sender in our first description of communications (Figure 14.1) really includes several components. Since all communication is carried on in some form of language, all communications must have some process of *encoding*, that is, of translating information into the specific form in which it is going to be transmitted. Taking an idea and converting it into words in normal conversation is an encoding process, but so is the act of a clerk filling in a form using the appropriate numbers and symbols so that the proper material may be drawn from stock. Needless to say, if the information is in code form, there must also be a *decoding* process in the receiver that extracts the information the code contains.

Selection

In addition to encoding, any sender carries out a process of *selection*. There are numerous reasons for this. One of these is to keep the amount of information going through a system at a reasonable level to avoid overloading the system. Another is to reduce noise by preventing other than desired messages from entering the system. We might also note there is both desired and undesired selectivity.

Much has been written about the vast amount of paper work which flows in any government agency or business organization. If, for example, a business executive were to read or even look at every piece of paper directed to him, it would be unlikely that he could do anything else during the day. Each day's mail brings a large number of letters, some vitally important, which must be read and others nothing more than advertisements or things about which he is totally uninterested. To help reduce the amount of mail getting to him, most executives assign their secretaries a screening activity. The secretary is expected to throw out the unwanted advertisements, route legitimate business letters to other people in the organization, and allow only those communications that really require her boss's attention to get to his desk. She may go one step further and put the more important items on top so that they receive prompt attention. The secretary in this case is performing in accordance with a program.

Another type of selectivity occurs when information wanted by some members of an organization is kept from entering the communications system or when information important to one individual is introduced into the system by him even though it may not really be what others in the system need.

Selectivity also occurs at the receiving end. An example of screening here would be a person listening to a conversation at a noisy party. If he allows the surrounding conversations to claim much of his attention, the chances are he will not get much of the message sent out by his principal companion. But by serious concentration he can, in effect, "close out" the distraction of others and get fairly accurate

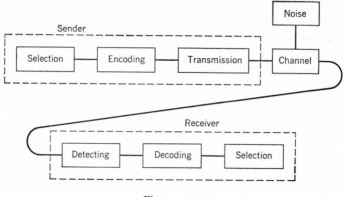

Figure 14.3

reception of his companion's message, a condition both desire. An extended model of communications system is shown in Figure 14.3.

Purposes

Much of communication is intimately tied in with the purposes or needs of the parties involved. We communicate in order to influence the behavior of others. If the communication does not accomplish this end, it is pointless even though the message may have been received quite clearly. Whether it accomplishes its intended purpose is to no small extent concerned with the needs of the recipient. At the same time, as noted in Chapters 2 and 3, perception and processes of selectivity are strongly influenced by the needs and objectives of the persons involved. This aspect of communications is not the major target of this chapter, and it is left to the reader to connect the content of earlier chapters to these aspects of communications.

A BASIC MODEL OF A COMMUNICATIONS SYSTEM 3

The elements labeled "channels" in our first version of the model also need elaboration. Thus far our illustrations have suggested that a channel is a simple link, such as a telephone wire, between two people. In organizations, however, channels are frequently not that simple. As we have noted, a channel may have parties on either end who are both senders and receivers. There may be a number of connected links in a network so that more than two people can be both senders and receivers. We may also have a situation where the communica-

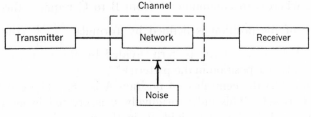

Figure 14.4

tions system consists of several links in series or a network (Figure 14.4) so that a message starting at one end of the system has to pass through several people or transmission units in getting to the other end. Sometimes links carry only certain types of messages, sometimes only in one direction. Many organization properties influence the channels of communication and hence organization performance. Some of the properties of different networks which constitute channels have been studied in the laboratory where examination is easier. Before reviewing these studies let us examine an important concept.

Centrality

In a network, one or more positions usually occupy a rather central location. A central position is the one closest to all other positions. Here distance is measured by the number of links which must be used to get from one position to another by the shortest path. In Figure 14.5, for example, to communicate from position A to C requires only

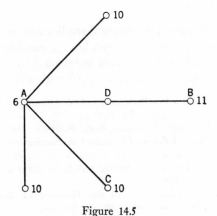

Figure 14.5

one link, whereas to communicate from B to C requires three. The centrality of the position is defined by formula $\dfrac{\Sigma d\ xy}{d\ \ xy}$ (the sum of all internal distances of the pattern divided by the total sum of distances for any one position in the pattern).[8]

In Figure 14.5 the centrality of position A is 7.8. The centrality of position B is 4.3. This index originally was created in an effort to determine the behavior of individuals in the network. As studies on groups were carried out, it became apparent that not all individual behavior was directly related to the centrality of the position held. Much of what was occurring seemed to center on the degree of independence of the position holder.[9] Others have computed different indices to measure independency, which take into account the number of communication links in the network, the number of communication links available to the individual, and the number of positions to which the individual must relay the information.[10]

Some idea of the significance of the independence of a position can be appreciated by consulting Figure 14.5. The person occupying position B really has no alternative open. He can communicate only with D and is probably going to be used primarily either to relay information to D or to execute orders coming from or through D. In contrast, A has considerable independence. He can communicate with four people and is in a position where he can collate and integrate information from a number of sources. This will put him in a unique position to make more adequate decisions than other members of the group. Consequently, he will be better able to make decisions and issue orders, in short, to assume a position of leadership.

Some Effects of Networks

There have been many experimental studies among work groups on the effects of different types of networks. A number of these investigations have *centered* on the factors influenced by, or the results of communications as measured by, the speed with which a task has been

[8] Alex Bavelas, "Communication Patterns in Task Oriented Groups," *Journal of the Acoustical Society of America*, 22, 1950, pp. 725–730, reprinted in Cartwright and Zander, *Group Dynamics*, Evanston, Row, Peterson, 1953, pp. 669–682.

[9] Harold J. Leavitt, "Some Effects of Certain Communication Patterns on Group Performance," *The Journal of Abnormal and Social Psychology*, 1951, 66, reprinted in Swanson, Newcomb, and Hartley (eds.), *Readings in Social Psychology*, New York, Holt, 1952, p. 123.

[10] M. E. Shaw, "Group Structures and the Behavior of Individuals in Small Groups," *Journal of Psychology*, 1954, 38, pp. 139–149.

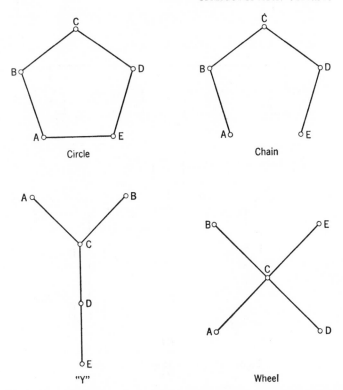

Figure 14.6. *Source:* Harold J. Leavitt, "Some Effects of Certain Communication Patterns on Group Performance," in Swanson, Newcomb, and Hartley (eds.), *Readings in Social Psychology*, New York, Holt, 1952, p. 114.

accomplished, the number of errors made, the morale or attitude of people occupying positions in the network, and the ability of the network to cope with ambiguous (noisy) situations.

In one series of studies a number of different networks, each having five positions, were tested. They are shown in Figure 14.6; the positions are indicated by the letters and the lines indicate the links forming the network. In the abstract they look somewhat unusual and foreign to the typical organization. A slight rearrangement, though, shows that most of these patterns are not uncommon. For example, the Wheel resembles a typical situation in which four subordinates report to a superior (Figure 14.7*a*). In the Chain illustration, one superior has two subordinates, each of whom have a single subordinate (Figure 14.7*b*). We might liken this to a small accounting firm where the owner has two accountants working for him, each of whom has an

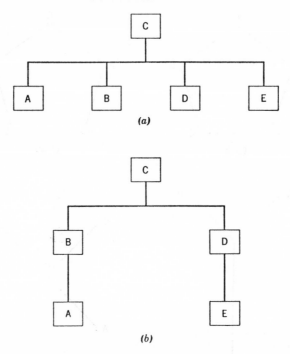

Figure 14.7. (a) Wheel; (b) chain.

assistant to do leg work, or to a head buyer who has two senior buyers, each of whom has an assistant buyer reporting to him.

In this series, the groups forming a network were assigned a simple problem.[11] Each member of the network was given a card containing five symbols: stars, triangles, circles, etc. Only one of these symbols was on all five cards. The group task was to find the common symbol. In conducting the experiments, the groups repeated this project fifteen times, with data collected on the length of time it took them to perform each trial, on whether their decisions were correct, on the attitudes of the group members, etc.

Overall Performance of Networks

These experiments yielded some interesting and, at times, unexpected results. One result showed that the time spent per trial tended to follow a similar pattern (Figure 14.8). The mean time per trial for any group tended to decrease with each additional trial, gradually

[11] Leavitt, *op. cit.*, pp. 108–125.

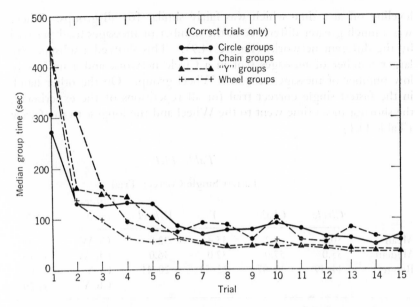

Figure 14.8. Median group times per trial. *Source:* Harold J. Leavitt, "Some Effects of Certain Communication Patterns," in Swanson, Newcomb, and Hartley (eds.), *Readings in Social Psychology,* New York, Holt, 1952, p. 115.

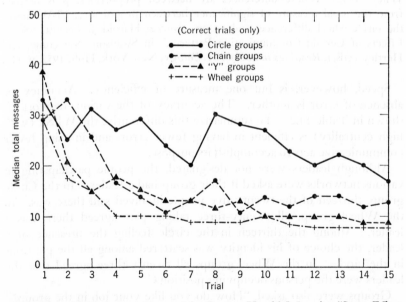

Figure 14.9. Median messages per trial. *Source:* Harold J. Leavitt, "Some Effects of Certain Communication Patterns," in Swanson, Newcomb, and Hartley (eds.), *Readings in Social Psychology,* New York, Holt, 1952, p. 116.

leveling off at a time which was fairly similar for all groups. There was a much greater difference in the number of messages used per trial by the different networks (Figure 14.9). This showed a substantially larger number of messages sent in a Circle network and a uniformly low number of messages sent in a Wheel group. On the other hand, in the fastest single correct trial for all repetitions of the experiment, the shortest mean time went to the Wheel and the longest to the Circle (Table 14.1).

Table 14.1

Fastest Single Correct Trial

	Circle	Chain	Y	Wheel	Differ-ence	p *
Mean	50.4	53.2	35.4	32.0	Ci–W	<.01
Median	55.0	57.0	32.0	36.0	Ch–W	<.10
Range	44–59	19–87	22–53	20–41	Ci–Y	<.05
					Ch–Y	<.20

* Significance of differences between means were measured throughout by *t*-tests. The *p*-values are based on distributions of *t* which include both tails of the distribution (see H. Freeman, *Industrial Statistics:* New York, John Wiley, 1942). Where differences are between proportions, *p* is derived from the usual measure of significance between proportions. Ci-W means the circle-wheel difference, and so on. *Source:* Harold J. Leavitt, "Some Effects of Certain Communication Patterns," in Swanson, Newcomb, and Hartley (eds.), *Readings in Social Psychology*, New York, Holt, 1952, p. 116.

Speed, however, is but one measure of efficiency. Accuracy or absence of error is another. The accuracy of the various networks is shown in Table 14.2. To summarize this differently, the Wheel (with high centrality) is efficient in having fewer errors and in using fewer communicative acts to accomplish its purpose.

Although leaders were not designated, the people participating in various networks were asked if their group had a leader. In the Circle group, thirteen of the twenty-five people involved said there was. In the Wheel group, all twenty-three taking part agreed there was a leader. Among the thirteen in the circle feeling the presence of a leader, the choice of his identity was scattered among all the positions in the circle. In the Wheel groups all twenty-three agreed that the leaders were the persons occupying position C.

Groups were also asked, "How do you like your job in the group?" Members of the Circle group indicated the highest level of satisfaction, next came the Chain group, then the Y, and last the Wheel group.

Table 14.2

Errors

Pattern	Total Errors (15 Trials)		Total Errors (Last 8 Trials)		Final Errors		Mean Number of Trials with at Least One Final Error *
	Mean	Range	Mean	Range	Mean	Range	
Circle	16.6	9–33	7.6	1–18	6.4	2–14	3.4
Chain	9.8	3–19	2.8	0–11	6.2	1–19	1.8
Y	2.6	1–8	0	0	1.6	0–5	0.8
Wheel	9.8	0–34	0.6	0–2	2.2	0–7	1.2

* p values Ci-Y < .02. *Source:* Harold J. Leavitt, "Some Effects of Certain Communication Patterns," in Swanson, Newcomb and Hartley (eds.), *Readings in Social Psychology*, New York, Holt, 1952, p. 117.

Performance by Position in Various Networks

The structure of the networks caused certain differences in the performances and reactions of group members. In general, the higher the centrality index, the larger the number of messages sent from a position. Conversely, the least central position sent the fewest messages. Those occupying the more central positions usually indicated they enjoyed their jobs more. Conversely, those with lower centrality tended to enjoy it less.

We can summarize the results of this study no better than Leavitt: "We may grossly characterize the kinds of differences that occur in this way: The circle, one extreme, is active, leaderless, unorganized, erratic, and yet it is enjoyed by its members. The wheel, on the other extreme, is less active, has a distinct leader, is well and stably organized, is less erratic, and yet is unsatisfying to most of its members." [12]   Of major interest is that the structure of a network influences the performance and attitude of the unit as a whole as well as the performance, attitude, and role of individuals within the unit.

The Ability of Networks to Cope with Ambiguity

In the experiments described, the items were clear cut, simple, and hardly ambiguous at all. In a variation of this study, each member of the group was given five marbles and asked to find the common color. As long as the colors of each marble were uniform, common, and

[12] Leavitt, *op. cit.*, p. 120.

easily distinguished, the groups performed exactly as in the preceding illustration. However, when marbles containing several colors in varying patterns were substituted and the groups were asked to find the common marble, the problem became much greater.   It was hard to describe the colors clearly.   Was it brownish red or rust?   And even more difficult to describe were the shapes in which the colors occurred.   In this situation, the Circle groups tended to overcome the problem quite readily and quickly get back to their earlier levels of performance.   The Wheel groups, on the other hand, had far more difficulty adapting to the situation and were still committing a large number of errors after many trials.[13]

Network and the Formation of Organizations

From the foregoing studies, it seems that the networks have a direct influence on the performance of the group.   This, however, is not the case, for there is an intervening factor of significant importance.

When assigned positions in a network, individuals were uninformed in regard to the structure of their networks or their positions in them. At first these people were unorganized in the sense that they did not see where their efforts fitted into a united whole, nor was there any central position directing and coordinating effort, to wit, a leader. Later experiments by Guetzkow and Simon established that the structure influenced the ability of the groups to develop adequate organization, and that it was the existence or absence of adequate organization which influenced performance of the network.[14]

In replicating Leavitt's study, they showed that the wheel-type structure most easily became "efficiently organized."   After relatively few trials, the organization that the structure imposed on group members emerged, whereupon they adopted it.   The circle structure, on the other hand, had two consequences: some groups developed an "efficient organization" and others did not.   Those that did usually had to spend considerable time deciding what would be the best form or organization for them.   When this decision was reached and the organization established, the groups performed quite adequately.   For example, fifteen Wheel groups averaged 0.46 minutes for their three fastest trials.   Among twenty-one Circle groups, the average for their

[13] Harold J. Leavitt, *Managerial Psychology*, University of Chicago Press, 1958, p. 197.
[14] Harold Guetzkow and Herbert A. Simon, "The Impact of Certain Communication Nets upon Organization and Performance in Task Oriented Groups," *Management Science*, **1**, 1955, pp. 233–250.

three fastest trials was 0.73. However, for three Circle groups judged as developing "efficient organization," the average for their three fastest trials was 0.472. The difference between the average of the efficiently organized Circle groups and the Wheel groups is not statistically significant.[15] The effect of structure on unit performance and on individuals finding their role can now be seen as the influence the structure has in either facilitating or actually forcing unit members into the stable set of interrelated roles we call an organization.

FORMATION OF NETWORKS

Networks are created by two different types of effort: formal and informal. Those classified as formal are consciously planned, facilitated, and controlled. Of many types, they fall into two principal classes.

One formal channel follows *chain of command*. Here communication is expected to flow from one subordinate to his superior, from that individual to *his* superior, or vice versa. In this arrangement, if the work of two departments is to be coordinated, the information flow passes through the managerial hierarchy. This flow greatly increases the centrality of the higher positions in the organization with consequences already touched upon. Actually, most information does not follow the chain of command. Were this to occur, many organizations, even of modest size, would flounder because of overloaded channels of communication. Most information flows through other systems.[16]

Great numbers of formal systems occur in contemporary organizations. They are spelled out in numerous procedural and organizational manuals. In brief, they designate what information a person has to gather, the form in which it is to be recorded, and the party to whom it is to be sent. Such formal systems further tell a person what information he should be receiving and, of course, give him the programs to use upon its receipt. Formal systems have grown so numerous and become so complex that individuals are often specifically assigned to the planning of new ones, improvement of existing ones, and elimination of unneeded ones.

Informally created networks arise spontaneously within an organization in response to the needs of organizational members. This for-

[15] Guetzkow and Simon, *op. cit.*, p. 248.

[16] E. Wight Bakke, *Bonds of Organization*, New York, Harper, 1950. See also Richard L. Simpson, "Vertical and Horizontal Communication in Formal Organizations," *Administrative Science Quarterly*, 4, 1959, pp. 188–196.

mation usually involves one person establishing contact with another although such contact is not formally required, at least in regard to the type of information which will flow through the contact. We have already referred to the general need of people for information about their world. In organizations like the army, where formal channels tend to be hierarchial in nature and convey relatively little and highly selected information which is not widely disseminated, we expect people to establish many informal channels. Anyone who has been in the army is familiar with the "grapevine" and the high prevalence of rumor. In spite of its highly informal nature, rumor is communication passing through channels related to a need, and, contrary to some general impressions, it can be quite accurate.[17]

Not infrequently the formal organization plans overlook the need for coordination in certain areas or at least the flow of information necessary for coordinative purposes. When this occurs, individuals in an organization often establish their own channels of communications, sometimes in the face of considerable difficulty. The obstacles may even be managerial rules or mores which have to be violated or circumvented in order to get a job done.[18] Other situations pose different problems. In the reorganization of British coal mining mentioned in Chapter 6, coordination between shifts was necessary but unprovided by management. The necessary communication links were established, as we saw, by the workers off the job by calling on members of other shifts in pubs or their homes.[19]

Before leaving this section, let us make clear an important point. We have been discussing the need for communication links to be satisfied by either formal or informal means. There is no guarantee that they always will be. A formally planned communication network may not bring about the transmission of necessary information. Members of an organization may not step in to establish an informal communications network. The possibility that these things will occur is very likely but by no means absolute. No formal plan ever takes into account all organization needs. The likelihood of voluntary, informal supplementation to formal organization inadequacy depends on the perception and motivation of organization members as well as constraints on their efforts.

[17] Theodore Caplow, "Rumors in War," *Social Forces*, **25**, 1946 and 1947, pp. 298–302.

[18] Donald Roy, "Efficiency and 'The Fix': Informal Intergroup Relations in a Piece Work Machine Shop," *American Journal of Sociology*, **60**, 1954, pp. 255–266.

[19] E. L. Trist and K. W. Bamforth, "Social and Psychological Consequences of the Long Wall Method of Coal-Getting," *Human Relations*, **4**, 1951, pp. 1–38.

ORGANIZATIONAL FACTORS THAT INFLUENCE COMMUNICATIONS

An extraordinarily large number of factors can influence communication. To mention, much less examine, all of them at this point would be difficult. In this section we focus on the effects on communications of various organizational elements already discussed.

Division of Work

Division of work tends to make it easier to communicate within an organizational subunit than between subunits. This can come about for several reasons. All members of an organizational subunit, such as a department, share a subgoal(s), and since the subgoals of departments are usually different this tends to popularize communications. The process of departmentalization is also one of the factors which groups people and determines, in part, with whom they come in contact. Part of this behavior springs from their sharing of some goals and purposes, and part from the interrelation of their activities. Last, division of work usually puts people within reasonable physical distance of one another.

Rules

In developing an organization, rules inevitably develop too. Some rules are formally presented in written form and distributed throughout the organization; others are informally developed, many times springing from past practices which have become widely accepted. Regardless of source, they can influence communication in a number of ways. One is by establishing rules about whom an individual can or must communicate with (channels), another is by influencing the content of messages, and a third by setting the form through which communications must take place: a letter, a prepared form, spoken, etc. Often rules also specify the code which must be used.

To illustrate some of these, there are organizations with clear rules saying that certain types of communications must "go through channels." For information from another department, an individual may, in this case, have to request his superior to take steps to obtain it. On the other hand, other organizations have rules stating that an individual (usually of managerial rank) is expected to go directly to anyone whom he thinks has information that can help him in doing his job.

Another type of rule may specify that a request for a particular service be submitted in triplicate, not duplicate, and that the service be identified by classification number. Hence, to hire an employee, a manager would have to fill in a specified number of copies of a personnel requisition form identifying the position to be filled according to some job classification number, and indicating the salary that will be paid by a number on a pay scale.

Many detailed rules for communication can be a source of great frustration to organizational members. Annoying though the "red tape" may be, one should recognize that many of the rules are intended to improve communications by (1) keeping out messages deemed unimportant which would function as noise, (2) keeping out unnecessary or unimportant messages which might cause channel capacity to be exceeded, or (3) combatting noise through the use of code. These are desirable objectives and when rules function to promote them, they are obviously justified. The problem is that it is extremely difficult to determine completely what information a communications system will need to transmit. An unfortunate and not uncommon consequence, therefore, is that rules are established that unintentionally block or distort necessary communications.

Stable, Dynamic, and Crisis Conditions

Thus, communications channels can get filled with routine matters which make it difficult if not impossible for the nonroutine to pass through. Hence, the conditions under which a communications system will be used are of major significance in evaluating or planning. We might begin with the observation that if we knew exactly what information had to be transmitted a system of communications would not be needed. Instead, we could write a complete program on whatever result we wanted to accomplish. In a fundamental way, a communications system exists because of ignorance and inability to define what information will be needed or available.

However, there are degrees of ignorance about the information to be communicated. In some situations a good deal is known about the types of information which will be important, and we are primarily concerned with items of detail which fall within fairly narrow boundaries. For example, we know that production information sent to a department would be concerned with the types of products that department is prepared to make. The information probably will specify such things as times, quantities, and particular models to be produced.   Tomorrow the same types of information surely will be used even though the times, quantities, and models may be slightly different.   Hence, in a stable situation we are able to define quite closely the types of information which will be transmitted.   We can, therefore, specify in considerable detail the capabilities required of the communications system.

But if a department is to make a radically new product, for which programs do not exist, we will need channels that, in addition to carrying purposeful information will also bring about learning (such as conveying instructions for fabricating the new product) and will provide feedback as to whether learning has occurred.   It may not be necessary to transmit information about learning every day, but the system must have this capacity when it is needed.

The third type of situation develops when an organization has to cope with not only stable and dynamic conditions, but also with crisis conditions where events of fundamental importance to its survival arise unexpectedly and have to be taken care of at once.   Consider a bomber flying through enemy territory.   The crisis could consist of an attacking enemy aircraft suddenly diving out of a cloud bank, a condition which must be handled immediately.   Whereas many other types of information *ought* to be transmitted through the plane, information relevant to the crisis *must be* transmitted.   Such critical conditions occur with far less frequency but require instant attention when they do.   Consequently, there are standing rules on bombers that intercoms are not to be used for personal conversations, which may be quite desirable, and even information relevant to the task will be interrupted and removed from the channel when a crisis arises.   Indeed, the intercommunications system on a plane may be unused for many hours during flight even though some of the persons on the plane have no other way of communicating with one another and hence must spend hours in virtual isolation.   Unused communications capacity is provided and tolerated because of the nature of the conditions which the aircraft is sometimes expected to face.

As we go from stable to crisis conditions, we see situations which influence the extent to which communications capacity will be utilized.   On highly routinized matters under stable conditions the use can closely approach channel capacity.   As a person moves to non-routine, crisis-type situations, rules and other constraints are introduced to maintain a greater degree of unused, standby, channel capacity.   Crisis represents not only a threat to the organization but often also a new set of factors which may not be effectively handled by the existing special language (codes, forms, etc.).   This situation can lead to inaccurate communication, overloading of channel capacity because of redundancy, or both.

Leadership

The effects of the leader on communications and the performance of work groups is easily recognized.   However, the casual reading of research in this area might appear to be contradictory.   In some situations authoritarian leaders who, among other things, put many restrictions on communications, seem to have the more productive units. Other reports show that more permissive or group-centered styles of leadership which usually promote a freer flow of communications are more productive.   This contradiction is more apparent than real.   Let us separate several elements.

We shall begin by visualizing a communications channel as containing a number of types of information—information relevant to the task, information for learning, information important to the social life of group members.   The leader influences the communications system in several respects: (1) he influences the selection that group members make about the information they put into the system.   By imposing certain constraints on the system itself these constraints prevent or at least hinder certain types of information from going through.   (2) He determines the network, including the directionality of channels, that will exist.   Earlier in this chapter we noted that feedback situations appear to be messy.   A number of people are sometimes talking at the same time; they seem to be talking on a wide range of topics, and some of their comments may not be at all respectful to the person nominally in charge.   The leader may look at such a situation and decide that this is inefficient and wasteful and that it perhaps also constitutes a threat to his position.   As a result, he may impose rules or give orders which prohibit communications on anything but task-relevant items. If this is a situation in which satisfactory programs already exist and there is sufficient group cohesion, this step may produce a more productive outcome.[20]   However, if the situation is one where adequate programs and codes do not exist and have to be developed or learned, as in the experiments reviewed, such actions restrict the learning and, in turn, the performance of the group.

Many times it is presumed that the democratic or permissive leader

[20] M. E. Shaw, "A Comparison of Two Types of Leadership in Various Communication Nets," *Journal of Abnormal and Social Psychology*, **50**, 1955, pp. 127–134.

is one who tolerates or permits a group to interact in a manner of its own choosing. This is not necessarily so. It has been shown, for example, that where groups are instructed to develop the best solution to a problem, the successful group is the one whose democratic leader is quite directly involved with controlling communications, seeing that *all* members of the group have an opportunity to participate, that one or two do not dominate the conversation, and that the quiet ones are drawn out.[21] This often involves considerable control of the communications system by the leader.

Filtering Effects

Since most communications systems in organizations are made up of people, it is necessary to give attention to a particular type of problem human beings raise for communications. Often when information passes through people as part of a communications system they delete or modify it. This is a filtering effect. Sometimes people do not "hear" what is said to them. Sometimes they do not send out information which they see as threatening to themselves, or perhaps as advantageous to others. Sometimes they send out inaccurate information which they believe people want to receive.

Filtering is a particular problem in the hierarchial flow of information when status and power differences have a significant impact.[22] In Chapter 12 it was pointed out that people in an organization who share concepts of organization goals can achieve voluntary coordination when there is an easy flow of information. This has been found to occur when status and power are deemphasized to permit a rapid, lateral (nonhierarchial) flow of information.[23]

Hierarchy

Needless to say, a person's position in an organizational hierarchy may bear a close parallel to his status position. Yet some aspects of communications have been more closely identified with a person's position in an organizational hierarchy than with his status. In one intensive study of an organization, it was found that people higher in a company organization tended to communicate more; that is, the vice-

---

[21] A. Paul Hare, "Small Group Discussions with Participating and Supervised Leadership," *Journal of Abnormal and Social Psychology*, 48, 1953, pp. 273–275.
[22] See Chapter 4 for details on the effect of status.
[23] Tom Burns and G. M. Stalker, *The Management of Innovation*, Chicago, Quadrangle Books, 1961, p. 125.

president was found to spend much more time in acts of communication than a foreman. The same study showed that people higher in an organizational hierarchy had more information than those lower down. This was true even when the information concerned events at a lower level.[24]

Individual Competence

People have a choice of whom they will deal with. They tend to direct their activities according to some pattern. Some we have already noted. One other which is of considerable interest is that people tend to direct their communication contacts toward members of their work group who are respected by them as being highly competent (Table 14.3). To begin with, competence is certainly one of

Table 14.3   Contacts Received per Hour and Competence

Contacts Received	Competence High	Low	Total
Many	5	1	6
Few	2	7	9
Total	7	8	15

Source: Peter M. Blau, "Patterns of Interaction Among a Group of Officials in a Government Agency," *Human Relations,* 7, 1954, p. 339.

the things which gives status. However, this factor can also be interpreted differently; that is, in order to do their jobs well, people go to those who can help them most, those they feel to be very competent.[25] By taking this idea one step further, we might point out that many times asking for help can be interpreted as indicating a lack of ability which a person might be reluctant to reveal to anyone, but more reluctant to disclose to his boss than to a fellow worker.

SUMMARY

This chapter dealt with an extraordinarily complex issue: communications. We gave attention first to a model of a communications

[24] Keith Davis, "Management Communication and the Grapevine," *Harvard Business Review,* 31, 1953, pp. 43–49.
[25] Peter M. Blau, "Patterns of Interaction among a Group of Officials in a Government Agency," *Human Relations,* 7, 1954, pp. 337–348.

system, examined some effects of communications on organizational behavior, and, last, pursued some of the factors in organizations which influence one or more portions of the system.

The model discussed identified the following elements: a selector and encoder embodied in the sender, a system of communication links which forms a network called the channel and actually transmits the information, and steps of decoding and selecting information for use which occurs in the receiver.

The movement of information through a system is influenced by two principal factors, its capacity and the noise within it. If the capacity of the system is not exceeded, the accuracy of the transmission of information is a function of the noise, which, in turn, can be combated by redundancy, which uses up more of the channel capacity, and by coding. Coding permits more information to be communicated but at a cost of reducing the independence of choice of the persons involved and of bringing about a greater delay in communication because of the necessity of encoding and decoding.

Many factors already discussed in organizations influence one or more aspects of communications systems. These, in turn, are affected by the type of conditions facing an organization.

15

Rewards and the Implementation of Motivation

Coordination ultimately rests on attracting and holding requisite personnel in an organization and on influencing them in some way to ·behave in accordance with one or more of the general coordinative systems. Largely this is a problem of motivation, of having people satisfy more of their needs at lesser costs in the organization than in any other way.

In Chapter 2 we noted that through motivation an organization controlled many of the means by which people satisfy their needs. How these means are developed and handled is the substance of this chapter. This chapter does not include all types of rewards and reward systems, but only those most directly involved with achieving coordination.

Need satisfaction was seen to be a roundabout process. A person manifests a certain behavior to achieve an objective which functions as a means to gratify some need. To satisfy some ego needs an individual might want a promotion which he knows he can obtain by performing exceptionally well in his present assignment. This combination of something he gives (behavior) to receive something else (objective) we call a reward. A reward contains two elements: something obtained in return for something else provided. The set of rewards in an organization are a principal determinant of the individual behaviors that influence organizational performance.

In this chapter we consider three topics: (1) the relationship between reward and need satisfaction, (2) the nature of the systems of rewards in organizations, and (3) some of the issues and problems in designing a reward system.

282

REWARD AND NEEDS SATISFACTION

The Search for Ways to Satisfy Needs

A need often can be satisfied by several sets of objectives and behaviors. A person may have a need for individual recognition satisfied through promotion, but may also find it fulfilled through receipt of a prize or some other honor. Furthermore, a person may achieve his objective of promotion by hard work in his job or perhaps by marrying the boss's daughter. A second point, often obscured, is that a single reward may satisfy several needs. A pay increase may give a person a feeling of security. It may also give him higher status. Last, the relationship between need and means is not always apparent. The obvious relationship first detected between a reward and a possible need satisfaction may not be adequate or possible. As a result, an individual may begin a search for some other reward-need combination which can be realized.

Consider a child who wants some recognition as an individual. In school he may see that pupils who obtain high grades receive recognition from the teacher. But after trying very hard he finds that he is just not capable of achieving grades sufficiently high to obtain the attention he wants. He may then observe that some children receive attention by taking part in the class play. Again, after trying, this child finds that he has no facility for the stage. Perhaps in despair, he creates a disturbance in the classroom teasing a child in front of him. Finally, this gets attention from the teacher. He is instructed to stay after school, and during detention is asked in a long and not entirely unfriendly conversation, "Why do you do things like that? Wouldn't you like to be like other people?" Strange though it might first appear, by raising a disturbance in class he has found a way to get the individual attention he so desperately wants. It is not too difficult to envision how, in a short time, when the temporarily satisfied desire for attention renews itself, he may revert to the previously successful behavior as the class "hell raiser." Thus, the means to satisfy needs are not always obvious. As a result it is useful to conceive people as impelled by a *search* for ways to satisfy their needs.

The search for a workable means of satisfying needs makes people try different behaviors to achieve objectives. Once a satisfactory, but not necessarily the best, reward has been found it is likely to be used in the future. We can say that learning has occurred. In any organization the individual is faced with the task of learning what rewards are available. Sometimes this is relatively simple because rewards are publicly announced in the form of policies on promotion, rules, and attached penalties, etc. Many rewards are not so explicitly stated or easily learned, making the search for them more extensive and more difficult.

Take the not untypical situation of a person who, wanting a position to satisfy some of his needs, knows that a promotion depends, among other things, on his "judgment." He is then faced with the necessity of exhibiting behavior that those who can recommend or deny his promotion interpret as reflecting judgment. Looking about the organization he may note that people are thought to be sound thinkers or to possess good judgment when they proceed with caution, never taking action until they have explored the consequences and have sounded out higher authorities to make sure of their approval. With judgment measured in these terms, he makes sure that he is never found to be acting precipitously or taking action without the knowledge or support of his superiors.

Needless to say, in another organization the behavior that leads to promotion may be entirely different. Hence, the search takes time and skill, and can result in frustration and failure. There is always the danger, for example, that the behavior of superiors may not be the type one should exhibit to receive a promotion. The blunt, frank talk employed by superiors may be the last thing they want to hear from subordinates. One executive disappointed in this way observed:

> As I told you before, I have been held back three years in the company because I got on somebody's blacklist. I am getting older and smarter about these things. I always used to say exactly what I felt was the thing to say but now I figure the company wants some other things from me so I'll play it their way. I don't want to be pushed back again.[1]

Effect of Rewards

All rewards do not have the same effect. Some have a great impact, others hardly any. The magnitude of the effect is influenced by many things, such as

1. *The intensity of the need.* The greater the need, the more impact a reward will have. The offer of $5 for helping an aged person across the street will have considerable influence on a person who has

[1] Paul R. Lawrence, *The Changing of Organizational Behavior Pattern*, Division of Research, Boston, Harvard Graduate Business School, 1958, p. 29.

just spent his last dime and wonders where his next meal is coming from. It would have relatively little effect, however, on a person who had just come from his financial counsellor, where he was reviewing his stock holdings and had found that his income will be $50,000 higher this year than last.

2. *The certainty of the reward.* People are likely to stick with a sure reward than to go after one which may be greater but is uncertain. We stay with a job where we are settled and know we have a place rather than go to another which may be a better position or be higher paying but where we are not sure of how things will work out.

3. *The cost involved.* One part of the reward is the behavior required. We can look on this as a cost. We may not like to work but are willing to do so for the pay we receive. However, some work is less desirable and therefore has a higher cost; we might not be willing to perform this less desirable work for the same pay.

REWARD SYSTEMS

Having considered the relationships between an individual and rewards we now turn to more general considerations of the provision of rewards and their distribution.

It is not uncommon to think of reward provision as a matter between a leader and a follower or a superior and a subordinate. At times it is, but not always. In fact, we seldom appreciate how often and in how many situations the leader or superior has very little influence on the provision or distribution of rewards. In a study of rewards sought by nurses in a number of large hospitals, it was found that the five most desired rewards were beyond the control of their immediate supervisors.[2] Among the satisfactions most desired by the nurses were relationships with patients, relationships with staff, opportunities for professional growth (Table 15.1) determined by procedures, rules, and structures. All these were, in fact, controlled by the organization.

What exists between nurses and their immediate superiors is similar to conditions found in many large organizations. The things people receive as rewards for being in an organization—pay, promotional opportunity, job assignments, etc.—are often controlled by policies, regulations, and staff positions but not by the immediate superior. A generation or two ago in the same organization a supervisor, such as a

[2] W. G. Bennis, N. Berkowitz, N. Affinito, M. Malone, "Authority, Power and the Ability to Influence," *Human Relations*, 11, 1958, pp. 143–155.

foreman, might not have had anywhere near the same number of constraints or limitations on his ability to distribute rewards. At that time he might well have been able to determine what type of employee he wanted, have handled his own recruitment and selection, set wages as long as they stayed within the budget, and placed workers on whatever jobs and in whatever groupings he felt desirable. In short, he would have been able to control a wide array of the tangible and intangible rewards that are of interest to people. Today in many large organizations lower level managers are not involved with the development of such rules and policies but merely with their application. They make decisions about whether particular rules or policies fit the situation or person.

Table 15.1   Reward Systems

	Usually Controlled by Supervisor	Usually Not * Controlled by Supervisor
† Satisfactions	0	88

* The nurse research associate on the project, a former supervisor of an OPD judged whether the satisfactions were manipulable by the supervisor. It should be mentioned that these items may be manipulable by the supervisor but are typically placed there by the organization and are only indirectly controlled by the supervisor.

† The rank order of satisfactions nurses would miss most if they left nursing are:

1. Relationships with patients
2. Personal satisfactions
3. Relationships with staff
4. Opportunity for professional growth
5. Hospital atmosphere

Source: W. G. Bennis, N. Berkowitz, M. Affinito, M. Malone, "Authority, Power and the Ability to Influence," *Human Relations*, 11, 1958, pp. 143–155.

It is possible to envision a continuum representing the degree of the organization control over rewards that ranges from a very loose condition, where the immediate superior has a great deal of control over the distribution of reward, to a very tight situation, where he has little control. Over time, especially in larger companies, conditions have been shifting to the tight end of this continuum. There has been great concern about the loss of autonomy of lower level managers. Some companies have made determined efforts to increase the lower managers' scope of authority, but as we shall see in Chapter 19, on decentralization, these efforts usually concern authority over the conduct of work and far less frequently over the distribution of rewards.

In any organization there are large numbers of rewards which influence the behavior of many people in the performance of their individual jobs and which influence integrated behavior. The development and distribution of these rewards are therefore complex, subtle, and important, controlled by organizational members, principally those in a position to influence greatly the structure of the organization. The shaping of a reward system is at times direct or indirect, hopefully deliberate and conscious, sometimes accidental and unintended. This chapter is concerned with not only the final distribution of rewards but also with the process by which they are allocated.

Basic Considerations of a Reward System

We have already noticed some of the fundamental considerations of a reward system; others, however, need to be identified.[3]

The behavior and objective that constitute a reward are both scarce. Whenever a particular item becomes common, or at least less rare, its influence decreases and, of course, vice versa.

Since an organization is allocating or distributing rewards it faces constraints; it cannot give out more than it has or is receiving. There is some slack in this, however. An organization could pay out more in wages than it receives in income for a short period, but not permanently. At the same time, people in an organization may be willing to receive less than they normally do or expect during a temporary "belt-tightening" situation to retain desirable long-term arrangements. The same holds true for intangible rewards.

Making decisions about the distribution of rewards is one of the most subtle, important challenges facing executives. First, they must maintain a proper balance between the rewards distributed and the resources to be drawn upon. Second, as already noted, they must distribute the rewards in such a fashion as to elicit the desired, integrated behavior. In Chapter 2 we explored leadership as a function which facilitates the satisfaction of people's needs, in terms of the individual leadership between a superior and a subordinate or small group of subordinates. Here we are concerned with the facilitation of need satisfaction through an organization where influential executives act indirectly through a structure which promotes such satisfaction.

[3] The following discussion has been adapted from Peter B. Clark and James Q. Wilson, "Incentive Systems: A Theory of Organizations," *Administrative Science Quarterly*, **6**, 1961, pp. 129–166.

Development of Sentiment to Support
a System of Reward

The effect of a system of reward extends beyond gratification of the immediate need. It does this through carryover, which influences the individual, or more precisely, the outlook or attitude the individual has toward the particular reward systems with which he comes into contact.

Robert Merton analyzed this effect in bureaucracies.[4] He noted that bureaucracies are organizations intended to accomplish certain tasks with the greatest efficiency. As a result jobs are designed with great precision. Specific rules and procedures are established for the execution of a job and precise standards are prescribed to determine who will be assigned to these jobs. To obtain a job an individual has to have high technical competence determined through an exhaustive, objective examination. Once he has obtained a job the individual has great security. Theoretically he can be removed only when incompetent, which would mean failure to apply the established rules, techniques, and procedures with accuracy. Advancement to higher positions is again based on objective examination of an individual's competence in the area of the higher position. Thus obtaining a job, keeping it, and advancing are dependent on the individual's competence to handle the technical aspects of the position involved, as individually measured by tests. None of these things depend on, theoretically at least, the opinion of the immediate superior.

People in bureaucracies learn quite early what is expected of them. They appreciate that their security and advancement rest heavily on their personal competence, and that there is a high certainty to the reward conditions which increase the intensity of the effect of the system. They often look on these arrangements as highly desirable and develop loyalty toward the system, or "positive sentiment" toward it.

What happens in regard to bureaucracy and tight organizational control of rewards seems equally applicable to individual executives when there is loose organization control of reward distribution. The individual who gains the confidence and favor of his superior, and is sure to be "taken care of," would be likely to accept and generate positive sentiment toward the system of reward distribution—in this case developing a strong personal loyalty to the superior.

[4] Robert K. Merton, "Bureaucratic Structure and Personality," *Social Forces*, **18**, 1940, pp. 560–568.

In returning to the continuum of the organizational control of rewards, we might say that at the loose end, where the supervisor has a great deal of control over distribution of rewards, strong personal loyalty toward him is likely to develop (Figure 15.1).   At the other end, where there is tight organizational control, strong loyalties are likely to develop for the organization and for the particular system of distributing the rewards.   Many organizations, of course, fall between these extremes, creating partial organizational control of reward distribution.   An example of this is a common situation where a central staff department sets up a wage plan that specifies the bracket for a job

High supervisory control of rewards	High organizational control of rewards
Loyalty to superior (Change of superior difficult)	Loyalty to organization (Change of work methods difficult)

Figure 15.1

and the wage range it will command but leaves to the supervisor great control over job assignment and the decision about whether the individual assigned will receive the top or bottom wage permissible.   In these organizations a supervisor has considerable freedom within definite boundaries.   The full extent of his freedom depends on his skill and ingenuity in finding the exact limits within which he must work. To no small degree, as we shall see in Chapter 22, the extent to which personal loyalties develop depends on the skill with which an individual uses the elements within his area of freedom.

Dysfunctional Consequences

The development of loyalties toward a reward system seems to have distinct advantages; this can also lead to a number of disadvantages. In a bureaucracy, for example, should there be any need or desire to change the organization, strong opposition would be likely to develop. To change the content of the job would mean that people would have to learn new techniques, new procedures, and new rules scrapping some of the old ones.   But these old rules and procedures represent considerable investment for organizational members who have spent much time and effort learning them and in developing skill in using them.   Second, to abandon these techniques is to give up a sure way of satisfying needs.   Change necessitates the expenditure of considerable effort in learning new techniques and rules, and means taking the risk that a person will not be able to perform the new procedures as well as those already known.

Where there is loose organizational control of reward distribution, the change in job methods or content does not have nearly as great an influence on the reward received and hence change comes more easily. At the same time, in the "loose" condition the possibility of a transfer to a new boss with whom the individual does not have the same personal relationship would be a considerable threat to the certainty of reward and would be strongly resisted (Figure 15.1).

The difficulties in changing job content, which can arise in bureaucracies, thwarts modification of organizational performance or of the goals toward which the organization is directed. As a condition facing an organization changes over time, this sort of rigidity renders the organization less compatible with its environment, less useful to the society about it.

Organizational rigidity is not the only consequence of strong sentiments developed toward a reward system under bureaucratic control. Presumably organizational members have both the organization objective and their own job objective in mind when they work. Yet because of the "loyalty effect" people at times come to see the rules, techniques, and procedures as ends in themselves and thereby play down or lose sight of the overall objectives of the organization or even the more specific objectives of their jobs. The feeling seems to be that if they perform the technique well, they will be rewarded even though the actual result is meaningless to the organization. This, of course, would not be serious if all the operations of a job were specified precisely. However, even in the most bureaucratic organizations there are unspecified things which people have to fill in for themselves or for which they have to adapt existing sets of instructions. If this is not done, coordination breaks down or the results of organizational efforts are unsuited to satisfying objectives.[5]

Having considered the effects of the development of positive sentiments toward the particular reward system, let us look closely at the process by which this occurs. It is not inconceivable that a person, on taking a job in a bureaucracy, will find the extensive detailed rules and procedures that largely eliminate the need for individual discretion confining and frustrating. He may feel that this is a stifling atmosphere for a well-rounded, independent individual such as himself. But, as we have also noted, attitudes often change. The things perhaps viewed undesirable at one time achieve considerable importance

[5] Merton, *op. cit.*

so that the desire to change roles diminishes and their precise execution induces pride. Exactly how this shift occurs is not certain, but part of the explanation seems to lie in the compatibility of a person's self-concept with the role he had to play.

Initially we hypothesize that the person's role-concept conflicts in a number of ways with the role he is playing. This conflict results in considerable personal strain and discomfort which over time can lead to one of two general changes. Either the person will abandon the role and seek one more compatible with this self-image or the self-image will change. If he stays in a bureaucracy, for example, he will begin to see himself as a public servant, a professional in his agency, someone who is capable of competently performing a significant and complex task which is important to society or the community. This produces a different self-image, one in which the person can take pride and which is compatible with the role he is now playing.[6]

MISMATCHING OF REWARD SYSTEMS

People may have many needs they think should be satisfied by organizational membership but which are not. This suggests that we should examine the kinds of rewards available in an organization and the needs people want satisfied. One way to study the matching of reward need and availability is to ask supervisors which rewards are available and then ask their subordinates which ones they want. The previously mentioned study of nursing personnel found that there was not a very adequate matching (Table 15.2). Of the fourteen different

Table 15.2

	Rewards Mentioned by Supervisors	Rewards Not Mentioned by Supervisors	Total
Rewards mentioned by nurses	3	6	11
Rewards not mentioned by nurses	3	0	3
Totals	8	6	14

Source: W. G. Bennis, N. Berkowitz, M. Affinito, M. Malone, "Authority, Power and the Ability to Influence," *Human Relations*, 11, 1958, p. 150.

[6] For an interesting discussion of the relationship between self concept and roles, see Theodore M. Newcomb, "Role Behaviors and the Study of an Individual Personality and of Groups," in Howard Brand, *The Study of Personality: A Book of Readings*, New York, John Wiley, 1954, pp. 331–345 and Paul R. Lawrence, *The Changing of Organizational Behavior Patterns*, Boston, Harvard University, 1958, Chapter 8.

rewards mentioned by the nurses and supervisory personnel, only five were both desired by the nurses and provided by the organization. Three rewards were provided but not mentioned at all by the nurses, and six which the nurses wanted were not provided by the organization.[7] How often mismatching of this magnitude occurs in organizations is hard to say, but it is common certainly and not unique to hospitals. We continually encounter executives who are disappointed at the lukewarm reception workers have accorded a newly renovated plant and workers who are disappointed because their superiors have failed to mention a job well done.

Mismatching of expected and provided rewards can occur in other ways. What might be a significant reward to one person, for example a superior, may be of only minor importance to another person, a subordinate. In the hospital study superiors and nurses were asked to rank rewards in the order of importance to the nurses. The nurses placed salary increases first on their list; the supervisors placed it fourth. The nurses said promotions were second on their list and supervisors placed this first (Table 15.3). It would be erroneous to

Table 15.3

Nurses' Ranking of Rewards Most Commonly Hoped for	Per cent	Supervisors' Ranking of Rewards Most Likely to be Given to Nurses	Per cent
1. Salary increase	33.3	1. Promotion	23.1
2. Praise	19.6	2. Praise	19.2
3. Promotion	14.7	3. Educational opportunities	15.4
4. Better job (more responsibility without promotion)	8.8	4. Salary increase	11.5
5. Educational opportunities	6.9	5. Report performance to higher-ups and put on permanent record	11.5

Source: W. G. Bennis, N. Berkowitz, M. Affinito, M. Malone, "Authority, Power and the Ability to Influence," *Human Relations*, 11, 1958, p. 150.

extrapolate these data too far. However, they do highlight the fact that many times there will be considerable difference in perception between superiors and subordinates regarding the importance of rewards.

[7] Bennis, Berkowitz, Affinito, Malone, *op. cit.*

PATTERNS OF REWARD DISTRIBUTION

Identification of rewards is one thing, distribution is another. The concern here is with the terms under which rewards are made available to organizational members. Quite apart from the intrinsic nature of the rewards, the manner in which they are distributed can have a profound effect on organizational performance.

Exchange

Perhaps the simplest and least charged of all reward systems is *exchange*. In its simplest form two parties strike an agreement whereby one of them will provide one element and the other will contribute or supply another. At the end of this exchange both may wish they had more, but probably feel that what they have received is reasonable and equitable. Exchange is the mode of distribution presumed to underlie classic wage and economic theory. It doubtless exists in many circumstances. However, there are times when exchange does not seem an adequate concept to explain what is actually taking place. Implicit in this concept is that each transaction can and probably will be different. People on the same level or in the same department will receive somewhat different rewards depending on what they have to exchange and on their relative bargaining position and bargaining skill at the time of the transaction.

Competition Against a Standard

For a number of reasons a second pattern has been chosen frequently for the allocation of rewards. This involves the establishment of a standard, and rewards are conferred on the basis of persons' meeting or exceeding it. This is the rationale for most incentive wage programs, as well as for many promotion programs in organizations and grading systems in educational institutions. In such a program, on meeting the standard people not only receive rewards from the organization but also a measure of their personal competence or performance; that is, the standards provide the basis for a self-evaluation of work. Intended or not, when such a plan is chosen, a method is introduced into the organization which is used to evaluate people and rank them in relation to others. Hence, it is possible with mode of reward distribution, as with others, to satisfy several rewards at the same time.

Competition for Preferred Positions

Any sort of measurement differentiates people in a social system and is to some degree a base for disharmony. However, as long as a standard is fairly fixed, clearly understood, apparently reasonable, and open to all, the effects probably will be minimized. But as soon as there is a preferred position in this competition (that is, a position which can be occupied by only one or a few people) a new, more potent type of competitive situation emerges. While the competition exists only against the standard, there may be mutual acceptance and sharing of experience differentiated by the extent of individual ambition. However, with a system in which only one or a few people can win or succeed, people compete vigorously among themselves to attain this preferred position. Efforts may be directed not only toward succeeding and meeting certain performance levels but also toward preventing others from doing so.[8]

An interesting example of such disruptive effects was found in an investigation of a government employment agency. In this agency the statistics on the number of clients placed in a job by interviewers was circulated to everyone in the office. This created a strong competitive attitude among the members of the agency. In order to get the best possible rating interviewers began hoarding job openings, which were scarce, rather than making them known to others in the office. As a result, some interviewers were able to have very impressive performances, while others could not because of not having access to all open positions. Needless to say, there was considerable hard feeling among members of the agency, and although some interviewers had very high placement records, the agency as a whole had a lower rate than similar units where competition was not as strong.[9]

In this situation there were really two competitions. One was the planned competition against a standard and the other the unplanned and initially unperceived competition for a preferred position. It was this second perceived competition which caused the difficulty. Many competitions for a preferred position are innocently established in an organization, as is often the case with positions or departments which check the performance of others, such as inspectors, quality control, accounting personnel, etc. They exist, in effect, to find when others are deviating from standards or are going wrong, thus creating the win-

[8] Effects of this type of situation on cohesiveness are discussed in Chapter 5.
[9] Peter M. Blau, "Cooperation and Competition in a Bureaucracy," *American Journal of Sociology*, **59**, 1954, pp. 530–535.

lose situation referred to in Chapter 5.   The inspector "wins" (justifies his job) when he shows that poor quality work is being produced; at the same time the production superintendent "loses."   The existence of such positions and arrangements has a significant impact on the behavior of organization members, particularly on their willingness to cooperate.

REWARD SYSTEM AND THE LEVEL OF NEED ACTIVATION

A reward, as we have seen, may have different meanings to different people.   Some of this difference, of course, could be a matter of individual taste and preference.   However, there are other factors which influence what is important to a person at a particular time, and many of these are either controlled or considerably influenced by the organization.   In Chapter 2, on motivation, we noted that people have different classes of needs and that there was something to be gained from considering these in an hierarchial arrangement.   Hence, if the need for safety of economic income were the one activated, the opportunity of participating in decisions about a new work layout would not be of much interest.   Conversely, when people's safety needs relevant to job security are satisfied, the offer of a reward which will give them additional job security is superfluous.[10]   This suggests that, in designing a reward system, managers in the organization must be cognizant of the level of need activation prevalent among organizational members and provide rewards which are congruent with the level.   To fail to do so is to create reward systems that are going to be unused or ineffective which leave unprovided, and therefore unobtainable, many desired rewards.

If an organization is to provide a reward system congruent with the level of need activation, the members of the managerial hierarchy must accurately perceive that level as it is conceived by organizational members.   Yet this perception is not likely to be too accurate (Table 15.2).   Why this occurs is difficult to explain concisely although some indications are contained in chapters on perception and the managerial hierarchy.   Regardless of how it occurs it is a real phenomenon, and to the degree that perceptions of organizational member needs differ from actual needs, the organization will probably be less efficient and a less satisfactory unit in which to have membership.

[10] For further elaboration on this point, see James V. Clark, "Motivation in Work Groups: A Tentative View," *Human Organization*, **19**, 1960–61, pp. 199–208.

SUMMARY

In this chapter we have considered an extremely difficult and slippery topic. People in an organization have certain needs which they expect to have satisfied to a degree through their membership in the organization. Hence, the adequacy with which the rewards available match the actual needs of members will be a measure of the effectiveness of the organization. This matching is not only imperfect, but it is also frequently much out of phase.

The meaning of rewards was explored at some length. We began by noting that an organizational member can be viewed as continually searching for ways or means with which to satisfy his needs. The intensity of the effect of these rewards depends on a number of considerations, among them the strength of the need they are to satisfy and the certainty of the reward. When a means is found to satisfy a need, and is used several times, an individual usually develops positive sentiments toward the means or the system behind it. There are advantages to this, but there are also disadvantages or dysfunctional consequences of organizational rigidity and displacement of goals.

We have considered the basic elements of rewards and began to consider their provision as an organizational matter, recognizing that the distribution of rewards is basically an organizational affair. A range of possible conditions was noted: at one extreme an executive is given great autonomy in the distribution of rewards, and at the other extreme the executive has no control—all rewards here being distributed by organization rules and procedures or organization members other than the immediate superior. These two "styles" were seen to influence the focus of member loyalty and the type of rigidity or inflexibility generated. The design of reward systems influences the type of prevailing competition, which can have differing effects on individual and group behavior. The more selective a reward system is in distributing a reward—that is, a reward system which gives certain positions preference over others—the likelier it is to increase competition among unit members and, therefore, create disruptive forces in addition to high levels of individual motivation.

Managerial Structure

O FTEN when people think of large or complex organizations they envision a structure of managerial positions (Figure 16.1) which shows departments, positions, and their reporting relationships. This structure, however, is only part of an organization. Hence, we explore this topic after having considered other things which in a sense are more fundamental to organizational performance.

As with many topics related to organizations, people in general know something about organizational hierarchies. It might be well to review briefly the highlights of more traditional concepts of hierarchy to identify them and point out where they fit in the material covered in this chapter.

In the traditional concept of organizational hierarchy, positions are arranged according to authority. The position at the top of the organization, in a business concern usually called the *president*, has the greatest authority. The next level, usually containing *vice presidents*, has delegated to it portions of the president's authority; hence, its scope of authority is smaller but is complete over all positions reporting to it. The next level of positions, perhaps called *department heads*, has a still smaller scope of authority, and so on down to the individual worker. A *manager* at any place in a hierarchy is responsible for the activities of all units or positions reporting to him. If this condition is to be met, he must (1) be thoroughly informed about what is taking place, (2) know clearly what is to be accomplished, and (3) be able to exercise complete control over everything under his jurisdiction. From these requirements follows a number of anticipated practices in organizations: (1) that each person will have only one superior (unity of command) who insures his activities to be precisely coordinated to accomplish subunit goals, (2) that there should be clear channels of communication up to the manager providing him with

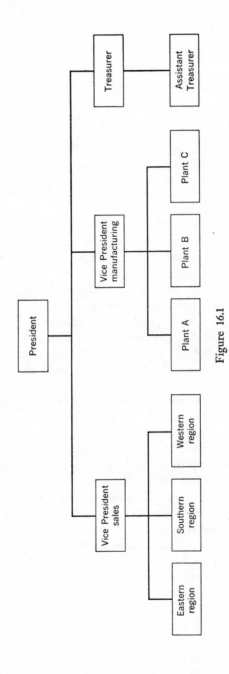

Figure 16.1

adequate information to make necessary decisions, and (3) that flowing down from him will be a series of orders which will be obeyed by all those in subordinate positions. Characteristic of this approach, therefore, information, orders and instructions, decisions, and acts of coordination and control are arranged in a vertical or hierarchial manner. In reality, some events in the management structure follow this pattern; a great many do not. Managerial structure as discussed in this chapter is viewed as consisting of a number of patterns of activity.

NATURE AND PURPOSE OF A MANAGERIAL STRUCTURE

Work, Operating, and Management Systems

To begin our discussion of what constitutes a managerial structure, let us return to the earlier discussion of systems. A method of analysis has been developed to help probe the topic without becoming bogged down in complex interrelationships. This approach begins by saying, "Let us take the system under investigation as an entity and study the relationship between what goes into the system and what goes out, and for the moment ignore what takes place within the system." A production system, such as the factory, is analyzed by studying the inputs in the form of raw materials, labor, machinery, etc., and their relationship to the output in the form of finished products or services, satisfactions, etc.[1] (Figure 16.2).

If a little more detailed but still very gross analysis is made, the content of the rectangle labeled "Factory" can be explored. We may find that it consists of a number of smaller systems, or subsystems,

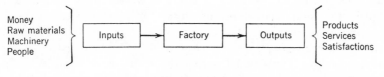

Figure 16.2

---

[1] The reader may at first think this is an overly simplified approach and unmeaningful; however, he should recall that much of our knowledge of the physical sciences is of this form. For example, we do not know what gravity is or the means by which it works; however, we can predict its effect. We say that given an input of a certain mass at a certain velocity into a particular type of gravitational field (equivalent of our square for the factory), we can predict the output of the item in regard to its velocity and mass.

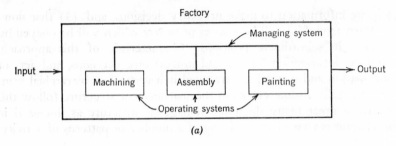

(a)

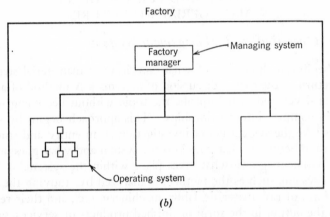

(b)

Figure 16.3. A factory consisting of operating and managing systems.

which represent departments performing manufacturing functions such as machining, assembly, and painting. We call this group of subsystems *operating systems*. These subsystems cover what each of the departments in the factory does; however, their sum does not explain the total factory performance, for it does not explain how these parts fit together. Hence, one other factor is found inside the factory: a *managing system*[2] (Figure 16.3), which is not directly involved with organizational output but is necessary to make the collection of operating systems meaningful. In essence, a management system includes any of those activities that are external to an operating system and are involved with integrating its efforts with other operating systems for the completion of an organizational objective. The

[2] These concepts are for the most part developed from A. K. Rice, *Productivity and Social Organization: The Ahmedabad Experiment*, London, Tavistock Publications, 1958, and Eric J. Miller, "Technology, Territory and Time," *Human Relations*, **12**, 1959, pp. 243–272.

managerial system could operate without any formal hierarchy at all. In actual practice the managerial system is largely facilitated by the managerial hierarchy. In this chapter we view the managerial hierarchy as the most important element in, and determinant of, the managerial system.

Returning to the analysis, each department or subunit in turn is divided into additional subunits, and these are integrated by another management system. Hence, each operating system can be considered as consisting of suboperating systems and a submanagement system. Ultimately, of course, a point is reached where the managerial system no longer can be differentiated from the execution of work. Here we reach a particular type of operating system called a *work unit*. In a factory this might be a worker on a bench; in the laboratory it might be the scientist with his instruments; and in certain areas, such as finance, it might be the vice president of finance negotiating with a bank. The distinguishing feature is that the work unit is at the end of the means-ends chain, where acts are performed that culminate in the accomplishment of basic purposes, rather than in those events that are concerned with managing these acts.

We have taken this approach for several reasons: (1) the basic systems approach provides us a useful theoretical base to integrate material not only in this chapter but also in the following chapters, (2) most of our attention until now has been oriented to, if not exclusively about, work units. A simple statement that the managerial structure is concerned with integrating the performance of work units might create the impression that this structure is fairly homogenous in nature. This approach clearly reveals that it is not, that it is a complex set of different things. The work system is determined by a number of factors, among them the *technical system;* that is, the sequence of operations required by the selected technology to make a product perform a service. Although the *work system* is molded by, and is frequently very close to, the technical system, it nonetheless is different. For example, the technical system may include the operations of casting, heat treating, grinding, and polishing. These would be spelled out in engineering blueprints and specifications. The work system might contain activities on the part of the employees to perform these operations in this general order, but may include other activities as well, such as storing the casting before and after operations, inspected parts, etc. (Figure 16.4).

Again, let us recall that systems are interrelated; therefore, although these systems are different, they have important reciprocal effects on each other. The technical system determines some of the principal

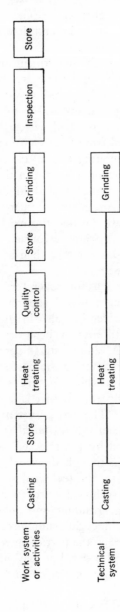

Figure 16.4

activities of work systems and their sequence. It also is one of the principal determinants of interdependency of the work system. The work system, on the other hand, can reduce the impact of the technical system by, for example, the introduction of stores at appropriate places, which will reduce the felt interdependency. In return, the success with which the technical system functions is totally dependent on the work system. The managing system may be conceived of as being next to the work system and interrelated with the other two. Hence, the requirements of the technical system filter through the work system to determine properties of the managing system. But the managing system, in turn, makes important decisions about the other two (Figure 16.5).

This scheme has been elaborated for two reasons: first, to show the interrelationship among various systems and the organization goals; second, to bring out the fact that the nature of the managing system at any one time will be determined by a number of things—the nature and the present state of both the technical system and work system and the nature and degree of organizational goals. The managerial system is continually changing to adjust to these variations. If the technology changes, as, for example, when a marketing company decides to switch from having clerks deal directly with customers to a supermarket operation, its managing system must of necessity change. If the goals of the organization change, say, from trying to serve the customer's immediate wants to trying to serve their more basic and less frequently changing ones (as might occur if a company decided to make plain muslin sheeting rather than fabric used in high-fashion clothes), the managing system must also change. We shall have more to say about the form and processes of these changes in Part Four. At this point, however, it should be clear that there is no final, absolute, ideal form for the managerial hierarchy to take. Instead, the effort must be to develop the best, or at least a satisfactory, managerial system for the particular set of goals and technical and work systems (among other things) faced. Since these things vary enormously, the

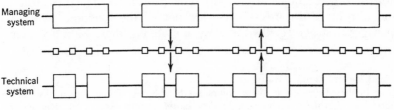

Figure 16.5

specifics of organizations will be as numerous as the individual's sets of conditions.   Each organization is, in a sense, unique.

Functions of the Managerial Structure

A partial answer to the question, of what purpose is the executive superstructure, is that it provides coordination for the work of the organization. This it can do through a number of means. First, it is the means for facilitating the mechanisms for coordination and control discussed earlier.[3] Second, the executive hierarchy defines subunit goals. If it does this well, work can be easily integrated; if not, co-ordination is difficult or impossible. Third, even with the best of intentions, actual organizations will have conflict. Subordinates who are in agreement on the objectives of the organization may see quite different ways of achieving these objectives. This leads to conflict which frequently has to be resolved through the exercise of higher authority. Also, as we have noted, people in different sections of the organization may perceive objectives differently. Thus, there may be more fundamental and difficult differences of opinion which will have to be resolved. In fact, sources of conflict could be listed almost endlessly which, without some means of being resolved, could seri-ously interfere with and perhaps prevent coordinated effort.[4]

The need for and the methods of coordination and control have received some, but not really adequate, attention from traditional organ-ization theorists when discussing the function of managerial structure. Also inadequately discussed, but nonetheless important, is the function of *allocation*. Frequently, this is taken to mean the allocation of capital resources to different uses as approached in economic studies. Needless to say, this is an important aspect of allocation. As we have seen, though, allocation also includes the assignment of people to different jobs or vice versa and the distribution of phases or elements in basic organizational processes such as control among various posi-tions, individuals, or both. Still another aspect which has received a great deal of attention in the last fifteen to twenty years is the motiva-tion of organizational members. The managerial structure provides and distributes rewards. These are not all the functions which the managerial structure fills but they are among those most frequently cited.

[3] See Chapters 12 and 13.
[4] For further discussion of these points, see Herbert A. Simon, Donald W. Smith-burg, and Victor A. Thompson, *Public Administration*, New York, Knopf, 1956, pp. 210–213.

Hierarchal Zones

The statement frequently is made that the work of the manager is the same anywhere in the organization; that is, all managers must plan, organize, motivate, coordinate, and control. In a broad sense this is true; however, the stress placed on these individual functions varies greatly in different managerial positions. The foreman may spend relatively little time planning and a great deal of time motivating and coordinating, whereas the senior vice president may spend a great deal of time planning and controlling but proportionally less in motivating. In fact, at times the differences between managerial positions, particularly when viewed along a hierarchical dimension, are so great that they appear to be distinctly different classes of work. For this reason many analysts have talked of zones or levels of management and pointed to the differences among them.[5]

The number of levels or zones varies somewhat with how they are defined. Here we consider three zones of management which seems not unreasonable in describing typical, large scale organizations. At the very top, there is the *institutional level.*[6] Here the environment of the organization is evaluated, and the basic organizational goals are established to fit the appraisal of the environment, the resources which the organization has at its disposal, and the objectives of organizational members. This level also makes the first of the means decisions that determine the basic ways in which the organization shall achieve these ends. Last, the institutional level makes fundamental allocative decisions about the organizational resources such as money, time, and people. In the business concern this is typically regarded as the work of the board of trustees and often it is. It should be noted, however, that whether the board actually assumes this role or whether it is carried out by the president and vice president who use the board as a compliant rubber stamp, is not the issue here. The important thing is that this function, which in the broadest sense of the word is a trustee function for the organization, must be performed.

Below this institutional zone is a *general management zone,* which is primarily concerned with taking the broad means-type decisions of institutional zones as objectives and translating them into more specific terms, processes, units, etc. This is where the basic divisions of the

[5] See, for example, Talcott Parsons, *Structure and Process in Modern Societies,* Glencoe, Free Press, 1960, particularly pp. 16–96, and Paul Holden, Lounsbury Fish, and Hubert L. Smith, *Top-Management Organization and Control,* New York, McGraw-Hill, 1951, particularly pp. 15–29.

[6] Parsons, *op. cit.*

organization are determined and where the general overall programs are established.   Here the fundamental decisions are made as to which system needs prominent attention, and furthermore, it is here that the results are carefully inspected to make sure the organization is meeting its objectives.   This level in a business organization is typically thought of as containing a president, top vice presidents, and top-level staff positions such as legal counsel, treasurer, and economist.   The emphasis is on the overall organization and is primarily concerned with planning and bringing about organizational adaptation to modifications in the environment (Figure 16.6).   We might call this the *facilitating function*.

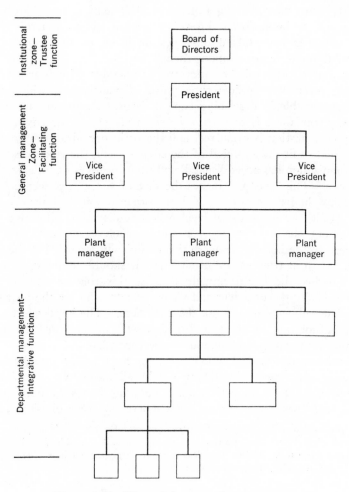

Figure 16.6.   Hierarchal zones of management.

Below the general management zone are those managerial positions that are primarily concerned with carrying out or achieving the more specific goals and objectives. These levels operate within fairly restricted boundaries. For them the products or services and basic means of making or providing them are determined; the objectives are set. They are primarily intended to bring performance to the point where it satisfies established objectives and conditions. They are directly concerned with the details of coordination, control, and motivation, in addition to funneling vast amounts of necessary information to higher levels. We might call this the *departmental management* zone comprising plant managers, general foremen, and departmental foremen, all of whom fill an integrative function.

The Anatomy of Management Structure

One of the dominant characteristics of management structures is their pyramidal form. A single head at the top gives way to progressively larger numbers of positions at each level down through the organization. There are several explanations for this pyramidal form. One is that as the overall organizational goal is subdivided into subgoals, the number of subgoals becomes larger with each progressive subdivision. If each of these subgoals is the responsibility of a department or a position, then these organizational units become more numerous as we move further from the basic organizational goals. Another factor which leads to the pyramidal form is that as the work of achieving a goal is divided, it leads to a necessity for coordination. A common method of achieving coordination is to have one person so placed that he can view the activities of others and see that they are integrated toward accomplishing a goal, that is, to use a hierarchy of positions to achieve coordination.[7] This leads to two important points in traditional organizational theory.

UNITY OF COMMAND. If subordinates are to have their efforts coordinated, it seems necessary that they receive instructions from a single source. Hence, in traditional organizational analysis, it is usually maintained that a subordinate should have only one superior or that there be a unity of command.[8] We cannot argue easily with the reasonableness of this concept. The difficulty is that this requirement is violated in varying degrees in almost every organization. As we

[7] For further discussion, see Simon, Smithburg, and Thompson, *op. cit.*, pp. 130–131.
[8] L. Urwick, *The Elements of Administration*, New York, Harper, 1943, p. 45.

shall see in Chapter 17, staff raises serious problems with the concept of units of command. Second, there are some organizations which have deliberately created units where a plant may be headed by two or even three coplant managers; and this multiple command extends to a number of other departments in the same organization. It should also be recalled that when discussing social groups, it was noted that a group might have several leaders. Hence, multiple leaders or superiors is not an "unnatural" condition. We might summarize this by saying that organizations tend toward unity of command and that typically a person will have one superior who is more dominant than others in influencing his behavior. It is also important to keep in mind that hierarchal supervision is only one way of achieving coordination. Therefore, the necessity for unity of command will depend on the complex of other means being used to achieve coordination as well as the type and degree of coordination needed.

SPAN OF CONTROL. Achieving coordination by having one person supervise the activity of others is limited by each one's work capacity; thus there is a limit to the number of people one person can supervise. The number of people reporting to a person is called the span of control. To coordinate the efforts of large numbers of people, it becomes necessary to divide the work to be supervised among a number of managers and, in turn, to have their efforts coordinated by a higher level of managers who also have their span of control limited by their work capacity.

Span of control is one of the important elements which determines the shape of the management hierarchy. If an organization has broad spans of control, it will have fewer levels in it and be flat in appearance (Figure 16.7a). If an organization with the same number of members has narrow spans of control, it has many more levels of supervision and a more peaked appearance (Figure 16.7b). If there are sixty-four workers to be supervised and the span of control is to be eight, there would be eight supervisors directing the workers and one manager directing the supervisors. On the other hand, if the span of control were four, the same number of workers would require sixteen supervisors who in turn would be directed by four managers, and these four in turn would be directed by one manager. Reducing the span of control by one-half therefore would increase the number of positions in the managerial structure from nine to twenty-one and increase the levels of supervision from two to three. Seldom, of course, is the span of control uniform throughout an entire organization. Generally speaking, spans become smaller the higher one goes in

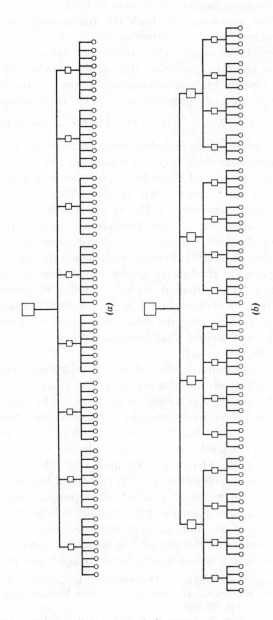

Figure 16.7

a managerial structure. Furthermore, even on the same level, there will be considerable variation in the span of control.

In view of its importance to both the functioning and form of managerial structure, it is not surprising that span of control has received considerable attention. One strategy of handling the span of control centers on the observation that as the number of positions reporting to a superior increases arithmetically, the number of possible interrelationships increases geometrically. This relationship is given by the formula, $C = N\left(\dfrac{2^N}{2} + N - 1\right)$. Here C is the total possible number of interrelationships including those between the superior and individual subordinate, those between a superior and several subordinates at the same time, and those between subordinates without the superior being a direct party. Hence, for three subordinates the number of possible relationships is 42, for 5 it is a 100, and for 10 it is 5,210.[9] If we assume that all these relationships are important to the performance of the unit and that the superior must supervise all of them, the number of interrelationships with which the superior would be concerned quickly reaches staggering proportions as the span of control increases. This situation has led a number of people to propose that the span of control should be kept narrow, particularly for positions higher in the managerial structure. There are recommendations that the span of control should not exceed five or six and that the ideal number is four.[10]

Such recommendations depend on two fundamental assumptions: (1) that all possible relationships are used and (2) that the superior must be involved with supervising all of them. The fact that it is possible for two people to interact does not mean that they will or have to. In fact, many *possible* interrelationships never take place. Many that do do not need supervision by a superior or require that he concern himself at all. Hence, it seems more reasonable to expect that the actual number of subordinates a superior could handle effectively would be larger than we might conclude from computations proposed by Graicunas, and indeed some empirical studies indicate this to be the case. In a survey of one hundred large companies (over five thousand employees), it was found that the median number of executives reporting to the president was somewhere between eight and nine (Table

[9] V. A. Graicunas, "Relationship in Organization," in Luther Gulick and L. Urwick, *Papers on the Science of Administration,* New York, Institute of Public Administration, 1937, pp. 181–188.

[10] L. Urwick, "Executive Decentralization with Functional Coordination," *The Management Review,* 24, 1935, p. 359. Similar proposals have been made by others, for example, Ralph C. Davis, *The Fundamentals of Top Management,* New York, Harper, 1951, p. 276.

16.1).   In a study of forty-one medium-size companies (five hundred to five thousand employees), it was found that the median number of executives reporting to the president was between six and seven (Table

Table 16.1   Number of Executives Reporting to President in 100 Large Companies (over 5,000 employees)

Number of Executives Reporting to the President	Number of Companies	
1	6	
2	...	
3	1	
4	3	
5	7	
6	9	
7	11	
8	8	
		Median
9	8	
10	6	
11	7	
12	10	
13	8	
14	4	
15	1	
16	5	
17	...	
18	1	
19	...	
20	1	
21	1	
22	...	
23	2	
24	1	
Total	100	

Source: Ernest Dale, Planning and Developing the Company Organization Structure, New York, American Management Association, 1952, p. 57.

16.2).   The median span of control in both cases was larger than those recommended on more theoretical grounds and, furthermore, the spans of control were larger for the larger companies where we might reasonably have expected them actually to have been smaller.[11]

[11] Ernest Dale, Planning and Developing the Company Organization Structure, New York, American Management Association, 1952, pp. 56–57.

Table 16.2   *Number of Executives Reporting to the President
in 41 Medium-Size Companies*

Number of Executives Reporting to the President	Number of Companies	
1	3	
2	. . .	
3	2	
4	2	
5	4	
6	8	
		Median
7	7	
8	5	
9	2	
10	4	
11	1	
12	. . .	
13	1	
14	1	
15	. . .	
16	. . .	
17	1	
Total	41	

Source: Ernest Dale, *Planning and Developing the Company Organization Structure,* New York, American Management Association, 1952, p. 59.

Findings such as these have caused some people to question seriously the strategy of narrow span of control and to endorse the counter-strategy, that of broad spans of control.   Research conducted in the Sears-Roebuck Company suggested that both employee morale and operating efficiency were closely related to the organization and that efficiency and morale increased with broader span of control and the resultant flatter type of managerial structure.[12]   Here giving a manager a broad span of control encouraged and in fact required that he give his subordinates a great deal of discretion or autonomy.   Hence, there was enforced decentralization.   As we noted under division of labor, increasing the scope of responsibility and area of discretion can have an important impact on individual performance and attitude. Moreover, by permitting a flatter structure with fewer levels of super-

[12] James C. Worthy, "Organizational Structure and Employee Morale," *American Sociological Review,* 15, 1950, pp. 169–179.

vision, lower members of the organization hierarchy have easier access to the top executives and top executives can be in closer touch with day-to-day activities at the work level. Also, with a broad span of control, supervisors were forced to restrict themselves to those things that were essentially their job and had to leave their subordinates to their own. In this way they developed a sharper differentiation between the work of the manager and his subordinates, which was found to be associated with improved employee attitudes and subunit effectiveness.[13]

The broad span of control strategy received support from a number of directions.[14] Implicit in some of these analyses is the assumption that what is really needed is separation of the superior and subordinate, in effect keeping the superior out of the subordinate's hair. This is the counterargument to the other strategy that effective organizational performance comes from a superior being directly cognizant of, and involved with, everything that takes place within his unit. We can perhaps unravel this further by referring to research which in some ways runs counter to the broad span of control strategy. In a study of an IBM company plant in New York it was found that as the company reorganized, decreasing the span of control of its first-line supervisors, the morale of the employees increased and so did productivity and the efficiency of the plant.[15] The important point to be noted is that during this period the company also carried out an extensive program of decentralization or, as it has sometimes been called, *job enrichment*. The activities assigned to the workers were increased considerably as was their area of decision making.

The result of much of this was that interaction between the workers and their superior actually increased. From earlier developments in Chapter 7 we would expect this increased interaction between superior and subordinate to lead to increased positive sentiments between the two, which it did. The nature of the interaction, however, was quite different from what existed before. Here the objective sought was more consciously shared by both superior and subordinate, and the superior's role was more one of helping and assisting than of directing.

[13] Robert L. Kahn and Daniel Katz, "Leadership Practices in Relation to Productivity and Morale," in Cartwright and Zander, *Group Dynamics, Research and Theory*, Evanston, Row, Peterson and Company, 1960, pp. 554–570.
[14] See, for example, Herbert A. Simon, "The Proverbs of Administration," *Public Administration Review*, 6, 1946, pp. 53–67 or Waino W. Suojanen, "The Span of Control—Fact or Fable?" *Advanced Management*, 20, 1955, pp. 5–13.
[15] F. L. W. Richardson and Charles R. Walker, *Human Relations in an Expanding Company*, New Haven, Yale University, Labor and Management Center, 1948, pp. 9–11, 86–93.

Hence, a differentiation between superior and subordinate roles actually existed.

It appears, therefore, that to specify one number as the ideal size for a span of control or one particular strategy as being preferable to another can lead to undesirable or confusing conclusions largely because these prescriptions grossly oversimplify a complex phenomenon. To determine the appropriate span of control for a given situation, it seems necessary to consider a number of other important factors.

Factors Influencing a Satisfactory Span of Control

The decision on a satisfactory span of control seems to depend on the nature of the situation defined by two broad classes of variables: the need for control and coordination imposed by the situation and the means used in the organization to provide this coordination and control. Let us consider the second class of variables first.

TYPE OF COORDINATION OR CONTROL CHOSEN. Implicit in much traditional organization theory in which a narrow span of control is proposed is the assumption that all coordination and control must come from the superior. If this type of situation exists or is sought, the work of the superior will be enormous. However, if the necessary coordination can be provided by a combination of means such as administrative systems and self- and group-control, as well as hierarchical control, the burden on the superior can be substantially reduced, and broader spans of control become more possible.

CONSTRAINTS ON SPAN OF CONTROL. The need for coordination and control varies according to the number of factors. As this need becomes greater, the ability of the individual manager to satisfy it through direct supervision may be exceeded. It is hardly possible at this time to list all the factors which influence the need for coordination. We merely note some of the principal ones.

DEGREE OF INTERDEPENDENCY. As noted in Chapter 12, the degree of interdependency in a work situation can vary enormously depending on the technology used, the objectives chosen, the basic organizational structure, etc. In brief, the greater the interdependency, the greater is the need for coordination.

SIMILARITY OF SUBORDINATES' JOBS. If the superior is going to direct the work of subordinates, he must know what the jobs are, how they are performed, and he must possess an array of information about the state of work in and around them. Consequently, the superior's job is much simpler when his subordinates do similar or identical work; there are fewer jobs for him to learn, and there is less confusion in his mind in turning his attention from one subordinate to another. The number of factors which can influence any of the work in his department is relatively less than if the jobs were more varied, etc.

DISCRETION EXERCISED BY SUBORDINATES. We might note two dimensions which can describe the subordinate's scope of discretion in decision making: (1) the range of things he can make decisions about. The foreman who can only make decisions about immediate work scheduling problems does not have the same range as a foreman who can make decisions about scheduling problems, housekeeping, hiring and firing employees, giving raises, etc. (2) The other discretion dimension is time. Here we mean the length of time which can elapse before a subordinate has to report to or check with his superior. The worker who is checked on by his boss every half-hour has a much shorter discretionary time span than the maintenance man who may go off on a job for four or five hours by himself, and he has far less time span than the salesman who may be on the road for two weeks at a time and only files a report when he comes back. As discretion of the subordinate increases, the demands on the superior decrease.

This scope of discretion exercised by a subordinate is in turn influenced by two other sets of factors. One concerns the capabilities of the subordinate. The subordinate who has learned the programs for his job is not likely to be checked on nearly as frequently as the new man who is using the program of activities for the first time. Another aspect of this situation is the motivation of the subordinate; the one who is interested in his work, motivated to do his job, requires less direction than one who is not. The other principal set of factors concerns the perception of the superior. The executive who assumes his subordinates lack initiative, maturity, or ability does not see them as very capable. Therefore in his mind he is not justified in permitting them a greater degree of discretion, which means that he must assume more control and direction.

STABILITY OF ENVIRONMENT. We have already discussed a number of ways in which the stability of the environment influences the need for coordination and control, but one important influence of an unstable environment has not yet been discussed.

As goals are broken into a hierarchy of subgoals through means-ends analysis, one of the important things which determines the exact nature of the subgoals is the environment facing the organization. If some element of this environment changes, one or more of these subgoals is likely to become inappropriate. If the environment changes rapidly and drastically enough, a number of subgoals are likely to need revision. To do this rapidly, it may be necessary for higher executives or managers, whose goals may not have needed changing to redefine subgoals for their subordinates to meet the new situation. Hence, in times of business crisis it is not uncommon to find decision-making powers being pulled up the hierarchy. Considering the instability of things facing an army in the field, perhaps we can see more readily why there is more insistence on retaining decision-making powers higher in the hierarchy and keeping the span of control narrow.

Linked Command Groups

In Chapter 6 on groups, it was pointed out that an important type of group, from the organizational point of view, was the command group consisting of a superior and his immediate subordinates. It is important to note, however, that the superior in one command group is usually the subordinate in another and a peer member of other groups. Most managerial positions, therefore, serve to link command groups, and it is often useful to think of an organization as a complex of linked command groups as illustrated in Figure 16.8. Such a concept makes it easier to grasp many problems in organizations. It brings out the complexity of the role held by an organizational executive who simultaneously holds superior-subordinate relationships in one group and horizontal peer relationships, in addition to subordinate-superior relationships, in the other. These are three different roles, which at times are conflicting, making difficult demands on the behavior of an organizational manager. The liaison nature of the man-

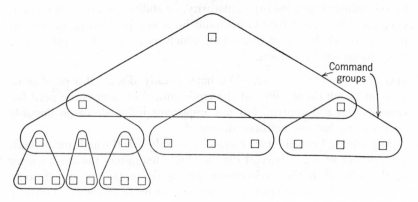

Figure 16.8

ager's position requires him to be a channel through which information, requests, and instructions flow.   On the other hand, since many
of the demands may be different or incompatible and the information
confusing, misleading, or threatening, he must many times act as a
buffer between these organizational elements.[16]   The stress and consequences resulting from being in a position requiring multiple roles is
discussed more fully in Part Four.

It may be well to pause and examine what this means for the individual executive in his daily work.   Let us consider a foreman directing his work group.   Popular thinking might envision him spending
most of the time giving orders and instructions to his subordinates and
in turn receiving instructions and orders from his superiors.   One
study of foreman behavior showed that a little over 26 per cent of a
foreman's interaction time was with his own immediate subordinates
and that a not quite 6 per cent of his time was engaged in interacting
with either his immediate superior or the superior's superior.   On the
other hand, he spent a little over 25 per cent of his day interacting
with people who were not in actual hierarchal relationship to him—
other foremen, and various service groups.   (Table 16.3).   We might

Table 16.3

Contact	Per cent of Time
Own operators	26.4
Other foremen	7.0
General foreman	4.6
Department superintendent	1.1
Other superiors	0.4
Service personnel	
Maintenance	2.5
Inspection	2.3
Material	2.6
Work standards	0.4
Other operators	3.8
All others	6.2
Total contact	57.3

Source: R. H. Guest, "Of Time and the Foreman," Personnel, 1956, 32,
pp. 478–486.

[16] For further development of linked command groups or (as they are also called)
overlapping teams, see Rensis Likert, New Patterns of Management, New York,
McGraw-Hill, 1961, Chapter 8; or Robert S. Weiss, Process of Organization,
Ann Arbor, Survey Research Center, Institute for Social Research, University of
Michigan, 1956, particularly Chapter 5.

also note that these interactions occur with a great many different people. In the particular study cited, foremen would interact with between twenty-five and fifty different individuals.[17]

This suggests that foremen spend relatively little time interacting with their superiors, about a quarter of their time interacting with their own subordinates, and about the same amount of time interacting with people outside of their own work group. Much of this interaction doubtless coordinates the work of their unit with other units in the organization. In short, these interactions form an integral part of the coordination of the work system.

The significance of this situation for the success of the foreman and indirectly of the organization can be seen in a study of an automobile assembly plant where there is a high degree of interdependency in the work system. Here it was found that the more successful foremen (as rated by their organizational superiors) spent more time interacting with people outside their own work group; whereas those who were rated less effective spent significantly less time interacting outside of their work group.[18] Furthermore, the more effective foreman directed these outside contacts to other foremen, that is, to peers (called horizontal relationships), to service or staff personnel (called diagonal relationships) such as inspectors and personnel department employees, or to workers reporting to other foremen whose services were necessary in facilitating the work of his own department.[19]

FACTORS CAUSING VARIATION IN MANAGERIAL STRUCTURE

Underlying much of the earlier discussion on the anatomy of organizational structure has been the theme that the various structural components can be arranged in a number of different ways depending on the particular set of factors which face the organization. In short, we may say that a satisfactory managerial structure is formed partially in response to a set of existing factors rather than in a way that conforms with a universal ideal. Some of these factors and their influences have been touched on briefly earlier in the chapter. Let us consider them in more detail.

[17] Robert H. Guest, "Of Time and the Foreman," *Personnel*, 32, 1956, pp. 478–486.
[18] Frank J. Jasinski, "Foreman Relationships Outside the Work Group," *Personnel*, 33, 1956, pp. 130–136.
[19] *Ibid.*

Degree of Interdependency

In general, the greater the interdependency of organizational units, the more challenging is the task with which the managerial structure is confronted. As noted previously, a concern such as Sears-Roebuck and Company, which has numerous retail outlets around the country, has a relatively low order of interdependency between these units. Consequently it has to provide fewer mechanisms to facilitate co-ordination. This means less need for procedural systems, horizontal coordination between peers, such as store managers, etc. It affords a definite advantage which permits a larger span of control with a flatter type of organizational form.

This form is in contrast to that of a company which has a high degree of interdependency among organizational units as, for example, a national airline where units on the west coast are closely inter-connected with those on the East coast because of necessity of individ-ual aircraft and passengers using and depending on both regional offices. This interdependency plus the problems of safety, govern-mental regulations, and other elements make geographical units much more interdependent. Consequently, we expect and find much more extensive use of administrative systems, that is, means to promote formalized interaction by providing, for example, various networks of communications open to executives. However, the demands of inter-dependency are so great that there is also extensive use of hierarchal control and coordination with the resultant narrower span of control and more peaked type of structure.

Environment

The environment in which an organization operates is always chang-ing. In fact, it is changing in several ways at the same time. It is often helpful to distinguish, as we have done repeatedly, between long-run changes which take months or perhaps years to occur, but are of fundamental nature, and short-run variations which may occur on a daily or weekly basis. The organization responds to these two in different ways. It may establish a managerial structure in response to a set of long-run conditions found at a given time, and then as these change over the years eventually adopt a new form of managerial structure to cope with the new structure. On the other hand, it may be impossible to change the managerial structure each time there is a short-run change. Instead, the managerial structure may be chosen which can cope with a range of conditions likely to be encountered in the short run.   Let us consider this in more detail.

Long-Run Changes

An interesting analysis of this sort of change is found in research that was conducted on the reorganization of a supermarket chain.[20] This was a medium-size chain of food stores which had grown and developed over many years.   At the time of the reorganization, the section of the company concerned with operating the stores, called "store operations," was organized in the following manner.   In each supermarket there were three managers: one for produce, one for groceries, and one for meats (Figure 16.9).   Each of these reported to an Assistant District Manager who was responsible for the same type of commodity.   He reported to a District Manager who was responsible for all three commodity areas.   It should be noted, however, that the Assistant District Managers received a great deal of information and were substantially influenced by the Assistant buyers in their commodity area.   This organization placed great emphasis on the commodities which the store sold but provided no single position concerned with the store as a whole.

This organizational form had its roots in an earlier phase of the company's existence.   Prior to the time of the development of supermarket-type stores the company was organized on commodity lines from the top of the organization down to the individual stores. Large food chains grew at this time, partially as a result of the advantage of buying in large quantities at lower prices.   However, there was a problem.   The commodities handled could spoil, particularly meats which required refrigeration; the goods had to be handled both rapidly and carefully to avoid undue loss and spoilage.   To put it in terms we have been discussing, the organization's success depended on (1) a volume-purchasing system and (2) a commodity-handling system.   There were, of course, many other systems in the organization but none was as crucial to its success at the time as were these two. The organization chart in 1954 was strongly influenced by these earlier conditions, and the primary emphasis of the organization was still on facilitating these two systems.

About 1954, however, company executives were becoming increas-

[20] The material for this section, unless otherwise noted, is drawn from Paul R. Lawrence, *The Changing of Organizational Behavior Patterns*, Boston, Harvard University Graduate School of Business Administration, Division of Research, 1958.

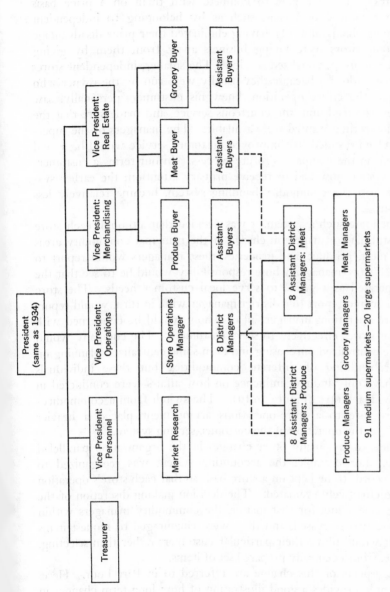

Figure 16.9. Supermarket partial organization chart, 1954. *Source:* Paul R. Lawrence, *The Changing of Organizational Behavior Patterns,* Boston, Harvard University, Division of Research, Graduate School of Business Administration, 1958, p. 16.

ingly aware that their competition (particularly the smaller, independent stores) (1) were able to compete with them on a price basis through a variety of means, such as by belonging to independent wholesaling chains, and (2) having eliminated their price disadvantage these competitors were taking business away from them by giving customers more personalized service. The smaller, independent stores were able to do this because they usually were run by the owner who supervised the entire operation, knew his customers personally, saw that they received uniform, courteous service, and made sure that the special items they wanted were available. The managers of the supermarket chain decided that improved customer service would be a vital ingredient in the company's future success. In our terms a customer-serving system now had to receive primary attention; the earlier systems, at least the commodity-handling system, became relatively less important.

To facilitate such a system, it was decided that although each store would still have managers in charge of the principal commodity areas such as meat, produce, and groceries, these managers would report to an overall store manager whose responsibility would be to see that the store operated as a whole to serve local customer needs. The store manager would report to a district manager who, in turn, would report to a store operations manager, all of whom would be concerned with operating stores effectively to serve customers. The company would still have centralized purchasing and even some centralized planning on the merchandising of different commodities, but these individuals would have only indirect influence on how affairs were conducted in the individual stores (Figure 16.10). The switch from a commodity-type structure to a store-operations arrangement placed a heavier emphasis on the operation of the customer-serving system.

Needless to say, many other changes in the organization paralleled this one. For example, the accounting system was reorganized to permit records to be kept on a store basis so that each store's operation could be effectively evaluated. The decision-making discretion of the store managers and, for that matter, the commodity managers within each store was increased, and they were encouraged to request items they felt would please their particular customers rather than selecting, as before, from a centrally prepared set of items.

Other aspects of this change are referred to in Part Four. Here, this example provides a good illustration of how long-term changes in the environment (the development of new marketing channels which permitted independent supermarkets to compete better on a price basis) ultimately led to a set of conditions which required a fundamental reorganization of a company.

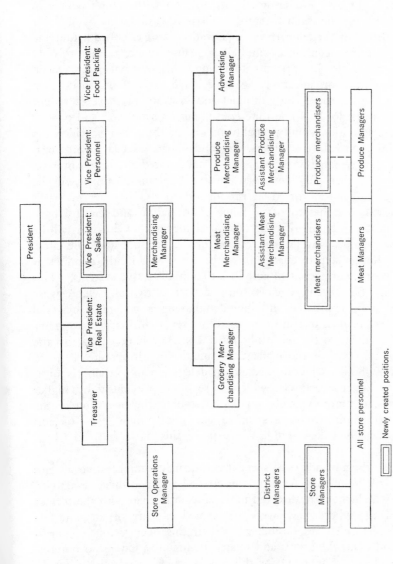

Figure 16.10. Supermarket partial organization chart, 1955. *Source:* Paul R. Lawrence, *The Changing of Organizational Behavior Patterns*, Boston, Harvard University, Division of Research, Graduate School of Business Administration, 1958, p. 70.

Short-Run Changes in the Environment

Let us begin by considering an organization with a high degree of interdependency between organizational units and faced by a stable environment. If the concern or organization has the coordination and control activities centralized in higher management, there probably would be considerable pressure to change this internal arrangement. First, since most organization executives have more work to do than they can handle, there is a continual and insistent pressure to reduce executive work loads. The time-consuming coordination and control of routine activities would probably be one of those things which top executives try to shift to others. Second, if this is a large organization, we can reasonably expect, as we have noted in the chapter on coordination, that the hierarchal flow of communications will be slowed down and distorted in proportion to the number of levels through which it has to pass. Since coordination and control have communications as one of their central elements, they in turn will be made less reliable. Additional reasons for the pressure could be cited.

One common step to change this situation is to shift the conduct of routine coordinative control activities to administrative systems. This is an important event, because now certain activities, which were formally undifferentiated and included among a general managerial activity, are broken out and described in a set of formalized programs permitting them to be uniformly repeated. We have called this the institutionalization of the managerial function.[21] It should be noted that although this sometimes results in delegation of certain responsibilities to lower executives, which were done previously by higher executives, it more typically involves assigning the operation of the formalized administrative system to an entirely new class of employees, usually called *staff*. We explore this more fully in Chapter 17.

With all the advantages of specialization, such administrative systems usually will be able to perform the control and coordinative activity toward which they are directed more efficiently than with the former arrangement, where they were performed as part of an undifferentiated hierarchal responsibility. When this occurs, much coordinative and control activity and related communications [22] do not follow the chain of command or the organizational hierarchal channels.

[21] See Chapter 8.
[22] See James G. March and Herbert A. Simon, *Organizations*, New York, John Wiley, 1958, pp. 160–161.

Administrative systems	Managerial control through hierarchal or voluntary activities
Stable environment	Unstable environment

Figure 16.11. Influence of short-run environmental stability on the location of control and coordination activities.

If conditions should change and become unstable, one of the requirements for specialization would be eliminated or at least reduced. This would reduce the utility of the administrative system and make it likelier that some other coordinative strategy, such as a hierarchy or voluntary activities, would assume conduct of the affected control and coordinative activities. Therefore we can envision a continuum (Figure 16.11) where, assuming an organization with a high degree of interdependency, there would be at one end stable environmental conditions, under which the organization would be predisposed to use a large number of administrative systems to facilitate control and coordination, and at the other end highly unstable environmental conditions where, under control and coordination, the management structure or voluntary activities would come through.

Existence of Group Values Which Facilitate Group Coordination and Control

In a study of a large governmental agency charged with supporting research, it was found that some managers reported spending a considerable amount of their time in administrative activities largely devoted to control and coordination whereas another group of managers, in sharp contrast, reported proportionally far less, and some reported none at all. Figure 16.12 illustrates that the administrative section of the agency contained executives who reported a high percentage of time spent on control and coordinative activities, and that the scientific section contained those who reported very little. It was also found that the hierarchical coordination absent in the scientific section was replaced with a high number of coordinative contacts among members of the section. In contrast, fewer coordinative contacts were carried out among members of the administration section. In the scientific section, the informal coordinative actions were often between people who had no formal relationship to one another.

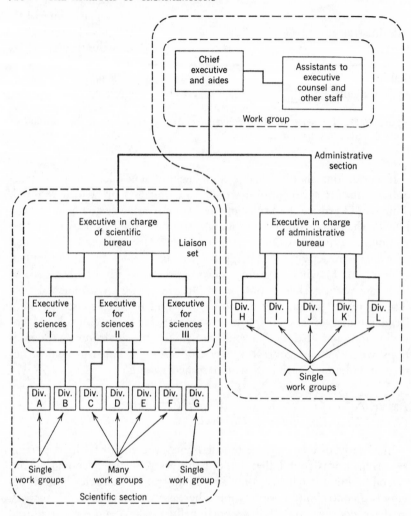

Figure 16.12. Government agency organization chart and actual structure. (*Note:* Dashed lines equal actual structural units.) *Source:* Robert S. Weiss, *Processes of Organization,* Ann Arbor, Survey Research Center, University of Michigan, Institute for Social Research, 1956, p. 57.

Further investigation disclosed that the members of these scientific sections, primarily scientists or individuals with scientific training, had brought with them from their education or previous work situations values which supported the free flow of information and made it each person's individual responsibility to: (1) freely give anyone the information he has, and (2) seek directly, from the best possible source, the information he needs.[23] An important factor was the sentiments individuals brought into the organization.

Organizational Decisions That Affect the Functioning of the Organization Structure

By this time it should be evident that decisions about certain aspects of organizational hierarchy can loop back through effects on organizational performance making still further design decisions necessary. There are many such situations. We consider two here.

DEFINING ORGANIZATIONAL UNITS CONTAINING IMPORTANT SYSTEMS. As noted in Chapter 8, an organization consists of many systems. Among the most important decisions made about an organization are those that identify its crucial systems and provide for their facilitation. This frequently can be done by placing them within a single organizational unit. Let us suppose, for example, that a manufacturing plant is making three products, 1, 2, and 3, and all three use three processes, A, B, and C. We have, therefore, at least two ways of organizing the work in the plant. We could set up three functional departments, each containing a different process (Figure 16.13a) or we could group the work on each product in a department; therefore, each department would contain each of the three processes (Figure 16.13b).

Let us assume that all coordination and communications flow through hierarchal channels. It can be seen that in the functional type of arrangement, work on a given product (for example, product 1) has to occur in all departments; if there is any problem in coordinating information, it must flow from the worker up to the foreman (S_1) and through the plant manager down another foreman (S_3) to the appropriate worker. In the product arrangement (Figure 16.13b) coordinative problems on product 1 are contained within one department; should there be any need for coordination between two of the workers, it would only have to pass through one foreman, a much shorter, simpler loop.

If we abandon the assumption that all coordination is carried out through hierarchal means, coordination would be handled even more easily in the product arrangement, because people working directly on the product would be able to communicate more readily with one

[23] Weiss, *op. cit.*, particularly pp. 58–62.

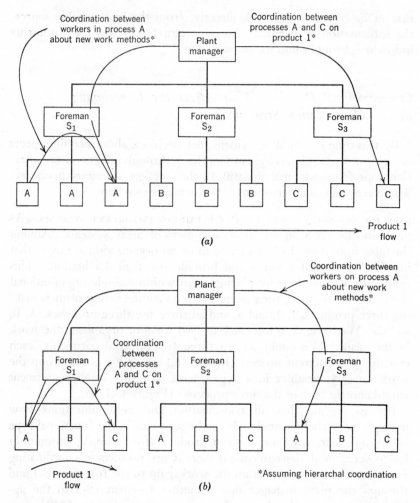

Figure 16.13. (a) Work grouped by functional departments; (b) work grouped by product departments.

another and thereby promote group and self-coordination.[24] Hence, if the system is to make individual products that are of prime importance, the purpose or product-type of organization is most advantageous since coordination of work on these is contained within the smallest possible organizational unit.

[24] Most of this discussion was drawn from James C. Worthy, "Organizational Structure and Employee Morale," *American Sociological Review,* **15,** 1950, pp. 169–179.

However, if the nature of an industry or technology is such that the coordination of information about technical processes is most important, the functional-type of organization may be most valuable. In such an organization information about process A circulates within the smallest possible unit. Hence, if one worker discovers a useful way of performing the function, it can be very easily circulated through the foreman or even directly to the other workers. In contrast, in the product arrangement, any information about the discovery of some new way of performing the process by a worker on process A, in the department making product 1, would have to flow through foreman, plant manager, and other foremen down to the other workers involved in the same process. The alternative of having workers communicate directly with one another is less likely because of spatial distances, job objectives, etc.

DECISIONS AFFECTING THE DEGREE OF INTERDEPENDENCY OF THE WORK SYSTEM. As noted before, the technical system imposes a certain degree of interdependency on the work system, but at the same time decisions can be taken to modify this effect. One important decision already discussed concerns placing stocks or stores of material between elements in the work system, which serve as cushions and reduce the interdependency. To put it another way, if stocks are eliminated or at least reduced, the interdependency that people and organizational units feel increases. If, at the same time, there is a delegation of responsibility to lower members of the organization, the combination of increased responsibility and increased feeling of interdependency leads to a change in the behavior of managers.[25]

SUMMARY

In this chapter we have examined the administrative superstructure of the work activities of an organization. We concerned ourselves with two basic points: (1) the anatomy of the structure, and (2) the variations and the factors causing modifications in this anatomy.

In discussing the anatomy of the administrative superstructure we noted that it served to carry out the managerial function of the organization, and considered as a whole, it was concerned with coordination, control, allocation, setting and adjusting goals, and regulation of the rewards system.

The managerial structure was described as being pyramidal in nature with more positions on each lower level which had authority and

[25] Richardson and Walker, *op. cit.*

responsibility, but a smaller area of decision-making autonomy. This was to be expected since the hierarchy also represented a hierarchy of goals, the goals of one level being the subgoals of the higher level. The hierarchy, then, was intimately related to the means-ends sequence.

An important element in determining the particular shape of the organization was seen to be the span of control—the number of subordinates reporting to a superior. The superior and his immediate group of subordinates are a command group and the organization can be considered a network of linked command groups.

These were the general elements included in the discussion of organizational anatomy. The specific form which these elements took was seen to be determined by many factors. We can conceive of one set of factors creating a certain administrative need or problem which must be satisfactorily handled by the managerial system. The managerial system meets this requirement by combining several subfunctions, a hierarchal system, a voluntary system, and an administrative system.

It is conceivable that the entire managerial functions could be provided by the hierarchal system and the values for the voluntary and procedural systems could be zero. More reasonably, though, we would expect all these systems to be in effect to some degree. Their particular combination or allocation of the managerial function among them is dependent on a number of things. Some were identified in this chapter: (1) stability of inputs and methods of the technical and work systems, (2) the similarity and complexity of activities in the work system, (3) the capabilities of the organizational members, (4) the possibility of self- or group-coordination, (5) the perception of higher authority. The magnitude of the administrative need or problem was seen to vary primarily according to (1) the stability of the environment of the organization, and (2) the degree of interdependence of the work system. This, in turn, was seen to be dependent on a number of factors, principal among them: (1) the technical system which, of course, was molded by the technology chosen and available and (2) the particular design decisions made in earlier phases of organization development and planning.

The basic theme in this, as with other chapters, is that although there are some regular aspects or components of organizations, they have no final form universal to all organizations. Instead, the managerial structure, as with so many other elements of organization, is the result of (1) the needs of the organization dependent on its objectives and the conditions faced and (2) the capabilities it has of coping with these needs in the form of its resources and the potentiality of the organizational processes available.   What emerges as the managerial structure, or system, is molded by and intimately connected with the technical, economic, and political elements surrounding it.   To attempt to study the behavior of managers without taking this into account, that is, to ignore that this behavior is part of a sociotechnical system, is to take a view so limited as to be meaningless for the understanding of organizations.

I7

Staff

F<small>EW</small> areas in formal organizations are more controversial than staff. The integration of staff activities and personnel into organizations is recognized as a source of continuing friction and problems. The very word "staff" is so clouded in its meaning and so loaded with unfortunate connotations that some authors are hesitant to use it.

At the same time, staff work looms large in contemporary organizations. In fact, there seems to be some evidence that the most successful and rapidly growing business concerns are those where staff positions are proportionally larger and increasing at a rate proportionally greater than in other firms.[1]

As suggested in the preceding chapter, staff is an aspect of the managerial hierarchy and important in its execution of the managerial function. We shall consider staff in two chapters. Here attention is given to what staff is and how it contributes to the execution of the managerial function. In Chapter 18 we deal with some of the more critical problems which surround the use of staff in contemporary organizations.

THE CONCEPT OF STAFF

As we shall see in Chapter 18, some of the problems stemming from the use of staff have their roots in popular and widely held theories of staff. However, these theories are inadequate to explain the nature of staff and are in conflict with much actual staff practice. Since the reader will encounter some of these concepts in actual organizations, let us begin by examining them and their limitations.

[1] Samuel E. Hill and Frederick Harbeson, *Manpower and Innovation in American Industry*, Industrial Relations Section, Princeton University, 1959, pp. 53–56, 70–71.

Review of Typically Held Staff Concepts

A typical discussion usually begins by observing that as an organization grows in size or conditions around it change, the work load of the individual executive increases, ultimately reaching a point where it exceeds his work capacity. At this juncture new positions are created to perform activities which help the executive do his job. Commonly these activities include assembling data about areas of future decision or gathering information about an area of organizational performance and reporting these to an executive, thereby relieving him of having to do so personally. One part of the typical concept holds that the function of staff is to assist the executive in a variety of ways in performing duties that he otherwise would have to do himself.

The range of decisions that executives have to make, particularly those at the top, is so broad that some are bound to be in areas unfamiliar to the executive and about which his knowledge and judgment is less sure. In such situations he may turn to others for advice, drawing on their knowledge, experience, and superior judgment to aid in making decisions. History tells us of young and inexperienced kings drawing on the knowledge of old royal courtiers in making decisions. A second part of the general staff concept is for the staff to supply special knowledge, skill, and the like needed by an executive.

Typical definitions, whether concerned with a position or a whole department, specify that staff assists, advises, and counsels the line executives and has no direct authority over any portions of the organization except, of course, immediate subordinates within a staff unit.[2] A fundamental implication here is that although staff is necessary in large and complex organizations, it is secondary in importance. Its basic purpose is to *serve* other important executives called *line executives*.[3]

Few organizations give staff members clear-cut authority to give orders to line executives. Hence, in a formalistic way they may fulfill the conventional requirements of staff, whereas in practice they are frequently in a position to influence directly what line executives do.

---

[2] For example, see Lewis A. Allen, "On Improving Staff and Line Relationships," *Conference Board Report, Studies in Personnel Policy, No. 153*, National Industrial Conference Board, 1956, particularly pp. 38–39, and Dale Yoder, *Personnel Principles and Policies—Modern Manpower Management*, New York, Prentice Hall, 1952, pp. 21–22.

[3] Leonard D. White, *An Introduction to the Study of Public Administration*, New York, MacMillan, 1955, p. 195.

Sometimes this influence is so great that the absence of a formal statement of authority is of trivial consequence. The unique position of staff men frequently permits them to employ the stratagem of the old top sergeant, who in attempting to get his men to do something not permitted by regulation says, "I can't make you do it, but I can surely make you wish you had." Typically, line executives often find themselves in a position where staff executives are, for all practical purposes, giving them commands.

Another feature which causes difficulty is that staff personnel frequently have higher status and better pay than comparable line executives.[4] For the line executive who had been told that staff is of secondary importance and is there to serve and assist him, this seems incongruous.

We explore other aspects of the problem of traditional staff concepts in Chapter 18. These should be sufficient, however, to illustrate that the more commonly held concepts do not fit contemporary organizations. We could look at the situation in at least two ways. One is to assume that theory is correct and practice is wrong, and that we must endeavor to bring practice into line with theory.[5]

The alternate course of action, to develop new theory more adequate in explaining actual organization, seems to be the more reasonable approach, and has received serious attention in recent years.[6] There is little doubt that within the foreseeable future we shall have a new theory to take the place of the more traditional staff concept. Whatever form this new theory takes, it will doubtless cease to consider staff units as being secondary in importance and principally intended to serve the line. Some inkling of the orientation which the new theory may adopt can be gathered from the terms which some writers are now using as substitutes or alternates to the word, staff. *Auxiliary departments* is being used to identify those departments that perform activities for the entire organization.[7] Or *adjective tasks* is used to define certain types of managerial work. The term is borrowed from jurisprudence where the distinction is made between sub-

[4] Ernest Dale, *Planning and Developing the Company Organization Structure*, New York, American Management Association, 1952, p. 74.

[5] For a development of this position, see Sampson, *The Staff Role in Management*, New York, Harper, 1955.

[6] For one summary of this work and proposals for new theoretical forms, see Robert Golombeiwski, "Toward the New Organization Theory: Some Notes on 'Staff,' " *Midwest Journal of Political Science*, 5, 1961, pp. 259–273.

[7] James G. March and Herbert A. Simon, *Organizations*, New York, John Wiley, 1958, pp. 195–196.

stantive law and adjective law.   In this context adjective is being used
as a synonym for procedural.[8]

In this chapter staff will be regarded as serving a role and having a
relationship different from that contained in the more traditional concepts.   At the same time, we shall continue to use the term, staff,
feeling that although its purpose and even its method of operation may
not be clearly understood, the term at least still serves a useful end.
As an analogy we might recall that at one time thunderstorms were
considered a manifestation of the fury of the gods, and therefore
served the function of warning men that they should mend their ways
and give appropriate offerings.   Today we understand them to be the
result of a complex physical phenomenon.   Dangerous and threatening, yes, but in a way entirely different from that understood by our
primitive ancestors.   Where early and contemporary man might differ
widely in their understanding of why a storm develops, they would
clearly be able to identify what a storm is: high winds, black clouds,
and probably rain, sleet, or snow.   So, too, with staff.   People may
differ widely on its purpose and how it operates, but they usually have
little difficulty in identifying staff positions.

Staff as a Specialization of the Managerial Function

The idea of staff as a specialization of the managerial function has
been mentioned.[9]   The argument is simple.   If the managerial function is conceived as a set of activities facilitating the work of the
organization, these activities can be carried out more effectively
through the use of division of work leading to a specialization of
managerial labor. [10]

THE PROCESS OF INSTITUTIONALIZATION.   Perhaps the nature of staff can
be made clearer by reviewing how many of the specialized [11] staffs
initially developed in American business concerns.   Seventy or more
years ago in many American manufacturing companies, the manager in
charge of a department handled all the managerial activities necessary.
He decided on equipment layout, hired and trained people, developed
schedules, etc.   At best he had a clerk who handled the few records

[8] John M. Pfiffner and Frank P. Sherwood, *Administrative Organization,* Englewood Cliffs, Prentice Hall, 1960, p. 125.
[9] Chapters 8, 9, and 17.
[10] This idea has been put forth by a number of writers, among them Ralph C.
Davis, *The Fundamentals of Top Management,* New York, Harper, 1951, p. 370.
[11] A distinction between different types of staff is made later in this chapter.

kept at that time.   As the volume of work in a department increased and the manager felt himself more and more pressed for time, often he would develop standardized ways of handling the routine managerial work necessary.[12]

By establishing a standard way of handling what today would be called *production-control* and *inventory-control* problems, the manager gained a number of advantages.   First, he did not have to make new decisions about each situation which faced him.   He merely applied the standard decision to a recurring type of problem.   Second, he had a check list which reminded him of what had to be done and when. Many of these procedures were written down and often had necessary paper-work forms prepared to support them.   Since a portion of the managerial work had standard programs prepared for it, it became possible to assign this work to someone else with the assurance that it would be done in a satisfactory way.   Hence, clerks were often hired to handle these embryonic production and inventory-control procedures.   In doing this, specialized staff positions were created.

This pattern of programming part of the managerial work and then assigning responsibility for it to a special position represents the institutionalization of the managerial function, a process which has continued for many years and led to many specialized staff departments. Even this simple illustration reveals a number of important characteristics of staff work.   First, it does not add any new functions to managerial effort.   Instead, it represents an institutionalization of managerial activities to handle a type of work or function which has grown so important or for which the volume of work has become so large and regular that it becomes desirable and often necessary to reap the advantages of division of work.   In the foregoing illustration, managerial work was divided in two different ways.   One was on the basis of managerial function, such as the planning and scheduling of the function of production control or the control aspects of inventory control, where staff personnel used established programs to plan work for the factory.   The other was division of work on the basis of phases of work performance.   Here planning, such as developing programs for production control, and setup of the staff work was handled by the line executive.   The execution was carried out by the newly appointed clerk.

Needless to say, division of work has many advantages for manage-

[12] For further details on the historical development of staff see Joseph A. Litterer, "Systematic Management: Design for Organizational Recoupling," *Business History Review*, 37, 1963, pp. 369–391.

rial activities just as it does for the performance of manufacturing work activities, and it also imposes the same necessity for coordination. In the illustration there are two classes of coordinative problems: to integrate the efforts of people performing different managerial functions and to integrate the planning and setup of staff work with its execution. As we shall see in the following chapter, these coordinating needs, often neglected, are the roots of many of the problems between line and staff.

One other consequence of the division of managerial activities is that the rest of the managers are excluded from doing the work that has been assigned to a specialized staff department. Hence, in a large company today it is usually impossible for a production foreman to run his own advertisement seeking new employees in a newspaper, although he once would have been able to do so. The necessity for this exclusiveness is not hard to understand when staff activity is viewed as a division of work. It is harder to understand and may even be considered unnecessary or illogical under the more conventional concepts of staff.

Such institutionalization has a number of distinct advantages for the successful performance of the managerial function. (1) Since the same program for the execution of managerial activities will be used repeatedly, it becomes worthwhile to expend considerable effort to determine the best possible one. (2) Since a particular set of activities are made the whole job of one person or department, it will be likely to be performed more efficiently because of the opportunity to build up special skills and knowledge, and because the activity is less likely to be neglected or handled poorly owing to the pressure of carrying out other different types of managerial activity. (3) Since some aspect of the managerial work has been delimited and defined in relation to a set of programs, its execution becomes less dependent on the individual skills of an executive. Under an arrangement where all executives carry out general managerial functions, very good employees may be hired because there are the skills, contacts, and patience to locate the best possible candidates for each job, where another man not possessing these attributes might hire less satisfactory employees.

Another aspect of this is that the organization is less dependent on the tenure of any one manager. Without any institutionalization, with each executive developing his own way of handling managerial activities, the programs and skills were exclusive with him, and when he left, they went with him making it virtually impossible for anyone else even to begin to handle that portion of the organization in the same way. With programs more explicitly established and known to more people, someone else can step into a position and at least know how to do the work even if he does not have the skill to do it as efficiently as the former occupant.

Staff Operation of Managerial Systems. In Chapter 16 we noted that the managerial function was concerned with facilitating the work system. The managerial function can be considered as a complex of systems designed to produce a wide array of results necessary for its completion. In a manufacturing plant, there would be a system to coordinate the flow of production which might well be developed in the fashion of the foregoing illustration. More concretely, staff positions and departments are often assigned the operation of procedural systems.

As previously noted, specific procedures formalized in an organization do not always include an entire system. An accounting system, for example, may include only one or two portions of the control cycle, leaving the others to be completed by less specific means. The same condition can be said to exist for many other staff departments and leads to another of the numerous sources of difficulties in regard to staff.

STAFF AND ORGANIZATIONAL GOALS. An organization consists in part of a progression of goals developed through a means-ends analysis. As the overall organization goal is successively broken into a hierarchy of subgoals, some of these goals become the objectives of subunits or departments and positions within the organization. None of the subunits developed in this fashion, however, would include staff positions or departments. Staff, as we have been discussing it, does not fit directly into the principal nesting of goals. In this light it is supplemental to the departments which evolve through means-ends analysis. It is in this context that some authors use the terms auxiliary or adjective to describe the fundamental nature of staff.

The units that evolve from means-ends analysis and which facilitate the main hierarchy of goals are usually called the *line.* They are the departments and positions most directly involved with the accomplishment of organizational goals. Whether a given department, position, or type of work is classified as line or staff depends on its relation to organization goals rather than to its possession of any unique or inherent properties. It is perfectly possible for a type of work to be part of a line department in one organization and part of the staff department in another or, for that matter, to be line at one time in an organization's history and staff in another.

An illustration of this second condition is the reorganization of the supermarket chain referred to in the preceding chapter. Prior to the reorganization, the levels below the district manager were organized on a commodity basis. The assistant district managers were assigned certain commodities, such as produce or meats, and held responsible for all phases of merchandising these goods in their district. Reporting directly to them were managers within each store responsible for all aspects of marketing the particular commodity in the store. They were line at this time. With the redefinition of subgoals the emphasis was on servicing the customer's needs in each store rather than maximizing efficient buying and handling of goods. A single store manager was responsible for all aspects of store operation for all commodities. He, in turn, reported directly to the district manager who again was responsible for all commodities. The work of the product-merchandising specialists (the former assistant district managers) now became staff positions, called "meat" or "produce" merchandisers. These merchandisers were to be technical advisors to the store manager on matters relating to their particular type of perishable commodity.[13]

TYPES OF STAFF

Thus far we have viewed staff as if there were only one form or type. This is not the case at all. There are distinctly different types of staff and the differences among them are considerable. We shall consider four basic types: the assistant-to, general staff, specialized staff, and operating services.

Let us begin by making a distinction between a person in an organization and the position he occupies. In the army there may be a person called General Jones who occupies the position of commanding general of the X division. Carrying out the activities necessary to perform the duties of commanding general is far beyond the capabilities of any one individual. Hence, he receives a great deal of assistance in executing this office. Even those portions of the office the general handles himself are very demanding on his time and energy so that it often becomes necessary for him to have a personal assistant to take over the many details, including social obligations, which press on him.

[13] Paul R. Lawrence, *The Changing of Organizational Behavior Patterns,* Boston, Harvard University Division of Research, Graduate School of Business Administration, 1958, p. 55.

The Assistant-To

The assistant-to is a personal assistant to an individual holding an office or position, usually an office or manager in the upper levels of an organization. His work is general and varied depending on whatever the superior decides to assign at a given time. Hence, the assistant-to may be asked one day to gather material for a speech, whereas the next day he may be asked to go and look over an area in the organization where there is a morale problem to obtain information for the superior. The following day he may be asked to entertain some people visiting the superior with whom the latter is not able to spend all his time. These positions are found in all large organizations. In business and government they are called the assistant-to; in military organizations, such as the army, they are called aide-de-camp.

In general, the assistant-to is to aid his superior in handling his own office. Ideally, there should be a great deal of rapport between these two parties so that the assistant-to can know how his superior would perceive and react to a situation. Hence, when the assistant-to is sent to look at a troubled portion of the organization, he should know clearly the sort of things his superior wants, including those items that can be specifically pinned down, and the intangibles, such as the "feel" of the situation.

The assistant-to can help enormously in bringing the gap between other members of the organization and his superior since he can circulate widely through the organization while the superior is often confined in his office. Many times other subordinates in the organization will want to know how the boss feels about a certain issue. They may not find it convenient or expedient to approach him directly. They may, however, quite readily approach his assistant-to to get some impression of the "boss's reaction." [14]

Because of his unique position—being close to his superior, being expected to funnel much useful but sometimes irregular information to the superior, and conveying irregular but valuable information to subordinates about and from the superior—the assistant-to is in a unique and delicate position with great potential power. Should he attempt to use or be suspected of using this potential power to his personal advantage, this could cause great difficulty in the organization and seriously impair his future when and if he thinks of moving to

[14] Most of this material on the assistant-to is drawn from Thomas Whisler, "The Assistant-to in Four Administrative Settings," *Administrative Science Quarterly*, 5, 1960, pp. 181–216.

another position.   Hence, when individuals are offered such a position, and such offers are frequently made to young, promising executives or officers, they are faced, on the one hand, with an opportunity of making valuable top level contacts and seeing how the overall organization operates, and on the other hand, with being in an extremely delicate position where they must be willing to devote their interests entirely to their superior and refrain from any personal exercise of ambition. An actual or perceived misstep on their parts may earn the personal enmity of other subordinates of the superior who are much senior in age and organizational rank.   Because of the unique properties of the assistant-to's position, it has been suggested that some conditions encourage its use, whereas others are likely to discourage it.

CONDITIONS FAVORING THE USE OF ASSISTANT-TO.   When there is high executive mobility, the assistant-to is seen as offering some distinct advantages: this is true of government, where bureau and department heads are politically appointed or the military, where a constant shifting and rotating of officers occurs.   The executive moving into a top post needs to know a great deal about his organization before he can be effective.   Much of what he needs to know is not the sort of thing which can be readily obtained through formal channels, namely, the informal norms of the executives, their personal capabilities, feuds, and coalitions, etc.   If he can obtain an assistant-to who has been in the organization for some time, the executive can frequently obtain this vitally important information.

Many executives occupy positions where they must maintain extensive contacts with the public, and consequently spend a great deal of time outside the immediate organizational setting, which makes it difficult to maintain close contacts with the organization.   Here again the assistant-to can help in maintaining an effective, personal link.

As an organization grows in size, the pressure on the personal activities of the executive and the number of people with whom he might feel it necessary to maintain some degree of contact becomes very large.   The assistant-to can relieve in these situations.

When there is considerable diversity in the positions or the units reporting directly to a superior, an assistant-to can be helpful in collating, synthesizing, and perhaps even predigesting much of the varied information which funnels into an executive position.

CONDITIONS NOT FAVORING THE USE OF THE ASSISTANT-TO.   Desirable though it often is in facilitating certain types of communication, the assistant-to position is nonetheless another link or step between the executive and the rest of the organization.   To be effective the assistant-to must learn a great deal about the organization and the executive; however, when conditions are changing rapidly, such as in the times of economic crisis or shifting technologies, the assistant-to may actually lag behind the requirements of the situation. Hence, we would expect the executive to go directly to those critically changing areas and not use the assistant-to.

General Staff

To go back to the military illustration, the general in charge of a division or army in the field has to be concerned with planning his next action against the enemy, translating it into specific plans and orders for units under his command, telling them where to be and when, checking to make sure that necessary supplies will be available at the right place and at the right time, etc. These duties are to be provided by the office of the general regardless of who occupies it. The pressures of time, however, make it virtually impossible for one person to make all these plans and arrangements. Thus, they tend to be allocated to other positions which, in effect, are part of the general's office. In the military, the positions identified with various aspects of planning are called the *general staff*.

Since one of the immediate objectives of possessing these positions is to have the work of the office of general handled expeditiously, the positions tend to be specialized. In the army, for example, these areas of specialization have become standardized into the G1, G2, G3, and G4 staff positions dealing with personnel, intelligence, operations and training, and supply and logistics, respectively. Typically, these staff departments gather information and prepare plans for their respective areas, present them to the general who, if he approves, authorizes their issuance. In other more routine areas, these staff officials can issue orders in the name of the commanding officer.

General staff is very commonly used in the military and frequently in governmental organizations, particularly in the federal government. It is not as widely used in business, although there is a growing tendency to add general staff positions concerned with overall planning at the top of large business corporations. In the military and in many governmental bureaus and agencies, it is not uncommon to find general staffs existing at many levels in the organization. In the army they appear attached to the office of the general commanding an army group, to the office of the general commanding an army, to the general commanding a division, and even further down.

In some ways, then, the assistant-to and the general staff positions are similar in that they focus on a particular point in the organization. However, the assistant-to is intended primarily to aid the individual filling an office in a personal way, an extension of the person enabling him to project his ideas and wishes to others in the organization and to sense more effectively what is going on in the organization. General staff positions are concerned with operating an office. They tend to be more specialized; whereas of necessity they have a close relationship with the person occupying a senior position, it is not as close as that of the personal staff. In a sense, the general staff positions are extensions of an office enabling an organizational position to fit better into the organization and function more effectively.

Specialized Staff

The third type of staff is the one which is referred to most frequently when problems and issues relevant to staff are discussed. These are staff positions which serve the entire organization or, at least, large sectors of the managerial structure. Positions here are more highly specialized than in the two former staff positions. Persons who fill these frequently receive considerable specialized training before they are qualified to assume these posts and are likely to spend the large part of their working careers in these specialties. Typical examples of such staff positions are accounting, quality control, economic forecasting, and the like. It is this type of staff position which we have largely had in mind in the foregoing discussion of the nature of staff.

Operating Services

Although quite different, operating services and specialized staffs do have the common feature of serving the organization as a whole, or at least large sectors of it rather than being focused on a particular person or position as were the types of staff discussed in the preceding section. The distinction between them is that the specialized staff facilitates the work of management while operating services facilitate the organization in a physical sense; that is, they are custodial in nature. Perhaps the distinction between the two can be made clear by a few illustrations.

We have observed that the managerial function was concerned with facilitating the work of the organization to accomplish its goals or purposes. We might say that the output of the managerial function or system is the facilitation of the work system to accomplish goals.

The illustrations thus far have considered organizations as comprising only one work system, and therefore, the managerial effort is directed toward facilitating this. No large organization is so simple. Most have several sets of objectives and work systems. Usually, some of these feed into other more fundamental work systems. A simple illustration is the plant cafeteria in a large manufacturing establishment. The output of the cafeteria is food for the employees. Providing this food is a managerial function in a typical manufacturing plant. The employees could bring their own lunches or go out to nearby restaurants or the company could contract with a caterer to supply food for the employees. This work system is of secondary importance and exists only to support or service the main work system. For that reason it is called an *operating service*.

In facilitating any work system, the managerial function is performed by the execution of a set of subfunctions. These functions may all be handled completely by line executives or, as we have seen, portions of the functions may be carried out by staff personnel. One of the functions management is concerned with is control. To help with this there are a number of staff positions which take over different portions of different types of control systems such as accountants, quality-control experts, attitude-surveying activities of the personnel department, etc. These specialized staff positions include the vast majority of those found today in large-scale business organizations.

The distinction between the specialized staff and operating services is illustrated in Figure 17.1. Here we are looking at the managerial function as a system. Among the outputs are the operation or the facilitation of various work systems. Some of these are the prime systems of the company leading directly to principal objectives. Some portion of the managerial effort in most organizations, however, is directed to the operation of service work systems which in some

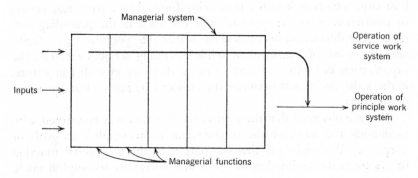

Figure 17.1

way support or assist the principal work system. In carrying out the managerial system or function to facilitate or operate any of these work systems, certain managerial functions have to be performed—such as coordination, part of which is carried out by production control in typical manufacturing organizations, and control, which is partially carried out by accounting.

The establishment of an operating service usually does not change the work of general line executives much, if at all. On the other hand, when a specialized staff position is created, it usually means that portions of the work of general line executives are being removed and concentrated in the position of the staff specialists. This may be considered an advantage of relieving the line manager of some activities which were part of an excessive burden or for some other reason beyond his ability to cope with adequately. The organization as a whole frequently benefits because the work can be more expeditiously handled by a specialist. Nonetheless, it does mean a reduction in the scope of things handled by the general line manager, and in this light has not always been regarded as either a blessing or an advantageous step. Because this type of staff looms so large in contemporary organizations, it is the target of discussion in the remaining portion of this chapter and Chapter 18.

This typology is but one of several ways of identifying different staff departments. We are dealing here with "ideal types" which we would not meet exactly in life. For example, the general staff sometimes does almost the same work as personal staff man, and the specialized staff also often fills general staff roles. Nonetheless, this scheme of classification is characteristic of what is usually found.

PURPOSES OF STAFF

We have generally described the purpose of staff as facilitation of the execution of the managerial function and the takeover of operations of systems that carry out a part of managerial subfunctions. Let us now examine the more prominent purposes or contributions of staff in greater detail. Few, if any, staff departments have only a single purpose; typically they have a principal purpose and several satellite ones. However, in the interest of discussion it is simpler to speak of a staff as having only one of the following purposes.

Facilitation of Organizational Control and Coordination

This purpose was cited in the illustration about how staff takes over the operation of procedural systems designed to coordinate or control portions of organizational activity. Staff positions having this purpose in a manufacturing company would be production control, quality control, budgets, etc. The need for this type of activity, and hence the need for this type of staff, arises very early in existence of most organizations; such needs are an outgrowth of the degree of the division of work and size. The underlying strategy of these staff activities is to keep the organization activity working toward goals.

Resource Acquisition and Maintenance

One of the prime concerns of management of any organization is to acquire the means by which organizational objectives can be accomplished. Such means usually consist of people, tools, raw materials, technical knowledge, etc. All too frequently resource acquisition is discussed as a one-shot activity. No doubt there are times in the history of any organization when there are major efforts in this direction such as acquiring the capital for a large, new business. However, if resource acquisition were a one-time event, it would not pose a problem that would justify the creation of a staff because it would not meet the condition of repetition of a single type of event that is necessary for specialization. Hence, we are concerned primarily with the continuing acquisition of resources which is carried on by organizations both to satisfy the demand of growth of the organization and to replace the losses. Resources can be lost in a number of ways: through being used up, as when machines gradually wear out; through being withdrawn, as occurs when employees leave because of quitting, death, or retirement; or as owners withdraw their capital.

Acquisition is not the only effort management makes in providing resources; it must also maintain them. We quickly think of the maintenance activities expended on machines or buildings, but we might also note the wide range of other resource-maintaining activities such as taking out patents on inventions and subsequently taking legal action against infringements of these patents.

This purpose of staff is fundamental to the creation, development, and long-term perpetuation of any organization, and we might do well to consider two departments which illustrate the extensiveness of the efforts in large-scale organizations—such as business concerns—to accomplish these purposes; one such is the personnel department. The task of the personnel staff is the management of a flow (Figure 17.2) where the organization is faced by a continual loss of personnel through death, retirement, or quitting for better opportunities which must be replaced by new employees if the organization is to survive.

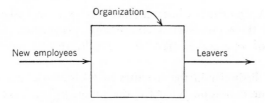

Figure 17.2. Personnel resource system.

In a company of 10,000 employees, this could amount to upwards of 200 persons a month, or almost 10 for each working day; this would be resource acquisition.

Considerable effort has been put into determining why people leave organizations. Some reasons for leaving, such as death and retirement, are unavoidable but many others are. Among these are the employees who leave because they are being underpaid, those who have talents they know are being overlooked and not utilized properly, or employees who feel they are working for bosses who are poor leaders. In contemporary organizations much effort is often put into detecting and correcting the sources of these reasons for leaving. Wage surveys are conducted to make sure that the organization's salaries are competitive. Training programs are instituted for foremen and other management personnel with the intent of making them better leaders and managers. These activities are usually carried on by the personnel staff as efforts to maintain the resource of personnel.

Staff as an Agent for Organizational Adaptation

There are many reasons organizations have to adapt. Business concerns have to adapt to the actions of competitors, the opportunities opened by new technologies, or the need for coping with new but powerful outside organizations such as labor unions. Universities have to adapt to new areas of knowledge and greatly increased knowledge in existing areas as well as to the pressure of increased student enrollment. Government agencies have to adapt to new public needs and diminishing of old ones. Although different, these changes entail common elements. In some way management has appraised conditions external or internal to the organization and decided that the organization must change and adopt modified or new goals at some place along the hierarchy of goals. A company whose scientists have discovered a new material, such as nylon, may be modified considerably as the new product is introduced with new opportunities and problems. A company whose engineers have found that in order to manufacture their goods at a competitive price they must increase their scale of operations may, as a result, decide to expand their business.

Although dissimilar in the specifics of their work, many staff positions seek out conditions vital for the organization; that is, they are performing an intelligence function and usually are proposing broad, basic policies or stratagems for the organization based on the information they have gathered. It is in this sense that staff positions are agents for organizational adaption. In recent years the number of these departments in large business concerns have grown rapidly and today we find departments for marketing research, market development, economic forecasting, long-range planning, profit analysis, to name a few concerned with this general purpose of adapting the organization.

Advice and Services

This purpose, so frequently cited in conventional theories of staff, is still basic to almost any staff department. It is different from the purposes just mentioned, however, in that this service is still performed largely on an individual basis whereas the others are performed for the organization as a whole. It is included here because almost every type of specialized staff department in fulfilling one or more of the aforementioned purposes is also available for any member of management to use as a source of advice or personal service. The personnel department does not look only at morale problems as a property of the total organization. Individual managers can go to the personnel department for advice in handling some morale problems in their departments. Obviously, providing advice and service constitutes a larger proportion of the activities in some departments than in others.

INTERNAL ORGANIZATION OF STAFF DEPARTMENTS

So much for *what* staff delivers to the overall organization. We now turn to *how* staff produces the services or results which the organization needs.

With personal staff this is a relatively minor problem. Such staffs usually consist of one or two or, at the most, a few people who report individually and directly to the person they serve. With specialized staffs, however, where the service is to the entire organization and the tasks frequently take on considerable complexity, larger numbers of people provide the result which creates the problem of how to organize them.

Division of Work of Staff Activities

Specialized staffs are intended to execute or, more accurately, aid in the execution of some managerial function. This becomes their main purpose or objective and the starting point for a means-ends analysis of the staff activity that defines the goal hierarchy of the subunit carrying out the work of this particular staff. We can, therefore, use general concepts of dividing work to begin the organization of staff departments.

Although all ways of dividing work are theoretically possible, these three are used most commonly:

1. *Division by purpose or what is delivered to the parent organization.* By applying the concepts of division of work noted earlier, we can consider a staff department as providing a number of outputs (similar to products or services), and it is possible to have principal divisions within the staff department separate work along these lines. For example, a legal department may provide legal services, but there are a number of different types of legal services a company may need, such as handling of real estate problems, drawing up contracts, and the handling of claims of people who have been dissatisfied with company products or injured on company property, etc. (Figure 17.3a).

2. *Division of work by recipient or recipient of the results of staff work within a large organization.* A staff department may be thought of as having a number of different groupings of clients who receive its services or products. Recipients can be classified in a number of ways: by their level in the organization (such as top, middle management, and worker levels) or by the area in which they are found, which in turn may be defined in several ways, such as geographical or departmental areas in the parent organization. For example, the legal department may have to provide its services to a company that has several divisions. Therefore, under a general legal council (Figure 17.3b) there might be principal staff departments concerned with handling all the legal problems of a particular company division.

3. *Division of staff work by step or function of the staff work.* Staff work, as any other, can be subdivided into functions which, when completed, culminate in the staff service or product. In the

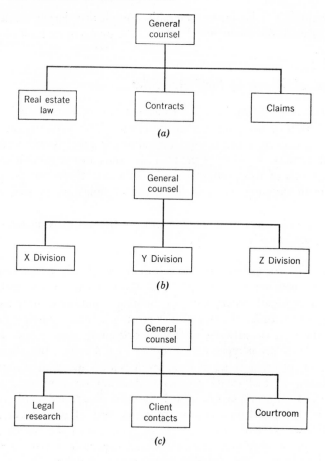

Figure 17.3. (*a*) Division by purpose or different types of legal service; (*b*) division by recipient; (*c*) division by phase or function.

legal illustration several functions might be necessary to perform the legal service. One such function would be contacts with the clients, finding out their problems, advising them on what they can do. Often, however, clients' problems can be handled adequately only by an extensive search of the law and judicial decisions so as to determine what advice to give the client. We might call this a *legal-research function*. Finally, the courts are essential instruments in the law, and many times a client's activities have to be taken to court; hence, there may be a courtroom function (Figure 17.3*c*). As always, functional division of work raises serious problems of coordination among subunits.

Allocation of Phases of Staff Work Activity

In illustrating the historical development of staff work we noted that this division of managerial activity had the same phases of performance as any other division of work: establishing a program for doing an aspect of the job, setting up through preparation of forms and arrangement of a work space, and executing a program. In this illustration staff positions, when created, were assigned only the execution phase —the other two being performed by line managers. Not until later were the setup and program-planning aspects turned over to staff. A central problem in deciding on an internal organization for staff is to determine how many phases of work activity will be allocated to it. This internal organization thus requires two principal decisions: one dealing with the division of work and the other with the allocation of phases of work activity. Let us consider three ways in which the work can be allocated.

1. *Staff allocated only execution of activities.* In the illustration we used, staff took over the program and facilities that were previously developed and set up by a line executive. This is to be expected under conditions where staff emerges as a result of work pressures on line executives who slough off part of their activities. Such a situation would be more typical in areas not having a particularly high degree of specialization and where the carrying out of the staff activity does not require a particularly high order of skill or education which might have to be obtained outside of the organization.

2. *Allocation of staff to set up, facilitate, and execute staff work.* A more advanced stage of staff development would be one in which staff members not only are intended to execute but also to set up and facilitate staff work. In more developed organizational situations, where staff work is carried out by a considerable number of people who may be separated widely both geographically and organizationally, there may be concern that all members of the staff subunit execute their work in the same way. Several things are done to facilitate this; one is to provide standard forms and tools so that all persons engaged in executing staff activities use the same implements.

Many times, however, uniform execution of staff activities depends as much on knowing the intent of the program as on knowing its content. To expedite this, many organizations turn the entire recruiting and training function of staff personnel over to the staff department. Staff executives then hire people whom they think have the training and other attributes to perform work in the way desired in this organization. Furthermore, they often bring newly hired persons into the central office where they can be trained and evaluated to make sure that when subsequently assigned to a field position, perhaps many hundreds of miles from the home office, they will understand what is to be done and why.

3. *Allocation of program development to staff units.* The third possible form of allocation, of course, is to turn over to the staff department the development of new programs for executing staff work. This has occurred in many long-standing staff departments in business organizations. In fact, this work has become so regular and important that it has often been institutionalized within the staff department itself. It is not at all uncommon in the accounting department of large business organizations to find positions or sometimes subdepartments devoted to the development of new programs for the staff activities. Figure 17.4 illustrates a manager of Accounting Development who has three subunits reporting to him. One of these subunits is devoted to accounting research, which primarily consists of keeping abreast of practices in other companies and the developments of accounting theory as reported in various journals and monographs. Another unit is concerned with accounting systems' planning, which in essence takes the findings of the research unit and translates them into specific programs or accounting systems for the company. The third subunit is concerned with accounting field services, where the new accounting systems are explained to the other staff personnel, instructions given in new techniques, and assistance is given

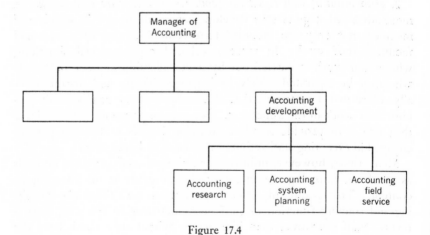

Figure 17.4

in working out problems encountered with the new procedures. Similar activities concerned with program development are found in many other lines of staff work such as manufacturing control systems, quality control, industrial engineering, etc.

When a staff department is allocated only the execution phase, it is far more dependent and subservient to the line than when it is allocated all three phases of work performance. By the time staff departments have been allocated all three phases, they are quite independent and autonomous within the parent organization. The range of control which line management has over the staff department has been reduced greatly. In these situations control is usually exercised at the top of the staff organization by executives (1) who are in a position to appoint the top staff officer and (2) have control over the particular set of objectives at the beginning of the means-ends chain of the staff work.

Staff Departments in Large Organizations

This topic leads to the observation that in contemporary, large-scale business organizations the more fully developed specialized staff departments constitute fairly autonomous subunits within the parent organization. Control over such departments is largely exercised at the top of the staff management structure, and the output of the staff in the form of services, etc. goes to all levels and areas of management. Within the foregoing broad issues of organizing staff work, there are more specific types of problems. One is how the staff work is to be arranged so that the staff department connects in a reporting relationship at the top management level and yet is able to funnel its services to all levels of the organization. This situation is complicated by the coexistence of top level or central staff departments, middle management staff departments, and plant, local, or regional staff departments, regardless of how staff work is divided.

SELF-CONTAINED LINE UNITS AND THE DISTRIBUTION OF STAFF WORK. If company policy attempts to make all line units as nearly self-contained as possible, local staff units logically would fall under complete control of the immediate line superior. A plant manager would have reporting to him the staff departments he needed such as personnel, accounting, etc. The decision as to how they are to operate and what they are to do would be a local one made by the plant manager, his local staff, or both. This practice enhances the execution of the managerial function with this subunit, but it does nothing to aid in the integration of the unit and other subunits in the organization. The alternative is to have complete control of all staff activities, which might be useful in promoting interunit coordination and control, but might also tend to overlook the peculiar problems of individual units, thereby denying them assistance in the execution of their internal managerial function.

The choice between these alternatives lies in part with the nature of the staff activity. Some, such as plant maintenance, have very little need for interdepartmental coordination. Thus, it is frequently possible to have this staff activity report completely to the subunit executive, or plant manager. On the other hand, if any form of accounting control is to be maintained for the entire organization, it is necessary that data be collected and reported in this same fashion in all departments to permit it to be combined and compared. Therefore, in accounting departments there is more necessity for centralized management of this staff activity and a lesser possibility of distributing the staff function exclusively to local subunits.

In actual organizations, many staff departments fall between the extremes of being completely distributed to local subunits or being entirely centralized at the top of the organization. A typical arrangement in many large organizations is for the top-level staff elements located in the central office to be responsible for the preparation and dissemination of programs for the execution of the staff work. Subunits within the organization then have control of the execution of the programs, and the setup and facilitation of the staff work is shared between the two. Accounting again serves as a useful illustration. The top levels of the staff activity prepare the overall accounting procedures, which are used throughout the organization. A local plant manager, for example, has direct control over the execution of accounting work in his plant, but it must be performed according to the centrally prepared program. Thus, the plant manager can determine what hours the accountants work, receive their reports, etc., but he is also accountable for accurate and prompt transmission of accounting data to higher management.

METHODS OF ACHIEVING INTERNAL STAFF COORDINATION. Division of work by function was seen to result in linked tasks which had to be coordinated to accomplish the overall end. Contrasted with this, division by product or service, or even frequently division by area, did not develop linked activities and, hence, did not have the same type of coordination problem. Needless to say, staff departments in which work is divided on the basis of function have the same problem. Here the reference is to the internal needs for coordination that arise within an organization as a result of division of work. Division by product or area may have problems of coordination arising from external conditions. In staff this may mean that the need for coordination will come from conditions not merely outside of the staff in the general management area, but external to the organization itself.

An illustration of such a case might be seen in a company which has to bargain with an aggressive, militant labor union. A common policy of such unions is that all union members must be treated equally anywhere in the company. Hence if employees in one plant have deductions made from their wages when they are late, whereas employees in another plant belonging to the same union do not, the company in all likelihood will receive a demand that all workers be treated the same and that none of them be docked for being late. Here the staff departments in the two plants are not linked internally; one cannot, for example, directly initiate action for another. However, if their practices relevant to members of this union are not coordinated, the staff departments can indirectly cause each other a great deal of difficulty.

We have discussed a number of steps commonly used to promote coordination, such as the central planning of programs and centralized recruiting and training of staff personnel. Many other techniques are used, among them meetings of all staff personnel and the use of audits.

Staff departments engaged in work more difficult to program, which is therefore more difficult to pin down in written form, are likelier to use meetings in which all the personnel in a given line of staff work are brought together periodically to discuss their work. These meetings may be annually, biannually, or even as frequently as monthly. The expense of transporting staff personnel who are scattered around the country to a central meeting may seem great; however, not to do this may lead to far more expensive and serious complications. An alternative is to have central staff personnel tour divisional and local staff offices to discuss problems, pass along latest techniques and programs, and to gather information about new problems which require attention.

Another technique is the use of audits. Personnel from the central staff unit survey the handling of work at the divisional and local levels to make sure that programs are properly used and that they are adequate. This procedure is obviously more usable in areas where staff work can become highly programmed as, for example, in accounting; here audits are primarily concerned with determining whatever local accounting activities are in line with prescribed and acceptable practices. However, audits also can be used in areas which cannot be thoroughly programmed. A number of people think personnel work is one area which should benefit from audit practices,[15] and other staff areas seem equally amenable to this approach.

Location of Staff Departments

Thus far we have treated staff as if all staffs ultimately reported to top management or were "plugged in at the top of the organization." Although this is true for many, it is not true for all. Some staff departments plug in only at the local level, whereas others are attached only to one division and not to others. The location of a staff department can be decided by using several criteria.[16] Among them:

1. *The greatest need.* Here staff is assigned to the division or hierarchal level where the service is most needed. Production and inventory control are needed mostly in production plants, which defines both a division and level. Economic analysis is most needed at the top of the organization.

2. *Importance of service rendered.* In general, the more important the service rendered by any organizational subunit, the likelier it is to be placed higher in the organization. For example, quality control is far less important in a company making whisk brooms than in a company making passenger airplanes. A failure of a whisk broom is a minor annoyance and may represent the loss of an investment that is under a dollar; the failure of an airplane in flight may lead to great loss of life, money, and reputation for the manufacturing company. As a result, quality control is likely to be attached at a relatively low hierarchal level in a whisk broom manufacturing company, whereas we may readily find it reporting to top-level management in aircraft manufacturing companies.

3. *Requirements for effective staff operation.* In brief, a staff department functions best when it is in a supportive or at least benign environment. For example, we could conceive of the possibility of placing a quality-control department because it is involved with control under the offices of the accounting department, which also exercises control activities. However, since the technology used in quality control is so different from that used in accounting, and furthermore since the types of control are so different, this probably would not prove to be a satisfactory arrangement—at least not as satisfactory as placing the quality control department under the engi-

[15] Dale Yoder, *Personnel Principles and Policies—Modern Manpower Management*, Englewood Cliffs, Prentice Hall, 1956, Chapter 22.
[16] This material is drawn largely from William Newman, *Administrative Action*, Englewood Cliffs, Prentice Hall, 1951, particularly Chapter 8.

neering department, where it would be in a more compatible technical environment, or even in the manufacturing department, where the purpose of its control would be more readily understood and utilized.

SUMMARY

In this chapter we began by considering the general purpose of staff to be able to assist in carrying out the managerial function. To do this, staff can assist managers and executives personally as personal staff or assistants-to. A staff might assist in carrying out the work of an office, such as the president of a business enterprise or the commanding general's office of an army, and thus be a general or positional staff. Or last, staff might do its work by assisting the organization as a whole, or at least large sectors of it, as do specialized staffs and operating services.

The work of personal staff tends to be general in nature and might cover a wide range of activities. General staffs tend to be more specialized although general staff officers often do not have specialized training in the work of their particular staff assignment. Specialized staffs and operating services tend to be the most highly specialized of all. These positions are frequently staffed by people who have received extensive, specialized training in their line of work. Operating services perform services for the organization, such as running the company cafeteria. Specialized staffs facilitate one, or part of one, managerial function; typical of these were accounting, quality control, economic forecasting, etc. Specialized staff are found to be growing rapidly in the last several decades constituting an important portion of the managerial structure of most business concerns and, for that matter, other large-scale organizations. Since they loom so large, both in size and in importance, this staff constitutes the "archetype" toward which the bulk of attention was given in this chapter.

Staff and particularly specialized staff were seen to constitute an institutionalization of the managerial function. Staff departments and positions were described in two respects: the type of division of work used to define the aspect of the managerial function handled by the staff and the number of phases of work activities included in the staff department. These same two dimensions were used to define the internal organization of a staff unit. In large-scale organizations having several hierarchal zones many staff departments functioned across all zones. The need for coordination, whether internally or externally induced, as well as other factors such as the overall organization style, influenced the distribution of the phases of work activities, program planning, setup or facilitation, and execution.   When this distribution placed more of the program planning and facilitation in the hands of either higher level staff positions or line management, the influence of these areas of the organization over staff activity and performance was increased.

Staff as an organizational element to support or assist the work of the managerial function did not fall directly along the means-ends chain of the organization.   Departments which did, and thus were in the primary hierarchy of goals, constituted the line.   Staff was concerned with supporting the management; to accomplish these goals it was in this sense auxiliary or adjective in nature.

Staff, notably specialized staff, although in general considered as aiding and performing many of the managerial functions, was noted as primarily assisting in the following areas: (1) coordination and control,   (2) resource acquisition and maintenance,   (3) as an agent of organizational adaptation, and   (4) counseling and service.

The importance of staff in handling the intricacies of the managerial function in complex organizations has grown over the years.   Important though it is, this growth has not been without problems, sometimes serious.   Some of these and of the reasons for them are discussed in Chapter 18.

18

Line-Staff Relationships

Life in the executive hierarchies of large-scale organizations has many strains as well as satisfactions. A chronic source of difficulty are the relationships between line and staff. These relationships are often fraught with arguments, confusion, and sometimes elaborate maneuvers to circumvent the other party's power or to create an illusion of compliance.

To no small degree these conflicts are generated and perpetuated by misunderstandings about the nature and purpose of staff and the relationship of staff positions to other managerial offices. Although not the only source of difficulty, these misunderstandings are particularly important because they cloud and conceal factors which contribute to other important causes. In this chapter we consider a few of the important reasons for conflict between line and staff positions. Some of them are unique to this particular source of difficulty; others are more general and can cause difficulty among any types of organizational positions.

STAFF AS A THREAT TO THE LINE MANAGER

Depletion of the General Managerial Function

We viewed the creation of staff as an outcome of the institutionalism of the managerial function; general, undefined areas of responsibility and activity were reduced by having specific responsibilities and activities separated out and assigned as jobs to other positions. In consequence, the general managerial function has been cut to several factors:

1. The individual line manager's job is trimmed, and to that degree made less important.

2. As the managerial work is institutionalized and a set of organizational programs developed, unique personal skills become less important.

3. As a general managerial function carried out by the typical line executive is reduced, that portion remaining (now smaller) becomes more easily defined and therefore more subject to control. Also as a consequence of having his scope of responsibility made smaller the line executive finds himself restricted to a smaller area of activity. Hence, he is less able to maneuver, to take the actions he thinks necessary to do his job, and to advance his purposes.

What are the consequences of this situation? They are feelings of frustration, isolation, detachment from the rest of management, and an overall pervasive feeling of being threatened. Careers built up and positions attained over years of lengthy service within one company become progressively less important, less influential, and place the occupant in a position of being less able to defend and protect himself.[1]

Staff as a Source of Change

Many staff positions noted in Chapter 17 are very much concerned with bringing about change. They generate plans and often play an instrumental role in implementing changes. Change can be a disquieting thing. In general, it seems that the less involved a person is in planning a change, and the less he knows about its purposes and meaning, the likelier he is to feel such a change as a hazard to his security. Seeing staff as the fountainhead of this threat, the line manager's negative feelings about staff as a threat to his security can readily be understood.

Staff Positions and Channels of Communication

Much of the interaction of the staff man is with people other than his superior. In a plant, the personnel manager in charge of local labor relations reports to the plant manager, who also has reporting to

[1] The effects have been noted in managerial positions at a number of levels—mostly typically, however, at the foreman or first-line supervisory level. For typical analysis, see Donald E. Wray, "Marginal Man of Industry: The Foreman," *The American Journal of Sociology*, 54, 1949, pp. 298–301; James H. Mullen, "The Supervisor Assesses His Job in Management," *Personnel*, 31, 1954, p. 105; Paul A. Brinker, "Supervisors and Foreman's Reason for Frustration," *Personnel Journal*, 34, 1955, pp. 101–103.

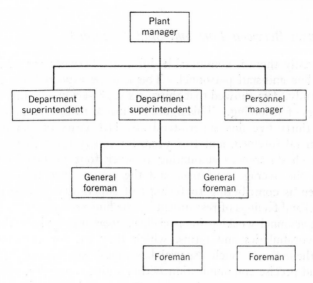

Figure 18.1

him a chain of department superintendents, general foremen, and foremen (Figure 18.1).   The individual foreman in such a situation looks at the personnel manager as an individual who has easy access to his superior, the general foreman, to the departmental superintendent, to the plant manager, and the personnel manager may be used as a channel of communication to speed the flow of information through the organization.   Therefore, when the personnel manager comes to discuss the details of a grievance filed against the foreman, the foreman probably feels that in addition to the advice and information being solicited, the personnel manager is also gathering data which he may report to "higher ups."   He may wonder what will happen if he ignores a suggestion made by the personnel manager.   Will the matter be dropped? When reporting the matter to "someone higher up," will the personnel manager say in an off-hand way, "Well, of course, the problem may take a little longer to solve than usual because of the attitude foreman X has adopted."   These fears may be groundless, but that they do exist is apparent to many who have worked in any sort of line-executive position.   Furthermore, the fears rest to a considerable degree on the awareness that the unique position of the staff man in communication channels makes such events possible.   Even without intention it is possible for the staff man's "advice" to have almost the weight of a command with the apprehensive line supervisor.

Differences Between Line and Staff Personnel

Frequently there is considerable difference between the educational level of line and staff personnel. This is to be expected, for as noted in one study, data showed that thirty-six staff personnel had a mean of 14.6 years of schooling. This figure compared to 13.1 years of schooling for thirty-five line superintendents, 11.2 years of schooling for sixty general foremen, and 10.5 years for ninety-three first-line foremen. Such differences amounting to over four years of education between the average staff man and the average first-line supervisor were seen as contributing to feelings of superiority among the staff personnel and feelings of resentment by the line managers.[2]

Staff personnel working in specialized areas usually have their own unique vocabularies and terms, which they use for communication among themselves. Such "special languages" are necesary for both quick and precise communication within a given specialty. However, when such language is used to communicate with people not in the specialty, the terms and phrases are meaningless and are a source of frustration contributing to a feeling of ignorance and inferiority. Staff personnel are frequently reported as using their special languages with line executives unfamiliar with them.[3]

In addition to these factors, line personnel frequently feel themselves different from staff on the basis of age in that staff personnel frequently are younger than the line executives with whom they are dealing. Furthermore, staff personnel tend to have a social life, both on and off the job, that is different from the line managers'.[4]

The Reward System for Staff Men

Patterns of reward for staff executives present some additional and complicating features. In the early part of his career a new staff man, if he enters a large, complex organization with highly developed staff departments, is likely to spend most of his working time in an environment particularly oriented to his professional specialty. The people around him will be specialists like himself, and it is likely that his superior will be a specialist in the same professional area. The behav-

---

[2] Melville E. Dalton, "Conflicts Between Staff and Line Managerial Officers," *American Sociological Review*, 15, 1950, pp. 342–351.
[3] See, for example, Chris Argyris, *The Impact of Budgets on People*, New York, Controllers Institute Research Foundation, 1952.
[4] Dalton, *op. cit.*

ior that obtains his position for the staff man, which, once he has it, will obtain for him rewards of acceptance by his peers and raises and promotions from his superiors, will be behavior derived from his professional area rather than from behavior that is of immediate concern to the overall organization. Hence, in dealing with line executives, the staff man is likely to feel quite confident and sure when he is insisting that standards and rules of his professional area be maintained rather than being bent to satisfy the immediate requirements of the line executive.

In a large staff department, the first few promotions the staff man receives will probably be within the department and this context. As he advances upward, however, the staff man is likely to become aware of the fact that sooner or later someone who is not a staff person will make a decision about his career. At some point a line executive makes the choice as to who will be the top staff member, and he may well look on things from a line point of view and not be particularly interested in professional values and standards. This outlook penetrates several levels down and, in effect, as a staff man moves upward in the staff department, he meets with a changing set of "acceptable" standards for his behavior. The closer he gets to the top of the staff organization, the more he knows that future rewards are dependent on his conforming more to the expectations of line than of professional staff colleagues.[5]

Staff officials at different hierarchal levels are likely to behave in accordance with slightly different reward systems, values, or perceived standards of acceptable behavior. This situation raises some difficulties within the staff organization itself; as higher staff officials appear more willing to accede to the demands of line officials at the expense of professional values, they are often seen by their professional colleague-subordinates as "selling out."[6] In this light it becomes easier to understand why staff problems often appear to be most intense among the lower levels of staff and line officials.

AN ORGANIZATIONAL ANALYSIS OF A
TYPICAL LINE-STAFF PROBLEM

Many problems, tensions, and conflicts between line and staff can be analyzed using concepts already developed. To illustrate this let us consider the description of events as they occurred in one company.

[5] For an interesting discussion of this and subsequent points, see Dalton, *op. cit.*
[6] *Ibid.*

This situation, while having a few unique properties, is in general typical of other companies with line-staff difficulties, and is illustrated in this rather lengthy quote (pp. 364–368).[7]

"This is a large multi-plant manufacturing concern decentralized along product lines into three operating divisions. Each division has its own internal, functional, and staff organization, including personnel administration. Plant managers report directly to the three vice presidents of divisions, who in turn report to the president. The company bargains with five craft unions, one of which represents the major share of the firm's production and maintenance workers. Negotiations are company-wide, since each union represents the employees of a particular occupation in all the separate plants.

"Before the company was unionized, the personnel function had little status in the company. The corporate personnel manager reported to a staff vice president in charge of services and was concerned largely with day-to-day administrative and clerical duties. After the unions gained recognition, he was promoted to the position of industrial relations director, reporting directly to the president. With the aim of preventing production holdups, the president told his newly established industrial relations director that he was holding him responsible for avoiding labor difficulties. 'Use whatever means you need,' he said, 'but keep us out of trouble.'

NEW LOOK IN LABOR RELATIONS

"Henceforth, the industrial relations director served as chief spokesman in negotiating the master agreements and headed a team of labor relations specialists from the central industrial relations office. All line managers, except possibly the president, were excluded from the negotiations, and did not receive reports on their progress. Though the wage settlement and basic matters of principle had to receive the president's approval, this was largely a rubber-stamp procedure.

"The industrial relations director also had a great deal of authority in interpreting the agreements once negotiated. While he sometimes consulted top line and staff people on the subject, the final decisions rested with him. Similarly, he handled all grievance cases that were not settled in the plants, and had complete authority to settle a grievance and to decide whether or not to take it to arbitration.

"Out in the plants, the middle managers and foremen played a role of

[7] Maynard N. Toussaint, "Line-Staff Conflict: Its Causes and Cure," *Personnel*, 39, 1962, pp. 11–15.

little consequence.   Despite criticism and obstruction from the unions, they were inadequately briefed on contract provisions and had received little training in the skills of managing people and handling grievances.   Consequently, the plant-level personnel people assumed an important role in interpreting the agreements and in handling grievance cases at the second step.   They occupied a difficult position, however, since they reported directly to the operating managers. Thus they had to secure line management's agreement on questions of interpretation or proposed grievance settlements.   The resolution of any disagreements was, of course, made by the central industrial relations director, often after a grievance reached him for settlement.

"Thus the labor relations function became highly centralized and specialized, even though this departed from the company's basic policy of decentralization.   This approach was considered necessary to preclude whip-saw tactics by the many unions, both in negotiating the contracts and in their administration.   Admittedly, it was effective in securing uniform labor relations policies and practices throughout the various plants.   And in terms of the industrial relations director's basic responsibility, it was indeed successful.   There were no work stoppages, and arbitration cases averaged only two a year.   Discussing his role, the industrial relations director made it clear that he regarded it as a substitute for line management in labor relations matters:

'Operating people are glad to be relieved of labor relations duties.   They don't have the patience to negotiate and handle grievances.   Those that aren't happy about it don't know what they have been saved from.   This kind of work requires a different kind of personality, interests, and skills.   I want a fuller recognition of the status of industrial relations and its appropriate organizational position.'

"But the plant and lower line managers were not so satisfied with this arrangement.   Many of them resented the "tightening up" of their activities, viewing it as criticism of their production methods.   In addition, they did not feel that standardization necessarily meant maximum efficiency in running the plants and in keeping costs down. They appointed 'personnel liaison representatives' to assist and represent them in daily labor relations problems.   These liaison representatives met periodically with members of the industrial relations staff to report local plant problems and complaints to headquarters, and to report back current labor relations developments throughout the company.

"This approach did not result in ideal union-management relationships in the plants either. The unions began to regard lower line management as unimportant and often incompetent. They took many of their complaints directly to the industrial relations director. The foremen, in turn, resented their loss of status and authority and felt they had no support from the top. Relations with the unions became insulting and abusive. As friction mounted, complaints and grievances arose over the pettiest details and legalistic interpretations of work rules.

THE CLASH

"Matters came to a head soon after the negotiation of a 'harmonious relations' clause in the master agreements providing for the union to discipline any union officials, and for the company likewise to discipline any foremen or others of its representatives, 'who shall conduct themselves in such manner as to bring upon the union or company, respectively, the proper reproach of the other.'

"The exact meaning of this clause was tested when one of the foremen issued a written warning to a union steward alleging that the amount and quality of the man's production had fallen below standard. The union objected to this action and took the grievance to the industrial relations director. In view of the new contract provision, the union contended that in no circumstance could management discipline a union official. The industrial relations director upheld this interpretation and rescinded the foreman's disciplinary action.

"Line management disagreed with this ruling. They did not think that the provision took away their right to enforce plant rules and production standards—'those things not related to the steward in his connection with the union.' Moreover, they strongly objected to the way this particular decision had been reached. A liaison representative described management reaction this way:

> 'This was announced as policy at a liaison meeting without any of us knowing about it. We were pretty sore since this was unilateral policy setting by the industrial relations director and top union officers. I was told to pass this on to operating people. The reaction was terrible, and I was caught in the middle. My plant manager was really burned up . . . I put my foot down at the next liaison meeting and demanded a written statement of company policy.'

"In response to questioning at the next personnel liaison meeting, the industrial relations director issued the following written statement:

'. . . In our union agreements, there is a provision that, in order to have harmonious relations, the company and the union each undertakes to discipline any of its members who bring upon the one organization the proper reproach of the other. . . . It is the responsibility of the management person to bring the action to the attention of this office through channels. This office will take it up with the business manager of the union calling upon him to exercise discipline to insure there will be no repetition of the incident. . . . In the case of the individual steward, though, he is not, in your opinion, or in the opinion of a number of people, a very likable or worthy person, he is nevertheless during the time he is steward, cloaked with the authority of the office. It is a union office, but it is the office of an official of a great and powerful organization and accordingly the office (whether or not the person) should be respected. . . . The unions have complained, and in some cases rightfully so, of a foreman's disrespect for the union. . . . If we are to have respect from the union officials for our management people, we must show to the union the respect as indicated here.

There was [also] some discussion as to the right of Personnel to enter into line supervision's dealings with the unions, but it was pointed out that the union as an organization looks to Personnel in its dealings with the company.'

"Line management now clearly understood that they were not to discipline union stewards. Any such discipline had to be administered by the union at the instigation of the industrial relations office. Nevertheless, they thought that the basic issue had not been resolved —their side of the story and their problems had been neither heard nor understood. As one middle manager expressed it:

'The industrial relations director is putting us in an impossible position. If we can't discipline stewards, it extends to workers. We are helpless, and all the industrial relations director does is softpedal it in our meetings. He gets philosophical, but we know it will hurt. His job is dealing with the union, and that's all he can see. His goal is to maintain our record of no strikes and no arbitration cases. . . . But we have to manage, and we're interested in our own necks on this case. We'll take it to arbitration without him. This one is critical. Unless we do, we're hamstrung in managing.'

"One general manager of operations decided to appeal directly to the president. But reportedly, all he got was a dressing down for 'interfering' with the industrial relations director's basic responsibility and authority. This served to clarify the prevailing structure of authority in union relations, but not to the satisfaction of the line people:

> 'Now we know how things stand around here. We knew the industrial relations director could make decisions on certain union issues, but we thought we could at least get a fair hearing if hurt badly. Now we know he can dictate to line management. This authority was delegated to him by the president, but it's no good. The only time we see the industrial relations director around here is when he comes down and tries to sell us something he has done to placate the union. He doesn't understand our problems, doesn't try to, and operating management doesn't like this appeasement policy. We think we have some pretty smart boys, too, and don't like this so-and-so. The industrial relations director got to the president first, but we'll get to him yet."

Separation of Planning from Execution

In this case, the union contract contained specific plans concerning how employees of the company were to be handled. These plans were established by the industrial relations department. Many of the contract's provisions, however, and certainly those under discussion, had to be executed by line officials. Although producing some distinct advantages, such a division of the phases of work performance can lead to a number of distinct problems, as it did in this case.

On one hand, the line executives were in the uncomfortable position of having their activities molded and directed by the planning contained in the contract, which in the line executives' eyes meant that they were being directed as to how to handle *their* people by the industrial relations staff personnel. Such a situation placed them in a status position inferior to the industrial relations specialist, since such prerogatives of direction usually go with higher authority and commensurate higher status.[8] On the other hand, the industrial relations staff man also found himself in an uncomfortable, although different, position. He had been charged by the company president to "keep us out of trouble" in regard to labor matters. However, he could only prepare plans for treating the company personnel. The actual treatment of these individuals was carried out by the line executives. The staff man in this case was in a position where even if he made the best possible set of plans, he might still have failed because of improper or

---

[8] See Chapter 4 on Status.

inadequate execution. Since he was not in a position to control directly the execution of plans, he was in a frustrating position. Seen in this light, we are not too surprised to find staff men frequently feeling that line executives act in ignorance, from stupidity, or in narrow self-interest. That is why staff men often go to top management to seek support for the proper execution of their plans.

Not all staff work has the same degree of separation between the planning and execution of work. In service departments—for example, a plant cafeteria—the staff is responsible for planning the work, that is, menus recipes, the layout of work, etc., and for execution through supervision of cooks, waitresses, etc. In these areas the amount of line-staff difficulty is usually considered to be less.

Different Goals—Linked Efforts of Line-Staff Departments

In the foregoing case the manufacturing department was one of a set of business functional departments. Its prime responsibility was to get a product made at a satisfactory cost within permissible time limits. To a line executive in a manufacturing department these functional goals were of major significance; any other objectives were secondary. Conditions or requirements which interfered with realizing these objectives were considered wrong or improper and in need of elimination. The industrial relations department, on the other hand, was one of a set of managerial functional departments. It was not only a different function but fitted into a different set of functions from the manufacturing department. The objective here was quite different. It was to "keep us out of trouble," and to this end the industrial relations staff bent its efforts.

These two different goals came into direct contact and conflict at the point at which action was taken in handling company employees who were members of unions. The line executives in this case saw the necessity for disciplining employees who were also elected union officials (such as shop stewards) as an essential act for maintaining discipline and control of their department to insure it would meet its objectives. This act, however, was directly opposite of what the industrial relations staff man saw as desirable in that when it occurred, it diminished the extent to which he was accomplishing his objective to "keep us out of trouble." The consequence, then, of establishing staff departments to administer the operation of different systems is that there are a number of actions which exist in two or more systems, and these may lead to conflict when the execution of one action reduces goal attainment in one system while increasing it in another.

Such situations are frequently brought to higher management for reconciliation. Management may choose to decide each instance differently by determining whether advancement toward a goal in one system more or less compensates the loss of another goal in a different system. Where these situations are frequent and conditions stable enough, management may take the next step of determining a decision role which says, in effect, that when an action leads to a gain toward accomplishing goal X in system A, at the same time diminishing the likelihood of obtaining goal Y in system B, the act must be avoided (or it could just as well say be permitted to be carried out). This step does not eliminate the problem, but sets up a standard way of dealing with it, and is one of the things the staff man will try to achieve in going to top management. In the case cited, the industrial relations director seemed to have obtained decision rules which favored the staff system and its objectives. The line people were not unaware of this, however, leading one of them to remark in the case, "The industrial relations director got to the president first, but we will get to him yet."

Different Perceptions and Systemic Linkages

Running through this case are comments which make it quite clear that the line manufacturing executives viewed the handling of personnel quite differently from the industrial relations director. The industrial relations director not infrequently looked on line managers as being narrow, provincial, and basically not interested in the overall welfare of the company.[9] On the other hand, the industrial relations director is frequently seen as placating the union and supporting union men at the expense of line executives.

Sometimes these charges are a result of the emotions that have been aroused. However, to a degree they also reflect conditions that have their roots in the organizational arrangements. If manufacturing line executives have a narrower outlook than the industrial relations staff executives, the roots for this lie in the existing structure. We have already talked about the restricted perceptions which often go with placing people in highly specialized units, especially those with fairly clear-cut objectives, enforced by a complex and effective system of reward and education. The staff personnel have a number of systemic linkages,[10] which influence their perceptions. The industrial relations director has many contacts with top management, particularly with the president, which in turn help him to achieve a broad, all-over

[9] Toussaint, op. cit., p. 11.
[10] See Chapter 10.

company point of view. Proportionately speaking, the industrial relations director also spends far more time in contact with union officials, particularly full-time, top-level union officials, than do line executives. Furthermore, the point of contact between these two parties are matters of direct and immediate importance to both.

In contrast, the line manufacturing executive seldom meets top-level union officials. He is in contact mostly with lower level union officials, and even then as only one of their many contacts during the typical working day. Second, when they meet in regard to an issue, they approach it from directions which make agreement and exchange less likely; the decisions made are often seen by the line executive as directly diminishing his possibility of accomplishing his ends. The industrial relations director, when making a decision about work assignments or work rule, is not making decisions about things which he will directly have to live with for the rest of the contract.

At the same time the lower union official when discussing a point of grievance or interpretation of the contract is usually in direct, continual contact with the person who files the grievance. Often they work in the same department. A decision which is unsatisfactory to the union member encourages him to confront the union official continually with his disfavor, and may ultimately mean the union official's loss of office in a union election. The higher level union official does not have to face a disgruntled union member regularly, and even dissatisfaction in one department or area of the union is hardly likely to be of direct immediate consequence for his tenure in office.

To summarize, when the line manager makes contact with the union, it is with less frequency and under less favorable circumstances. The lower level union official approaches such contacts in an equally unfavorable light. The outlook of both higher union officials and top-level industrial relations men are much more favorable. Systematic linkage is a particular type of relationship which does much to help explain the differing outlooks shared by staff and line personnel.

In this analysis we have attempted to show that many of the line-staff problems are of an organizational nature which can be detected by using the relatively simple concepts developed earlier in this book. These are hardly all the problems or all their sources. Furthermore, no attempt has been made to propose corrective action. Rather, the effort here has been directed toward analysis or, perhaps more precisely, toward diagnosis and not prescriptions. The problems analyzed, however, have tended to center on two topics. One of these was a particular set of organizational elements and their arrangements or, to put it somewhat differently, the way in which an organization was defined. Second, was the perceptions which organizational members have developed as a consequence of being in the organization. We study these issues a little more fully to see if further examination not only clarifies the problem but also begins to show possible solutions.

ORGANIZATIONAL DEFINITION

Division of Managerial Work and Requisite Coordination

The establishment of staff departments, as we have seen, grows out of a division of managerial work on a functional basis. Any division of work requires some coordination among the subdivided units, but the needs are of a particularly high order when this occurs on a functional basis. A key issue is how to provide for coordination of managerial units subdivided in this manner.

Traditional staff concepts had a built-in solution for this problem resting on the assumption that staff was in a subordinate, supportive role relative to line executives. In this sense it was implicitly line's responsibility to see that staff was used properly, and furthermore it was line's implied authority to determine when staff would perform and in what way. Traditional staff ideas thus took care of the problem of line-staff coordination through a crude decision rule; staff was subservient to line. Its efforts would be coordinated with line effort at the time and in the way line executives thought necessary. As we also saw earlier, regardless of the apparent utility of this decision rule, practice does not conform with the requirements of theory. The issue is if this widely quoted decision rule is not effective, how is the functionally subdivided managerial work coordinated? We explore this question within the framework of three of the modes of coordination discussed earlier.

VOLUNTARY COORDINATION OF MANAGERIAL WORK. All too frequently we receive the impression that there are formal means provided for the coordination of managerial functions. Almost by default there seems to be the decision to let the necessary coordination be provided through voluntary means. Although a great deal of coordination is provided via this strategy, there are many conditions in an organization which diminish its effectiveness. Let us look briefly at some of the elements which frustrate voluntary coordination.

A brief review of the elements in the influence model in Chapter 1 suggest that staff and line people behave in different influence systems. Located in different areas of the organization with diverse contacts they receive separate stimuli which, especially in light of their respective educational and professional backgrounds, is likely to lead to distinctive evoked sets. For the moment let us consider the different sets of perceived consequences to alternatives. In the case cited, the shop steward is seen by the line executives as an element in maintaining their control over employees in the production process. An action against the shop steward, perceived by line personnel as increasing their control, was seen by the staff personnel as leading to a deterioration of union-management relations. For both line and staff personnel the consequences of alternate courses of action are partially influenced by higher management, which, made more compatible, would do much to bring the resultant behaviors into closer coordination.

A second factor that makes voluntary coordination of line and staff difficult are their perceptions. Through the perception model presented in Chapter 2 we can see that they receive dissimilar information because of the differing natures of their work, positions in the organization, interaction with people, possession of role concepts, and their different reference groups. It is not surprising, therefore, that they have different perceptions and behave in different ways.

PROVISION OF ADMINISTRATIVE SYSTEMS. Coordination of managerial work can be facilitated by establishing procedures for performing certain aspects of managerial work, such as the procedures established to hire new personnel or to request maintenance. There is seldom, if ever, any group of people established to oversee or facilitate such procedures. Further methods are usually developed by one of the parties whose work is to be coordinated from the point of view of, "What do I need to do my job?" Joint development of procedures is uncommon. Often the program to develop coordination is established unilaterally. Needless to say, such procedures often fall short of what is needed. Perhaps the closest we come to having some personnel assigned to the operation of a coordinative system is in the development of program or product management units, where one person or a small group of people is charged with the responsibility of coordinating all work on sharply defined projects or areas.[11]

HIERARCHAL COORDINATION. The third strategy for promoting coordination is to have higher executives provide it. However, the coordination of managerial work by higher managers is all too frequently sadly neglected. This is not to say that higher managers are oblivious to problems of coordination, but usually they focus their attention on

[11] Joseph A. Litterer, "Program Management: Organizing for Flexibility and Stability," *Personnel*, 40, 1963, pp. 25–34.

coordination at the work level. That is, they will be very much concerned with provision of a production-control system to make sure that work on a product moves smoothly, but they tend to ignore the intervening levels of management whose work also has to be coordinated. The result is that many, and often simple, steps to facilitate coordination are either neglected or poorly handled. One example of this situation may be seen when a higher manager is approached by a subordinate with a proposal which he subsequently approves. Too often in approving the manager does not ask himself who besides himself will have to know about this decision, both to support it and to keep it from interfering with their other work. The number of things about which the executives in organizations will complain, "I just didn't know about that," is enormous. They range all the way from changing an executive's office location and failing to tell others with whom he has to work, changing telephone numbers and failing to notify even the operator on the switchboard, to far more important issues, such as changing basic policies about the quality of a product but failing to notify the sales department or the advertising department.

Some of the omissions are ludicrous and would seem artificial to anyone who has not been in a large organization, where they may occur numerous times. The very obviousness of such omissions suggests how extensive must be the failure to provide coordination through hierarchal means. Perhaps one fruitful thing that can be done is for higher management to focus more attention on the middle range of executives between them and the work site and attempt more directly to facilitate the requisite coordination.

The Problem of Boundaries

In dividing work there is always the problem of determining where one unit ends and the other begins. Dividing on a geographical basis, this is often fairly simple. The border between Indiana and Illinois could be chosen as the dividing line between sales areas. Other ways of dividing work and other areas in which work is divided make it increasingly more difficult to define boundaries sharply and clearly. For example, suppose a company introduces a new product which is so different that it is going to require, among other things, considerable retaining of existing salesmen. To facilitate all this work on the new product, a product manager position is created having among its responsibilities the duty to see that the salesmen receive the necessary training. Just what is the relationship between the salesmen and the product manager?   Can the new manager call the salesmen to a two-day training session on the new product?   If he does this, of course, the company loses two days of sales effort by all the salesmen, a matter of no small concern to the area sales manager who may not want the training at this time since this is the selling season for the concern's regular line of products.   The boundary in this case is much harder to define and more likely to be neglected.   In the area of managerial functions it is hard to fix boundaries clearly and sharply.   The oft quoted ideal of organizational definition, to have departments and decisions mutually exclusive, is very difficult and in fact often impossible to attain.

One partial solution has been to define boundaries in a conditional fashion.   We say that under one set of conditions the boundary is located in position X, and under another set of conditions it is located in position Y.   An illustration arises in the area of quality control in many manufacturing enterprises.   It is often stated that the quality control department has no direct authority over production.   It can specify the standards the product must meet, the types of tests which must be performed, and may even make the tests itself, but beyond this it has no influence in the conduct of the production operation *except* when the quality of the product is consistently below requisite standards; *then* quality control may have the overriding authority to stop all production until higher quality work is assured.   A similar pattern is often found in safety work.   A safety engineer may have no control over work in a factory except in those situations which he deems to be hazardous to life; then he may have the authority to shut down operations or to order people away from a location, overriding, if necessary, the authority of the regular line executives.

The establishment of conditional boundaries does not eliminate all conflict between line and staff personnel.   The reaction of typical line executives when the quality control manager "shuts down" his production line is usually quite spectacular.   However, the ensuing discussion will probably revolve around issues of the quality of the product or the ways of producing a quality product and not around issues of whether the staff man has any authority over production.   In short, defining things even in this limited way tends to move the discussion from an area of relative unprofitability for the organization to one where it is likelier to focus on issues which are of real concern in obtaining organizational objectives.   Still another solution plays down superior-subordinate relations, and stresses the complementary nature of functionally specialized positions.   Here the staff is viewed as colleagues rather than subordinates of line.

UTILITY OF CONFLICT

Much of this chapter is focused on the problem of conflicts between line and staff personnel and to a smaller degree on conflict among staff personnel themselves. This discussion might imply condemnation of all conflict. This is hardly the case. Conflict is dysfunctional when it absorbs organizational efforts and resources without producing anything, when it deflects attention from basic purposes, and perhaps when it leads to actions which consciously or unconsciously sabotage and subvert primary organizational objectives. On the other hand, conflict in some forms and areas can be extremely useful for the organization and in fact may be essential. Some recent investigations suggest that from conflict comes much organizational change.

Consequently, the issue is not whether conflict should be eliminated, it is to define those areas where it should be permitted and how it should be handled. Organizations that possess the capacity to deal adequately with conflict have been described as follows:

"1. They possess the machinery to deal constructively with conflict. They have an organizational structure which facilitates constructive interaction between individuals and work groups.

2. The personnel of the organization is skilled in the processes of effective interaction and mutual influence (skills in group leadership and membership roles in group building and maintenance functions).

3. There is a high confidence and trust in one another among members of the organization, loyalty to the work group and to the organization, and high motivation to achieve the organization's objectives. Confidence, loyalty, and cooperative motivation produce earnest, sincere, and determined efforts to find solutions to conflict. There is greater motivation to find constructive solution than to maintain an irreconcilable conflict. The solutions reached are often highly creative and represent a far better solution than any initially proposed by the conflicting interests." [12]

The essential theme here is that out of conflict will come a new synthesis superior to what existed before and perhaps superior to any individual point of view existent in the conflict. How this comes about has hardly been explored. Likert mentions a need for skill in interpersonal relations. Organizational adaptation frequently proceeds through a new arrangement developing informally, which, after

[12] Rensis Likert, *New Patterns of Management*, New York, McGraw-Hill, 1961, p. 117.

proving its worth and becoming accepted, is formally adopted. The first informal development, however, may be contrary to previously established procedures and in a sense a violation or a subversion of them; or the informal procedures may be an extension of a function for internal political purposes.[13] Conflict, resting in part on different perspectives of what "ought" to be, is one of the avenues for opening new directions for the organization or one of the ways of moving in new directions. This is not only useful but also vital for organizational survival. The question, therefore, as we view conflict is not, "How to eliminate it?" but, "Is it conflict of such a type and within circumstances where it will contribute to rather than detract from organizational interests?"

SUMMARY

This chapter focused largely on the problems which exist between line and staff personnel and to a smaller degree in the conflicts and problems which exist in any managerial functional department. Considerable attention has been given to the roots or bases for these problems and conflicts. Most of these problems are of an organizational nature, and yield to analysis using concepts and relationships thus far developed. This analysis does not produce automatically simple and universally applicable solutions to these problems. It does, however, clarify both the specific sources of the problem and the requirements which solutions must meet. It also helps to define more clearly those areas of conflict which are of dysfunctional nature for the organization and those that serve some important purpose, such as initiating changes in the organization and its objectives. The underlying assumption of this chapter, therefore, is that the problems frequently cited between line and staff personnel or even among staff or line personnel themselves are not issues that require direct and special solutions but, in effect, are conditions that grow out of a more fundamental and broader set of organizational issues which are or should be the real objects of attention. Whether a conflict is good or bad for an organization, whether a conflict can be made useful for an organization, depends not so much on manipulating the conflict itself as on the underlying conditions of the overall organization. In this sense, conflict can be seen as, (1) a symptom of more basic problems which requires attention, or (2) an intervening variable in the overall organization to be considered, used, and maintained within certain useful boundaries.

[13] For discussion of these see Melville Dalton, *Men Who Manage: Fusions of Feeling and Theory in Administration*, New York, John Wiley, 1959, Chapter 10.

19

Organizational Style:
Decentralization

An architectural student learns that there are such things as beams used to support ceilings and floors, that beams have length, width, and depth, and that knowing the load on a given length of beam enables him to compute the cross sectional area. He can make similar computations about the heat loss through walls of certain materials, the compressive forces on foundations which determine their dimensions, and numerous other elements, all of which are necessary in designing a building. These elements enter the analysis whether the architect is working on a house, an office building, or a railroad station. They also enter into the design of a Cape Cod cottage as well as a contemporary house. The appearance of the buildings not only depends on these elements but also on the purpose of the building and the style of architecture chosen. So, too, an organization. There are elements common to all organizations which can be used to make governmental agencies, hospitals, armies, and business concerns. Also, organizations for these purposes can vary considerably, depending on the style chosen. In this chapter we consider some of the ways in which organizational elements can be put together to create different styles of organization.

Although many factors influence the style chosen, two are dominant. First, style may be substantially influenced by the *conditions* faced. In a hot, dry climate buildings with thick walls made of clay and small windows may be very desirable, because the walls absorb the intense heat of the day slowly, keeping the interior cool, and then slowly radiate the absorbed heat at night when the temperature often falls considerably. In hot and humid areas materials that are less affected by moisture must be used for the construction of walls and

378

frequently it is more desirable to have open construction, which permits the greatest movement of air. In a northern climate walls constructed of wood, a material often easily available and with high insulation value, may be far more common. These conditions and materials substantially influence the architectural style possible. Similarly, in an organization the conditions faced determine to no small extent the organizational style possible.

The other major factor is *preference*. The architect's choice of style will be largely governed by the client's preference and, frankly, his own. In an organization the founder, the owner, or the larger organization of which it is a part will have an important influence on the style chosen.

THE CENTRALIZATION–DECENTRALIZATION DICHOTOMY

The organization styles which have received the greatest attention are those of centralization and decentralization. In centralization all, or at least most important, decisions are made by one individual or a very small group of individuals. Usually this occurs at the top of the organizational hierarchy. Decentralization exists when decision making has been thrust down in the hierarchy so that lower managers, and perhaps even employees at the work level, make as well as execute organizational decisions. Ideally we can think of a dichotomy with one end having organizations which are centralized, where all decisions made at one place and executed throughout the organization, and the other end having decentralized organizations where decision making is carried out at the lowest possible level in the organizational hierarchy. For convenience and ease of exposition it is possible to think in terms of one topic, degree of decentralization, rather than two. The remaining portion of the discussion focus was largely on decentralization, its advantages and limitations usually being the reverse image of these qualities in centralization.

Decentralization has received considerable attention in American industry, and many advantages have been claimed for it.[1] Among the advantages seen are that decentralization creates more meaningful jobs for lower managers and workers, creates a better, more meaningful social climate, permits problems arising to receive prompter and more knowledgeable attention, requires less precise coordinative systems and efforts, and permits greater organizational flexibility and adaption.

[1] For typical discussions, see James C. Worthy, "Organization Structure and Employees' Morale," *American Sociological Review*, 15, 1950, pp. 169–179; and Peter F. Drucker, *Concept of the Corporation*, The John Day Company, 1946.

Decentralization can and does have all these advantages and more; however, some business concerns and even government agencies have been greatly disappointed in attempting to utilize this style. Such disappointment seems to rest in part with an overly simplified conception of decentralization and the failure to recognize some of the conditions that must be met before it can be successfully adopted. We consider some of these under two broad headings: the complexity of decision making and structural constraints on decision making.

COMPLEXITY OF ORGANIZATIONAL DECISION MAKING

Uncritical acceptance of a statement which describes decentralization as a shifting of decision making in a downward direction in an organizational hierarchy leads to an inadequate understanding of the topic. Much of the difficulty centers around the thinking that decision making is a monolithic element which can be transferred *en masse* from one organizational location to another. Decision making as an event cannot be handled in that fashion. Let us consider some "dimensions" of decision making.

We have already discussed one dimension, the individual's scope of discretion in decision making. This was found to have two components. One was the range of things about which an individual could make decisions, and the other was the length of time he could go before reporting to some other position or department.[2]

Autonomy of Decision Making

There can be great variations in the autonomy that individuals have in decision making. Some individuals in some situations need not report their decisions to anyone. On the other hand, there are situations where a person, having decided what should be done, must obtain permission before executing the decision. In many organizations, for example, an executive's decision to buy a piece of equipment must be approved by his superior and sometimes his superior's superior. Between these extremes there are a number of intermediate arrangements; for example, an individual may be able to make and execute a decision but be required to file a complete report later. The degree of autonomy may vary both with the location in the organization of the position held by the decision maker and the subject of the decision. To illustrate, the executive in charge of a manufacturing division may have complete authority to make any type of decision on production

[2] See Chapter 10.

schedules. He may have to check first with the budget department or a control-manufacturing staff department before he can spend money on capital equipment.

Participation and Decision Making

Often decision making is thought of as a single act carried out by an individual. It may be, but in an organization a number of people are often involved. Furthermore, it is never a single act. Decision making has a number of steps or phases.[3] First, a problem is defined or a need for decision recognized and established. Second, information is gathered about the problem. For example, what are the causal factors? What are the conditions that have to be considered along with the problem and related to it? Third, various solutions to the problem or issue are sought. This is, in a sense, a search process. Fourth, the consequences of carrying out the various courses are analyzed. This exploration includes not only determining the advantages but also the cost of each course. Fifth, the possibilities and their consequences are compared and a choice made among them.

It is possible for these phases to be carried out by one individual. It is also possible for a number of individuals to be involved in one or more of the steps.

The decision making with which an executive toward the lower end of the organizational hierarchy is involved can be described in terms of the range of things about which he can make decisions, the degree of autonomy he has, the number of times he has engaged in one or more of the phases of a top management decision, etc. To put it differently, we increase decentralization by increasing the range of topics about which he can make decisions, his discretionary time span, his degree of autonomy, or his efforts in one or more phases of a top management decision.

STRUCTURAL CONSIDERATIONS

Although the degree of decentralization is to a considerable extent an arrangement of the administrative process it is subject to influence by a number of other elements. One of these is the structure of the organization. There is no structure of decentralization, but there are certain limits imposed by the structure of the organization beyond

[3] The decision-making process has been described by a number of authors. See, for example, Peter F. Drucker, *The Practice of Management*, New York, Harper, 1954, particularly Part 7.

which decentralization will not be effective or cannot be effective without additional cost.   Sometimes the cost can be so high as to make decentralization impossible.   Let us consider this situation.

When organizational units are set up on a basis of function there is a high degree of interlocking among their activities; therefore, considerable effort is employed to facilitate the necessary coordination.[4]   In Chapter 16 we considered a plant making three products: 1, 2, and 3, all using the same three processes—A, B, and C.   If the departments in the plant are arranged on a process basis (Figure 19.1), all workers performing process A report to one foreman (S_1).   All those performing process B report to another foreman (S_2) and so on.   In turn, all foremen report to the plant manager.   In this way all three products have to pass through all three departments.   It is easy to envision what would happen in the other departments if (S_1) decides to have his department take its vacation in April when the rest of the foremen were expecting their vacations in July.   Departmental vacations have to be taken simultaneously; and decisions about vacations cannot be taken independently by foremen.   They either have to be taken by foremen as a group or by a higher authority to whom they all report, a plant manager.   If the decision is to be taken by the collective action of the foremen, we could expect some expenditure of time and effort in arriving at a consensus.   If decisions about vacations are

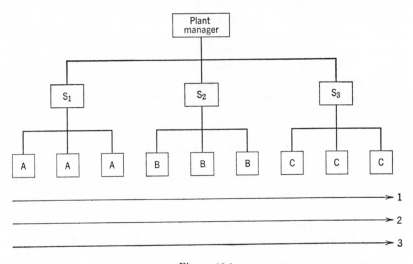

Figure 19.1

[4] See Chapter 12.

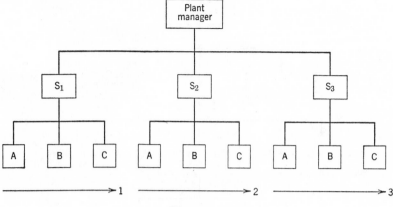

Figure 19.2

not delegated to the foremen but left as a decision to be made by the plant manager, considerably less man-hours will be spent in arriving at a decision.

On the other hand, if the work in the plant were grouped on a product basis (Figure 19.2), each foreman would have reporting to him workers who performed all the processes in the making of one of the products. Here each foreman would be responsible for all phases of making the product and would therefore be in a position where he could be delegated considerable decision-making powers. A decision by (S_1) on vacations would not have the same serious consequences for the other departments. Moreover, this arrangement relieves the plant manager of making many decisions or the foreman of meeting to reach consensus.

More generally, in order to obtain coordination without undue expenditure of effort we can carry delegation only to the point where substantial functionalization begins.[5] Only here will a position control a sufficient number of the interlocking elements to permit reasonably autonomous decision making. The key item is the point at which substantial functionalization begins. Since there are a number of different types of functionalization—management function, business function, manufacturing function—there may be a number of different minimum levels of decentralization. For example, in Figure 19.3 showing a company organized on a product basis, the vice president in charge of the division handling product B could be delegated decision-making powers in all aspects of that product. Beyond this point be-

[5] For further discussion of these points, see Worthy, *op. cit.*

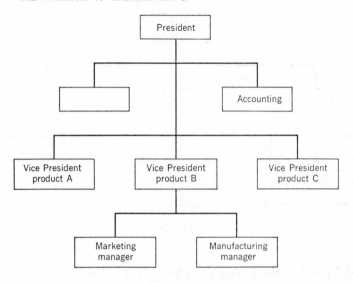

Figure 19.3

gins partitioning of work on the basis of business function, and he can-not effectively delegate any decision-making powers in regard to the overall business aspect of product B to anyone below him in the hier-archy. Similarly, the vice president's superior cannot effectively dele-gate to him any decision-making powers in regard to any other prod-uct. But, the vice president in charge of product B can delegate sub-stantial decision-making powers concerning the execution of manufac-turing functions to the manufacturing manager. Furthermore, there are some things that would not be delegated to the vice president in charge of product B or for that matter any other product, such as de-cision on the programs for accounting. Decisions of this sort will in all likelihood be reserved for the president or his immediate staff work-ing at the top level of the organization, or both, for there is a great need for coordination of the form and timing of accounting data.

In summary, the extent to which decentralization can be carried depends on certain structural properties or, more accurately, it de-pends on the nature of the particular forms of functionalization en-countered. As a result, in organizations there are some things which of necessity are and will remain undelegated. In that sense they are centralized, whereas other things can be delegated far down in the organizational hierarchy to promote substantial decentralization on these matters.

Administrative Costs of Decentralization

Other ways of promoting coordination, as we have seen, have included administrative systems and decision rules.   What effect, then, will these factors have on organizational efficiency, particularly when considered in the light of the possibility of carrying decentralization beyond the point of substantial functionalization (or where there is a high degree of interlocking)?

This situation has been explored by Marschak.[6]   He suggests envisioning a company that has two production facilities and two market areas.   The production facilities have different cost structures, and the prices offered by the customers in each market area for the company's products vary considerably.   The basic decision to be made is which bids from customers are to be accepted, considering the prices offered and the costs at which the company's production facilities can manufacture the items.   Complicating this decision is the fact that the company has no idea about the bid price of the next offer, but it does know the probable distribution of prices.   For example, if a high bid is received from one market area, the company is likelier to receive a high bid rather than a low one from the other market area.   Considering the complexity and uncertainty of the situation, the executives in the company will make decisions about accepting and assigning orders with the aid of decision rules designed to optimize profits.   Marschak analyzes two conditions under which these decisions can be made: centralized conditions, where executives at a central point (headquarters) possess all available information; and decentralized conditions, where local executives (regional sales managers) make decisions using the limited amount of information available to them.   He concludes that using appropriate decision rules, under these two conditions the centralized situation will produce a higher average profit than the decentralized.

This illustration considers only the selling prices and the actual costs of production.   The administrative costs necessary to facilitate centralized decision making have not been weighed.   All available information could be collected at one point by bringing together the regional managers, but this would be at the expense of the salaries paid to them for the time spent in connection with the meeting, their transportation expenses, etc.   A communication system could be set up which would funnel all the information in the organization to a central

[6] Jacob Marschak, "Efficient and Viable Organizational Forms," in Mason Haire, *Modern Organization Theory: A Symposium on the Foundation for Research on Human Behavior*, New York, John Wiley, 1959, pp. 307–320.

point where the decision could be made.   Again setting up and operating such a communication system would have its costs.

This brings us to the heart of the issue.   Centralized decision making may not be worth using in situations where it has only a *slightly* higher average profit than would be achieved by decentralizing past the point at which functionalization begins this arrangement; the profit differential may not be sufficient to cover the costs of the administrative machinery necessary.[71]   The choice between a centralized or a decentralized style under these conditions is dependent on their relative *profitability and their relative administrative costs.*

Decentralization and Interdepartmental Administration

Let us draw together points made at several places throughout this chapter.   The less independent are the units within an organization to be decentralized, the greater will be the task of bringing coordination among them.   Needless to say, units within an organization are never completely independent.   We have reviewed some of the factors which influence the independence of organizational units.   The degree and nature of this interdependence will be largely determined by the decisions of higher or central management.   Some, such as decisions about the basic type of division of work, have already been referred to; others of great importance and complexity have not.

Many problems grow out of the need for some way of determining how well decentralized units are performing.   In business concerns one strategy is to consider each unit a profit center and to measure its success by the margin of its income over its costs.   This appealing solution has a number of serious problems.   These are the most important.

JOINT COSTS.   As part of an organization, decentralized units have to bear some overall organization expenses, such as the president's salary, costs of research and public relations, etc.   The problem is how these costs are to be allocated.   Any method chosen seems to have problems.   A simple illustration discloses some of them.   Assume a company has three divisions each with sales of ten million dollars a year and company overhead costs of three million dollars.   Should the company allocate these joint costs on the basis of sales?   If one division, let us call it Alpha, has costs of eight million dollars, it will still

---

[7] Marschak refers to "complementarity" between members' actions, in the following sense: ". . . the effect of one member's action depends on what his colleague is doing," *op. cit.,* p. 317.

show a profit of one million.   Another division, Beta, however, has costs of nine million, and its share of the joint costs eliminates all profit.   If rewards are based on profits earned, the managers in Beta division will not be very well satisfied.   Suppose, now, that these costs were allocated on the basis of capital investment.   Alpha division with twenty million dollars invested would get two million in overhead costs, while the other two divisions having five million invested each would get 0.5 million in costs.   Now Beta is making a profit and Alpha is not.   There are, of course, many other possibilities, but the point has been established that the allocation of these costs is an arbitrary decision by higher management which can substantially influence the apparent performance of the decentralized units.[8]

INTERDEPARTMENTAL PRICING.   In large companies some departments make products or offer services which are used by other departments. Many problems center on the question of how much the using department will be charged for the product, or how much the producing department will receive.   Suppose that the Alpha department is making a product for seven dollars a unit which is used by Beta department, and one which also can be bought from an outside supplier for ten dollars.   Should Beta be charged ten dollars for Alpha's product? If so, should the manager of Beta be forced to buy from Alpha or will he be permitted to give his business to an outside supplier?   If Beta's costs are high and profits practically nonexistent, its manager may feel that he is not getting any benefit from being in the company.   Should the product be priced at cost?   If so, the manager of Beta would be as delighted as that of Alpha was displeased.   Again, these decisions will be made in accordance with rules and policies made by top management, decisions which will markedly influence the profit made by the decentralized units.

INTERDEPARTMENTAL TRANSACTIONS AND ALLOCATIONS.   In any organization there are innumerable transactions of goods, services between departments, and allocation of resources and costs among them.   In decentralized organizations these activities may be administered by higher or central management or by interactions among the managers involved.[9]

[8] For further discussion of these and related points, see Martin Shubik, "Incentives, Decentralized Control, the Assignment of Joint Costs and Internal Pricing," in Charles Bonini, et al., *Management Controls*, 1964, New York, McGraw-Hill, pp. 205–226.
[9] Certain aspects of how these decisions are made among managers are discussed in Chapters 21 and 22. The reader may also want to see Leonard R. Sayles, *Managerial Behavior*, New York, McGraw-Hill, 1964, particularly Chapter 4.

Staff Activities for Decentralized Operations

Most of this discussion has been set in the context of the line or operating area. But decentralization also raises some important issues in regard to staff. First, how are staff activities to be organized in order to aid the degree of decentralization chosen? Second, what degree of decentralization is to be permitted within staff departments?

ORGANIZING STAFF TO AID THE DEGREE OF DECENTRALIZATION CHOSEN. In Chapter 17 it was pointed out that large corporations are likely to have staff departments existing on a number of levels. A typical arrangement is to have a home office staff department, a division staff department, and a plant staff department. In an organization where decentralization has been substantial, the tendency would be to make the staff manager at the plant level report to the plant manager (Figure 19.4). Higher staff positions in these cases serve as sources of advice and programs for performing the work of the staff departments at the plant and divisional levels. Conversely, if there is a high degree of

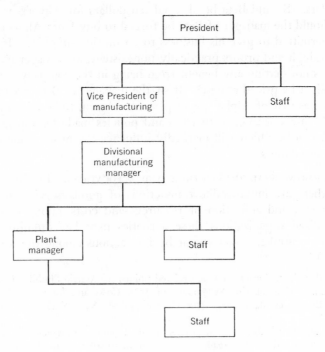

Figure 19.4

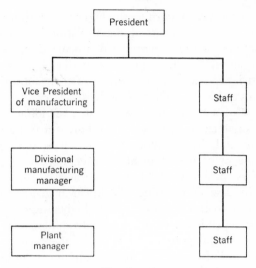

Figure 19.5

centralization, the staff man reports to the higher staff authorities and has only an advising, nonaccountable relationship to the local plant manager (Figure 19.5).

Simon and his associates found that for the controllers department, at least, the tendency was for all the work of the department to be organized on a decentralized basis when the prime company plan favored decentralization.[10]   That is, the data would be gathered at the lowest possible level and ledgers and accounts would be set up to bring the data together for the lowest administrative unit.   Although this has been the common tendency Simon raised the question as whether it really has been necessary for things to be done this way.   The issue he raised is a rather interesting one.   Does centralization in the operating or line departments necessitate parallel decentralization within the staff department?   This question needs further analysis.

OVERRIDE

Although higher management can delegate responsibilities, it cannot transfer them.   The ultimate responsibility is always theirs.   Essentially the same holds for authority.   Although certain authorities could

[10] Herbert A. Simon, George Kozmetsky, and Gordon Tyndall, *Centralization versus Decentralization in Organizing the Controllers Department*, New York, Controllership Foundation, 1954.

be designated for lower executives, the higher executive always has the final authority.   Certain aspects of these relationships should be made explicit in the case of the decentralized organization.   Even in a decentralized organization where lower executives have a great deal of autonomy and independence, the exercise of their authorities is always subject to an override by higher executives.

This concept of a higher, usually latent, overriding authority provides a useful organizational notion.   Authority may be thought of in an intermittent and discontinuous fashion.   It is different from the commoner concept of management by exception, wherein the lower executive refers problems to higher authority for decisions and actions.   In the case of override, the lower manager may not have brought a matter to the attention of the higher executives, and they may act quite independently of any request from him.

The concept is analogous to an airplane under the control of an automatic pilot.   This piece of control equipment guides the plane toward the destination making adjustments in course and elevation when necessary.   It is in complete control of the plane, perhaps during many hours of flying.   However, at all times, the pilot is in control; it is quite possible for the pilot to place his hands on the instruments and immediately take control of the aircraft from the automatic pilot.   The advantage to the pilot is obvious.   It relieves him of a great deal of detailed concern and permits him frequently to give attention to other matters, yet, at the same time, does not interfere at all with his ultimate control of the plane.   The only time there could be any danger, of course, is when he is negligent of his overriding responsibilities.   The parallel holds in an organization.   Override enables top management to be freed of many details in the rather immediate operation of the organization; its final authority reposes in a latent, not an active, state.

LEADERSHIP IMPLICATIONS OF DECENTRALIZATION

Participation

In describing how decentralization operates in companies, investigators report that the top executives frequently consult with the several levels of executives beneath them, asking for ideas, soliciting their opinions as to the consequences of proposed courses of action, and inviting their participation at several steps in the decision-making process.   Participation seems to be an essential aspect of decentralized operations.   It does a number of important things.   First, it elicits many ideas and information which perhaps will be unobtainable by any other means.   Second, it gets the lower executives involved in the fundamental decisions of the organization.   When a decision is finally made, these individuals are much likelier to accept it than if the decision were handed down as an edict.   Participation is also perhaps the most effective way to make sure that the policies of the organization are completely understood, not only in their letter but also in their intent.

A willingness to encourage participation reflects a certain style of leadership, one hardly compatible with a highly authoritarian system. Therefore, it should be apparent that a company desiring a decentralized mode of operation must be willing to adopt certain aspects of a permissive leadership style in order to encourage the participation of lower executives in decision making. The relationship between leadership style and participation in decision making and, hence, to decentralization is shown in Figure 19.6.

Closeness of Supervision

When a decentralized mode of organization is in effect, it is quite obvious that the higher executives are not really in a position to supervise the lower executive very closely.   This absence of close supervision will have a definite effect on the morale and attitudes of those in lower positions, as was mentioned in the chapter on leadership.   Thus,

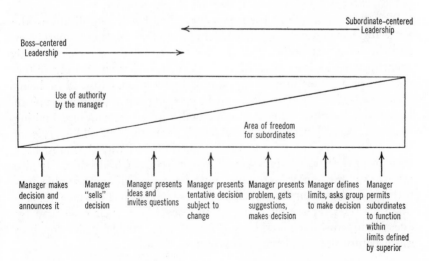

Figure 19.6. *Source:* Robert Tannenbaum and Warren Schmidt, "How to Choose a Leadership Pattern," *Harvard Business Review*, 36, no. 2, 1958, p. 96.

by its very nature, decentralization creates certain aspects of leadership which have been found by other studies to be exceedingly valuable for promoting satisfaction.

Selection and Training

For any executive to be willing to delegate substantial amounts of responsibility and authority to subordinates, he must possess a high degree of confidence in their ability to handle matters in a way that will reflect credit on both of them. A subordinate who fails not only brings disgrace to himself but also to the superior to whom he reports and who is held accountable for his performance. It is unlikely that many men will delegate freely to those in whom they do not have considerable confidence. This means that the selection of executives in a decentralized style of organization is of the utmost importance. They must have the capabilities which will permit them to handle their responsibilities. Since a generally recognized point in management today is that executives are made rather than born, this means that any decentralized organization must of necessity be deeply concerned with training and developing executives to perform efficiently and competently in their posts. The development of managerial skills is a long, complicated process, and must take place not only in formal training programs but also on the job through rather intimate and extensive contacts between the senior, and presumably more competent, executive and the junior man who is developing.

The three implications for leadership raised by decentralization—the need for participation, the virtual impossibility of close supervision, and the basic responsibility of the senior executive for developing his subordinates—indicate that the senior executive has an entirely different role as a leader in a decentralized organization. Instead of being concerned with issuing orders and in carrying out a directive-type of leadership, he must be more concerned with understanding, inviting cooperation, and developing the people beneath him. This style of leadership is involved with handling situations in a way that must have time to bear fruit. It is not a short-run style of leadership. It also means that the senior executive must be a man of considerable maturity who is willing to let subordinates, whose performance reflects upon his own reputation, struggle and develop in their own way by occasionally making mistakes as they, in turn, gradually develop into more mature and competent executives.

SUMMARY

Decentralization is one of the major organization styles. However, it is much more than merely an edict as to where decisions will be made. Although not directly a matter of structure, real decentralization is possible only when there is a compatible organizational structure available. Certain types make it virtually impossible, whereas other types make it more easily possible.

Decentralization has some definite implications for the type and methods of control used. It is a control centered to a great extent on performance, leaving subordinates a considerable degree of latitude to choose the methods of achieving desirable performance results. A decentralized mode of operation is possible only when certain leadership patterns are in existence. By its very nature, it is fundamentally a definition of leadership which bears important implications for the way higher authorities look upon their subordinate managers and employees.

In a decentralized operation the subordinate is viewed as a source of information and ideas and permitted a wide latitude of discretion. To be successful, therefore, this type of operation is dependent on selecting many people with great capabilities for still higher levels of effectiveness rather than depending on a few competent top executives supported by larger numbers of executers of their orders.

Part Four

Change and Adaptation

20

Growth and Structure
of Organizations

THE first three sections of this book considered organizations under steady-state conditions. They dealt with various structural forms and some of the internal processes that go with them but did not examine the questions of which forms organizations are likely to take, how organizations change from one form to another, or what internal efforts are involved in changing the form of an organization. These and related questions are discussed in this section.

Organizational change is one of the less developed areas in the study of organizations. This, then, will be only an introduction to an extraordinarily interesting but complex topic. We shall really consider two topics: very long-range change characterized by growth and aging, and shorter term changes in which an organization adapts to shifts in its internal and external environment.

The immediate concern is with what might be called the "biological" aspects of organization, changes that accompany growth and aging. We are all too familiar with stories of business enterprises which started as one-man shops and burgeoned into globe girdling corporations having hundreds of thousands of employees to make necessary a plea for recognizing that organizations grow. Indeed, this is so widely accepted that we sometimes neglect to notice that many organizations do not grow. Many are founded, grow to a small size of perhaps 10 or 15 employees, and then continue at that size for many years. In this chapter we are concerned with relatively few organizations, those that grow and grow. These are the very large organizations which play such a dominant role in modern society. Our concern is with the processes by which they have been able to develop in this way and achieve such large-scale proportions.

GROWTH OF ORGANIZATIONS

Growth as a Process

In speaking of organizations, growth and size are sometimes used interchangeably, which can sometimes lead to considerable confusion. Growth is a process internal to the organization which brings about certain directions of development. In a biological sense growth has a "natural" connotation. It is a process which occurs under *normal* conditions or when nothing restricts or inhibits it.[1] Size, on the other hand, is something which results from growth. To suggest, as is sometimes done, that a change from one size to another is growth confuses effect with cause. Such a view may also obscure the fact that growth can be manifest in ways other than changes in size. To say that a company of 10,000 employees has added 500 new employees may not suggest any major developments relevant to growth. To know that these new employees are all engaged in a type of work new to the company, such as research and development, suggests that some remarkable growth has occurred. Size is only one of the results of growth.

Size is an important aspect of growth. And since it has the advantage of being easily observed and measured, it receives considerable attention in the following discussion.

Conditions for Growth

External conditions. The external conditions for growth are numerous and fairly obvious. Among the most important are: the demand for the organization's output; the possibility of obtaining a special opportunity, such as a monopoly through patents or franchise; the high cost of entry to the field which may keep other organizations from being launched to exploit developing demand; ability to obtain easily, or for that matter, not to obtain, needed inputs. These are a few of the more important external conditions which may influence the process of growth.

Advantages of scale. One of the most commonly cited advantages of large size is the ability it provides to utilize the advantages of large-scale production. We can state this differently and more precisely by saying, growth resulting in larger size occurs when the technology

[1] Edith T. Penrose, *The Theory of the Growth of the Firm*, New York, John Wiley, 1959, p. 1.

employed permits economies or advantages at a larger scale of operation.

It has been found in manufacturing that many industries have a J-shape cost curve. This means that a small manufacturing operation can gain advantage of lower cost through expanding until a certain point beyond which any further increase in size does not bring about a significant reduction in cost. To talk in this condition about growth as being "permitted" by the technology may be misleading. If other companies are already established at or are larger than the optimal size

Table 20.1   Proportions of National Industry Capacity Contained in Single Plants of Most Efficient Scale, for 20 Industries, per Engineering Estimates, Circa 1951

Industry	Percentage of National Industry Capacity Contained in One Plant of Minimum Efficient Scale	Industry	Percentage of National Industry Capacity Contained in One Plant of Minimum Efficient Scale
Flour milling	1/10–1/2	Rubber tires and tubes [7]	1⅜–2¾
Shoes [1]	1/7–1/2	Gypsum products [8]	2–3
Canned fruits and vegetables	1/4–1/2	Rayon [9]	4–6
Cement	4/5–1	Soap [10]	4–6
Distilled liquors [2]	1¼–1¾	Cigarettes	5–6
Farm machines, except tractors [3]	1–1½	Automobiles [11]	5–10
Petroleum refining [4]	1¾	Fountain pens [12]	5–10
Steel [5]	1–2½	Copper [13]	10
Metal containers	1/3–2	Tractors	10–15
Meat packing: [6]			
fresh	1/50–1/5		
diversified	2–2½	Typewriters	10–30

[1] Refers to shoes other than rubber.

[2] Capacity refers to total excluding brandy. Costs refer explicitly to 4-year whiskey, packaged.

[3] Refers primarily to complex farm machines.

[4] Optimal balanced integration of successive processes assumed. Inshipment and outshipment largely by water assumed; optimal scale may be smaller with scattered market and land shipment.

for low-cost operation, a new firm in the industry may be impelled to expand rapidly to optimal size or be forced to suffer a severe competitive disadvantage. As Table 20.1 shows, the most efficient scale for a plant in some industries may amount to a sizable portion of the total national capacity.

Financial efficiency is a major advantage of larger scale operations. Large-scale operations permit purchasing in large quantities, which usually permits a company to receive and sometimes compel lower prices for the things purchased. Larger companies often find it easier to attract money for loans and investments and therefore acquire funds at lower cost. Furthermore, through centralized handling of funds they may be able to get by with less cash on hand and be better able to make temporary investments of surpluses at an advantage. Without these and other advantages of scale, growth would be restricted if not actually prohibited. The next condition for growth is the possibility of realizing the advantages of division of work. The general aspects of this condition have been discussed. We refer to more specific analysis later.

FACTORS IN GROWTH. One of the key components in the growth process is the existence of unutilized or at least underutilized resources.

Footnotes for Table 20.1 continued:
[5] Refers to fully integrated operation producing flat rolled products. Percentage figures are based on capacity circa 1950; subsequent growth of national capacity would lead to slightly lower percentages today.
[6] Percentages are of total nonfarm slaughter; diversified operation includes curing, processing, etc.
[7] Purchase of materials at a constant price assumed; production of a wide variety of sizes assumed.
[8] Combined plasterboard and plaster production assumed.
[9] Refers to plant producing both yarn and fibre.
[10] Includes household detergents.
[11] Plant includes integrated facilities for production of components as economical. Final assembly alone—1 to 3 per cent.
[12] Total includes conventional pens and ballpoints, but plant specialization by price class assumed.
[13] Assumes electrolytic refining.

Source: Joe S. Bain, Barriers to New Competition, Cambridge, Harvard University Press, 1956, p. 72.

The term "resources" covers the broadest possible scope here to include capital, productive capacity, talents of personnel, ideas, etc.   There are two principal parts to this argument.   First, seeing an unutilized resource organization, officials will attempt to put it to use leading to new activities or new outputs.   A newspaper that uses its presses only five hours a day to print its editions may take on the printing of advertising material to utilize the presses during the remaining portion of a normal eight-hour shift.   However, to do so probably would require the addition of extra salesmen or artists and layout people or laborers to handle delivering of the goods.   Hence, growth would be evidenced by a larger volume of business, a more varied number of outputs, and probably an additional number of employees. The second part of the argument is that there will always be un- or underutilized resources for two reasons.   The first is that resources cannot be added in exactly the size needed.   That is, we may need a man only for five hours a day, but union regulations may tell us to hire him for eight; consequently steps taken to make better use of one set of resources may mean the acquisition of still additional resources, which in turn can only be partially utilized.   The second reason is that new ways of utilizing existing resources are continually coming to mind.[2]   Initially a contractor may have seen the possibility of using his equipment to construct houses.   With experience and more information he may learn that he can use his resources to better advantage building commercial structures.

Another factor to be taken into account with organization growth is the overutilization of resources.   To reduce the burden, supplemental resources are added and growth occurs.   Machines can be run at excessive speeds for a while but eventually management will be compelled to do something, such as buying an additional machine, before the first becomes permanently damaged by its excess load.

The existence of overutilized resources helps explain why unused or underutilized resources may not be permitted to remain in that condition even though the managers to whom they have been assigned are uninterested or apathetic about their utilization.   Managers in charge of overutilized resources may demand that the underutilized resources be employed to reduce the pressure on their units or on themselves. The manager whose department has far too much work may put pressure on higher executives to have employees, machines, or both transferred to his unit from departments where they are not being fully employed.   This leads to an increase in the number of employees or

[2] Penrose, op. cit., p. 66.

units in his department and to a modified form for the entire organization.

Needless to say, several of these factors may be in effect at the same time. One resource may be underutilized and another overutilized. Steps taken to make better use of the underutilized resource may end up causing it to be overutilized and a new resource to be underutilized. It is perhaps best to envision a constantly shifting pattern of under- and overutilized resources compelling an organization to grow.

An underlying assumption is that the manager in an organization has a desire to make the best use of the organization's resources or opportunities. Certainly without such motivation growth is unlikely to occur.

DIRECTION OF EXPANSION. The next question is, "In which direction will growth occur?" There is no simple answer. Expansion is influenced by a combination of the aforementioned factors. What resources are unutilized? What supplemental resources are needed to put to use additional resources available? Last, what opportunity for using the underutilized resources are perceived by members of the organization? These considerations have to be coupled with others pertaining to overutilized resources. A direction of expansion suggested by the underutilized resources that would require still greater use of other already overutilized resources hardly would be followed immediately. On the other hand, a direction that would both permit greater use of underutilized resources and reduce the demand on overutilized resources would very likely be followed.

Without further exploring the complexities of this issue we can recognize the point that a direction of expansion for any organization is circumscribed by its resources, the conditions it faces, and its manager's perception of resources, conditions, and opportunity. Hence, we should not expect to find any organization expanding in totally new directions or expanding in great jumps. Nor should we expect to find an organization moving directly to the very best utilization of its resources. It will move in those directions that are immediately approachable from its present position, choosing presumably the best among these courses. But even the best of these may not permit the ultimate use of resources of the organization.[3]

Size and Form Considerations of Growth

One point barely mentioned is that growth may, and often must, result in changes in both the size and form of the organization. This

[3] Penrose, *op. cit.*, particularly Chapter 5.

can be illustrated colorfully by pointing out that if the giant in the fable *Jack the Giant Killer* were to exist many times larger than normal man, he could not have the same form as man and be able to function. That is, if the giant were to have the same proportions as normal man but were a hundred or a thousand times larger in size, his bone structure, for example, would be entirely inadequate to support his huge person.[4] The problem is that the giant must conform to the square-cube law so well known to biologists. This says that if the giant were a thousand times the size of man his volume would increase 10^3 and so roughly would his weight. His area would increase 10^2; hence, the cross-sectional area of his bones would increase at a far lower rate than the weight which they had to support. As a result, if the giant were to attempt to stand his leg bone would break. Hence, the form of man would be inadequate for a much larger being. The much larger being would have to walk on four legs like the elephant or float in the ocean like the whale. The same rule holds true for organizations. Larger organizations require different organizational forms than the smaller. Let us consider the general outline of these size-form changes.

Changes in Organizational Form

SIMPLE TO COMPLEX ORGANIZATIONS. Coordination of individual efforts was seen as one of the prime characteristics of organizations. A simple organization exists where efforts of small groups are coordinated by the group itself without someone filling a separate coordinating role. In essence, coordination is intrinsic to the group. This might be the case of two men paddling a canoe or lifting a heavy log. As the group becomes larger this intrinsic regulation or coordination breaks down and it becomes necessary to have a separate or coordinating unit; usually such a unit takes the form of a supervisor and the development of a higher structure. A unit in which coordination is realized through a separate integrating unit is called a complex organization.

This change in form from simple to complex organizations, therefore, should be accompanied by improvement in the overall performance of the unit. One study which clearly showed this examined the efficiency of retail stores in England. Here the number of employees per store was compared with both the overall efficiency of the store measured in sales turnover (Figure 20.1) and the sales per person.

---

[4] D'Arcy Thompson, *Growth and Form*, Second Edition, Cambridge England, University Press.

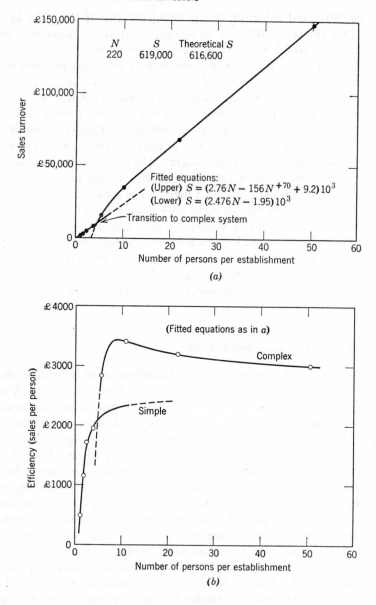

Figure 20.1. Size-output function of complex systems. (Data are based on 1950 census of retail establishments.) (a) Relation between sales turnover (S) and size of establishment (N); (b) comparative efficiency of simple and complex organizations. *Source:* P. G. Herbst, "Measurement of Behavior Structures by Means of Input-Output Data," *Human Relations,* **10,** 1957, p. 343.

The impact of the transition from simple to complex organization form on sales turnover is shown in Figure 20.1*a*. The relative efficiency of simple and complex organizations measured in terms of sales per person is shown in Figure 20.1*b*.

UNIVERSAL TO SPECIALIZED MANAGERS. When complex organizations first emerge, a superior directs a small group of subordinates. If this is a small firm, this superior, who is also probably owner and manager, handles all management functions. As the organization grows and the number of employees increases, he doubtless will employ other managers who will do essentially the same as he. Eventually, it will become expedient to add staff, assigning it special management functions and at the same time largely delimiting other managers from these functions. This is a switch from universal to specialist managers. In short, staff is added because the universalist form of management becomes progressively inadequate in the emergent complex organization to cope with coordinative problems as the organization grows and increases in size.

In a series of longitudinal studies Haire found this to be essentially the case. In a study of a number of companies from their inception he saw that as their size (measured in total number of employees) increased, the percentage of employees in staff positions rapidly increased and then stabilized at a fairly fixed percentage. (See Figure 20.2 for data on one of his companies.) The pattern may be described in more detail as follows: once a company reaches a certain minimal size, and the surprisingly low figure of eight employees is given, there begins a rapid increase in staff positions. As the number of line positions grows linearly, the staff grows by some exponential function until a point is reached at which both grow at similar rates.[5]

FUNCTION TO PURPOSE DEPARTMENTALIZATION. Ultimately it becomes impossible to integrate all vital activities and functional departments even with numerous staff groups. At this point the organization changes from a functional departmentalization to a product or, we might say, *purpose* form of departmentalization.

This is how the shift occurs. Functional departmentalization makes best use of the advantages of specialization of individual skills, machinery, etc. As the organization grows, the coordinative task between

[5] Mason Haire, "Biological Models and Empirical Histories of the Growth of Organizations," in Haire (ed.), *Modern Organization Theory: A Symposium of the Foundation for Research on Human Behavior*, New York, John Wiley, 1959, pp. 272–306.

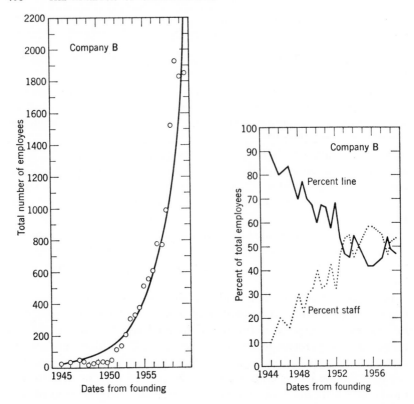

Figure 20.2. Percent of line and staff personnel. *Source:* Mason Haire, "Biological Models and Empirical Histories of the Growth of Organizations," in Haire (ed.), *Modern Organization Theory: A Symposium of the Foundation for Research on Human Behavior,* New York, John Wiley, 1959, pp. 280, 288.

functional departments increases; at the same time, the marginal economy resulting from specialization decreases while the marginal cost of coordination rises. Ultimately a point is reached at which functional departmentalization is inadequate. Here a switch is made to a product organization, or departmentalization which is more self-contained and has lower coordination of cost.[6]

Let us draw together these central relationships. As an organization, having a form characteristic of its size, increases in size the means of coordination usually associated with this form becomes increasingly inadequate until finally it is so inefficient that either growth must stop or a new means of coordination be provided. Generally this entails

[6] James G. March, Herbert A. Simon, *Organizations,* New York, John Wiley, 1958, p. 29.

the institution of a new organizational form.   Thus, intrinsic organization soon breaks down leading to coordination through higher means and the development of complex organizations.   Continued increase in size reaches the point where the requisite coordination cannot be provided through universal managers and hierarchal forms.   This situation in turn leads to the development of formal coordinative systems and staffs—specialist managers.   Further increases in size make the combination of formal coordinative systems, hierarchal coordination, and intrinsic coordination inadequate for the total coordinative demand leading to a newer organizational form.   This form does not support a new type of coordination.   Instead it marks the break-up of the unit into smaller, more easily coordinated wholes, forming product or purpose departments.   Major coordinative efforts occur within these units.   Very little coordination must occur between them. Continued increases in size are now possible, because the newest organizational form has reduced the *need* for an elaborate coordinative system rather than, as with earlier progressions, providing a new *means* of coordination.

We might pause momentarily to examine the impact of computers on this program.   Until the advent of computers much managerial work, which included the operation of formal coordinative procedures, was carried out largely on a hand-labor basis.   As a result, computers probably will increase the size at which coordination breaks down in a functional form of organization.

We have been considering only certain types of organizational forms influenced by only one organizational dimension.   Needless to say, many important organizational dimensions influence form.

CHANGES IN DISTRIBUTION OF EXTERNAL-INTERNAL ORIENTED POSITION. The volume-surface law regarding the giant in the story *Jack the Giant Killer* has also been applied to organizations.   The question has been asked, "As an organization increases in size should not the number of outside positions, those that primarily deal with elements of the organization's environment, increase more slowly than those that relate to internal matters, such as production control?"   Or to be more exact, should not the inside and the outside positions increase in accordance with cube-square law?   Haire studied this point and found that it did.   Data on one of the companies he studied is shown in Figure 20.3.   Here the cube root of internal employees is plotted against the square root of external employees.   The results yield a remarkably good fit to the predicted straight line.[7]

This same point, relationship between external and internal employees, was studied on a cross-sectional basis using 62 concerns in nine

[7] *Ibid.*

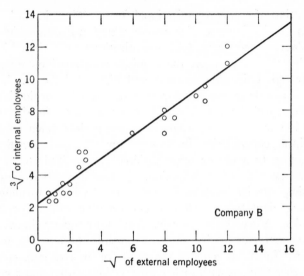

Figure 20.3. *Source:* Mason Haire, "Biological Models and Empirical Histories of the Growth of Organizations," in Haire (ed.), *Modern Organization Theory: A Symposium of the Foundation in Research on Human Behavior*, New York, John Wiley, 1959, p. 286.

different industries. The same relationship was found to hold although the correlation was not as good. In Haire's study the correlations ranged between 0.95 and 0.99. The cross-sectional study had a correlation of 0.80.[8]

Another change that seems to accompany increased size is a larger span of control for supervisors (Table 20.2). In companies having from 20 to 50 employees, supervisors were found to be responsible for 11 to 12 employees. In companies with over 200 employees span of control increased to 21. At the lower hierarchal levels this is to be expected. As staff positions are added and the managerial work becomes more specialized, the lower levels of supervision have a reduced scope of responsibility. This presumably would permit them to supervise larger numbers of subordinates.

Managerial Advantages of Scale

These different forms of organizations are essentially different forms of managerial hierarchy, that is, those levels of organization above the

[8] Seymour Levy and Gordon Donhowe, "Exploration of a Biological Model of Industrial Organizations," *Journal of Business*, **35**, 1962, pp. 335–342.

Table 20.2

Average Number of Employees per Supervisor		Top and Middle Management as a Per Cent of Total	
Size of Firm	Average Number Supervised	Size of Firm	Per Cent in Top and Middle Management
20–50	11.5	20–50	13.6
50–100	14.0	50–100	10.5
100–200	12.0	100–200	5.9
Over 200	21.0	Over 200	4.1

Source: Mason Haire, "Biological Models and Empirical Histories of the Growth of Organizations," in Haire, (ed.), *Modern Organization Theory*, New York, Wiley, 1959, p. 296.

direct workers.   To put this important point another way, organizational growth is intimately connected with the structural form in which the managerial function is carried out.   Although we have been observing that increased size requires a different form of organization, we might also note that increased size permits the managerial hierarchy to take on different forms.   Specialization within the managerial hierarchy becomes possible permitting the function to be performed much more efficiently.   Duplication of certain efforts can be eliminated or reduced.   The volume of managerial work reaches the level where the minimal unit, the whole man, can be hired to provide special skills and services as contrasted to the condition often found in smaller organizations where there may be a need for one-quarter of an accountant and lawyer, and one-half of a line executive.   In short, as the organization increases in size, the larger managerial group becomes progressively more capable of carrying out its overall responsibility than it was at a smaller size.[9]

As a result we would expect the number of people involved in carrying out the managerial activities—including line-staff managers and clerks, secretaries, etc. who help them—to decrease a percentage of the total group as a company grew larger.   Some investigators have found this to be the case.[10]   Other investigators have shown the ratio of number of personnel carrying out the managerial function to the rest of the employees to be increasing with size.   Analyzing the data

[9] Penrose, *op. cit.*, p. 92.
[10] F. T. Terien and D. C. Mills, "The Effect of Changing Size on the Internal Structure of an Organization," *American Sociological Review*, 20, 1955, pp. 11–13.

more carefully Anderson and Warkov suggest that the contradiction is more apparent than real. Their explanation is:

1. The relative size of the administrative component *decreases* as the number of persons performing identical tasks in the same place increases.

2. The relative size of the administrative component increases as the number of places at which work is performed increases.

3. The relative size of the administrative component increases as the number of tasks performed at the same place increases [or] as the roles become increasingly specialized and differentiated.[11]

Growth, as we have seen, results in an increase of organizational size and usually in a change of organizational form. The change in form can occur in a variety of ways. There are apparently certain patterns in these changes making them to some degree predictable and understandable.

ORGANIZATION SIZE AND BUREAUCRATIZATION. One change in organizational form obliquely referred to in the preceding section needs to be made explicit. As an organization grows partially resulting in larger size, there will be an increase in internal confusion, inefficiency, etc. This in turn leads higher management to desire, search for, and install methods of controlling the performance of lower organizational members to make individual and overall organization performance more predictable. Often this takes the form of more precisely specified duties and responsibilities, formally designated rules and procedures, and more insistence on individual competence—in short, the installation of bureaucracy [12] and the institutionalization of the management function.

This shift to a more bureaucratic form of organization has a definite impact on the organizational members. The loose, flexible, personalized way of conducting affairs diminishes and in its place comes closer control to what must be and what must not be done. Relationships between jobs and people become more formalized, less personal. There is a greater emphasis on personal competence and less on per-

[11] Theodore Anderson and Seymour Warkov, "Organizational Size and Functional Complexity: A Study of Administration in Hospitals," *American Sociological Review*, **26**, 1961, pp. 23–28.

[12] For further discussion of this see Max Weber, *From Max Weber*, New York Galaxy Books, 1958, pp. 196–216, translated by H. H. Girth and C. Wright Mills; and Oscar Grusky, "Corporate Size, Bureaucratization and Managerial Succession," *American Journal of Sociology*, **67**, 1961 pp. 261–269.

sonal acceptability.   As a result the organization becomes less dependent on the services of particular individuals.   Organizational members may come and go or shift locations with less impact on the overall performance of the organization.   Bureaucratization, therefore, would make it possible for a higher rate of turnover to exist in organizational positions.   This has been found to be so in a study of 53 of the 500 largest business concerns in the United States.   The 26 largest companies, assumed to be more bureaucratic, were found to have a significantly higher rate of succession in the highest administrative post than the 27 smallest in this group.[13]

ORGANIZATIONAL AGING

Let us return to the biological analogy; biological organisms not only grow but also age, and so apparently do organizations.   As organizations age some of their problems change.   With the changing problems new groups of organizational members better able to cope with the new problems rise to dominant positions.   Let us review some points covered in Chapter 8.   The initial problems are of two types: acquiring the basic resources in the form of funds, tools, locations, perhaps patents and certainly key personnel; and setting the basic direction or policy of the organization.   Once these conditions have been satisfied there is the necessity of making the organization work successfully enough to justify its existence—that is, to legitimatize the organization.   To the business enterprise, this would be producing a product or service customers want.   In a hospital it would be giving enough competent medical service to the community to make patients, physicians, and the community feel that it performed a useful medical function.   But goods and services must be produced efficiently, or more accurately, in line with conditional objectives.   Hence, a third effort would be to achieve internal efficiency.

All three classes of problems may be handled by the same individual or group of individuals.   There is evidence to suggest, however, that each class of problems will be best handled by different individuals or groups.   In a hospital the initial problems of resource acquisition and study of policy may well be best dealt with by trustees who likely will be members of the general community and have access to resources and an understanding of the type of service the community needs.   However, they are unlikely to be able to handle the problems of rendering good medical service.   This problem can be handled most competently by the medical staff.   Once the hospital is established,

[13] Grusky, *op. cit.*

this second problem begins to emerge and the medical staff probably will assume a major influence in the hospital's operation. With acceptance by the community established, the problems of internal efficiency come to the fore. To handle these problems may require skills, outlooks, and a role different from that of the medical specialists. At this stage a professional administrator, neither a trustee nor a medical specialist, may assume a dominative role. In business concerns the lines of demarcation do not seem as sharp but the same general pattern apparently exists.[14]

Size and the Internal System

Although growth may be regarded as a natural process, it would be wrong to think that it occurs without some "costs." One of the many costs occurs in conjunction with the internal system and the individual. Generally speaking, the larger the organization becomes, the more extensive is the use of the division of labor, which has a number of consequences. Job content becomes smaller resulting in a more limited range of activity, and less control by the individual over his activities. Second, as jobs become more numerous several things occur to increase status differentiation. First, there are more levels in the organization, leading to status differentiation based on hierarchal position. Jobs are more restricted and can be differentiated on the

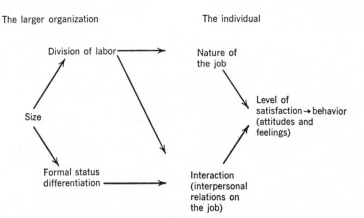

Figure 20.4. *Source:* Sergio Talacchi, "Attitudes and Behavior: an Empirical Study," *Administrative Science Quarterly,* **5,** 1960, p. 405.

[14] Charles Perrow, "The Analysis of Goals in Complex Organizations," *American Sociological Review,* **26,** 1961, pp. 854–865.

basis of skill, materials worked on, etc. These status differences belong with the number of other things that interfere with the possible or required. The changes in the external system will have strong implications for the internal system, leading ultimately to a shift in attitudes of individuals in the organization. The general pattern of restriction of activities and of interaction can be reasonably expected to lead to a lowering of possible sentiment toward the organization. The relationship between these elements are shown in Figure 20.4. In a study by Talacchi there is a general negative relationship between organization size and level of employee satisfaction. In the sample of 93 companies there was a negative correlation of −.67, significant at the 5 per cent level.[15]

SUMMARY

In this part of the book the examination of organization under steady-state conditions shifts to those of *change*. This chapter considers the grosser organizational changes—those that might be called the biological changes of growth and aging. Though fascinating, they are extraordinarily complex and as yet little is known of them. Sufficient material is at hand, however, to indicate the general patterns of these changes and some of the factors connected with them.

Organizational forms resulting from growth are numerous and serve a number of broad classes of functions. One function which received considerable attention was that of providing greater coordination or integration and control made necessary by the larger organization size. This function was seen to lead to emergence of differentiated hierarchal roles, the establishment of formalized procedures for coordination, and the establishment of special departments, such as staff, to operate them, which last can be viewed as part of a larger movement toward a more bureaucratic form of organization.

Ultimately, an organization was seen to reach a size where these steps were not capable of providing adequate coordination and control leading to a fundamental shift from functional to purpose or product form of departmentalization, which reduced the necessity of organization coordinative systems. This central theme, that growth leading to larger size engenders progressively more complex problems of coordination which, in turn, must be supported by more adequate organizational forms, is supported by longitudinal and cross-sectional studies of business organizations. These studies showed that as

[15] Sergio Talacchi, "Attitudes and Behavior: An Empirical Study," *Administrative Science Quarterly*, 5, 1960, pp. 398–420.

organizations increased in size, the proportion of internally oriented positions increased more rapidly than the proportion of externally oriented positions. The internally oriented position is concerned primarily with the problems of coordination and integration.

These are the results of organizational growth which stems from the existence of both underutilized resources and overutilized resources. However, in addition to the existence of these, there must be certain conditions which permit or facilitate growth. These were largely seen as financial, technological, and managerial advantages of scale. Given the necessary internal factors and faced with an auspicious environment, organization growth leading to size and form changes will in all likelihood occur as a natural phenomenon.

Organizational Adaption

GROWTH is only one form of organizational change. Organizations can be properly considered to be a continual process of change: changing internal work methods to improve the accomplishments of objectives; changing objectives; and adjusting to depleting resources, shifting competitive patterns, and fluctuations in the business cycle. These and many other types of change are always taking place in organizations.

Little is known as yet about organizational adaption. There are apparently an extraordinary large number of factors which can bring about organizational adaptions. The organization elements and processes involved in adaption are only partially identified among many levels of organizational systems. Such a complex phenomenon would take considerable time to explain to any satisfaction even if it were fully understood. For the space and the meager knowledge available at the moment, all that is possible now is to present the broad outline of the elements in and the determinants of organizational adaption.

ORGANIZATION VARIATION AS A RESPONSE

Organizational adaption can be studied in a number of ways. One is to examine the variations in one organization as elements in or about it change. Another, to study the variation among organizations which are confronted with different conditions. Let us take the second approach and examine some variations among organizational properties which develop as a response to different environmental conditions. The first three parts of this book focused on integration and productivity under steady-state conditions; now we are concerned with the "fit" of an organization to its environment and with the fit of the parts to an organization.

Differences in Managerial Autonomy

In a study by Dill [1] the influence of environment on the managerial autonomy of two companies was examined. Managerial autonomy was the degree of freedom from influence an executive possessed. Two types of autonomy were examined: *upward autonomy*, that is, freedom of second-level executives from influence by the owner-manager who headed the concern; and *horizontal autonomy*, that is, freedom from influence by peers. In the first company, Alpha, executives had relatively less upward autonomy than those in the second, Beta, company. In Alpha (1) the president initiated more tasks for his subordinates; (2) the president was more frequently involved as a participant in subordinate tasks; (3) key executives made decisions less often; and (4) executives were more often restricted to tasks of "collecting information" and "preparing proposals." The first-line executives at Alpha Company were also found to have less horizontal autonomy in that they (1) had more of their tasks initiated by peers than those at Beta, and (2) more often had peers as coworkers on tasks than executives at Beta and had more interaction with peers and peer subordinates than those at Beta. In short, the executives at Alpha Company had less upward and horizontal autonomy than those at Beta.

Differences in Environment

These differences in managerial autonomy were seen as organizational adjustments to different environmental conditions by these two concerns. The executives in both companies had contacts with the company's environment. It was found that the executives in Alpha tended to deal with the same or closely related markets, unions, governmental regulatory bodies, and suppliers. The executives in Beta Company came into contact with a more differentiated environment. Executives dealt with different markets; they dealt with different unions, different regulatory bodies, and different suppliers. As a result, there was less need for their individual decisions to be coordinated. Second, feedback from the environment had a much greater impact in Alpha Company than in Beta. Third, in the immediate or short-run time span there were more drastic economic and market changes confronting Alpha Company than Beta Company. Last,

[1] William R. Dill, "Environment as an Influence on Managerial Autonomy," *Administrative Science Quarterly*, **2**, 1958, pp. 409–443.

communications between Alpha Company and its environment could be more readily handled in written or symbolic form.   This made it less necessary for the executives of the company to come into direct contact with suppliers, customers, and the like.   Such was not possible in the Beta Company, and in order to maintain effective contact the executives often had to engage in face to face meetings with important people outside the concern.   These differences are shown in Table 21.1.   In brief, the autonomy of executives was found to be less when:

Table 21.1

	Alpha Company	Beta Company
Differentiation of customers, suppliers, unions, and regulatory bodies faced by key managers	Little	Great
Short-run stability of environment	Relatively unstable	Relatively stable
Adjustment required by feedback from environment	Much	Little
Demand for direct interaction with environment	Little	High
Upward autonomy	Low	High
Horizontal autonomy	Low	High

Source: William R. Dill, "Environment as an Influence on Management Autonomy," *Administrative Science Quarterly*, 2, 1958, pp. 409–443.

1. The executive dealt with a less differentiated set of customers, suppliers, and government regulatory bodies.

2. The company was more closely coupled with its environment through feedback.

3. The environment was less stable in the short run.

4. The precision of communications was greater, requiring less interaction with environment.

This research showed the connection between certain organization characteristics and environmental properties.   This relationship did not direct the way the company should be organized internally.[2]   The environment did, however, specify the conditions or effects the internal arrangements of the company would have to produce.   Each concern probably had a number of different approaches or strategies it might have followed in coping with the environment.   These would

[2] Dill, *op. cit.*, p. 435.

Figure 21.1

have specified the things to be accomplished and the general ways these results would be achieved. For our purposes we call these specifications *policies*, which may be either formally specified or informally developed (Figure 21.1).

POLICY AS A DETERMINANT OF ORGANIZATION VARIATION

The role of policy as an intervening element between environment and the organization can be extended by examining research which has investigated these relationships. One study compared two textile mills in the same Indian city selling to the same market, using the same type of processes and machinery, and of approximately the same size.[3] In mill A, the managing agent handed down the policy that the mill would make products that were most immediately in demand and would give the greatest short-run profit. Since fashion changed rapidly, this meant the mill frequently had to change the characteristics of the product sold. Mill B, on the other hand, adopted the policy of producing those fabrics that would have long-run demand and on which it could build a reputation for quality. This meant that product changes would be few and seldom.

To support these different policies, it was necessary to develop different organizational forms. In mill A the executives reporting directly to the managing agent felt relatively little autonomy. They frequently received orders or instructions from him on what to do, and they were expected to report several times a day on what had been accomplished. On the other hand, in mill B the executives reporting to the managing agent had considerable autonomy, receiving very few orders and instructions from him and having to report infrequently. The frequent changes in product in mill A led to frequent shifts in the organization, particularly personnel changes, which in turn led to numerous expressions of dissatisfaction and a relatively high turnover rate among the managerial personnel. The stable product mix in mill B led to the opposite conditions.

Several other interesting organizational differences were noted. In

[3] Kamla Chowdary and A. K. Pal, "Production Planning and Organizational Morale," *Human Organizations*, **15**, pp. 11–16.

mill A regardless of its formal chart most managers—that is, production managers, department managers, and assistant department managers—reported directly to the managing agent making the organization quite flat and centralized. In mill B the hierarchal order of reporting relationships was managing agent, production manager, department manager, and assistant department manager. Furthermore, when there were corrections or changes in products, these were likeliest to come directly from the sales manager to the department manager or assistant department manager involved. In mill A this information went through the managing agent to the department manager involved. Last, there were considerable differences in the shift arrangements in the two mills. In mill A most of the senior and junior executives worked on the day shift, and only a few junior executives worked on the night shift, thereby permitting the executives to have maximum contact with the managing agent. In mill B there was almost an equal distribution of both senior and junior executives between the two shifts. These and a number of other differences between the two mill organizations are shown in Table 21.2.

Policy then specifies particular goals or targets and the approach to be taken to accomplish these. To support the policy, certain organizational forms develop. As a relationship this has been stated as: "Structure follows strategy." [4] Figure 21.2 summarizes the main thread thus far. In light of a particular environment, certain goals and strategies leading to these goals will be formulated as a policy. Given this policy as compatible, an organizational form must be developed.[5]

Determinants of Policy

Since policy is seen to have such a central role in determining organizational form, it seems necessary to examine it further. Here we do not attempt to specify what are the best policies. Instead, we examine some of the principal influences which determine what a policy may be.

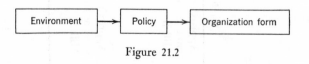

Figure 21.2

[4] Alfred Chandler, *Strategy and Structure: Chapters in the History of Industrial Enterprise*, Cambridge, MIT, 1962.
[5] For earlier discussion of the different types of objectives, see Chapter 8.

Table 21.2

	Market	Number of Spindles	Number of Looms	Product Policy	Manu-facturing Program	Superior Reporting to:		
						Production Manager	Department Managers	Assistant Department Managers
Mill A	Approximately same as for Mill B	45,000	850	Change to meet immediate demand to get maximum profit for each product	Frequently changed	Managing agent	Managing agent	Managing agent, department manager, production manager
Mill B	Approximately same as for Mill A	37,600	500	Produce same product regularly; maximize quality image.	Only minor changes	Managing agent	Production manager	Department manager

Table 21.2 (Cont.)

	Group of People Worked with	Composition of Night Shift	Work Assignment of Managerial Personnel	Changes in Manufacturing Program	Turnover of Managerial Personnel	Frequency of Check Up by Managing Agent	Perceived Autonomy of Department Heads
Mill A	Changing	Principally junior managers	Frequency changed	Managing agent	High	High	Low
Mill B	Stable	Same as day shift: both senior, four junior managers	Stable	Sales manager	Low	Low	High

Source: Kamla Chowdary and A. K. Pal, "Production Planning and Organizational Morale," *Human Organization, 15,* pp. 11–16.

ENVIRONMENT. By environment we mean the portion of the world external to the organization with which it comes in contact. Influence of some external institutions on the formation of organization policy have been touched upon. There are other environmental influences not yet examined.

Most of the environmental influence examined so far has been concerned with how organization outputs have been integrated into the operation of a larger social system. Does the organization deliver the products and services the public wants? Does it handle its obligations to individuals in other organizations in an acceptable fashion? Another set of issues revolves around the compatibility of an organization's operation with the expectations of the environment.[6]

This issue of compatibility of one organization's method of operating with the expectations of the larger society and the organizations in it centers more on norms than on products. It is concerned with such questions as how the organization hires and fires its personnel. A current topic would be: What does the company do with employees displaced by automation? Another set of issues revolves around its support of important social institutions. Does the company, for example, support higher education by establishing scholarships, by giving research grants, and by endowing new buildings or does it regularly refuse to give any such support? The list can be endless. These topics center on the basic issue of how compatible the organization activity, often internal, is with the values of the society around it and actions of other comparable organizations.

This environmental influence can be regarded as establishing a series of conditions with which organizational behavior must be compatible. If not, the organization can probably expect some consequences either in the form of a loss of any support from society or the development of some means by which the larger society can insure that organizational performance will meet minimal expectations. An illustration of this second situation would be the development of laws and institutions in the 1930s to constrain activities of business concerns in their dealings with labor unions.

RESOURCES. Resources an organization has or can reasonably expect to obtain influence both what it can hope to accomplish and the means it can use to do this. An organization with a million dollars of capital could think of building a supermarket store, but it would be hardly feasible for it to think of going into the steel business. To be com-

---

[6] The following discussion comes largely from Talcott Parsons, *Structure and Process of Modern Societies*, Glencoe, Free Press, 1960, particularly pp. 16–58.

petitive as a steel producer, the company would have to operate plants of such a size that it would need hundreds of times more capital than on hand.

Resources influence policy, and subsequently organizations, in several ways other than by restricting goal considerations. Certain organizational elements may be necessary to attract needed resources. For example, having a steady supply of uniquely qualified employees may be particularly crucial to the success and survival of organizations such as law firms, universities, research institutions, etc. To attract particular types of young lawyers, some leading legal firms have made substantial rearrangements of their internal operation in order to be able to give the new lawyers the type of experience they want, thereby making it desirable for them to come to the firm. This has, at times, entailed special rotational schemes giving new lawyers experience in a variety of different legal matters, rearranging some of the activities of senior members of the firms to give the new lawyers a "richer" set of professional experiences as well as getting the senior members of the firms into more of a coaching rather than directing relationship. Many activities have been incorporated under positions such as personnel director which are relatively new additions in firms of this sort.[7] Some observers have claimed that some business concerns have added research and development departments to their organization primarily to attract investors rather than to develop new products for processing.

TECHNOLOGY. In a crude sense, technology is knowledge of a way of doing something. Such a definition permits us inclusion of not only manufacturing processes, which we might well first think of, but also of ways of carrying out business and managerial functions. We consider these in turn. Obviously the technology available limits and constrains the policies which can be established. Forty years ago there was no point in establishing a policy of having 24-hour delivery to customers from a company plant if the concern served anything more than a very restricted area. Today with the development of the jet airplane and air freight service it is possible to think in terms of 24-hour delivery from a plant site to almost any major city in the country. Nor would there be any point to having an objective of making nonrusting steel until the development of stainless steel and the current development of ultrapure metals.

[7] See Erwin O. Smigel, "The Impact of Recruitment on the Organization of a Large Law Firm," *American Sociological Review*, **25**, 1960, pp. 55–66.

This broad definition can include business technology. For example, in marketing the self-service store can be considered a technological arrangement different from direct service through a clerk, as was the way of handling marketing until the last generation. The development of this new technology permitted new policies and organizational forms of development.

We would be remiss if we did not consider the managerial technologies used to carry out the managerial function. Until recently many, in fact most, managerial activities had to be carried out on a hand-labor basis. That is, the work of management was carried out by individuals using the very simplest of tools—paper, pencil, and occasionally typewriters, adding machines, and other simple mechanical tools. The structure of positions and departments we have grown to think typical of business concerns was molded in many ways by the hand-labor nature of management technology. The advent of high-capacity, high-speed computers permits managerial work to leap from a hand-labor level to an automated level almost overnight. The full implications of this possibility are only sketchily understood at the moment; yet there already seems ample evidence that there will be a dramatic shift in many policies. In some instances, companies will go from a decentralized to a centralized organizational style. In other instances, such developments will permit concerns to operate at a size which previously would have been impossible, such as has already occurred in instances of large insurance companies.

A PRELIMINARY GENERAL STATEMENT OF ORGANIZATION ADAPTION. Three classes of policy determinants—environment, resources, and technology—constrain policies of any organization and, thereby, the organizational form (Figure 21.3). A change in any one of these at the very least requires a reexamination, probably a policy change, and then a change in organization.

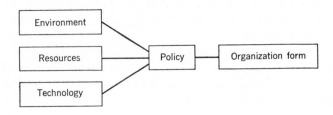

Figure 21.3

Processes in Policy Change

Our emphasis, until now, has been largely on the constraints on policy formation and change. Let us now consider some of the processes by which these occur. Much of the process of policy change revolves around the twin conceptions of (1) the need for change, and (2) the possible way of changing. In reality, it is not the change in one of the constraints which brings about a change in policy, but rather a perception by some organization member or members that the change in the constraint requires a change in policy. A dip in business activity interpreted by key corporation officials as a minor variation may not lead to any change in credit or inventory policy. In other companies, other executives may interpret it as a major economic downturn necessitating important changes in these two policies. Hence, the mechanisms of perceptions, discussed earlier, are important processes in policy change.[8]

THE INITIATION OF INNOVATION. Although the general discussion has focused on how a change in one of the determinants of policy results in a change in policy, it is erroneous to presume that all changes in policy occur through a sequence of events which begins with some organizational member actually observing a change in one of these determining factors. Organizational members never know all the facts pertaining to these determining factors, as would be necessary in order to proceed in this fashion. As a result, a limited number of factors are often observed with varying degrees of consistency. In actual practice it is more common to evaluate the performance of an organization and formulate new policy when that performance is different from the one desired; that is, the organization operates as a closed system. The detection of a need for new policy and the initiation of the process of obtaining it, which we call *innovation*, obviously causes a delay in adaption. This practice, however, affords great economies by reducing the number of things which have to be observed and the intensity with which they have to be examined.

CYBERNETICS AND ORGANIZATIONAL ADAPTION. We have already considered cybernetics as a process leading to changes in organizational activities to bring performance within acceptable levels. We now examine cybernetic processes at a level where the adjustment of activities within policy and program specifications is not sufficient, and the

[8] See Chapter 3.

policy and program themselves have to be regarded as subject to change.

As an illustration let us assume that we have a going concern that has a stated policy which says all orders received by the factory must be shipped within 10 days. This, then, is a standard criterion for successful plant performance. There is also a policy which says that the company will maintain no finished goods inventory but adjust production to meet demand by working overtime when necessary. For a while these arrangements are satisfactory, and variations in productive demand change the number of hours worked. Then comes a period when sales are particularly good and the number of overtime hours increases to the point where any further increases will require the company to pay double time for additional overtime work, in accordance with the union contract. Furthermore, let us assume that there is a company rule that says there will be no double-time payments to any employees. Hence, if orders increase beyond this point, performance (as measured by prompt shipment of goods) will not meet the standard, and a cycle of events will begin that lead to some corrective action.

However, the new action is not specified. It must come through some innovated process. It may be a modification of the 10-day rule, a relaxation of the no-double-time payment rule, or the establishment of a second shift. As the innovation process suggests an alternative policy, its likely influence will be examined. Will changing the 10-day rule endanger the company's marketing image? Will changing the double-time payment rule increase the cost of the product so much as to eliminate profit? These and many other questions are raised and examined by comparing the consequences of proposed optional policies with criteria of satisfactory organizational performance.

It may be, of course, that no other course can be found which will satisfactorily meet the standards used. If this is the case, another cycle of examination in which the standards themselves are open to change will probably begin.[9] Is it important to have the reputation of being a company that makes prompt deliveries and etc.? (Figure 21.4.)

The question not yet explored is, How are policies formed? More specifically, how are objectives chosen for an organization and plans developed to achieve objectives? A closely related question is, Who establishes organizational objectives? It would be simple to say that the owners through the board of directors or through their appointed

---

[9] For further elaboration of this process, see James G. March, and Herbert A. Simon, *Organizations*, New York, John Wiley, 1958, Chapter 7.

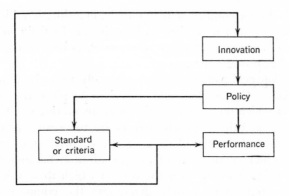

Figure 21.4.   Initiation of innovation of policy.

chief executive set the objectives by way of some rational process. Although this is a tidy and uncomplicated explanation, it does not reflect organizational realities. Goals for an organization are established by a number of people, only some of whom are owners. Although rational processes may be used by individuals to develop their proposals or to defend their proposals, it is quite obvious to any observer that other processes are also involved. Integrating proposals of several people into working objectives for an organization is a task of major proportions. One recent theory suggests that organization goals are determined by coalitions.[10] The explanation begins with recognizing that people come into an organization with an array of goals. Their goals are both different and ranked. Some are extremely important and others are desired but hardly essential. A coalition will be formed among some organization members on the basis of the complementariness of their individual goals. These *complementing goals* are in effect the organization goals.

The term, complementary goals, is used in loose fashion. It could mean that some parties would share the same goal. It could also mean that two individual goals mesh together nicely to support a more inclusive, umbrella form of goal. For example, a sales manager may want to increase sales and feels he needs to have a new product to do so. A research manager may want to expand the efforts of his department to advance the knowledge of the field and also to develop new products. Hence, both are interested in expanded research and development programs. At the extreme end, it may merely be that indi-

---

[10] Richard Cyert and James G. March, *Behavioral Theory of the Firm*, New Jersey, Prentice Hall, 1963, Chapter 3.

vidual goals do not conflict as, for example, in a situation where a plant manager may want a new plant to be quite modernistic and the sales manager may have no preference whatsoever, as long as the new plant quickly makes products he can sell.

In discussing goal formation there are really two classes of goals to keep in mind. One is the actual objectives people may have for the organization which must possess this complementariness. The other is the more personal things people may desire for a number of reasons. These may include things like wages, special privileges, or a certain form of conduct on the part of the organization because the person happens to think it right. It is the way in which these side payments will be allocated which largely determines the composition of the coalition. It is the complementariness of the goals of coalition members that determines the goals of the organization.

This is one of the numerous double relationships we have discussed in the past. Goals, coming from a coalition, depend on who the coalition members are. On the other hand, a particular set of coalition goals will determine who will be coalition members. For example, a group of engineers, financial people, and production specialists may have a company but may recognize that to have it succeed they will need a sales executive. Upon recruiting a sales executive into the organization and coalition, they may find that he has a slightly different combination of goals causing a shift in those found to be complementary. The organization goals will therefore vary, both as the composition of the coalition changes and as the goals for the company and individual members change. Such a view of the formation of organization goals makes the constant shift of specific organization goals more understandable.

Coalition Formation: Bargaining

This theory holds that the key process of coalition formation and, therefore, of coalition-goals formation is bargaining. In a primitive arrangement we often think of a person contributing X number of hours' work for Y number of dollars' pay. In coalitions, the process includes a number of other important elements. In addition to monetary payments, the individual receives commitments about how the organization will operate. The sales manager may insist on what he calls "adequate advertising." One form of this advertising might be to have all the salesmen's cars made to look like a replica of the company product, for example, a hot-dog roll. He thinks such actions are necessary for him to do his job well. The rest of the policy-forming executives may feel that this will detract from the dignified image they would prefer their company to have. However, since this is not a vital issue for them, they are willing to give up this point and make a policy commitment that salesmen's cars will be used to advertise the company products.

An important point about bargaining over side payments, such as policy commitments which this illustration reveals, is that many of the objectives bargained for are "given up," or perhaps a more accurate term, "contributed by" other members of the coalition. Hence, it is not primarily dividing up the profits of organized efforts but the allocation of the collective contribution of coalition members. In the foregoing illustration, the other executives gave up some of their ideal image of the company to permit the sales manager to receive something he felt to be very important.

Stabilizing Coalitions

Bargaining goes on continuously within organizations as individuals' objectives change, as the opportunities they see change, and as their power changes, etc. This seems to make things very unstable. Actually, although some bargaining over objectives is always under way, many commitments and objectives have great stability and persist for long periods of time. This stability comes about in a number of ways.

First, people have limited time and energy, and bargaining over goals consumes great amounts of both. Hence, in order to accomplish goals, people seem willing, once a basic agreement has been reached, to let it stand. It may not be perfect from their point of view, but it is perhaps not so bad as to justify the effort of seeking a better arrangement, which might never come about anyway.

Second, to make any basic agreements work, there has to be an enormous number of sub- and sub-subagreements worked out. Many of these are informal, even unconscious, accommodations that people working together make to each other. Change basic objectives and these formal (such as reward systems) and informal (such as norms) arrangements will also change. The cost of changing such sub-agreements, accommodations, and arrangements may be so great that basic objectives are not changed even when most people recognize the necessity.

Third, many organizational institutions which reflect and support coalition objectives and side payments have a life span during which time the goals stay fixed. Budgets reflect objectives and since they are usually fixed for at least a year, they fix goals for that period. The definition of organizational units (for example, positions and departments, reflect objectives), and although the terms of these units may not be definite, they do tend to persist and therefore perpetuate the attainment of certain objectives. Thus the allocation of capital resources in budgeting and the allocation of functions in a division of work both reflect and stabilize objectives.

Fourth, previously institutionalized elements and accommodations become models for subsequent ones. Last year's budget becomes a model for next year's. The organization of current sales divisions becomes the model for new ones.

Coalitions and Changes in Objectives

This view sees the individual in a coalition as the source of changes in objectives. The individual who sees that changed economic or social conditions have made new objectives desirable can propose and bring about changes. The person whose power has increased may be able to obtain side payments he has always desired but only partially achieved. The individual who sees that current objectives are not, and perhaps never can, be obtained may suggest new and more reasonable objectives.

SUMMARY

Organizational change is an extraordinarily complex process. We have looked at it as an adjustment to a shift in some of the determining factors of resources, which include tools, raw materials, patents, money and people, technology, and the environment. This impact or adjustment is not direct, however. It is transmitted through formally and informally derived objectives and plans for achieving them, which we have called policies. These are, in turn, formulated or arrived at by a number of means; for example, as a result of coalition formulation within the organization, a coalition is formed on the basis of the complementariness of individual objectives for the organization and bargaining over side payments for individual objectives.

The organization then adapts to a wide array of demands. These include the objectives of the coalition, the individual wishes of coalition members, and the demands of society for certain products and services as well as the demands of society that the organizational mode of operation be compatible with societies' values and standards.

Individual Managerial Practices

THROUGHOUT this study attention has centered on the determinants of behavior. Examining these one at a time, as we have, can lead to the desirable but usually unattainable concept that the various influences on behavior mesh in a nonconflicting or supporting pattern. More typically, some are nonsupporting of one another and some are in conflict. Conflict may lead to the individual's choosing one over the other. At times, however, the conflict of influences produces a totally new and unexpected type of behavior, not the direct result of any of the clashing elements but of the conflict itself.

In this and the final chapter of the book we return to examining the individual. We now look at him as living in a multiorganizational or multisystem world. We cannot consider these all at the same time, but we can consider a few in combination. We examine particularly the manager and especially his behavior that deviates from formal organization prescriptions or the expectations of higher management.

PATTERNS OF DEVIATIONS

Strategic Leniency

Consider a plant where a number of rules are in effect, one of which states that production workers must stay around their work area unless they are on breaks or going to the restroom; another says that there shall be no smoking anywhere in the plant except in private offices, restrooms, or the cafeteria. One day a foreman walking by the open door of the stockroom sees several of his production employees sitting on boxes and crates smoking. This is indeed an awkward situation. The production employees have violated at least two rules. The stockroom attendant has violated several others. As a member of management, which created the rules, the foreman might take immediate action to stop the infraction and to punish the offenders. He may do this, but let us assume he chooses to say nothing, close the door, and walk on. In short, he not only permits violation of organization rules but also actually helps to cover them up.

What are we to make of the foreman's behavior? One quick explanation might be that he is "weak," unable to fill his job as a superior. Perhaps. But there is some indication that the weak, insecure superior is the one most likely to use rules and the sanctions they carry with them.[1] The crucial element is that the use of the rules and the administration of their accompanying punishments is something within the control of the foreman. That is, "the rules . . . created something which could be *given up* as well as *given use*." [2]

By withholding punishment, by deliberately not using a rule, the foreman permits the men in the stockroom to obtain some things they really want—freedom to move around, smoke. But the men doubtless recognize quite clearly that obtaining these things is possible only if the foreman continues to withhold the application of rules and punishments. Obtaining these things makes them dependent on him and not on the organization as a whole or on a reward system. His power over them thereby increases, and he can use this expanded power to influence their behavior in many other areas, such as bending informal codes and work restrictions to meet production schedules, which are important to the foreman, or following his instructions and orders where his legitimate authority may not be clear. Should they fail to follow his instructions and orders in these instances, the next time he can break up the smoking group in the stockroom and send them back to their work positions or go one step further and impose the punishments which should accompany the violation of this rule.[3]

Two points are of such importance that they need elaboration. First, in developing a pattern of strategic leniency, the foreman basically takes into account needs and desires of subordinates which are not being satisfied by the formal organization. This reverts to the earlier discussion on motivation and a superior's role in facilitating the satisfaction of needs. Close application of organizational rules can often interfere with the satisfaction of these needs, and as we have seen close supervision, which would be necessary to enforce all the rules, is

[1] For discussion of this topic, see Alvin W. Gouldner, *Patterns of Industrial Bureaucracy*, Glencoe, The Free Press, 1954, particularly pp. 93–96.
[2] Gouldner, *op. cit.*, p. 174.
[3] For further discussion of this see Peter M. Blau, *Bureaucracy in Modern Society*, New York, Random House, 1956, particularly pp. 70–79.

often accompanied by low productivity and negative employee attitudes.

The second aspect of strategic leniency which bears attention centers on the function of this action in building the personal authority of the superior. In large organizations, which have well-established systems of rules enforcement, the rules vary over time. Sometimes they are meticulously followed and punishments regularly administered, whereas at other times they are often neglected and when invoked entail nothing more than a warning rather than more severe punishment. One explanation for this is that personal authority or power is hardly permanent. It has to be built up between two or more individuals. Second, it tends to erode as conditions change, as the irritation of dependency encourages people to break away, or as permitted deviations come to be seen as rights. The explanation, therefore, is that although a superior initially needs to establish his personal authority or reinforce it as it appears to be slipping, he is likely to enforce rules to remind subordinates, in effect, that they have been benefiting from his personal discretion and not from any inalienable right. Put another way, if subordinates receive things they consider their due or right, they are hardly likely to regard the receipt as strategic leniency, and this has little, if any, usefulness in building personal authority.[4]

Mock Compliance

Often the deviation between formal organization rules and actual behavior is involved with a more complex pattern of events, as when a rule is actually being violated but on the surface appears to be complied with.

Dalton described an interesting example of this in his MILO study. Here, the central office was trying to obtain control over and reduce the quantity of parts kept in inventory for maintenance purposes in the various departments of the MILO plant. Control over the purchase and inventory of these parts was nominally to be in the hands of an executive who, although he worked in the plant, was to receive his orders directly from the central office. Among other things, he had been instructed by his superiors in the central office to engage in surprise inspections to determine whether maintenance-parts inventories actually exceeded the permitted levels by some considerable amount. Such inspections, if carried out, would have ultimately led to reduction in these stocks. For the inspection to take place would,

[4] For further discussion of this topic, see Gouldner, *op. cit.*, p. 53.

in the eyes of the production managers at least, have seriously reduced their ability to have their department function well. On the other hand, not carrying through the order for spontaneous inspection would have been so obvious that some action by a higher executive could be anticipated which might ultimately lead to the same reduction in maintenance parts stocks.

The solution lay in mock inspections. The executive who was to make an inspection would let the executive in charge of the area know his plans, stating when the inspection would begin, where it would begin, and the route it would follow. By varying the starting point, starting time, and route this official could appear in his report to be meeting the basic conditions of surprise inspections. Knowing this in advance, the executives in the plant could easily make sure that the illegal stocks and material were moved to locations where they would not be uncovered.[5]

This sort of deviation is possible only when (1) there is a more elaborate plan covering how the rule will appear to be observed when it is actually being ignored, and (2) there is cooperation among a number of people on both sides of the rule.

The foregoing, fairly elaborate illustration of mock compliance came about because of the inadequacy of an earlier and simpler form, that is, the filing of fictitious reports. This was a fairly simple expedient which often required no coordinated group or elaborate preparations. When the executive had to file reports on the stocks of replacement materials in inventory, he simply turned in figures which he knew would be approved. Such practices are all too frequently found in a large-scale organization. They exist not because it is impossible to stop them but because it is not reasonable to make the effort to do so. Carrying out the extensive checking necessary to make sure all rules are observed, would exceed the capabilities of any organization. However, this does not mean that mock compliance is always undetected; in the MILO Company higher officials instituted spot surprise checks as a half-way point to 100 per cent inspection.

Exchange

Exchange is the allocation of organizational resources through unofficial channels. It takes many forms, but an example drawn from the army may serve to describe the general phenomenon. A sergeant may want some paint to finish up a room or two in his barracks. However,

---

[5] Melville Dalton, *Men Who Manage: Fusions of Feeling and Theory in Administration*, New York, John Wiley, 1959, pp. 47–49.

he may not be able to get the paint through official channels for quite more individuals.   Second, it tends to erode as conditions change, as camp and simply by asking for it receive it as a favor.   He knows that sooner or later the person from whom he receives the paint will probably call on him for some return favor such as the donation of some leftover poles with which to make a fence.   Exchanges do not always involve only two parties; some time in the future the individual from whom the sergeant receives the paint may have a friend or acquaintance who needs the surplus poles.   The giver of the paint may, therefore, introduce his friend to the sergeant and explain his need for some poles for a fence.   In short, the credit of the favor can be expended in a number of ways.   Such exchange systems can at times become quite complex.

In a highly organized bureaucracy, such as the military, there are usually quite specific rules as to how resources will be allocated. Hence, the existence of an exchange system is, in varying degrees, contrary to the overall intent of the rules.   There would be considerable concern if exchange systems existed wholly for the personal benefit of the individuals involved.   Sometimes, of course, this occurs, such as when the mess-hall food for personal consumption is exchanged for a better place in the barracks.   However, many exchanges are more in the nature of the illustration given earlier.   They aid a person in the managerial hierarchy in doing or carrying out his official duties by permitting him to acquire things which official channels would not provide at all or at least in time.

Informal Specialization

We have often mentioned specialization almost as if it were something that had to be imposed on individuals, something that was normally to be avoided.   This is hardly the case, for many times individuals seem to modify their work in a way which makes them more specialized than is intended by the formal organization.   This often occurs in functional-type departments when a foreman may deliberately exceed quantities stated on a production run, feeling that he can do a better job that way.   For example, he may say that, "Once I have opened up a carton of raw materials I might as well use them all up and therefore produce five thousand rather than three thousand widgets."   Or, the setup time to produce widgets is so long that he decides to get the most use from it and produces five thousand rather than three thousand.   His rationale may be that sooner or later he will use these items.   From his point of view he is doing a good job for the company.   Actually, of course, he may not because the storage and inventory charges may be so great as to eliminate the savings he thinks he is making by the larger run.   Furthermore, the company may not use any more widgets and then his effort will be a complete loss.[6]

THE ROLE OF MANAGERIAL DEVIATION

How can we interpret these managerial deviations from expected organizational behavior?   A first impression might suggest that they are disloyal or self-seeking.   The illustrations used have been chosen especially to suggest that the answer is not that simple.   Managers may be trying to do their jobs in a way that seems best to them.   More specifically, the illustrations chosen show these managers trying to get greater personal control over their unit, trying to acquire the resources with which to work, and trying to use the first two to accomplish what they see as the thing that their group can do best.   Does deviation in managerial practices always signify such "good" intent?   Hardly. However, such a demonstration establishes that all deviations should not be considered "bad," and that instead some might have usefulness for organization.

The manager is placed in the position, in effect, of building his own position through a number of factors.   First, no organization, however carefully designed, considers all things its members must do.   In short, the formal program is never 100 per cent complete.   Second, as far as these formal prescriptions go, they may at times be inadequate, conflicting, or detrimental to the purposes for which they are intended. Even if they were fairly complete and adequate at one time, conditions may have changed somewhat since they were originally conceived and they are now to some extent out of date.   On the other hand, any individual manager cannot see the whole organization, understand all its purposes, or all the problems facing it.   Only a relatively small section is within his immediate vision.   The rest is only vaguely known, if at all.   All this is compounded by the fact that to know what to do requires information; as we have seen, communication systems are far from perfect either in the accuracy of transmission or the timeliness of presentation.   We could extend this further, but the general picture has been outlined; the individual manager is not, and probably never will be, in a position to be told what should be done to

[6] See, for example, R. L. A. Richardson, Jr. and Charles R. Walker, *Human Relations in an Expanding Company*, New Haven, Yale University Press, 1948, p. 68.

benefit the organization in every instance. The individual manager must always have some degree of latitude of discretion and some degree of control over people and resources. This eliminates the possibility of a tight, closely coupled organizational system. Of necessity there must be slack, give and take, and local variations. Even in building a bridge there is permit for sway, settling, and other variations rather than attempts to build a completely rigid and stable structure; to do so would be impossible. Surely in something so much more complex and difficult to specify as organizations the need for leeway and slack must be greater. While this makes organization design simpler in some ways, it makes it more complex in others.

Managerial deviations rather than being viewed as something to be eliminated have to be taken into account as a fact in organization planning. Such an approach is neatly summarized by Dalton:

> The logically conceived plans of one executive level are variously altered by subordinate levels to fit their shifting social relations as well as the emergencies of work. Inspired by fear of unofficial reprisals the alternations are often concealed and, therefore, not incorporated into future planning so that the organization is always out of date in some sense. Therefore, while planning must in general be logical, it must also be abbreviated and even loose in some areas to allow latitude for social contingencies. Achievement of organizational goals intertwines with individual and group ends near and remote from those of the firm.[7]

THE INDIVIDUAL IN A MULTIORGANIZATION WORLD

As indicated at the outset of this chapter, we are concerned with the interrelation among various aspects of organizations, particularly as they converge on the individual manager. Hence, we can look at the individual and say he is partially motivated by his own internal needs. He is influenced by the informal organization of which he is a member and he is also influenced by the formal organization in which he has a position. Actually, we can extend this even further and say that at one and the same time the manager is in a command group of which he is head. He is in another command group in which he is a subordinate and he is also a member of a peer group, all in addition to being a member of the formal organization.[8]

[7] Dalton, *op. cit.*, p. 68.
[8] See Chapter 16.

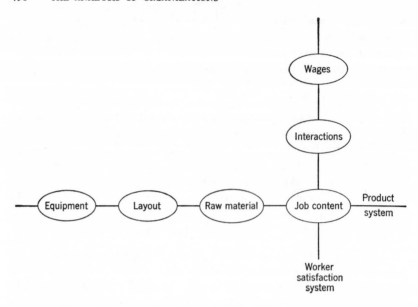

Figure 22.1

Single Acts, Multiple Effects

One result of this is that a manager finds himself in a world where even the simplest act on his part can have multiple and often conflicting results. For example, he is concerned with such things as raw materials, tools and machinery, the layout of equipment, the development of jobs, and the assignment of people to jobs, all very important in producing a product. We might call them elements in a product producing system. At the same time, he deals with other things such as wages, interactions, job contents, job assignments, etc., which influence the satisfactions of his subordinates. We might call these elements in an employee-satisfaction producing system. The point is that some elements appear in both systems (Figure 22.1). Hence, when he changes one item, or commits one act, it influences both systems. A change in job content to improve the efficiency of the product system may substantially reduce the satisfactions the person working at the job receives. Since a single act may be involved with numerous systems, the acts of the manager can be seen to have multiple, complex, and difficult-to-trace consequences. The manager who attempts to trace all these effects will be paralyzed into inaction. The manager who pays attention to just one is courting disaster. His task then is to find and understand those of real importance.

Role Conflict

A role is a set of expectations people have about the behavior of a person in a position.[9] The problem of concern here centers on the fact that different groups of people may have different sets of expectations about a person in a particular job or office. Hence, on the one hand, a manager's subordinates may expect, because he is boss, that he will take an interest in their personal problems, that he will "go to bat for them upstairs" when they have problems with the organization's bureaucracy, such as getting periodic wage increases on time or leaves of absence. They may also expect him to bend organization rules and procedures to accommodate their personal problems when needed, such as permitting them to leave early or occasionally come in late. The superiors of the same individual, on the other hand, may expect him to keep a tight rein on things, keep people in line, keep costs down, and stay on top of the situation. At the same time he is in a group of peers of other managers on the same level who probably expect him to cooperate with them by occasionally lending them extra personnel or rearranging their work schedules so that work can get to the next department a little more quickly and help out in a tight situation.

The list could be extended, but the pattern makes clear that whereas all expectations about a position are not in conflict, some are, and some of these are very important. The manager facing these sometimes conflicting expectations from superiors, subordinates, and peers is placed under considerable strain and is in some way going to have to accommodate them. A number of responses by the manager are possible.[10]

1. He can adopt a hierarchy of role obligation, that is, he can say to himself that the expectations of his superior are always more important than those of his subordinates or his peers. Of course the peers or subordinates may be the dominant group. Carried to an extreme, role expectations from one or perhaps more groups will be repudiated, such as the manager who says his employees are nothing to him but things with which he gets work done or the worker who says or seems to say

[9] E. Jacobson, W. E. Charters, and S. Lieberman, "The Use of Role Concept in the Study of Complex Organizations," *Journal of Social Issues*, 7, 1951, pp. 18–27.
[10] For the most part ways of dealing with role conflict discussed are taken with some modification from Jackson Toby, "Some Variables in Role Conflict Analysis," *Social Forces*, 30, 1952, pp. 323–327.

that for him the management is just the enemy and the only people who count are fellow workers.

2. He may use screening devices which usually involve the rules. In essence this means that the boss while doing something unpleasant and against the expectations of his subordinates says or implies that "It is not I who is doing this to you. I'm merely following the orders of superiors or the rules they have established and there is no way either of us can escape." Of course the reverse is also possible. A manager can go to his superiors and claim that for him to install such and such a rule with his group would lead to serious consequences, such as a wildcat strike, consequences far more serious than are justified by the rule. Thus, he has an excuse for not living up to the expectations of his superiors because of the unfortunate conditions with which he is faced.

3. The manager may use rituals to reduce the expectations from one or more groups. Rituals may take many forms, such as excessive politeness or formality. He may use formal names, for example, such as Mr. Jones rather than Bill, all of which although polite are less personal and make it more difficult for a person to press certain expectations for reasons of friendship or personal regard.

4. He may use deception where one or more groups are led to believe that expectations are being fulfilled. We discussed this earlier in this chapter.

5. He may stall. Many expectations decrease in intensity with time. The manager faced with one expectation from his superiors to act one way and another from his subordinates may deliberately stall until the need for action has disappeared or the concern of one or perhaps both parties has diminished.

6. The manager may lead a double life. An individual is seldom in contact with more than one group at a time. He may, therefore, attempt to play an approved role in each group while he is involved with it, shifting as he goes from one to the other. This, of course, is most possible in the area of expressing expected attitudes, such as, "all workers are lazy" or "management is out to exploit us," and most difficult in the areas where specific acts must be undertaken which can be observed by the various conflicting groups.

7. He may escape from the field. This is the solution used in other frustrating situations—to quit, to find another job.

8. He may succumb to illness. Psychological strain imposed by role conflicts can lead to personality disturbances and actual physical illness.

Duplicate Sources of Legitimate Influence

This section is in some ways closely related to the preceding one. It concerns, however, those problems confronting a manager when he must face several forces of influence, each of which he can somehow consider legitimate, the overdefined situation. The word influence has been chosen rather than authority because the latter has a number of special meanings, none of which seems fully adequate. Moreover, the effort required to integrate these multiple definitions to cover the phenomena under consideration does not seem warranted.

FORMAL RULES OR DUTIES AND SUPERIOR'S ORDERS. In this situation the manager or officer in an organization has certain specific rules telling him what he can and cannot do and also a superior who gives him an order which, were he to obey it, would cause him to violate one of the rules. An illustration is the navy disbursing officer who has quite specific rules about how he discharges his office. He may receive orders from his superior, the commander of the ship, which would cause him to violate these rules, such as paying men a few days early when the ship is in port.[11] The orders of superiors particularly in the military organizations are to be followed, often presumably without question, and yet the rules for the disturbing officer are clear cut; violation of them might damage his career and in some cases bring criminal prosecution. How can the officer resolve this conflict of duplicate sources of influence? He can decide the rules are more important than an order from a superior and can stick to his guns and rule book. The hazards of this course are rather considerable; the superior files regular fitness reports on him which will substantially influence his future career. He can relinquish authority in some degree by saying, in effect, to the superior, "I will do this under protest with a direct order from you, and will file my protest in written form." A third course is to treat the rules as a guide and the superior's orders as final and in this way perhaps adjust to the situation. The displeasure of the superior in not having his orders followed is sure. Being detected violating a naval regulation is a possibility and often a remote one at that.[12]

STAFF MEN, STAFF SUPERIORS, AND LINE MANAGERS. Staff personnel in any organization frequently find themselves in this position. They

[11] For background for this illustration see Ralph Turner, "The Navy Disbursing Officer as a Bureaucrat," *The American Sociological Review*, 12, 1947, pp. 342–348.
[12] *Ibid.*

simultaneously face a request by a line executive to permit a deviation in certain rules, such as not filing of a report on time, a group of colleagues who have a professional standard which insists that this is unethical and unprofessional, and a superior who insists that the line is to be served by the staff which should do everything in its power to facilitate the work of the overall organization.

The somewhat reverse situation exists for line executives who may receive strong pressures from their immediate line superiors to increase production and equally strong pushes from staff personnel to maintain quality or have the production line shut down.

There are many other instances of duplicate sources of influence which can be found in any large-scale organization. The general result is usually the same; whatever the manager does he is bound to appear to be in violation of what is proper by at least one and perhaps by all. The psychological strain for the individual in such situations can be considerable. Yet, as also noted in Chapter 8, he obtains an area of discretion not found in the exactly defined organization.

SUMMARY

In this chapter we examined the behavior of individual managers in large, complex organizations and have addressed ourselves particularly to the question concerning the way in which and why their patterns of behavior deviate from what is or could be expected. On the one hand, they were seen as steps taken to permit the individual manager to do his job more effectively by developing a greater personal control over his immediate work situation or to acquire the resources necessary for his area of responsibility to perform well. On the other hand, these were seen as adjustments to conflicting pressures which permit the individual manager to continue to function under what otherwise would be an intolerably stressful situation.

These accommodations have been viewed as useful on two counts. One, they may provide the necessary flexibility and adaptions to permit the organization to function well. Two, they permit the individual manager to reduce the tensions of living in a complex, multisystem organization to a point where he can continue to function usefully. We further explore the situation of the individual manager in a multiorganization world in Chapter 23.

23

Changing Organizational Behavior

In the preceding chapter we began an examination of some of the factors which contribute to a lack of congruency between formally prescribed organizational behavior and the actual behavior of organizational members. In particular, we saw how the individuals and groups with which a manager comes into contact influence behavior in a way to make it noncongruent with the expectations of higher management. We were primarily concerned with the effects of the internal system in which the manager finds himself and other factors such as reward systems.

This analysis left unexplained a number of other fairly common patterns in which managerial behavior deviates from prescribed ones. There is, for example, the situation in which a manager may want to comply with the prescriptions of higher management but may behave in a way which, in effect, misses the mark. The child who wants to "help Daddy" while he is painting, having seen him mix clear chemicals with the paint, and mistakenly pours a large quantity of gasoline into the paint bucket, provides a crude illustration of this phenomenon. Then there is the situation in which, unlike those discussed in the preceding chapter, the deviation is clearly publicized; that is, the manager is a maverick. For the individual to assume, and the organization to permit, a maverick role to emerge requires some different accommodations from those we have discussed. To explain these and similar patterns of behavior requires building on concepts developed earlier.

Although not essential for these behavior patterns to occur, change nonetheless tends to dramatize their existence and often highlights the causal factors. For this reason Chapter 23 discusses change situations. The first section extensively examines a fundamental change in an organization. Later sections deal with changes concerning only one person.

NONCONGRUENCY OF FORMAL-TASK ROLE AND
SELF-IMAGE ROLE

Organizational change may take a number of forms. Locations may change; for example, a company may build a new plant and transfer existing personnel to it. Duties which people in an organization perform may change, as when a new product or procedural tool is introduced. Changes of this sort, relatively speaking, have less impact on the functioning of the organization than does a change in organizational style, as would eventuate when an organization shifts from a centralized to a decentralized mode of operation. In this case, the physical surroundings may remain pretty much the same and many technical aspects of work may be unchanged in that people might work on the same products using the same technologies. The change in the relationships among people, however, may be very great and have a profound impact. To explore this, we continue the analysis of the decentralization of the supermarket chain that we began in Chapter 16.[1]

By way of review, a medium-size supermarket chain having grown successfully over the years was faced with increasing competition from a source over which, until recently, it had had a distinct advantage. Local, independent companies, now operating a single or few stores, had become able to stress service and selection to the local customers which the chain found difficult to match with its highly centralized organization. Top management made the decision to reorganize, create a new position of store manager, and have the person in this position operate as much as possible like an independent businessman. Within the constraints imposed by the overall system—centralized buying, advertising, personnel policies, etc.—the individual store manager was to make all decisions in a way to maximize his store's performance. He or his subordinates would have control over selection of items (within the array the chain carried) to be marketed in the store. He would be responsible for layout, inventory policies, hiring of personnel, determining shifts, and who would be on them.

This necessitated radical changes in many organizational personnel regarding what they did and how they looked at their jobs. Store managers were to be selected for the most part from current store personnel, particularly grocery managers. In the highly centralized

[1] Unless otherwise noted material in this section is taken from Paul R. Lawrence, *The Changing of Organizational Behavior Patterns*, Boston, Harvard University, Division of Research, Graduate School of Business Administration, 1958.

organization they had been primarily accustomed to receiving orders and then executing them. Strong emphasis had been placed on obedience and compliance. Whether the order advanced company welfare was not something about which store personnel had to concern themselves. Further, district managers had been primarily concerned with transmitting orders and information from top management to store personnel, giving commands of their own, and meticulously checking to see that store personnel properly carried out the instructions given them. It was recognized by management that the changes intended would not result simply from the issuance of an order. Such things take time. In this chapter we are concerned with some of the fundamental reasons for this. To restrict the scope of the discussion, we focus primarily on the district managers. They obviously played a crucial role in how well and how completely the store managers would make the transition. They were also faced with the fact that they kept the same titles and were concerned largely with the same stores. For them the change was concentrated on the most critical areas, that of the relationships with their subordinates and the style of leadership employed in these relationships.

In the new organization plan prepared by top management the district manager's role basically changed from one of directing store personnel to supporting and assisting them in carrying out their responsibilities. They were to convey information, not orders. They were to help the store manager make decisions, not to control him to see that he complied with decisions made by someone else. The full meaning of the change could not be easily conveyed in the usual organization chart or job description. A more inclusive concept was needed.

What we have been explaining are in essence the expectations of top management about how subordinates will behave in order to carry out a new organizational plan. The term expectations gives the clue that what we are really dealing with are a set of formal roles, that is, behavioral expectations about a positionholder arrived at through conscious planning. This formal role contains not only descriptions of duties but also many descriptions of actions, interactions, and for that matter, viewpoints, attitudes, or, as they would be called in a Homans scheme, sentiments. It would seem useful, therefore, to translate what this new organizational plan meant for the district manager into a statement of a formal role containing prescriptions for sentiments, interactions, and activities. Such a statement might be as follows [2]:

ACTIVITIES. The district manager was still expected to spend most of his time going from store to store in his territory, ob-

[2] *Ibid.*, pp. 63–64.

serving and talking with his subordinates. He was, however, expected to spend more time looking over perishable departments because of his loss of the assistant district managers. He was also expected to spend more time on planning functions and less on "firefighting" current problems.

INTERACTIONS. The district managers were expected to provide opportunities for the subordinate store managers to assume more decision-making functions. They would have to converse with their fledgling store managers so that these men would assume greater responsibilities and discharge them adequately. This meant that in their interactions with their subordinates they were expected to make a fundamental change toward adopting a more problem solving two-way type of communication. They would also have to strike a relatively even balance between the amount of time they spent talking to their subordinates and the time the subordinates spent doing the talking to them. . . .

SENTIMENTS. Like the store managers, the district managers were expected to conceive of themselves as more independent, self-sufficient business men who were concerned with the long range well-being of their districts. They were even to think of their role as superiors as being more that of teachers and developers of the capacities of their store managers.

RESPONSES TO NEW FORMAL-TASK ROLES

After the reorganization the behavior of some district managers very soon fit the new formal-task role requirements. Others did not fit too well and some hardly fit at all. These responses are described in detail.

General Reaction of District Managers to the Reorganization

One of the district managers (hereafter referred to as DM1) viewed the reorganization in the following way:

I know most all of the district managers will tell you they are sorry the assistant district managers' system is gone. They miss not having those men as their assistants. Well, I think it was a good system but I think our present system can be better whenever we get it working right. I think the store manager's system is working out fine because I think of the store managers as my assistants and I can do a better job with them than I ever could with assistant managers . . . The store manager is my representative in the store . . . I have to keep watching myself on working consistently through the store manager.   Every once in a while I slip back into that habit of speaking to whoever happens to be handy when I see something I don't like but you really lose the effectiveness of what you are trying to do if you do that.   Sometimes I have to remind other people, too, that come into the store to deal with the store manager.[3]

Contrasted with this was the reaction of another district manager (called DM3) who expressed himself as follows:

I am one of the few people that doesn't like this new set up with merchandisers and store managers.   I thought the old way much better.   I had a team operating in my territory that you just couldn't beat but I'm not arguing with them.   I'm doing what I'm told these days.[4]

In the case of DM1 the individual seems to support the new plan and to echo some of the important attitudes specified by top management.   The store managers should be allowed to run their own show. The district managers should not interfere, etc.   DM3, on the other hand, is flatly opposed to the new plan and apparently also to what it stands for.   He is, however, going to comply.

Changes in Interaction as a Result of the New Organization Plan

Among the other expectations of top management was that the interactions between the district manager and the store managers would become more equal, more information would flow both ways, and a more equal balance would develop between the initiation of topics and length of time they were discussed.   In this study Lawrence recorded data on the interactions of various district managers and store managers; some of these are shown in Figure 23.1. One factor noted is that relative to store managers DM1 speaks less, 58 per cent to 42 per cent, than DM3, 75 per cent to 25 per cent.   Within this overall allocation of interaction there is also a difference of a distribution of topics.   Both DM1 and DM3 still give far more directions and suggestions than their subordinate store managers but the pattern shifts from 28 to 2 for DM3 to 15 to 5 for DM1.   Furthermore, if they are to support and assist their store managers, we expect not only a reduction in directions but also an increase in advice or

[3] *Ibid.*, pp. 150–151.
[4] *Ibid.*, p. 169.

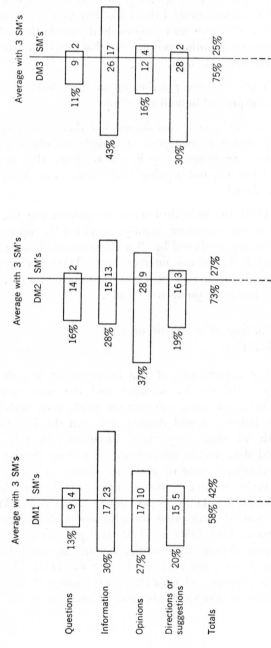

Figure 23.1. Percentage of DM and SM talking time by categories. *Source:* Paul R. Lawrence, *The Changing of Organizational Behavior Patterns*, Boston, Harvard University, Division of Research, Graduate School of Business Administration, 1958, p. 134.

other helpful statements, such as opinions. Conversations between DM1 and his subordinates have 27 per cent of the time allocated to this topic, whereas between DM3 and his subordinates only 16 per cent of the talking time is devoted to this category.

As to the specific topics covered during these discussions (Figure 23.2) DM1 spends the greatest percentage of his time talking with subordinates about personnel, 48 per cent as compared to 11 per cent for DM3.   On the other hand, for the supervisor in the old centralized approach there was considerable emphasis on control and compliance. One aspect is setting up and maintaining adequate records.   Consistent with this DM3 spent 47 per cent of his time discussing record systems with his subordinates as compared to 22 per cent for DM1.   Without exploring the other data in Figure 23.2 in more detail, let us note that the warmth or friendliness of the relationship between two people can perhaps be indicated by the amount of conversation which is not on business topics, that is, small talk.   There is fourteen times as much of this in the conversations with DM1 than with DM3.

One of the final aspects of the interaction pattern examined here is who initiates new topics for discussion—district managers or store managers?   Figure 23.3 shows that whereas the district managers al-

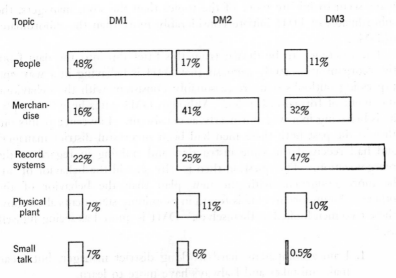

Figure 23.2. Percentage of DM and SM talking time by topics. *Source:* Paul R. Lawrence, *The Changing of Organizational Behavior Patterns,* Boston, Harvard University, Division of Research, Graduate School of Business Administration, 1958, p. 137.

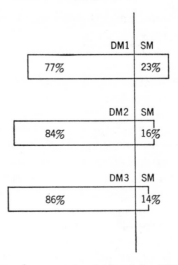

Figure 23.3. Percentage of new topics initiated by DM's and SM's. *Source:* Paul R. Lawrence, *The Changing of Organizational Behavior Patterns,* Boston, Harvard University, Division of Research, Graduate School of Business Administration, 1958, p. 138.

ways seem to initiate more of the topics than the store managers, the subordinates of DM1 initiate considerably more than the subordinates of DM3.

The inference to be drawn from this brief dip into the data from the reorganization study suggests that DM1 is behaving in a way and expressing outlooks that are reasonably consistent with the behavioral statement of formal-task roles. Although DM3 states he will comply, he is behaving in a way not nearly as consistent. Lawrence points out that in the past both these men had been successful district managers and had received the same instruction and training in regard to the reorganization. The question then is why should the behavior of one be more congruent with the new plan than the behavior of the other? An important clue is found in examining statements about how these two men looked at themselves. DM1 is quoted as seeing himself as: [5]

1. I am a competent, hard-working district manager, but I can make mistakes and I always have more to learn.
2. I am a person who says what I think to anyone even if it is unpopular, but I am willing to accept good ideas from any source.

[5] *Ibid.,* pp. 145–146.

3. I face up to unpleasant realities about myself.
4. I am something of a nonconformist.

He then goes on to say that as a superior he sees himself as:

1. I do not want to dominate the thinking of my subordinates.
2. I want to push responsibility on them as fast as I can and get them to answer their own problems.
3. I operate by giving them my advice and suggestions and taking a keen interest in their problems and suggestions.
4. I treat different employees differently and do not expect perfection.
5. I look for administrative ability as the primary requirement for my subordinate superiors.
6. I candidly tell my subordinates where they stand with me.

This picture of himself enables DM1 to fit closely the concept of what is expected of him. He, in effect, is doing what comes naturally. To put this more abstractly, DM1's behavior matches well with the formal task-role prescription because his self-concept is fairly similar to this role prescription. In this situation not only is it easier for DM1 to do what is expected of him, but he feels better about it, more comfortable, more secure.

Perhaps these last points can be illustrated by examining what it was like for DM1 before the reorganization and under the centralized, authoritarian style of organization. Speaking for himself he says at one point, "I have always been something of a maverick in this organization." [6] In short, he seems to have seen himself as different in what he did and the way he looked at things. The maverick's position usually is not a particularly comfortable one. It is different but one in which a person places himself and where he can understand the difference between how he sees himself and what is expected of him. It is not the most comfortable position, but it is far less uncomfortable than some others, which are of concern when a person feels he should conform to what higher management expects of him but in so doing finds himself undertaking tasks or occupying positions which he basically feels are not right for him, are "immoral," "below his status" or "not what a natural man would do." Here there is no relief for the tension and strain. These persons experience considerable inner conflict and feelings of insecurity.

Let us move along to examine the situation for DM3. Lawrence summarizes DM3's self-concept as:

⁶ *Ibid.*, p. 152.

1. I am a systematic and tough supervisor who gets things done.
2. I am an all around expert on running supermarkets.
3. I am too honest and forthright for my own good.

In discussing his subordinates he says:

1. I tell my subordinates what to do, answer their questions, and follow up to see that things are done.
2. I expect my subordinates to listen to my instructions, then to do them without a lot of arguments.
3. I expect subordinates to be aggressive in getting things done with their own subordinates.

He goes on at one point to say:

I find in my own experience that I can work much better with people under me who have learned to accept my criticisms and welcome them instead of those who seem to be fighting them.

And still later:

I like a supervisor who is really the boss, really running things, a take charge guy.[7]

This self-concept would fit fairly well with what was expected under the earlier authoritarian, centralized mode of operation. Here DM3 was probably quite comfortable. However, the role prescriptions for the new decentralized organization do not match his self-concept, and there is some evidence of strain and conflict in his opinions of the new organizational form.

Yet DM3 feels that it is his duty to follow orders. He wants to conform to what is expected. When he does this, several things happen. As already noted, he behaves in a way which violates his self-concept and causes considerable stress and feelings of insecurity. Furthermore, even though he is attempting to comply with what is expected, the best he can do is to live according to the letter of the law. He certainly will miss the intent, for he has no real idea of what it means. However, organizational behavior and particularly that of executives is so complex and varied that it can never be completely programmed. Between the general guide lines received the individual must fill in a multitude of details in order to perform effectively. Not really understanding what is intended DM3 has an extraordinarily difficult job in adequately filling in these unprogrammed portions of his behavior.

[7] *Ibid.*, pp. 163–165.

We may recall a cartoon popular a few years ago which showed an irate Sunday school teacher with a large stick in his hand and a ferocious scowl on his face glowering at his small, frightened charges saying, "You're going to get brotherly love for each other even if I have to beat it into you."

ADAPTIVE RESPONSES TO INCONGRUENCY OF FORMAL-TASK ROLE PRESCRIPTIONS AND SELF-CONCEPTS

Let us consider this topic in more abstract form.   Basically there are two primary elements: the formal-task role and a person's self-concept.   If these are fairly congruent, quite a comfortable, workable arrangement eventuates (Figure 23.4).   On the other hand if they are incongruent, some tension, conflict, and feelings of insecurity are to be expected.   Since it is not easy to comfortably live with these feelings, we can reasonably expect the person involved to produce some adaptive responses in an effort to reduce the tension and security.   Although there is no way of predicting exactly what adaptive response will occur, there are a number which occur fairly typically.

Leaving or Withdrawal from the Situation

Here the individual tries to escape. He may quit, go to another job. Even if he does not physically leave the job, he may psychologically withdraw from it. He becomes apathetic, listless, does not seem to care.[8]

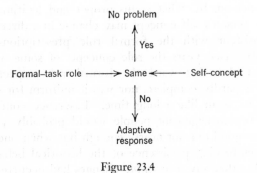

Figure 23.4

---

[8] See Chapter 22 for some general responses to role conflict.

Change the Formal-Task Role

Here the person involved takes an action he hopes in one way or another will cause the expectations others have about him to change. He may, for example, argue about the reorganization, pointing to its weaknesses, hoping to discredit the change, and perpetuate the old form. More subtly, as seen in the preceding chapter, he may try to achieve a situation in which the new formal plan, despite being on the books, is regularly circumvented, and everyone knows that some deviation from it is not only permitted but also expected. He may engage in some political activity which at one extreme could lead to revolt or at least the replacement of key figures so that the new power structure would install a new set of expectations, more compatible with his self-concept.

Agree to Disagree

In this sort of arrangement the parties involved remove the uncertainty of compliance with the formal role prescription by recognizing that one or more people are going to deviate and that they will be recognized as being different or "mavericks."

Change Self-Concepts

No one's self-concept is fixed throughout his whole life; they all change. However, the change is exceedingly slow, much slower than most of us might recognize. Since our self-concepts do change, we usually sense that it is to no small degree influenced by what is expected of a person, by what seems proper and legitimate.[9] Hence, given time, a person's self-concept may change in a direction to make it more consistent with the formal role prescriptions. Lawrence found that after two years the role concepts of some of the district managers had shifted toward the formal role expectations. The movement was hardly complete, nor was it uniform for all personnel. Last, two years seem like a long time. Lawrence concludes at one point, "The top management people would probably view the two years' result as good but not nearly enough but when one looks at the built-in self-reinforcing persistence of the historical behavior pattern, it is remarkable that any *discernible* changes had occurred."[10]

[9] See Chapter 15 on Reward Systems for some aspects of this topic.
[10] *Ibid.*, p. 204.

As an exercise we might review the things previously identified which influence perception, particularly our perception of ourselves. Among those covered thus far are reference groups, particularly cosmopolitans and locals, the culture as it influences the sentiments a person acquires in growing up, and the education, both of a formal and informal nature, that takes place within an organization, such as that which comes about through reward systems.

OTHER SOURCES OF VARIATION IN FORMAL-TASK ROLE

Reorganization is not the only way in which the formal-task role facing an individual can change. This can also occur through moving within the organization to a new position. Whereas a horizontal shift of position brings some variation in role prescription, vertical movements to a higher position in the hierarchy are likelier to bring about a more drastic change. We review briefly some of the more important ways in which role prescription may change with vertical mobility.

Span of Discretion

As we have seen, the content of a job or, to be more accurate, the content of a role varies with different location in the organization. In some positions the occupant has very little discretion as to what he shall do or when he shall do it; in others he may have a great deal. In short, the span of discretion a person may have can vary considerably with his position in the organization. We have already identified some important dimensions of discretion: range of decisions (that is, the number of different things about which a position holder can make decisions) and the reporting-time span (that is, the length of time an individual can go without reporting back to a superior).[11] In general, as we go from lower to higher positions in the organization these two dimensions increase.[12]

There are several other time dimensions to be considered. These are the immediacy with which a decision has to be made and the time in the future over which decisions have an effect. For example, a foreman may be faced by the fact that an employee on an assembly line is ill and does not show up for work one day. Almost immediately he has to make a decision about the matter, for he cannot afford to have a gap in his assembly line left very long. His decision may be

[11] See Chapters 16 and 19.
[12] Much of the following discussion is drawn from Elliot Jaques, *Equitable Payment*, New York, John Wiley, 1961, particularly Chapters 5 and 6.

to borrow an employee from another department to fill in for the day. Hence, the decision influences events for approximately a 24-hour period. Foremen live in a world where their decisions are immediate and have an effect over relatively short periods of time—a day, a week, seldom more than a month. As we go higher, these time dimensions increase. At the top level of a company a decision may be able to be delayed for considerable periods of time, sometimes almost indefinitely. Furthermore, when made their effect may be stretched for months, a year, or in many cases many years into the future. Table 23.1 shows the time perspectives found to exist in a plant for four levels of supervision.

Table 23.1   Time Perspectives of Decision Situations
at Four Levels of Management

Time	Works Manager (per cent)	Division Superin- tendent (per cent)	Depart- ment Foreman (per cent)	Shift Foreman (per cent)
Short (0–2 weeks)	3.3	54.2	68.0	97.7
Moderate (2 weeks to year)	46.1	41.4	30.4	2.1
Distant	50.0	4.3	1.5	0.0
Total	99.4	99.9	99.9	99.8

Source: Norman H. Martin, "The Levels of Management and Their Mental Demands," in W. Lloyd Warner and Norman H. Martin, Industrial Man, New York, Harper, 1959, p. 281.

In general, as an individual goes higher in the organization, he is expected to handle a greater discretionary span. Some people welcome this, but others find it a strain, quite different from their traditional ways of operating and looking at themselves. They are without the guidance that comes from the pressure of an immediate event and frequent review by a superior. Consequently, most learn to work for much longer periods of time without any real knowledge of whether they are going right or wrong.

Weighting of Task Role Components

We have already noted the variation in the discretion a person has in choosing the tools to handle his job that may occur with hierarchal positions. There are also other variations. It is sometimes suggested that the skills necessary for an executive position are the same at all

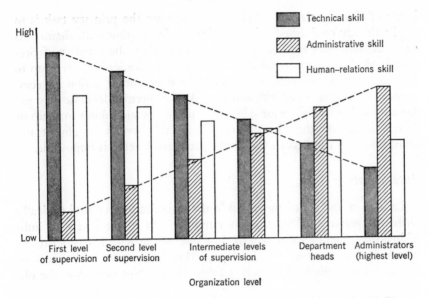

Figure 23.5.   Relative importance of different supervisory skills.   *Source:* Basil S. Georgopoulos and Floyd S. Mann, *The Community General Hospital,* New York, Macmillan, 1962, p. 238.

levels.   Perhaps so, but not in the same proportion.   At lower levels of supervision close to technical operations technical knowledge and skill can loom far more important than at, for example, the president's level.   Although ability to deal with people, interpersonal, or human relations skills is important at the first level of supervision, it can reasonably be expected to be more important at higher levels of management, because here a person is required to have more subtlety and discretion.[13]   The arrangement between these two skilled components of managerial positions and a third area, namely, administrative skills, is shown in Figure 23.5.

Degree of Structure

Among other things that can change in the work of the executive as he moves upward in the organization is the degree of structure about his job.   This can occur in several ways.   First, the range of responsibilities that come under his concern increases.   Second, at the lower

[13] Basil S. Georgeopoulos and Floyd G. Mann, *The Community General Hospital,* New York, Macmillan, 1962, particularly Chapter 9.

levels of the organization as problems come up the primary task is to apply already established rules or solutions for coping with them. As the executive goes further up in the organization, the number of prepared solutions or prepared alternatives rapidly diminishes. It is up to him to decide if anything at all should be done and, if action is necessary, to determine what it should be. At the foreman level he may get by with going to a superior with some problems and asking for help or instructions. At the vice-president level this would be almost unthinkable and, needless to say, at the president level it is impossible.

Interaction

Last, as an individual moves up in the organization we find typically different patterns of interaction required. At lower levels an individual may spend a great deal of time interacting with his associates or peers, but as he goes up the ladder this interaction with peers or associates may diminish sharply (Table 23.2). Not only does the ob-

Table 23.2   Superordinate-Subordinate Associational Contacts at Four Levels of Management

Contact	Works Manager (per cent)	Division Superintendent (per cent)	Department Foreman (per cent)	Shift Foreman (per cent)
Superordinate	29.4	21.9	28.9	20.4
Associate	1.9	6.9	4.4	18.4
Subordinate	68.6	71.2	66.7	61.2
Total	99.9	100.0	100.0	100.0

Source: Norman H. Martin, "The Levels of Management and Their Mental Demands," in W. Lloyd Warner and Norman H. Martin, Industrial Man, New York, Harpers, 1959, p. 289.

ject of his interaction change but the nature of the interaction also changes. At the foreman level interaction is often direct, close, face-to-face. Higher in the organization it becomes indirect, and more so if it is carried on through telephone conversations, larger meetings, correspondence, etc. (see Table 23.3).

Thus, we have reviewed briefly some of the ways in which the work and the world of an executive changes as he advances vertically in an organization hierarchy. The things he has to do or is expected to do change dramatically. The man who sees himself as a person who likes to work with concrete, tangible problems, who does best when he works closely with others, and who likes to know where he stands in regard to what he has been doing may find this picture of himself quite incompatible with the realities of higher level positions. We may, therefore, find the lack of congruency between self-image and formal-task role requirements occurring for this reason.

Table 23.3   Frequency of Direct versus Indirect and Group Contacts at Four Levels of Management

Contact	Works Manager (per cent)	Division Superin- tendent (per cent)	Depart- ment Foreman (per cent)	Shift Foreman (per cent)
Direct	30.76	71.18	77.61	84.31
Indirect	56.41	25.42	19.40	15.68
Group	12.82	3.38	2.98	
Total	99.99	99.98	99.99	99.99

Source: Norman H. Martin, "The Levels of Management and Their Mental Demands," in W. Lloyd Warner and Norman H. Martin, *Industrial Man*, New York, Harpers, 1959, p. 290.

SUMMARY

This chapter can be summarized in Figure 23.6. We have given primary attention to the congruency or lack thereof between the formal-task role and a person's self-concept. When they are non-congruent, we expect tension, strain, discomfort, and insecurity to increase, leaving a person to choose some sort of adaptive response to reduce these conditions. Among those noticed are leaving or withdrawing from the organization, attempting to change the formal-task role, agreeing to disagree, forced compliance, and last changing one's self-concept. A person's self-concept is in part a product of his culture, reference groups, and his education and training. The formal-task role can vary through change in organization design and through change of a person's position within the organization. Last, but hardly least, we might add that a change in the personnel in the organization, such as the appointment of a new superior, or for that matter, new subordinates, may also change the formal-task role.

This chapter completes a cycle and the book. We began by looking at the individual and examining certain basic aspects which influ-

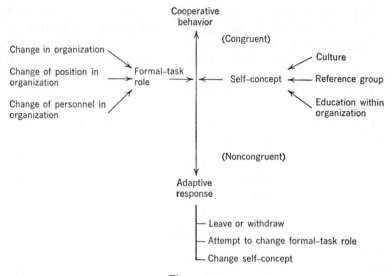

Figure 23.6

ence his behavior. We then proceeded to study organizations building one layer on top of the other: the small group, the complex organization, the environment of the organization. Particularly in the last two chapters we have reversed this process and, in effect, slicing vertically through these layers of abstraction have asked how does a person behave when he is at one and the same time a unique individual, a member of a particular group, an occupant of a position in a formal organization—all of which exist in a culture, environment, or society? The particular focus in this discussion has been on how well individual behavior complies with the behavior prescriptions or expectations of formal organizations. This is but one of several perspectives that could have been taken. Considering the nature of the book and its target audience this seemed to be the most relevant and useful one.

We shall close the book in stating an objective which, hopefully, has been clearly demonstrated throughout the book. Namely, we have been studying organizations to identify the principal factors they contain and to understand some of the important relationships among these factors. The effort has been to understand how a complex system operates. There have been no detailed specifications of how organizations *ought* to operate nor any detailed programs of *how* to operate organizations. It is hoped with a better knowledge of organizations that managers, both current and future, will be able to make better decisions about them.

Index

461